W9-AZS-693

PRESS FREEDOM

AND

COMMUNICATION

IN

AFRICA

EDITED BY FESTUS ERIBO AND
WILLIAM JONG-EBOT

Africa World Press, Inc.

P.O. Box 1892
Trenton, NJ 08607

P.O. Box 48
Asmara, ERITREA

Africa World Press, Inc.

P.O. Box 1892
Trenton, NJ 08607

P.O. Box 48
Asmara, ERITREA

Copyright © 1997 Festus Eribo and William Jong-Ebot

First Printing 1997

All rights reserved. No part of this publication may be reproduced, stored in a retrieval system or transmitted in any form or by any means electronic, mechanical, photocopying, recording or otherwise without the prior written permission of the publisher.

Cover and Book design: Jonathan Gullery

This book is set in Souvenir and Trajan

Library of Congress Cataloging-in-Publication Data

Press Freedom and Communication in Africa /editors, Festus Eribo, William Jong-Ebot
    p.   cm.
    Includes bibliographical references and index.
    ISBN 0-86543-550-2. – ISBN 0-86543-551-0 (pbk.)
    1. Government and the press–Africa.   2. Freedom of the press–Africa. I. Eribo, Festus, 1950-   II. Jong-Ebot, William, 1954-
PM4748.A35P74 1997   97-13289
323.44'5'096–dc21   CIP

CONTENTS

PART 2
ARABIC SPEAKING

PART 3
FRANCOPHONE

PART 4
LUSOPHONE

INTRODUCTION

Festus Eribo

William Jong-Ebot

Studies about Africa in the last few decades have often been lacking what Klein (1992) has called a "historical consciousness." Africa has been dubbed the "dark continent," a "confusing place," where hunger, poverty, corruption, instability resulting from ethnic conflicts and autocratic governments are rampant. It has been portrayed as a failed continent which needs help (Hawk, 1992). The electronic media in particular have provided viewers worldwide with gruesome pictures of starving Somalis, their gun-toting soldiers and United Nations rescue efforts without any focus on background or context.

In analyzing contemporary Africa's success or failure, the focus is often on the extent to which a particular country is "democratic" or "developed" as indicated by such measures as Gross Domestic Product or per capita GNP. The picture that often emerges at the end of most analyses is that of a continent still learning to crawl, let alone walk. Diamond (1993) notes: "On virtually every measure of economic and human development, African countries are clustered among the poorest and most miserable in the world."

While Africa's misery is not in dispute, scholars ought to attempt to avoid "scholarship shaped by our passions" and examine any society, particularly a complex region like Africa, by also "studying how it came to be" (Klein, 1992).

The mass media institution, a necessary component of any democracy, developed in Europe and was transplanted into Africa during the colonial era. Today the media are in the forefront of the war for democracy in Africa, along with students, civic organizations and political parties. But the media too are a contradiction. Having been organized to serve the needs of the various colonial administrations, they became, at independence, ideological tools of the new African leaders, and were brought under state control and made to sing the praises of dictators in the name of national unity and development. As late as 1990, Ghana's Minister of Information still expected his country's journalists to act as partners in development. "What we need in Ghana today is a journalist who sees himself as a contributor to national development. This country does not need watchdogs" (The Democratic Journalist, 1990).

African journalists operate under some of the most controlled conditions — stringent and often draconian laws enacted to make them "willing tools" and cheerleaders of inept and often corrupt governments. Given such a state of affairs, one cannot simply slide through Africa's media troubles without an analytical and comprehensive look at other factors, both internal and external. Zaffiro (1993) notes with respect to studying African broadcasting that one needs "to unavoidably and deeply enter the realm of political and social policy analysis." One also ought to examine the historical path through which a country's media traveled, so as to pick up whatever "habits of mind" its journalists and leaders inherited. Examining the symptoms rather than the underlying causes of contemporary Africa's media stagnation and so-called failure is a somewhat fast track approach.

A few studies of the continent's media in recent years reveal monumental problems — economic, social and political. Ochs (1987) notes that many African countries do not have "basic media" because they lack the economic resources. Even where such media exist, they are controlled by authoritarian leaders, thus making Africa "a continent that gags its press." Mytton's (1983) analysis of the role of the media, particularly radio and television in Africa, provides a few case studies indicating that while radio, for example, may be capable of speaking directly to a large audience, centralization, along with political control of the media, often lead to less freedom to question government policies.

Hachten (1993) says the media in Africa have failed to "grow and prosper" because African governments have not promoted the political and economic climate which would lead to independent, critical, and economically viable media. Instead, African leaders have controlled and suppressed the media, resulting in what he calls a "kept press" whose role is that of a "cheerleader supporting unpopular leaders and their policies."

Faringer (1991) attempts a limited look at press freedom in Africa. She examines the media in Nigeria, Ghana, and Kenya — three former British colonies — criticizing "development journalism" without distinguishing it from "development-support communication."

There have been four main problems with contemporary studies of the African media. First, there is the underlying assumption that the Western media are free and should be the "guiding light" for all other media systems, including those of Africa. Second, there is a neglect of other forms of communication in Africa, such as word of mouth, dance, art, traditional music, and oral literature, which have existed in Africa for centuries. Many Africans live in rural areas and often depend on other forms of communication, in addition to radio, for information. Third, there is a failure to recognize that the media in African countries formerly ruled by Britain, Belgium, France, Spain, and Portugal, all emerged from colonialism with different communication models and today operate in ways somewhat different from each other. Fourth, there is no thorough examination of the external, along with the internal factors, that affect media performance in Africa. More attention is often focused on the internal factors.

A cursory look at the history of the continent reveals a pattern of domestic and external factors militating against realistic development of the people and nations of Africa. Davidson pointed out in 1992 that Africa is a continent of "contradictions." To fully understand any of its people or institutions, one needs a broader picture, not just snippets of information designed to support some truth-cum-myths about the continent.

There is perhaps no exact point in history when the continent's contradictions began but one can obviously point to 1885, when it was arbitrarily carved up among European countries who all had varying ambitions and no regard for the ethnic, linguistic or geographic features of the people. Whether Africa had nations, cultures, or a civilization, a tradition of political organization prior to 1884 is not the issue. What is at issue is that the continent's past has caught up with its present, making any movement forward difficult.

One of the continent's most visible contradictions is its more than seventy years of life under foreign rule. What emerged after those years were, in some cases, artificial units rather than countries, barely ready or prepared for the tasks of nation-statehood. Each "departing" colonial power left its indelible imprint or colonial "habits of mind" which are visible today among the continent's rulers, people, institutions and actions. Mazrui (1993) notes that "the damage of enslavement and colonization does not lie in the past. The damage is here; the damage is now . . . The long-term effects of slave raids and colonization are part of the brutal legacy of the present day."

One expectation or rather contradiction was the thinking that, armed with European parliamentary models and other inherited institutions, the new African leaders would simply "democratize" those legacies, "develop" and become modern nation-states just like the Europeans. However, as Davidson (1992) notes, the importation of "non-African scenarios and solutions," particularly the concept of democracy, could not take hold in Africa after colonialism because the political, economic and social conditions which nurtured the concept in Europe were absent in Africa. There was no economically viable working class or "middle strata" to promote democracy as was the case in France and Britain.

The political environment in existence during colonialism did not encourage democracy. For example, there was no freedom of speech, thought, or the press, except in a few cases under British rule. Instead of democracy, the new African leaders degenerated into authoritarian single-party or military dictatorships, created huge bureaucracies and ushered in "politics of clientelism" and later, of "kingship corporations." Klein (1992) notes that a new "bureaucratic class" or "entrenched elites" now emerged, "used power to maximize their privileges and take unto themselves an excessive part of the national wealth." From 1960, the continent watched a number of "sit-tight leaders" glorify and enrich themselves and their cronies at the expense of the masses. Democracy, known as the right of a people to participate in governing themselves, particularly by electing and voting out their leaders, was not practiced by the colonial masters in Africa and so it was no surprise when the African rulers practiced the dictatorship of their colonial masters but not the democracy.

The world economic order in which the new African countries found themselves in the 1960s was another contradiction. As a continent endowed with significant natural resources, Africa has often served as a supplier of raw materials for European and North American factories and importer of expensive finished goods. Ill-advised and grandiose development projects since gaining political independence, the continent's economic dependence on the same powers that supposedly set it "free," unequal trading rules dictated by the dominant industrialized powers, and mismanagement and corruption by its leaders have led to a deepening impoverishment of the continent. This is evidenced by stagnating or falling per capita incomes, debt burdens, civil wars, famine, hunger, weak trade and investment records.

Experts say Africa badly needs peace and stability, in other words, democratic governments so that it can begin meaningful and sustainable economic development. But such economic development will not come unless other factors, such as international trade policies, are revised. Warren Christopher (1993), former U.S. Secretary of State, acknowledged that " . . . protectionist barriers still impede Africa's competitiveness and its prospects for growth." So while democracy may bring peace and stability to Africa, a fundamental restructuring of the present world economic order has to be a part of the democratic package.

As the second wind of change, popularly dubbed the "Second Liberation" continues to blow over Africa, it is appropriate to examine the scale of press freedom in the liberation. If flourishing political and economic realms are the key to better media growth and performance, then Africa may just be poised for such conditions. But change will not come easily, for old habits are hard to break. In the post-cold war years, hopes of reaching the political kingdom and eventually the economic kingdom have been strengthened by the heroic efforts of Benin, Mali, Zambia, and Namibia. These countries took the first steps in the democratic process by electing their own leaders. Now they need to sustain democracy and continue the march forward.

In other African countries, however, the transition is still stuck in the mud. Examples from Kenya, Cameroon and Senegal illustrate that while some African leaders are prepared to permit democratic pluralism, they are reluctant to permit democracy, and specifically the mechanisms for fair participation. In those countries, the opposition, thanks to the governments in power, lacks a coherent agenda and undisputed leadership while the governments still use the armed forces to maintain the status quo—official corruption, harassment of the opposition, economic mismanagement and decline, and political misrule. Most of the so-called democratic revolutions are just cosmetic exercises, given that the same elites are still in control, enjoying the same privileges, and trapped in what Mutua (1993) calls "the politics of ethnicity and patronage."

While the concept of a competitive free press was born with this second liberation, many of the alternative media are being squeezed and not allowed to contribute to the democratic process. According to an International Press Institute's 1992 World Press Freedom Review, pre-publication censorship is still obligatory in Cameroon; in Algeria, several publications were suspended by Presidential decree No. 92-320 and a few journalists were detained.

When the Nigerian military government led by Ibrahim Babangida annulled the June 1993 presidential election claiming it was fraudulent, it mounted a strong assault on the press, shutting down five newspapers which had fiercely opposed the cancellation of the election. A decree in late June, 1993 enabled the government to "proscribe or seize and confiscate any publication if it contains any article or material which is likely to disrupt the process of democracy and peaceful transition to civil rule" (Adams, 1993). The Babangida government's battle to control public opinion began in 1986 after the weekly *Newswatch* was temporarily shut down for implicating the government in the assassination of Dele Giwa, the magazine's editor-in-chief. The squeeze on the media intensified in early 1993 after critical reports by weekly newsmagazines revealed stalling tactics regarding the transition program and disunity among military rulers.

These examples indicate that the liberty of the African media is still fragile at best. To understand the future direction of the continent's mass media, one needs a comprehensive examination, one lodged in the historical as well as the contemporary realms. This book attempts such an analysis, with studies of media development and performance from Anglophone, Arabic-speaking, Francophone, and Lusophone Africa. Contributors provide some background on the ideology of communication as well as media growth or the lack of it during the colonial period. They then turn to the media in the post-colonial period, examine media growth and performance, providing some glimpses of the problems facing the institution on the continent.

From Anglophone Africa, Kwadwo Anokwa examines the press performance and freedom under different regime types and styles of press control in Ghana. The author notes that due to direct government controls, official restrictions and censorship, the press has become an instrument of propaganda and an ideological mouthpiece of civilian governments and military regimes. The authoritarian press concept in Ghana uses a number of controls to prevent any criticism or public debate of the nation's policies or leaders. Since the former Gold Coast achieved independence from Britain on March 6, 1957, Ghana's press has functioned under nine regimes, five of them military and four civilian. Also press control has changed hands under different administrations. It is difficult to perform as real watchdogs of the freedom of expression and protectors of the people's interests under such uncertain circumstances. This study is significant because regime differences may have far-reaching implications for the development of press freedom in Ghana.

In her treatment of Kenya, Carla Heath identifies three distinct press traditions (models) governing press-state relations which she says have provided the "principal themes as well as points of contradiction and controversy in Kenyan press discourse." Her essay examines each press model, including a brief historical account of the media within each model, discusses the contradictions inherent in each model and reviews the press debate regarding Kenya's return to multi-party politics. She says the dominant press model in Kenya is that of a privately-owned commercial press as found in "liberal bourgeois democracies."

Festus Eribo examines the internal and external factors affecting press freedom in Nigeria, particularly the politics of ethnicity, religion, military authoritarianism, international news flow, pluralism, and new technologies. He notes that ethnicity and religion may cause political and social divisiveness but may contribute to the plurality of voices and opinion in the Nigerian media. Military authoritarianism, on the other hand, has consistently violated press freedom in Nigeria. He states that whatever freedom of press exists in Nigeria is the cumulative result of internal and external factors such as international news flow, media exposure, democratic spirit, ethnicity, new technologies and pluralism.

Anthony Giffard, Arnold de Beer, and Elaine Steyn take up the special case of South Africa which, they say, has entered a period of momentous change, peaceful reform, and the first universal franchise elections. Major changes have taken place. More surely will follow. The authors examine the tasks the media have to overcome in the transition from the apartheid regime to a new and democratic South Africa, noting the serious structural and political constraints. These include ownership of the media, which are firmly in the hands of the white minority; penetration by blacks into the board rooms (appointments) of white-owned English-language newspapers (which may be easier than being appointed to the board of directors of Afrikaans newspapers); government monopoly over broadcasting; censorship laws intended to muzzle the opposition; and the economics of launching new print media. Unlike other formerly colonized African countries where the colonizers "left" after colonialism, South Africa's whites, the authors note, are there to stay, thus there is no master plan to determine media policy and predict what is to come. Whatever media emerge in South Africa will depend on the extent to which existing media are willing to open up and admit people of other races.

Paul Grosswiler's essay traces the press history of Tanzania during colonization and since independence, leading to the opening up of the media in the last decade. Describing the emerging media democratization, his study of media worker perceptions about press freedom issues reveals several approaches that combine elements of socialist and Western media philosophies in a "third way" that transcend either global media system's way of thinking. Press freedom has progressed in Tanzania with the emergence of a half dozen privately-owned newspapers since the late 1980s and the emergence among journalists of attitudes embracing press freedom and a private press. Tanzania's democratization demonstrates the close connection that can exist between a socialist country that has attempted to achieve cultural autonomy since independence in 1961 and the pursuit of press freedom.

Melinda Robins' treatment of press freedom in Uganda points out the inherent problems with the leadership and iron fist. The victims are the people, the journalists and freedom of expression. Journalism, the author notes, is a dangerous business here. Robins notes that whatever freedom the press has today can only be measured against what has existed before. For example, the killing of some journalists and detention of others incommunicado by Idi Amin resulted in a contagious chilling effect even in the post-Amin era. The nightly news on government-owned media is a string of official releases. While no official censorship exists, there are subtle ways to control the press in Uganda.

With respect to the Zambian media, Francis Kasoma examines the legal and extra-legal government efforts to limit press freedom. The author raises some salient issues on the future of the mass media in this former British colony.

Tendayi Kumbula examines Zimbabwe media's "contradictory gyrations" since independence in 1980 while providing a glimpse of the media under white minority rule prior to independence. He outlines steps taken by the Mugabe government to wrestle the media away from white control and analyzes media performance under the Mugabe government, particularly with respect to development journalism, control of and interference with the media, and the Zimbabwe Mass Media Trust charged with setting overall policy and direction for all media in Zimbabwe.

James Napoli and Hussein Amin examine Egypt's media during colonialism and under Presidents Nasser, Sadat, and Mubarak, focusing on the legal, political, bureaucratic and social limitations of the country's contemporary media. Although the press, which includes opposition newspapers, is described as free by Mubarak's government, it is characterized by great ambivalence that expresses itself in a fawning semi-official press. Perhaps a study of freedom of expression and the press under the Pharoahs could have been an interesting scholarship but we are told by Napoli and Amin that the press in Egypt was established by Napoleon Bonaparte in 1798.

Mohammed Galander and William Starosta examine the post-colonial Sudanese press during periods of responsibility and irresponsibility, freedom and restrictions, unity and political infighting. The authors found ironic instances of press freedom during selected periods of military rule, and cases of relative press repression under otherwise democratic regimes. The analysis distinguishes the party-owned, party-affiliated, and non-party press. Galander and Starosta highlight the positive legacy of the non-party Sudanese press as an agent of responsible and constructive public dialogue, working under conditions of increasing government control.

From Francophone Africa, Allen Palmer notes that Beninois journalists are trying to reinvent a democratic form of journalism after years of French colonial rule and decades of Marxist-Leninist post-colonial government. The author points out the commitment of the journalists to the profession despite economic underdevelopment, lack of training, and political provocation.

Writing on Cameroon, a country which has been through three colonial administrations, MacDonald Ndombo Kale notes that the socio-political, cultural, and economic realities of any country should be taken into account in analyzing press freedom. He points out that a Eurocentric approach is inadequate in understanding press freedom in Cameroon because it fails to consider socio-political exigencies. He examines press freedom in Cameroon from a non-Western perspective. This examination is followed by Andre Jean Tudesq's analysis of the problems of press freedom in Cote d'Ivoire.

Minabere Ibelema and Ebere Onwudiwe writing on Zaire (now Democratic Republic of Congo) note that the philosophy of control has applied to much of the country's political and media history. They note that the colonial Zairian press was an instrument of colonial rule, geared toward the needs of Belgians in the Congo. The press, they note, continued its propaganda role after colonialism merely changing masters and serving a different elite. Under President Mobutu, it has been kept under leash and, despite the reintroduction of multi-party politics in 1990 and a rejuvenated press, the fate of the country's media will depend on a resolution of the problems of a post-Mobutu era.

Writing on Lusophone Africa, Festus Eribo examines elusive press freedom in Angola, starting with the colonial period. The author also examines the impact of the continuing struggle in Angola on the development of the mass media and the meaning of press freedom in a guerrilla-propelled media system. The study seeks to identify major political and structural factors which influenced the contents, purpose, and operationalization of the press in colonial and post-colonial Angola.

There are now 54 countries in Africa, all active members of the Organization of African Unity with the exception of Morocco. The 15 countries covered in this volume have a total population of about 416 million people, representing approximately 60 percent of Africa's 700 million people.

References

Adams, Paul. "Nigerian Press Squelched in Battle to Sway Public

Opinion," *Christian Science Monitor,* Aug. 6 1993: 7.

Christopher, Warren. "A New Relationship" *Africa Report,* July/August 1993: 38.

Davidson, Basil. *The Black Man's Burden: Africa and the Curse of the Nation-State.* New York: Times Books, 1992: 205-207.

Diamond, Larry. "International and Domestic Factors in Africa's Trend Toward Democracy, Eribo, Festus, et al., eds." *Window on Africa: Democratization and Media Exposure,* Greenville, NC: East Carolina University, March 1993.

Faringer, Gunilla L. *Press Freedom in Africa.* New York: Preager, 1991.

Hachten, William A. *The Growth of Media in the Third World: African Failures, Asian Successes* Ames: Iowa State University Press, 1993: 34.

Hawk, Beverly G. ed. *Africa's Media Image.* West Port: Praeger, 1992.

Klein, Martin A. "Back to Democracy: Presidential Address to the 1991 Annual Meeting of the African Studies Association" *African Studies Review,* 35:3 (Dec. 1992): 9.

Mazrui, Ali. "Who Should Pay for Slavery?" *World Press Review* Aug. 1993: 22.

Mutua, Makau wa "Ticking Time Bomb," *Africa Report* July/August 1993: 22.

Mytton, Graham. *Mass Communication in Africa.* London. Edward Arnold Publishers, 1993.

Ochs, Martin. *The African Press* Cairo: The American University in Cairo, 1987: 14, 23.

The Democratic Journalist, "Whither African Journalism?" April 1990: 6.

Zaffiro, James J. "Broadcasting and Politics: Radio Botswana Since Independence." Paper delivered at a conference on radio broadcasting, Institute for the Advanced Study and research in the African Humanities, Northwestern University, Evanston, IL. April 9-10 1993: 1.

PART 1

ANGLOPHONE

CHAPTER 1

PRESS PERFORMANCE UNDER CIVILIAN AND MILITARY REGIMES IN GHANA:

A REASSESSMENT OF PAST AND PRESENT KNOWLEDGE

Kwadwo Anokwa

INTRODUCTION

Since the former Gold Coast achieved political independence from Britain on March 6, 1957, Ghana's press has functioned under nine distinct regimes, five of them military and four civilian. The control of Ghana's press has changed hands from civilian regimes, which came to power through constitutional channels and democratic elections, to military regimes, which circumvented constitutional channels and took over power through coup d'etats or force of arms. Since Ghana's independence, the press has functioned under military regimes for over 20 years, a period which surpasses the functioning of the press under civilian regimes.

This study seeks to determine whether differences in regime types and styles of press ownership and control influence the successful functioning of the press in Ghana. This is important because regime differences and methods of press control may have far-reaching repercussions for the growth and development of the press in Ghana. To derive a better understanding of this study, the author presents an overview of Ghana, followed by a discussion of the press and censorship under colonial rule, the post-colonial controls and censorship, and the criticisms of the press by the powerful political elites of the Fourth Republic in Ghana.

GHANA: AN OVERVIEW

Ghana's contact with Western Europe goes as far back in time as the 15th century, when the Dutch and the Portuguese went there in search of gold and later, slaves. In the latter part of the 19th century, the British colonized most of modern Ghana and named it the Gold Coast. The British colonialists set up a wide spectrum of organizational, infrastructural, and physical systems to govern the existing traditional systems of Adansi, Denkyira, Akwamu, Ga and Fante. After years of political agitation by Western-educated Ghanaian elites, the first African Government was formed in March, 1951 by the Convention People's Party (CPP) with Dr. Kwame Nkrumah, as the leader of Government Business. On March 6, 1957, the Gold Coast and the British Trust Territory of Togoland, hitherto a United Nations Trust Territory, became an independent unitary state within the British Commonwealth under the name Ghana. The country derived its name from ancient Ghana, one of the earliest of the greatest empires of Western Sudan about 800-1076 A.D.[1]

In July 1960, under a new constitution, Ghana became a Republic with Nkrumah as its first Executive President. Nkrumah combined the roles of Head of State and Prime Minister. His first few years of rule in Ghana were politically tranquil. In 1961, however, there was a serious strike of railway workers, followed in 1962 by an unsuccessful attempt on his life. Nkrumah's government began to tighten its grip on the nation with increasing

4

use of the Preventive Detention Act, which allowed Nkrumah's administration to jail political dissenters without trial. This breach of human rights also had terrifying effects on journalists. Another assassination attempt on Nkrumah in 1964 was used by the Convention Peoples Party (CPP) government to justify a referendum that turned Ghana into a one-party socialist state. Nkrumah was subsequently sworn in as life President of Ghana. Two years later, on February 24, 1966 the army and the police seized power in a relatively swift and bloodless coup d'etat, while Nkrumah was visiting the People's Republic of China.[2]

In explaining why they toppled Nkrumah's government, the principal architects of the coup "emphasized their resentment at Nkrumah's interference with the army, his mismanagement of the Ghanaian economy, his repressive politics and the widespread corruption, intrigue and sycophancy of CPP functionaries."[3] General J.A. Ankrah, the Chairman of the National Liberation Council (NLC), a council of four soldiers and four policemen, formed to govern Ghana, said Nkrumah was removed by force in accordance with the oldest and most treasured Ghanaian tradition that a leader who loses the confidence and support of his people and resorts to arbitrary use of power should be deposed. Whatever the reasons for the coup d'etat, it ended almost ten years of uninterrupted rule by Nkrumah and his CPP government. The coup also brought an end to the non-competitive one-party socialist political system of Ghana, and ushered in an era of military-cum-police rule in Ghana and of musical chairs between civilian and military regimes. A succession of coups and counter coups with intermittent civilian administrations followed the General Ankrah's 1966 coup. The following military and civilian rulers have at different times headed the various governments in Ghana since the fall of Nkrumah: General Joseph Ankrah, General Akwasi Afrifa, Dr. Kofi Busia, General Kutu Acheampong, General Fred Akuffo, Flt. Lt. Jerry J. Rawlings, and Dr. Hilla Limann.

Table 1
Civilian and Military Regimes in Ghana: 1957-1997

Regime	Dates	Leaders
National Democratic Congress (NDC) Fourth Republic, (Civilian Regime)	1993 to Present	Flt. Lt. Jerry J. Rawlings
Provisional National Defense Council (PNDC), (Military Regime)	1981-1993	Flt. Lt. Jerry J. Rawlings
People's National Party (PNP) Third Republic, (Civilian Regime)	1979-1981	Dr. Hilla Limann
Armed Forces Revolutionary Council (AFRC) (Military Regime)	June 1979 to September 1979	Flt Lt. Jerry J. Rawlings
Supreme Military Council II (SMC II) (Military Regime)	1978-1979	Gen Fred Akuffo
National Redemption Council (NRC) Supreme Military Council I (SMC I)	1972-1978	Gen. Kutu Acheampong
(Military Regime), Progress Party (PP) Second Republic, (Civilian Regime)	1969-1972	Dr. Kofi A. Busia
National Liberation Council (NLC) (Military Regime)	1966-1969	Gen. Joseph A. Ankrah Gen. Akwasi A. Afrifa
Convention Peoples Party (CPP) First Republic, 1960-66 (Civilian Regime)	1957-1966	Dr. Kwame Nkrumah

At one point the military officers resulted to bloody means to clean house. On June 16, 1979, Acheampong of the National Redemption Council and Supreme Military Council I (NRC/SMC I) and General Utuka, a former head of the Boarder Guard were taken to the Teshie firing range, near Accra, and publicly shot after a brief trial by a hastily assembled revolutionary court. On June 26, 1979, more military officers were condemned and immediately executed by firing squad. They were General Akuffo of the SMC II regime; General Afrifa of the NLC regime; Rear Admiral Joy Amedume, former navy commander; Air Vice-Marshal George Boakye, former Air Force Commander; Major-General Robert Kotei, former chief of defense staff; and Colonel Roger Felli, former commissioner for foreign affairs. The executions shocked many Ghanaians, but there was intense pressure from the lower ranks of the army for more executions. Leading Armed Forces Revolutionary Council (AFRC) members later said they were faced with the choice of agreeing to these executions or being executed themselves. For instance, Rawlings has noted that in 1979, the AFRC didn't have too much of an opportunity to construct. Much of the regime's time was spent preventing further destruction. He said the AFRC needed to exorcise anger in order to avoid further loss of lives.[4]

Chazan (1983) has also observed that "these public executions signaled not only the termination of the already fallacious myth of the nonviolence of Ghanaian politics, but, more to the point, the deadly serious determination of the AFRC to wipe the political slate clean."[5] The handing down of revolutionary military justice was not confined to the generals and former heads of state. The nation trembled. The writing on the wall was clear. The media and the public were indisputably cowed by this public display of macabre scenario which they had to contend with in Ghana.

Ethnically, Ghana is a diverse country. There are over 75 different languages and dialects associated with a distinct ethnic group. Based on population size, linguistic affiliations, common cultural attributes and common myths of origin, Ghanaians may be divided into four major ethnic groups. There are the Akan, Mole-Dagbani, Ewe and the Ga-Adangbe. In terms of religious affiliation, Ghana is also a diverse society. Forty-three percent of Ghanaians are Christians; 12 percent are Moslems; 38 percent belong to Ghanaian traditional religions; and 7 percent have no religious affiliation. The British imposed English as the official language, and it was retained as the language of administration and education after gaining independence—ostensibly to help promote national integration. In addition to English, five major local languages are used for public communication, including radio and television broadcasting. They include Akan, Ga, Ewe, Dagbani and Nzema.[6]

Some of the problems facing the country include the deterioration in terms of trade; brain drain and local capital flight; the expulsion of Ghanaian workers from neighboring countries; and the smuggling of Ghanaian agricultural products such as cocoa and minerals (gold and diamonds) overseas to take advantage of higher prices, and the under-development of mass media infrastructure.

Both Ghanaian military and civilian regimes, in cooperation with Western industrial trading partners (the United Kingdom, Germany and the U.S.A.), and the World Bank and the International Monetary Funds have initiated a number of national economic programs to reverse the downward trend of the Ghanaian economy. The programs include the restoration of crop services; provision of agricultural extension services and credit facilities as well as incentives to increase agricultural production to achieve self-sufficiency and to increase exports; the pursuit of exchange rate policy; monetary and financial discipline; and measures aimed at addressing some of the structural weaknesses of the economy. The Ghanaian cedi has been progressively devalued from its level of C2.75 to the dollar in April 1983 to about C899 in 1994 and C2,025 in June 1997. Sixty percent of export earnings is devoted to payments of external debts. Since 1983, the World Bank and the IMF have invested over $2 billion in Ghana. Payments to the IMF alone rose from $19 million in 1986 to $207 million in 1988.[7] Clearly, the country has not achieved economic independence.

THE PRESS AND COLONIAL CENSORSHIP

The origins of the Ghanaian press and press laws date back to the nineteenth century. The first British colonial paper in the Gold Coast, *The Royal Gold Coast Gazette* was established in 1822 by Sir Charles MacCarthy, the first British governor of the Gold Coast settlements. The *Gazette* served as an official organ of the British colonial administration. African participation in the press industry began in 1857 with the establishment of the *West African Herald* by the Bannerman brothers. Following the demise of the Herald in 1873, a number of nationalist weeklies were established by Africans to help promote self-rule in Africa. The first nationalist daily newspaper, *The Times of West Africa,* was established by Dr. J.B. Danquah (a lawyer) in 1931. The majority of colonial newspapers established between 1931 and 1949 were owned and edited by highly educated Africans (mostly lawyers) who sanctioned freedom of the press and criticism of the colonial regime.[8]

Under colonial rule, several press laws were passed to muzzle the African press. The laws included The Newspaper Registration Ordinance of 1894 (Cap 116) and the Book and Newspaper Registration Ordinance of 1897 (Cap 12) which "enjoined a newspaper editor to send returns of the total circulation as well as the title of the newspaper, its offices, printers and publishers to the Colonial Secretary. In addition, the printer was expected to print his name and address on the first and last pages of the newspaper;"[9] and the Criminal Code (Amendment) Ordinance of 1934 also known as the Sedition Ordinance (Ordinance No. 21 of 1934). Section 330 of the Criminal Code of 1934 specified that "any person who published any seditious words or writing or was found in possession of any newspaper, book or document or any part thereof or extract therefrom that contained seditious words or writing and who did not show to the satisfaction of the court that at the time he was found in such possession he did not know the nature of its content was guilty of an offense."[10]

The editors of the African press were virulently critical of these press laws and fought hard to get them abolished by the colonialists. Commenting on the oppressive nature of the Newspaper Registration Ordinance of 1894, *The Gold Coast Methodist Times* noted: "It is reported that the local Legislative

Council contemplates the promulgation of an ordinance to create censorship over this journal and other organs of the Protectorate. If this were so, it would be a grievous fault and should be fought grievously. Freedom of the press, holds such an exalted position in Her Majesty's dominions that to establish law dramatically opposed to it, would mean ruin and devastation to the party or parties so offending. Why should colonial servants seek immunity from criticism—something Queen Victoria could not enjoy."[11]

A number of African newspaper editors and owners were prosecuted under the above laws. For instance, Attoh Ahuma, the nationalist editor of *The Gold Coast Methodist,* and Charles Newton, the printer of *The Methodist Journal* were prosecuted under the Book and Newspaper Registration Ordinance of 1897. Also, between 1936 and 1937, Nnamdi Azikiwe of Nigeria (Editor of *The African Morning Post*) and I.T.A. Wallace-Johnson of Sierra Leone (a writer of the *Post*) were prosecuted under the Criminal Code (Amendment) Ordinance of 1934. Azikiwe and Wallace-Johnson were prosecuted for "publishing a seditious article and for possessing material that contained seditious words."[12]

Newspapers owned and edited by Africans, and a small number of business and church organs featured prominently during colonial rule until the establishment of the *Daily Graphic* and *Sunday Mirror* in 1950 by Cecil King, the British newspaper magnate of the London Daily Mirror Group. The *Daily Graphic* (a daily) and the *Sunday Mirror* (a weekly) were established for political as well as economic reasons. They were set up to promote British colonial policy in Ghana and to earn foreign exchange for the British owners. It is important to note that shareholding in the Graphic Company was limited to British investors. The two papers received massive financial support from British banks for its operations in Ghana. They also enjoyed the patronage of British colonial officials, including the Governor. The British owned *Graphic* and *Mirror* became the most effective public communication media in Ghana because of financial security, modern equipment and good management and a well trained indigenous editorial staff. Although the *Graphic* was editorially staffed by Ghanaians, Sierra Leonean journalist, Bankole Timothy, was appointed the editor of the paper. In terms of circulation and content, the papers performed better than the Ghanaian owned independent newspapers such as the *Ashanti Pioneer* established in 1939; and the *Evening News,* founded in the early 1950s by the first president of Ghana Dr. Kwame Nkrumah. Due to their high circulation or readership in both urban and rural settings, the British owned papers were also more effective than the Ghanaian owned papers in stirring up political awareness among Ghanaians.

Post-colonial Controls and Censorship of the Press

Whatever contribution the British owned *Graphic* made toward the struggle for Ghana's independence, the paper never won the confidence and support of Ghanaian nationalist leaders, including Nkrumah. Nkrumah and other nationalist leaders viewed the *Graphic* as a relic of colonialism and a propaganda tool of opposition leaders.[13] Consequently, Nkrumah and the nationalist press launched a relentless campaign of mudslinging against the *Graphic* and its British owners. In post-colonial Ghana, Nkrumah sought not only to Africanize Ghana's press but also to use the press as an instrument of political development in Ghana and elsewhere in Africa. Nkrumah was committed to Pan-Africanism and socialist ideology.

Nkrumah believed that the independence of Ghana would be meaningless unless it was linked to the total liberation of the Continent of Africa. He argued that " just as in capitalist countries, the press represents and carries out the purpose of capitalism, so in revolutionary Africa, the press must present and carry forward our own purposes."[14] It was against this background that in 1958, Nkrumah established the *Ghanaian Times* to challenge the dominance of the *Graphic* and the *Ashanti Pioneer,* and to serve as the ideological mouthpiece of the CPP regime. The Nkrumah government and the party-controlled *Guinea Press Limited* provided necessary funds for setting up the *Times.* In its first editorial, the *Times* (published in Accra), stated its philosophy and functions as follows: "Our policy will be to support the government in power and wherever necessary we shall criticize it objectively. We believe unalterably that socialist policies of the CPP government are wisely and soundly conceived."[15] Nkrumah appointed party functionaries as editors of the *Times* to promote his socialist ideology.

On July 2, 1962, Nkrumah's government took over the ownership and control of the *Daily Graphic* at the request of the Daily Mirror Group. The British proprietors of the Graphic sold the paper to Nkrumah because they did not want to operate under Nkrumah's CPP government. Also, the law of Ghana forbade the wholesale repatriation of their profits. Under the law, foreign investors in Ghana were obliged to reinvest 60 percent of profits in their own businesses. The remaining 40 percent was, of course, subject to stringent foreign exchange controls before its repatriation. The change in ownership marked the surrender of the independence of the *Graphic,* and other independent newspapers in Ghana.[16]

In 1962, Nkrumah and the CPP government subjected the *Pioneer* to official censorship by appointing a government official to the editorial board of the independent paper which is (published in Kumasi, the Ashanti regional capital and a stronghold of Nkrumah's opponents). The city editor of the *Pioneer,* Kwame Kesse-Adu was arrested and detained in the Usher Fort prison for four years for "destructive criticism" of Nkrumah's CPP government. In order to consolidate government control of the Ghanaian press, Nkrumah passed a Newspaper Licensing Act in 1963. This press law required newspaper publishers to obtain a license, renewable annually, from the ruling regime.[17] In addition, Nkrumah established government corporations to run Ghana's mass media institutions, including the *Daily Graphic,* the *Ghanaian Times,* the *Evening News,* the Sound and Television networks of the Ghana Broadcasting Corporation (GBC), the Ghana News Agency (GNA), the Ghana Film Industry Corporation (GFIC), and the Ghana Institute of Journalism (GIJ) which was established under the Ministry of Information to train journalists in Ghana and elsewhere in Africa. By all indications, Nkrumah's reign was a period of healthy growth for the state-owned media although the era was also characterized by authoritarian methods of press control and complete rejection of private ownership and control of the media in Ghana.[18]

Following Nkrumah's overthrow on February 6, 1966, the NLC regime maintained the majority of the media institutions established by Nkrumah. It kept and operated the *Graphic, Times,* GBC, GNA, GFIC, and GIJ—as state-owned media institutions. It eliminated Nkrumah's *Evening News* but licensed the publication of a number of party newspapers, including the Pioneer, the Echo and the Star for Busia's Progress Party (PP) and the *Evening Standard* for K.A. Gbedemah's Native Alliance of Liberals (NAL) Party, and the *Legon Observer,* published by a group of University of Ghana professors.

The NLC like its predecessors, promulgated a number of press laws to ensure control of the private and public press in Ghana. For instance, under the "Rumors Decree" of October 1966, the NLC circumscribed domestic news, even though it lifted censorship of news accounts sent overseas from Ghana. The NLC in a subsequent decree of November 26, 1966, indicated that no one could sue the owners, publishers or editors of the government-owned newspapers for defamation without authorization of the Attorney General, an appointee of the NLC military government. In 1968, the NLC passed Decree 226 to place the Ghana Broadcasting Corporation under the jurisdiction of a statutory corporation and to redefine the objectives of the media.

Decree 226 of 1968 stated in part: "The objects of the Corporation shall be to undertake sound, commercial and television broadcasts, to prepare in the field of culture, education, information and entertainment programmes reflecting national progress, aspirations and to carry on an external service of sound broadcasting."[19] The NLC's policy in respect of Ghana's broadcast media followed the authoritarian pattern of control introduced by Nkrumah and his CPP socialist regime. In other words, the broadcast media were to have no utility or purpose other than serving the needs and aspirations of the ruling NLC military regime.

When the NLC left office in 1969, the military regime bequeathed the democratically-elected civilian regime of Kofi Busia with mass media institutions controlled by the government. As soon as he entered office, he tried to move Ghana's mass media policies in a libertarian direction. He repealed the Newspaper Licensing Act in 1970. He made personal changes in the top management positions in Ghana's mass media institutions, including the dismissal of Cameron Dodoo, the editor of the state-owned *Graphic,* for opposing the Busia regime concerning its call on African countries to have a dialogue with apartheid South Africa. Busia encouraged the establishment of a number of private and independent newspapers, including the *Palaver Tribune,* the *Voice of the People,* and the *Spokesman,* which was stridently critical of the Busia and Progress Party administration.20

When Acheampong overthrew the Busia administration in a coup d'etat in January 1972, he quickly restored the authoritarian method of press control. The military regime of Acheampong issued a decree indemnifying the state-owned press against libel suits which had been filed by the opponents of the regime, who alleged that they had been defamed by articles appearing in the state-owned press. In March 1973, Acheampong reinstated the "Newspaper Licensing Decree" and the "Rumors Decree" to tighten control over Ghana's media institutions. The Acheampong regime also used economic measures to establish its control over independent papers which were critical of the regime's policies. For instance, the *Echo* and *Legon Observer* ceased publication under Acheampong's regime because the regime refused to allocate these independent papers foreign exchange to import newsprint. Acheampong also arrested and detained top editors of the independent press, including the editors of the *Pioneer,* the *Believer* and the *Echo.* Acheampong introduced official and self censorship in the Ghanaian press system through threats of dismissal, harassment and military interrogation of Ghanaian media practitioners and managers.

It is important to note that Acheampong's authoritarian press policies did not deter the anti-Acheampong movements from criticizing the government. In May 1978, these movements launched a number of "revolutionary" papers which called for an end to military dictatorship and a return to a multi-party democratic system of rule in Ghana. These papers included two university student publications: the *Missile* of the University of Cape Coast, Cape Coast; the *Focus* of the University of Science and Technology, Kumasi; the *Voice of the People,* an underground newsletter of the People's Movement for Freedom and Justice (PMFJ); the *News Bulletin* of the Association of Recognized Professional Bodies; and the *Catholic Standard,* a weekly organ of the Catholic Church in Ghana.[21]

General Akuffo, who overthrew Acheampong's SMC I regime in a palace coup in May, 1978 sought to reverse the authoritarian press policies of Acheampong. He released journalists and politicians detained by Acheampong during the campaign for "Union Government," a non-party system of government. Akuffo's approach to the press led to the establishment of two party papers: the *Star* of the Popular Front Party (PFP); and the *Gong Gong* of the People's National Party (PNP). The approach by Akuffo and his SMC II regime led to the resumption of publication by two independent papers: *The Believer;* and *The Legon Observer.* [22]

During the AFRC short rule, the grip on Ghana's mass media was never let loose. Rawlings and his AFRC regime maintained complete control over the state-owned media. After repealing the press laws passed by the Acheampong regime, the AFRC took steps to appoint Elizabeth Ohene as the new editor of the state-owned *Graphic.* The appointment was made immediately after Ohene, literary editor and columnist of the *Graphic,* had published a column strongly criticizing the executions carried out by the AFRC. Critics of the AFRC viewed the appointment of Elizabeth Ohene as a mechanism by the AFRC regime to control the *Graphic.* In a reply to her appointment letter, Ohene said, "she had long been opposed to arbitrary government interference of this sort in newspapers," and asked to be made acting editor only until things were more settled. The appointment of Ohene was also seen as an attempt by Rawlings and the AFRC regime to undermine the Third Republican Constitution. The new constitution, promulgated by the AFRC, insisted that a Press Commission should be responsible for choosing a government body, which would in turn be responsible for appointing an editor of the state-owned press. Thus, Rawlings and the AFRC administration had no authority to either appoint or dismiss the editors of the state-owned *Graphic* or *Times.*.[23] The AFRC mishandling of the Ohene's affair and its authoritarian approach to the press convinced the regime's opponents that the AFRC revolt was not meant to restore public accountability, constitutional government and press freedom. However, Rawlings and the AFRC regime ruled Ghana for about four months and handed over power to the People's National Party (PNP), the civilian government of Dr. Hilla Limann, which secured 71 of the 140 seats of the unicameral legislature. The transfer of power to the democratically elected PNP government of Limann allowed Ghana to return to constitutional rule for the third time in its first twenty-two years of political history.

Limann was sworn in as president and head of government by Rawlings on September 24, 1979. When he assumed office, he took the necessary measures to restore libertarian press structures in Ghana. He inaugurated the 12-member Press Commission on July 25, 1980. Limann used this occasion to articulate his conception and belief in the libertarian ideas of the press in particular and free expression in general. He said:

> I shall, as elected President of Ghana, be forever prepared to submit to the acid test of public judgment the claims of those who may think that they represent the public more than me or any other political leader. Bluff, snobbery and arrogance on all sides must now cease, so that the Press Commission can function in the way that it has been envisaged by those who have never had any personal ax to grind. I have long been one of the protagonists myself. Since the functions of the Press Commission have been clearly spelt out in the Constitution, I can do no more than reassure its members and our journalists that my government will respect, uphold and defend the Constitution and thus do everything in our power to help the Press Commission discharge its obligation, in the overall interest of the public to which we are all to varying degrees accountable.[24]

Chapter 22 of the Third Republican Constitution of Ghana makes provisions not only for the establishment of the Press Commission but it also defines the functions of the Commission; sanctions the independence of journalists; and prohibits press licenses. The chapter, which was entitled "Press Commission," may be summarized as follows:

Establishment of the Press Commission: Article 192 (1) : This article notes:

> There shall be established, within six months after the coming into force of this Constitution, a Press Commission which shall consist of (a) one representative each nominated by (i) the Association of Recognized Professional Bodies; (ii) the Ghana Bar Association; (iii) the National Development Commission; (iv) the Universities of Ghana; (v) the owners and proprietors of the private press; (vi) the Association of Writers; (vii) the owners and the proprietors of the private press; (viii) the Christian Council and the national Catholic Secretariat; (b) two representatives nominated by the Ghana Journalists' Association; and (c) two other members one of whom shall be a woman.

Functions of the Press Commission: Article 193: This article states:

> The functions of the Press commission shall include: (a) the appointment of the chairman and other members of the governing body of any public corporation established for sound or television broadcasting, the press or other media of mass communication or information; (b) the assistance where necessary, in the procurement and distribution on an equitable and non-discriminatory basis of the facilities and services required for the efficient and independent operation of the press and other media for mass communication or information; (c) the making , by constitutional instrument, of Regulations for the registration of

newspapers and other publications; (d) the making, by constitutional instrument, of Regulations for the registration and licensing of other media for mass communication; (e) the taking of measures to ensure the preservation of press freedom; and (f) the taking of measures to ensure the maintenance of the highest professional and journalistic standards in the mass media including the investigation and adjudication of complaints made against members of the press.

Independence of Journalists: Article 194: The article states:

> Subject to the provisions of article 193 of this Constitution, the Press Commission shall not exercise or purport to exercise any control or direction over the professional functions of a person engaged in the production of newspapers or other means of mass communication.

Prohibition of Press Licenses: Article 195: This article notes:

> Subject to the provision of article 193 of this Constitution, Parliament shall have no power to enact an Act requiring or authorizing any authority to require a person to obtain or maintain a license of any kind for the establishment or operation of a newspaper, publication or institution of the press or other media for mass communication or information.[25]

During his tenure, Limann repeatedly committed himself to accepting the rule of law and the verdict of democracy in his approach to the mass media in Ghana. He observed that "the history of the press in Ghana since independence had not been endearing because press men and women had found it difficult to perform as real watchdogs of the freedom of expression, which also protects interests of the people of the country." Limann, who sanctioned privatization of the mass media, enjoined the Press Commission and mass media institutions in Ghana to develop true independence by being financially independent. He said:

No truly respected newspaper or journal has ever subsisted on the taxpayer's money. This is the deeper reason for my appeal through parliament in my last Sessional Address, for ways and means to be found for ensuring a really free press in every sense of the term. Now that the Press Commission has been set up, I hope that its members will seriously and quickly direct their attention to this most vital point in the fulfillment of their role and functions. As you are very well aware, the willful suppression of nationally important information in favor of distortions, can be harmful to a free press, particularly at the period of its early development when the reach of newspapers is still rather limited.[26]

Limann did not last long in office to implement his liberal press policies. On December 31, 1981, Rawlings and the military seized power again through a coup d'etat. Rawlings cited corruption and economic maladministration as the reasons for his "second coming." The Third Republican Constitution (including the Press Commission) was abolished, parliament dissolved, and the five political parties which contested the right to run the Third Republic were proscribed.

The Provisional National Defense Council (PNDC) headed by Rawlings was established to run Ghana. Immediately on assuming office, Rawlings reversed Limann's liberal press policies. He dissolved the Press Commission and urged Ghana's press to serve as the vanguard of the "Holy War" and direct the course of the December 31, 1981 revolution.[27] Rawlings accused Ghana's press of sowing the seeds of despair and pessimism that made Ghanaians refuse to be masters of their own destiny. The Ghanaian press, he asserted, would be doing a great disservice to the nation if it chose to please men in authority instead of serving the interest of the underprivileged and the defenseless. He further noted that the press had allowed the over-enthusiasm and over-simplified ideological ideas of a minority of its personnel to create a misleading image of the December 31, 1981 revolution at home and abroad.

Following his criticisms of the Ghanaian press in 1982, Rawlings dismissed the editor of the *Graphic,* George Aidoo; and the editor of the *Mirror,* Addo Twum. Three other senior journalists were sent on indefinite leave; they included Elizabeth Ohene, who turned down Rawlings' offer of appointment as editor of the *Graphic* in 1979, when Rawlings served as the head of the AFRC regime.[28] Rawlings and the PNDC regime appointed Kojo Yankah, a staunch supporter of the December 31st revolution, as the editor of the *Daily Graphic.* Following this appointment, the paper was renamed the *People's Daily Graphic* ostensibly to remind the personnel and readers of this national daily newspaper that the *Graphic* belongs to the "people" (the masses in Ghana) and must therefore be used to promote their interests and aspirations. The PNDC Secretary for Information, Joyce Aryee supported direct government control of the press. Speaking late in 1983, Aryee said:

> I don't see the press as lying outside the political institutions that we have. This is where I feel that people ought to realize that the press differs from country to country. In a situation like our, where we need to conscientize [sic] people, and where we have an illiteracy problem, you use institutions like the press to do the conscientization.[29]

The PNDC passed a number of decrees to muzzle the press and to prevent criticism of the policies of the regime. These included the Newspaper Licensing Law (PNDC Law 211), which stifled the growth and development of the private press; and Preventive Custody Law (PNDC Law 4), which allowed indefinite detention without trial of persons critical of the regime. Following a coup attempt in June 1983, the PNDC regime detained the owner, editor and a reporter of the *Free Press,* which represented the sole voice of dissent in Ghana's print media. Commenting on the detentions, the Information Secretary, Joyce Aryee said, they had nothing to do directly with what the *Free Press* wrote but that it was part of a larger issue of a systematic destabilization program that seemed to be around. She said it may have been reflected in what the paper wrote, but she would rather see this as a coincidence. Workers supporting the PNDC regime occupied the premises of Tommark Advertising, publishers of the *Free Press* and called for the independent paper to be turned into "a people's press to print people's news." It must be noted that the owner of the *Free Press,* Tommy Thompson, was released from detention after suffering a stroke requiring hospitalization. The editor, John Kugblenu, and a reporter, Mike Adjei were not released until June 1984. Kugblenu died soon after his release from prison.

Kojo Yankah, the PNDC-appointed editor of the *Graphic* was suspended later in 1983 following publication of a front-page story describing a conversation between a member of the PNDC, Amartey Kwei, and the Chairman of the PNDC, Rawlings, minutes before Kwei was executed for his part in the murder of three Ghanaian Judges. The state-owned *Times,* a competitor to the state-owned *Graphic,* supported the PNDC regime's suspension of Kojo Yankah. Commenting on the case, the *Times* noted that the *"Graphic's* insensitive front page scoop had made the Head of State's talk look like a device to vindicate the regime, when Rawlings' real concern was that even if his comrade had lied in his attempt to save himself, he would at least die with the truth on his lips."[30]

The draconian press policies of the PNDC regime was not limited to the print media. During the PNDC rule, several top officials of the Ghana Broadcasting Corporation were either dismissed or prematurely retired. The PNDC regime of Rawlings employed several economic and legal means to impose authoritarian methods of press control in Ghana. As a result of the authoritarian methods of control, Rawlings and the PNDC regime succeeded in making Ghana's press a handmaiden of the government. Rawlings in commenting on the performance of the press noted:

> Some of our journalists—fewer than formerly—I am glad to say—still produce the sort of bland, non-controversial, sycophantic material that was formerly the order of the day. Their aim seems to be to please authority, or, at least, not to offend it. In the process,

they neither interest nor educate their readers or listeners. But when I criticize the press, there are two types of reactions. One is nervousness that they are going to get into trouble for doing something wrong; the other is indignation at being dictated to."[31]

THE POWERFUL VERSUS THE PRESS

Since the 45-year-old Flt. Lt. (retired) Jerry John Rawlings was sworn into office as Ghana's Fourth Republican president on January 7, 1993, he has established a 15-member National Media Commission to promote the freedom and independence of Ghana's press. Rawlings has noted that "all that has happened during the last decade (of PNDC rule) cannot be divorced from today's constitutional order—No one can fail to appreciate the significance of the 31st December Revolution in bringing Ghanaians to the threshold of the Fourth Republic, and in establishing firm principles of social justice which will make the constitution a living reality—to do so would mean distorting Ghana's history and putting aside those vital lessons which would indeed enrich this phase of Ghanaian experience."[32] He further notes that his inauguration as Ghana's Fourth Republican president and Commander-in-Chief of the Ghana Armed Forces constitutes "a collective pledge to observe and defend the provisions of the constitution,"[33] including provisions in Chapter 12 of Ghana's Fourth Republican Constitution.

Chapter 12 of the 1992 Constitution which is entitled, "Freedom and Independence of the Media," defines the following: freedom and responsibility of the media; responsibility of the state-owned media; limitation on rights and freedoms; and media rights and freedoms to be additional to fundamental human rights. The Constitution also makes provisions for the establishment of a National Media Commission; functions of the Commission; the appointment of Board Members of the state-owned press; appointment of editors; and the independence of journalists.[34]

The Chairman of the National Media Commission, Mr. Kofi

Kumado, has noted that the Media Commission "has no mandate to curb media practitioners except where they have put freedom of speech and media in danger."[35] Speaking to journalists at the first meeting of the Media Commission, Kumado said, "Ghanaian journalists should not consider the body as a threat to their professional judgment and that the commission would not adopt a confrontational stance in dealing with complaints by members of the public[36]." He added that "the people of Ghana, in their wisdom, and because they valued freedom of speech and media, have decided that the media should be vehicles for the creation of a pluralist open society."[37]

President Rawlings and the NDC government have accused Ghana's private press of being stridently critical of the ruling government and its leadership. For instance Mr. P. V. Obeng a former member of the PNDC and now the Presidential Adviser on Government Affairs, has noted that "the government's tolerance of the press maligning members of the government has its limit."[38] He added that "the private press in particular has inflicted a lot of battering on the government with a view to creating antagonism between the government and the people."[39] Obeng noted that Ghana's new "democracy should be seen as a means to achieving development and progress and not to destroy."[40]

Mr. Justice D.F. Annan, speaker of Parliament and former PNDC member, has also criticized Ghana's private press for portraying the House as a mere rubber stamp and for relegating it to a position of inferiority. He said, "It is about time we looked at the issue critically. The dignity of MPs must be respected and that is why constitutionally it is an offense to do something that affronts the dignity of Parliament."[41]

Ghana's First Lady, Nana Konadu Agyemang Rawlings has also indicted the private press for "misusing the freedom of expression to spread falsehood."[42] She expressed doubt about the quality of training and professional competence of some of the editors of the private press. Mr. Kofi Totobi Quakyi, Minister of Information of the ruling NDC and the PNDC has also condemned the private press for being virulently anti-Rawlings, and has hinted that the tolerance of the NDC government is running out. [43]

The Acting Chief Director of the Ministry of Health, Mr. Alfred Onyina-Mensah has also told civil servants not to hold press conferences or divulge information to the press because such actions may be punished by the authorities. A citizens group called Friends of Democracy has also accused the private press of being "unprofessional, unconstitutional, un-Ghanaian and irresponsible."[44] The group which claims it has collected 1,000 signatories from all walks of life in Ghana, has pleaded with the National Media Commission to investigate the actions of the private press. The group led by the Rev. Dr. R.C. Lawson also accused the press of "publishing tendentious articles to bring the person and office of the President into disrepute. President Rawlings has also characterized Ghana private press as "having nothing good in stock but lies and falsehood."[45]

Mrs. Valerie Sackey, the director of the Public Affairs Secretariat at the Office of President Rawlings in reacting to Ghana's private press criticism of the NDC government noted: "There is no struggle between Ghana's private press (*The Ghanaian Chronicle, The Statesman, The Independent, the Ghanaian Voice,* the *Free Press,* the *Guide,* and the *Weekly Insight*). There is no clampdown. There is no siege. There is, however, considerable disgust on the part of the public as well as on the part of those who have to put up with the constant barrage of smears, innuendoes and vicious rumors from those who have run berserk with press freedom."[46] She added:

> Responsible journalism requires that the facts be checked and enquiries be made before going to print. Official sources are prepared to assist enquiries being made in good faith. It is unacceptable to publish unverified allegations and abusive untruths, and to continue to repeat the same allegations even when they have been responded to, with the argument that unless the editors are sued, the allegations must be true. It is even less acceptable for some sections of the private press to portray legitimate criticism of such unethical journalistic practice as an attempt by government to muzzle them.[47]

The editors of two privately-owned papers, *The Statesman and the Free Press* have reported that they have been sent death threats for being critical of the ruling NDC regime. The state-owned *Graphic* has written an editorial to condemn those who sent the death threats. The *Graphic* editorial noted: "Whatever the disagreements we may have, it must be as close as it can be to the end of the road for any nation when its editors face the threat of death for the pursuit of their professional duties."[48]

DISCUSSION

The foregoing discussion shows that the press in Ghana is circumscribed and limited by socio-political and economic conditions of the country. It also shows that past and present regimes in Ghana differ in their political ideology and method of press control. The evidence in this study and those of previous scholars suggest that the functioning of the press under past civilian and military regimes is characterized not only by an authoritarian method of control but also a Libertarian method of control. The evidence points to an authoritarian method of control under the governments of Nkrumah, Afrifa, Acheampong, Akuffo, and Rawlings' AFRC and PNDC.

The evidence also suggests that the functioning of the Ghanaian press under colonial rule, Busia, Limann, and the ruling NDC of Rawlings point to the liberal direction and social responsibility approach. These three regimes were democratically chosen under multi-party elections.[49] Despite the abrupt changes in government, the unsettling political upheaval, the chaotic economic conditions, and the strains and stress of nation-building that the Ghanaian press has experienced, the press has not failed to perform its societal functions, including transmission of news and information, providing a forum for public debates and education and interpreting policies of the government, transmission of entertainment, providing avenues for buying and selling and setting the public agenda.[50]

It is important to note that in spite of the democratic election in 1996, the strains and pressures facing the Ghanaian press will not be eliminated until there is civilian control of the military and a financially strong independent press. Several scholars have noted that the overriding determinant of press performance and contents is not multi-party structures and written constitutions but the political ideology of those who finance and control the press. [51]

NOTES

1. *Africa Year Book and Who's Who 1977.* London: Africa Limited; 435-452 passim. Also see Thomas A. Howell and Jeffrey P. Rajasooria, *Ghana and Nkrumah.* New York: Fact on File, Inc., 1972, 145-157 passim.
2. Ibid.
3. T.C. McCaskie, "Ghana: Recent History." In *Africa South of the Sahara,* Sixteenth Edition. London, England: Europa Publication, 1986: 480.
4. *Africa Contemporary Record,* Vol. 24, 1981-1982. London: Africana Publishing Company, B498.
5. *Africa Forum,* Vol. 2, No. 2, 1992: 10.
6. Donald Ray, Ghana: Politics, *Economics and Society. Boulder,* Colorado: Lyne Riener Publishers, Inc., 1986, xiv-vii. Also see E.A. Boateng, "Ghana: Physical and Social Geography." In *Africa South of the Sahara 1994,* Third Edition. London, England: Europa Publications Limited, 1993.
7. Baffour Agyeman-Duah, "Ghana, 1982-6: the Politics of the PNDC," *The Journal of Modern African Studies,* 25. 4 (1987): 613-642 passim. Also see *West Africa,* 28-February-6 March 1994: 367.
8. See K.A.B. Jones-Quartey, *A Summary History of the Ghana Press,* Accra, 1974.
9. Yaw Twumasi, Press Freedom and Nationalism Under Colonial Rule in the Gold Coast (Ghana), *Journal of the Historical Society of Nigeria 7.* 3 (Dec. 1974): 504-506 passim. Also see Yaw Twumasi, "The Newspaper Press and political Leadership in Developing Nations: The Case of Ghana 1964 to 1978," Gazette 26 (1980): 1-6 passim.
10. Twumasi (1980), op. cit. Also see Sylvannus A. Ekwelie, "The Genesis of Press Control in Ghana," *Gazette,* Vol. XXIV, No. 3, 1978: 197-206 passim.
11. Ekwelie, op. cit., 197. Also see *The Gold Coast Methodist Times,* 31 July 1897.
12. Ekwelie, op. cit., 198-203 passim. See Twumasi (1980) , op. cit., 5-6.
13. William Hachten, *Muffled Drums.* Ames, Iowa: The Iowa University Press, 1971: 89-95 passim. Also see Eddie Agyemang,

"Freedom of Expression in a Government Newspaper in Ghana," in Olav Stokke: The Scandinavian Institute of African Studies, 1971.

14. Kwame Nkrumah, *Ghana: Autobiography of Kwame Nkrumah,* Edinburgh, 1957, Introduction.
15. Hachten (1971), op. cit., 168-169.
16. Agyemang, op. cit.
17. Twumasi (1980), op. cit.
18. Hachten (1971) op. cit.
19. *National Liberation Council Decree* (N.L.C.D. 226), Accra, State Publishing Corporation.
20. Twumasi (1980), op. cit.
21. Ibid.
22. Ibid.
23. *Africa Contemporary Record,* Volume 12, 1979-1980 London: Africana Publishing Company: B502-503.
24. *Democracy and Ghana: Select Speeches of President Hilla Limann.* London: Rex Collings, 1983.
25. *Constitution of the Republic of Ghana,* 1979. Tema, Ghana, Ghana Publishing Corporation.
26. *Democracy and Ghana,* op. cit.
27. *Daily Graphic,* Jan. 5, 1982: 1
28. *Africa Contemporary Record,* Vol. 14, 1981-1982. London: Africana Publishing Company, B422.
29. *Africa Contemporary Record,* Volume 16, 1983-1984. London: African Publishing Company, B436-437.
30. Ibid.
31 *African News,* Sept. 19 1988: 8.
32. *West Africa,* 18-24 Jan. 1993: 52.
33. Ibid.
34. *Constitution of the Republic of Ghana, 1992,* Tema: Ghana, Ghana Publishing Corporation.
35. *West Africa,* 18-24 Jan. 1993.
36. Ibid.
37. Ibid.
38. *West Africa,* 25 April-May 1994: 740.
39. Ibid.
40. Ibid.
41. Ibid.
42. Ibid.
43. Ibid.
44. *West Africa* 21-27 March 1994: 550.
45. Ibid.
46. *West Africa,* 30 May-5 June, 1994: 961-962.

47. Ibid.
48. *West Africa,* 16-22 May 1994: 866.
49. For findings in previous research, see Twumasi (1980), op. cit., S. T. K. Boafo, "Ghana's Press under the PNDC: Performance under Confinement," Gazette, 35: 73-82, 1985, K. Anokwa and Osei-Mensah, Aborampah, "The Mass Media, Political Attitudes and Behavior in Ghana," *Gazette* 37, 1986: 139-154.
50. See K. Anokwa and Michael Salwen, "Newspaper Agenda Setting Among Elites and Non-elites in Ghana, *Gazette,* 41, 1988: 201-214.
51. Twumasi (1980), *op. cit.,* Jeffrey Herbst, *Politics of Reform in Ghana, 1982-1991.* Berkeley, California: University of California Press, 1993: 163-164, Herbert J. Altschull, *Agents of Power: The Role of the News Media in Human Affairs.* New York: Longman, 1984; Pamela Shoemaker, *Building a Theory of News Contents: A Synthesis of Current Approaches,* Journalism Monographs: 103, June 1987.

CHAPTER 2

COMMUNICATION AND

PRESS FREEDOM IN KENYA

Carla W. Heath

INTRODUCTION

The press has been a key actor in the construction of the modern nation state (Gellner 1983; Hobsbawm 1990; Anderson 1991). Newspapers, pamphlets, primers, mail order catalogs, and other print media have taught readers what it means to be British, French, Italian, or "other." They have standardized "national" languages, stimulated commerce, disseminated political intelligence, and whipped up support for foreign wars. The electronic media, beginning with the telegraph, extended this national project and facilitated the integration of national economies into an international economy. Satellites, computers, and telecommunications are presently transforming that international system into a transnational or global one.

In Europe, the nation state was the base upon which the international economic system was built. In Africa, the modern media of communication were employed to integrate African economies and peoples into the international market economy; only later were they harnessed to the causes of nationalism and nation building. As a consequence, the press in Africa has often served international commerce better than it has served national development. Such is the case in Kenya.

The Kenyan press has, to use Professor Mazrui's phrase, a triple heritage. Contemporary state/press relations, journalistic practices, and public expectations have been shaped by three conflicting yet interwoven sets of ideas about the role of the press in a new nation: the liberal/commercial; authoritarian/development, and advocacy/protest traditions. The ideas, like the media themselves, had their origins in Western Europe; the ways in which they have been interpreted and intertwined are particular to Kenya.

THE LIBERAL/COMMERCIAL TRADITION

The oldest tradition in Kenya is that of a privately owned, competitive, commercial press such as is generally associated with bourgeois democracies. The press in this tradition is "independent" in that it is not owned by government or subject to official censorship. The news media are expected to be watchdogs for citizens and to provide them with the information they need to make decisions about public affairs and to be wise consumers of goods and services available in the market. In addition, they are to serve as fora for debate on public issues (Siebert 1956b; Altschull 1984; Curran and Seaton 1988).

Although couched in liberal rhetoric, the liberal/commercial tradition is essentially conservative (Ainslie 1966, 215). The modern commercial press is an industry requiring enormous capital outlay in addition to a substantial operating budget for labor, fax, telephone, computer, and wire services. It must operate in accordance with industrial principles. Furthermore, because the commercial press is chiefly financed by advertisements placed on behalf of other industries and services, or is subsidized by revenues from profitable enterprises owned jointly with the media outlet, it typically espouses an editorial position that is pro-business and supportive of a "stable" political environment (Altschull; Curran &

Seaton). Labor, except as a problem for business, is generally ignored (Parenti 1986); language and stories that might inflame communal or class passions are not run. Instead, editors select—consciously or unconsciously—copy that attracts the sorts of audiences advertisers hope to reach. In a developing nation like Kenya, this means urban populations with cash incomes: civil servants, employees of commercial establishments, and factory workers as well as salaried bureaucrats and independent business persons.

The commercial press tradition was firmly established in the colonial era. European and Asian commercial, political, and social interests were served by a number of newspapers and magazines, the most influential being the *East African Standard,* founded as the *African Standard* in 1902 (see Ainslie 1966; Barton 1979; Mwaura 1980 for historic overviews). The origins of broadcasting were also commercial. From 1928 until 1958 international telecommunications companies provided radio services in exchange for a monopoly on providing external telecommunications services in the colony and 90 percent of the revenues from annual receiver fees (Heath 1986a, ch. 3). Like the settler press Kenyaradio catered to the interests and tastes of its target audience: European civil servants, missionaries, and settlers. Light entertainment, European music and drama and news from the BBC linked widely-scattered Europeans to each other and to Britain. As the Asian market for radios and goods advertised on the radio grew, programs in Asian languages were added. Services for Africans were provided by the state.

In 1962, on the eve of independence, all broadcasting was turned over to a consortium of British, North American, and Kenyan media concerns that agreed to take responsibility for radio and to introduce television. The decision to privatize broadcasting was related to the Colonial Office's efforts to assure continuity of British influence by economic and cultural as opposed to political means (Pratt 1982; cf. Karikari 1992). Television with foreign films, BCINA news films, and advertisements from multinational corporations was to be a powerful ally in this project.

The Kenya Broadcasting Corporation (KBC) was not a commercial success; within two years it was badly indebted to the Kenya government. The KBC was nationalized in 1964; however, advertising was retained and television continued to be dependent upon foreign news and entertainment programs.

The commercial press today is comprised of three newspaper groups: the *Standard,* the *Nation,* and the *Kenya Times;* the Kenya Television Network (KTN), and numerous periodicals. Foreign interests are still prominent although well placed Kenyans have managed the papers and sat on the boards of directors for over two decades. The commercial media rely heavily on sales and advertisements, the majority of which are placed by subsidiaries of multinationals operating in Kenya (Jouet 1984).

Standard, Ltd., which publishes *The Standard* and *The Standard on Sunday,* is a subsidiary of Lonrho, a London-based conglomerate which has substantial investments in Kenya as well as southern and central Africa. Lonrho's ownership of *The Standard* illustrates the inter-dependent nature of international capital/press/state/comprador relations in Kenya. Nicola Swainson (1980) has described in detail how Lonrho, beginning with the purchase of the *East African Standard* in 1967, acquired significant investments in all the major areas of Kenya's economic sector. Alliances with the ruling class were cemented by appointing prominent Kenyans to boards and managerial positions in local subsidiaries. Local managers drew upon Lonrho's resources for investment capital for their own enterprises while the conglomerate financed its regional expansion with locally borrowed money (Swainson 1980, 273-284).

The Standard was used to project a climate of opinion favorable to international business and to attack Kenyan nationalists who opposed Lonrho's takeovers (Ochieng' 1992). Editorial control was vested in people who understood the wisdom of supporting the government of the day and the value of pro-international business economic policies. Both Kenneth Bolton, who was Editor-in-Chief at the time of the Lonrho takeover in 1967, and George Githii, who held that position from 1980-1982, had close ties with the ruling circle through their friendships with the powerful anglophile Attorney General Charles Njonjo (Barton, 83; Ochieng', 38). When Henry Gathigira was Editor-in Chief (1975-80), it was Foreign Minister Njoroge Mungai who influenced and protected *The Standard* (Ochieng', 62).

Because of its colonial heritage and foreign ownership, *The Standard* has been associated with European interests in Kenya. It still carries somewhat more international business news than its rivals and *The Standard on Sunday* magazine is more likely to feature stories about European celebrities than African peasants. It did not take a clear Kenya African National Union (KANU) or opposition position in the 1992 election campaign (WR,1 1/1/(3:53).

Nation Printers and Publishers publishes four papers: *Daily Nation, Sunday Nation* and Kiswahili counter-parts, *Taifa Leo* and *Taifa Jumapili.* Over 60 percent of the company's shares are traded on the Nairobi Stock Exchange but control rests with the paper's founder, His Highness the Aga Khan, spiritual leader of the Ismali Muslims.

The Aga Khan's interests in Kenya range from rural health care to a chain of tourist hotels. Kenya has been a principal beneficiary of the Aga Khan Network (DN 4/24/92:8), the largest and one of the most respected private development organizations operating in the Third World. The network "emphasizes self-sufficiency, sound management, a good knowledge of local conditions, and the most appropriate technology...[it also] stresses the promotion of private enterprise and venture capital" and seeks to expand hard-currency revenue by using "local resources that are renewable and geared to export" (*Christian Science Monitor* 12/27/88:8). Self-sufficiency, private enterprise, and export-oriented projects are likewise key elements in the state's economic program as is cooperation with private charitable institutions (Kenya, 1965; 1989).

As the group's name suggests, the papers have been associated with the new nation since they were founded in 1960. *The Nation* is the leading paper with daily and weekly circulations of 200,000 and 252,940 respectively, more than double the combined circulations of its two rivals (DN, 6/23/90:11). It is perhaps the boldest of the Nairobi dailies and, as a result, has had more brushes with authorities than the others. *Nation's* reporters were barred from parliament for four months in 1989. With the return to multi-party politics, the *Nation* has been quite clearly identified with the opposition (WR 1/1/93:53) leading the

Minister of Information and Broadcasting, Johnston Makau, to accuse the paper of "fanning tribal sentiments 'by being partisan'" (DN 5/14/93:32).

The third group, *The Kenya Times, Sunday Times, Kenya Leo, and Kenya Jumapili,* was established by the ruling party, the Kenya African Union (KANU), in 1983. Since 1988 it has been owned by the Kenya Times Media Trust (KTMT), a joint venture between KANU Investments and Maxwell Communications. Following an agreement with President Moi, the late Robert Maxwell invested 30 million pounds sterling in the newspapers and brought in technical advisers and modern presses in an effort to make the papers more competitive (Heath 1992, 45; Ochieng', 148-155). According to Philip Ochieng', Editor-in-Chief between 1988 and 1991, KANU Investments is only a paper company and "never invested even a cent in the venture since it was relaunched in February 1988." Furthermore, KANU and the government owe the group "hundreds of millions of shillings" (Ochieng', 154). However, according to Nation Group chairman, A.A.A. Ekirapa, "the government has allowed the *Kenya Times* to import newsprint, equipment and spare parts duty free" and it has a monopoly on government advertisements and notices of tender (DN 6/23/90:11).

Ochieng' maintains that the *Kenya Times* "has often been much busier in its content, more vigorous in its analyses and greatly more courageous in its exposition of corruption in government and the private sector than have the privately-owned newspapers" (Ochieng', 148). Nevertheless, they are clearly KANU papers. *The Kenya Times* runs a regular party section on Saturdays and, with the reappearance of multi-party politics, news reports, editorials, and commentaries have tended to reflect and support the party line.

The Kenya Times Television Network is a UHF subscription service available in Nairobi. When it opened its service in March 1990 it was publicized as a Kenya Times Media Trust (KTMT) enterprise. However, late in 1991 Jared Kangwana, then chairman of the trust, announced that neither Maxwell nor the KTMT had ever held any Kenya Television Network (KTN) shares (DN 12/18/91). A projected partnership with a South African company, M-Net, which would have infused much needed capital into the business, did not materialize (Heath 1992).

Interestingly, the Kenya Times Television Network has not been associated with KANU in the public mind perhaps because its local news service appeared to be independent of the government, frequently covering stories Kenya Broadcasting Corporation-Television (KBC-TV) ignored. However, in March 1993, viewers were suddenly told that the local news service would be discontinued as the Kenya Broadcasting Corporation and the print media were "adequately serving the news market, and the news service was not commercially viable for commercial network" (WR 3/5/93:19). The announcement was met with anger from viewers and skepticism from opposition politicians who saw the move "as part of President Moi's strategy to muzzle the Press" (DN 3/2/93:1-2). According to *Nation* sources, the Kenya Television Network was, in fact, doing well; advertising revenue had doubled in the previous year, with 40 percent of it coming from news-related advertisements (DN 3/3/93:24).

There are dozens of periodicals covering a wide range of subjects published in Kenya. The best known news magazine is *The Weekly Review* published by Stellagraphics, a Kenya owned company, and edited by Hilary Ng'weno. *The Weekly Review* is notable for its detailed coverage of Kenyan politics and business. Although *The Weekly Review* has given close attention to controversial events and issues, it has never been banned or Ng'weno charged with sedition. The magazine eschews sensational headlines; it is careful to present all positions and options, and its criticism is unmistakably "constructive."

AUTHORITARIAN/DEVELOPMENT TRADITION

The authoritarian/development tradition is rooted in the ancient notion that certain people: philosopher kings, priests, and male house-holders are, by virtue of their heritage, education, gender, or race, wiser and more capable of understanding the complexity of public affairs than are other people. It is, therefore, their duty to look after, uplift, and make decisions for others in their household, plantation, or nation (Siebert 1956a; Smith 1973, ch. 1). Such paternalistic beliefs can be found in the philosophy of public service broadcasting as espoused by the British Broadcasting Corporation (Broadcasting Research Unit, 1985) and in what has been called development journalism (Altschull 1984: 149-160) as well as in Lenin's theory of the press (Lenin, [1901] 1972) and the practices of Chinese Maoists (Lee, 1990).

The contradictions in the authoritarian/development tradition in Kenya are most evident in the state's broadcasting system. As the only real mass medium, radio has the potential to be a principal vehicle for national integration and development; however, that potential has been regularly subverted by the tendency of the state to subordinate the interests and needs of the popular classes to those of the ruling elite.

The authoritarian/development tradition in Kenya was initially informed by European assumptions that the mass media were powerful forces of influence and persuasion (Ellul, 1965) and useful "instrument[s] of advanced administration" as well as "for the enlightenment and education of the more backward sections of the population" (Great Britain Colonial Office 1937, 5-6). It was also informed by the first wave of American development theory that argued that national unity, modernization, and development could be hastened with the proper use of the mass media (Lerner, 1958; Pye, 1963; Schramm, 1964). State control of the press, especially broadcasting, has been justified on the grounds that the country was engaged in a war against poverty, disease, and ignorance and could afford neither the time nor political risks associated with a free and open debate about public policies and leaders (Mytton, 1983).

Broadcasting as a means of social control was introduced by the colonial government during the Second World War. The African Information Service (AIS) leased facilities from Cable & Wireless to air broadcasts in African and Asian languages in an effort to gain support for the war; community receivers were placed in markets and schools, and listening groups encouraged (Heath 1986a, ch. 4). The colonial state's interest in broadcasting peaked in the 1950s during the State of Emergency. The AIS dramatically increased the number of hours and languages of its broadcasts and "loyal" Africans were employed to broadcast programs intended to persuade rebels to surrender and to convince other Africans that it was in their best interests to remain loyal to the Crown. As the rebellion was contained and steps to effect majority rule and political independence taken, radio was used to counter nationalist propaganda emanating from Cairo and Moscow and to encourage African listeners to adopt or retain favorable attitudes towards Britain and British culture (Ibid. 118-124).

By the time of independence, assumptions that broadcasting was a powerful weapon and an essential instrument of modern state administration were part of Kenya's bureaucratic and political culture. In moving the second reading of the Kenya Broadcasting Corporation (Nationalization) Bill in the House of Representatives, Achieng' Oneko, then Minister of Information, Broadcasting, and Tourism, declared

> Our primary objective is not profit-making but rather that these powerful weapons should become instruments for the constructive development of our country . . . (Kenya, House of Representatives: *Official Record*), vol. 3, pt. 1, 24 June 1964, cols. 531-33).

From 1964 until 1989 broadcasting was run as a government department by the Ministry of Information and Broadcasting (MIB) and known as the Voice of Kenya (VOK). In 1989, the system was turned over to a parastatal and directed to operate in accordance with commercial principles (The Kenya Broadcasting Corporation Act, No. 15 of 1988). It is financed by advertisements, revenues from dealer and time-of-purchase receiver fees, and government subsidies. The Ministry of Information and Broadcasting continues to operate the Kenya News Agency (KNA) and a training center, the Kenya Institute of Mass Communication. With Unesco support, it publishes several bimonthly Kiswahili regional papers that have a total readership of about 110,000 (DN 5/15/93:3).

Of the three radio services, the Kiswahili Service is the principal channel of political and economic integration. Historically the service with the most powerful transmitters, it can be received nearly everywhere in the country. It broadcasts exclusively in Kiswahili, the national language, and is thus accessible to mobile urban Kenyans and villagers with some schooling. It carries national news and ceremonies; reports of events in parliament; Kenyan—but not vernacular—popular music; "development" programs in which the ideology of the national elite is embedded, and advertisements for inexpensive consumer goods produced in Kenya by subsidiaries of TNCs. It is the radio service most often heard in *matatus* and buses and in food kiosks and bars along the highways. It is by far the most popular channel making it the Kenya Broadcasting Corporation's principal earner of commercial revenue.

However, national integration is hindered by the very system intended to achieve it. Much of the public lacks confidence in the Kenya Broadcasting Corporation as a source of news and information, referring to it as the *Kanu* Broadcasting Corporation. The KBC has frequently been criticized for failing to report on major events and for giving too much attention to the ruling party. A principal bone of contention in the 1992 election campaign was the KBC's failure to cover, except in negative ways, opposition parties and even to refuse to carry paid political ads from those parties until a month before the election (WR, 11/27:8). The lion's share of the KBC's operating budget goes to support the Presidential Press Unit (Heath, 1986a, 254). The Presidential Press Unit has its own well equipped mobile unit and employs the most seasoned journalists and camera people in the KBC. All news broadcasts lead with and are dominated by reports of the president's activities and speeches prepared by the unit. A Vice-presidential Unit has been added with comparable functions and objectives.

Association of development programs with the voice of the ruling party makes those programs suspect. In addition, cultural and ecological diversity make "national" development programs irrelevant (Durrani 1985, 150) and inaccessible to those—mostly women and the elderly—who do not speak Kiswahili. In theory the Vernacular Services are supposed to compensate for these lacunae; in reality they carry little more than translations of national news and vernacular music. Few resources have been allocated to support programming originating in rural areas. There are no mobile units or travel money for such purposes, and recording equipment, which is in short supply, is typically reserved by senior producers who prefer to work in the city.

Participatory, grass roots communication which media scholars like Paul Ansah (1992) and Magaga Alot (1982) maintain is essential for genuine development has not been given serious attention in Kenya. The only real effort in that direction, a Unesco sponsored FM community radio station in Homa Bay, was dismantled in 1984 with no notice or official explanation after only 30 months of operation. Although the 10 watt transmitter had a range of only 22 km and most people in the area did not have FM receivers, its potential for "subversive" activity was apparently feared (Heath 1986b).

The English Service is a hold over from Kenyaradio and the European Service of the first KBC. For years it was justified on commercial grounds as it catered to foreign visitors and business people. Today, it can more correctly be seen as an educational service for the upwardly mobile. It is used for Schools Broadcasts in the morning and Adult Education in the afternoon. English is the language of instruction beyond Standard 3; parents encourage their children to listen to the news in English so that they will do well in school and on exams. Even rural Kenyans, especially those who do not speak a Bantu language, may prefer news in English over Kiswahili because they see the former as the language of "success."

Television is still an elite, urban service; in 1992 there were only 320,000 licensed TV sets in the country (KT, 12/24/92:16) (many of these in hotels); reception of KBC-TV was limited to major urban areas: Mombasa, Nairobi, Nakuru, and Kisumu. The channel, which is not commercially viable, has, in effect, been subsidized by ad revenues from the Kiswahili Service (VOK, Commercial Billings 1979-1983).

The Advocacy/Protest Tradition

The advocacy/protest tradition is the tradition of using the press to criticize an existing political regime, economic policies, or social structures and to empower people so they can work for change. The "press" in this tradition includes wall posters, newssheets, and audio cassettes of protest songs as well as legally registered periodicals. Content ranges from cogent legal argument, well substantiated exposés of corruption, and explications of the social consequences of established policies and practices to inflammatory polemics and seditious calls to arms.

Like the liberal/commercial tradition, this tradition is grounded in Enlightenment notions of human rationality, popular sovereignty, and a free marketplace of ideas. But, because publications in this tradition question established political and economic practices and institutions, they must depend upon sales and subsidies for funding.

If the Kenya commercial press has been associated with economic integration and the state broadcasting system with social control, the advocacy/protest press has been a response to those forces. As Africans acquired European education and became familiar with the workings of a modern state, they began to publish newspapers in African languages. Many early nationalists had a hand in these papers which were intended to educate Africans in the ways of their colonial masters so that they could undertake modern economic enterprises and effectively seek redress for grievances against employers and the state and to rally support for the struggle for independence (R. Achieng' Oneko, interview, May 11, 1984; Alot, 1982, ch. 1; Scotton, 1975).

The advocacy press did not die with independence but the objects of its protest changed from settlers and the colonial state to Kenya's new elite and the neocolonial state. Over the years there have been numerous short-lived publications produced by individual dissidents or shadowy organizations. With the return to multi-party politics in 1991, many new publications associated with and backed by political organizations have flooded the newsstands (WR 2/19/93:17-18).

Of particular importance are the publications backed by

mainstream institutions, notably the National Council of Churches in Kenya (NCCK) and the Law Society of Kenya (LSK). Because these organizations are well respected and well connected at home and abroad, their publications cannot be easily dismissed by the government at which much criticism is leveled or foreign diplomats and representatives of donor agencies. The commercial press frequently comments on and paraphrases articles from the advocacy press, especially when issues are impounded or banned and editors are arrested and charged with sedition. In this way voices of protest are extended and legitimized.

In the tradition of advocacy journalism begun in the 1920s, magazines like *BEYOND, Society, Finance and the Nairobi Law Monthly* have combined nationalism, education, and protest. The editors and publishers operate on the assumption that a well informed, articulate citizenry is fundamental to a democratic society. People must understand their rights, know how to exercise them and when they have been abridged. The original purpose of *Society* as stated by its editor and publisher, Pius Nyamora, was to express society's "desires and dreams in life in a way that is Kenyan" and give particular attention to the cooperative movement *(Society* 8/88:2). Within a few months features about cooperatives were replaced by features about human rights advocates and populist critics of the KANU government and praise for President Moi was replaced by praise for Amnesty International and Africa Watch for exposing human rights abuses in Kenya and for US Ambassador Smith Hempstone who openly supported those who called for an end to single-party rule.

The *Nairobi Law Monthly,* which is sponsored by the Law Society of Kenya, began as a law news magazine that would present "on a regular basis information pertaining to law in a legal context" and be a law magazine of record (NLM 9/87:1). Within a few months the staff added a monthly column on general principles of law intended to promote legal education and rights awareness. By 1990, that had become the *Nairobi Law Monthly's* major purpose (11/90:1). Issues have been devoted to laws regarding labor, tenants' rights, elections, detention, and customary law. Of particular concern to the *Nairobi Law Monthly* were acts by the state that abridged fundamental constitutional rights and principles. Articles advocated an independent judiciary, freedom of expression and movement, and the right to a fair and timely hearing when charged with a criminal offense.

The *Nairobi Law Monthly's* editor, human rights lawyer Gitobu Imanyara, has called the *Nairobi Law Monthly* "a mouthpiece of the wind of change" (Imanyara, 1992). Certainly, articles by prominent Kenyan jurists, scholars, and clerics drew international attention to the depth of corruption and systematic way in which the KANU government was undermining the nation's legal system. These may have contributed to the Consultative Group of donors' decision to suspend aid in 1991, a decision that has been credited with forcing President Moi to agree to permit the registration of opposition parties (Widner 1992).

The language of the *Nairobi Law Monthly* is less populist than that of *Society;* it is the careful language of law. But, several pages in each issue are devoted to letters. Like the pre-independence protest press, these frequently voice criticism in poetry and allegory. But, unlike their predecessors, these publications are accessible only to those who read and understand English. They may be voices for the people but not of them.

DEGREES OF FREEDOM

The Kenya imagined by the country's leaders is a young nation struggling to be recognized as a modern liberal democracy that plays an active role in global affairs. Central to this image is a privately-owned, competitive press limited only by law, journalists' commitment to social responsibility, and ideological consensus. The laws which limit the press today can be traced to colonial legislation which was intended to control the nationalist press (Carter, 1970; Heath, 1986a).

Freedom of expression is constitutionally protected and constitutionally limited. The rights to assemble, speak, and publish may be limited in the interests of defense, public safety, order, health, and morality or to protect the rights and property of others (The Constitution of Kenya, 1983, Sec. 70; 79). Preventive detention, a tool used by the colonial state, is sanctioned by the constitution (Sec. 83) although not by the public, independent journalists or opposition politicians.

All publications must be registered and publishers of newspapers and periodicals appearing quarterly or more frequently are required to post a shs.10,000 bond as security for fines or damages resulting from libel (Books and Newspapers Act, 1960). "In the interest of public order, health or morals, the security of Kenya, the administration of justice or the maintenance of the authority and impartiality of the judiciary" the Attorney General may ban the importation, printing, possession, and distribution of particular publications (*Penal Code* 1970 Cap. 63 Section 52). Films, videos and plays may be censored (Film and Stage Plays Act (1962).

The press is also limited by laws of libel, sedition, and treason. In matters of libel, liability depends upon the fact of defamation not intention; the defendant must establish that the matter is not only true but was published for the public benefit (Kinuthia and Kariuki 1989). Sedition is broadly defined, encompassing intent as well as effect (Ghai & MacAuslan 1970, 453). Provoking communal or class hatred, discrediting or showing disrespect for the President or "cherished central institutions" along with seeking to overthrow the government or established laws are all grounds for charges of sedition (Ibid.; Moi, 1993).

As important as the laws themselves is the way in which they have been interpreted. In the eyes of many Kenyan legal experts, agents of the state have overstepped the limits of the law. Police have raided news kiosks and seized and impounded publications without first identifying offending statements or giving publishers the opportunity of a hearing to defend their statements (*NLM* 3/88:4). The Attorney General's order of March 14, 1988 banning "all past and future issues of BEYOND" was thought to be "so broad as to be unreasonable" (Murungi 1988). Charging a man wearing a T-shirt with a "V" and the slogan "1990 is the year of Victory" with possessing seditious material was regarded as absurd (*NLM* 11/90:8).

Not all media have been equally susceptible to state intervention. By definition, the most closely supervised are the state media: the Kenya News Agency, Ministry of Information and Broadcasting services, and the Kenya Broadcasting Corporation. As in the colonial period, the most susceptible to police swoops and bans are the media that employ vernacular languages and address concerns of the popular classes: vernacular newssheets, street and community theater, community radio, and audio cassettes. Independent publications of protest in English or Kiswahili are also vulnerable.

The National Council of Churches in Kenya's *BEYOND,* which had drawn attention in the commercial press and parliament for articles alleging misappropriation of harambee funds (WR 7/18/86: 5-6) and criticizing KANU's system of queue voting in primaries, was banned in March 1988 following an article alleging election irregularities which the government regarded as "partial and tribal" (WR 3/18/88: 18-19).

Society, Finance, and The Nairobi Law Monthly have been objects of numerous police actions. *The Nairobi Law Monthly* was banned in October 1990 after eight months of threats by members of parliament and after its editor had been charged with sedition for an article on the 1990 multi-party debate (*Society* 4/91: 27; *WR* 10/5/90: 21-23). Even after dissent was sanctioned with the registration of opposition parties, issues of *Society* were impounded and its editor charged with sedition. In April 1993, Fotoform which printed *Society, Finance,* and other magazines was raided; 30,000 copies of *Finance* were impounded; the presses were dismantled, and the firm's supervisor taken in for questioning by the Criminal Investigations Division (WR 5/7/93: 19). Both the editor and the printer were charged with sedition.

At first glance the commercial press appears to have been relatively free from state interference and harassment. The foreign-owned press has not been nationalized; it is not subject to prior official censorship, and no issues have been impounded. However, Members of Parliament who have personal political quarrels with the press regularly raise the specter of nationalization; editors have received midnight phone calls and been hauled in by the Criminal Investigations Division for questioning, and several prominent editors have been forced to resign because their papers' proprietors feared official retribution for critical editorials (Barton; Ochieng'). This sort of harassment has been fairly mild in comparison to that in other African countries. For the most part, the commercial press is controlled by self-imposed restraints that are the product of economic concerns, journalistic values and practices, and ideological consensus.

As in older democracies, the press and the state are in a symbiotic relationship (Bennett, 1988; Herman and Chomsky, 1988). Because of the way news has been defined, public affairs are grist for journalists' mills. The press depends upon politicians and government officials for stories and upon the Kenya News Agency for much of its local news. Because of the licensing law and the possibility, however remote, of nationalization, the foreign-owned press is beholden to the state for its existence. It is likewise dependent upon the state to maintain economic practices that are favorable to TNCs upon whom the papers depend for ad revenues. As Philip Ochieng' has put it:

> Some absentee owners, expatriate or locally-hired managers and editors are often even more enthusiastic with the blue pen than are local politicians. They have an even greater stake in the economic structure of the Third World country concerned and the political stability necessary for the perpetuation and consolidation of that structure (Ochieng', 74)

Only when that stability and structure are threatened is the commercial press likely to actively oppose the government. Such a situation occurred in Kenya in the late 1980s. Global recession, a growing national debt, double digit inflation, dislocation from structural adjustment programs imposed by donors coupled with wide-spread corruption, fiscal mismanagement, and increased human rights abuses resulted in serious tensions and increased demands for political, economic, and social reform (Nyang'oro 1990; Widner 1992).

Beginning in 1990, the commercial press joined the advocacy press in publishing editorials and commentaries which drew attention to corruption and the erosion of human rights. Once opposition parties were legalized in December 1991, the commercial press became an important forum for public debate on the new multi-party order. A close reading of that debate indicates clear support for reform not revolution. Although the particulars varied from writer to writer and paper to paper, the overwhelming message was support for transparency in government and business, respect for human rights, rule of law, and an end to violence on the part of the state and angry citizens.

For its part, the state is dependent upon the commercial press. While the state broadcasting system has a virtual monopoly on the dissemination of official news to villagers and pastoralists in remote areas of the country, in the cities and big towns, the government's voice must compete with the Kenya Television Network, newspapers, and advocacy periodicals which have greater credibility precisely because of popular perception that radio is the Voice of the President or KANU. Therefore, the state must rely upon the commercial press to disseminate information and ideology. Whether they are pleased with the newspapers or not, all government officials and politicians read them every day; copies of all the dailies are to be found in government offices where they are read by junior and senior staff as well as citizens seeking assistance or information from those offices.

The state clearly benefits from the existence of a healthy competitive press. It sends a signal to the world that Kenya is a liberal democracy that tolerates diversity of opinion and is friendly to foreign investment (Mwaura). The state needs the capital, technical know-how, jobs, and social services provided by Lonrho, Maxwell, the Aga Khan, and corporations and organizations that advertise in the private and public media. Just as these corporations profit from a hospitable political economic climate: law and order, docile labor, and attractive tax breaks, so does the state profit from the press' efforts to promote and legitimize those policies.

The commercial press stands firmly behind the ideal of freedom of the press; arrests of editors, Criminal Investigations Division swoops on printing establishments, and bans elicit sharply critical editorials in the commercial press and protests from the Kenya Union of Journalists. However, it is critical of the "excesses" that reflect badly on the press as a whole (Elderkin, 1992; Alot, 1993) and accepts the notion that the press must be responsible. In October 1992, under pressure from Attorney General Amos Wako, a group of journalists led by Hilary Ng'weno published a code of ethics for journalists and announced that "a self-regulating press complaints commission [would] be established in due course" (WR 10/30/92: 16-18). The code asserts editorial "responsibility for all matter, including advertisement[s] published in the paper" and protection of confidential sources of information. It affirms that "the fundamental objective of a journalist is to write a fair, accurate and unbiased story on matters of public interest." Unintentional inaccuracies and distortions should be corrected promptly and "a fair opportunity to reply" should be given (Ibid.).

CONCLUSION

There are three press traditions in Kenya; the strongest is the liberal/commercial tradition. The strength of this tradition is due to several factors: it was firmly entrenched in the colonial era; it is in accord with the Republic's political economy and the image many Kenyans have of their country, and it mediates between and extends the voices of the state and advocates for change. The three traditions and the many voices within each tradition give the impression of pluralism. But, it is pluralism limited to those who can read or can understand English or Kiswahili. The logic of the market demands that the commercial press cater to those in the modern sector of the economy. The state which might be expected to provide services that are not commercially viable (Ng'weno 1991) has not risen to the challenge, preferring to use the media it controls to project the president as a symbol of the nation and to extend the authority of the state rather than enable social development. The advocacy press apparently believes that it is elite Kenyans and foreigners, not the ordinary people who can best effect change.

Peter Ochieng' angered fellow journalists (WR 8/7/92:15; DN 8/14/92:2) by writing that questions of press ownership and constitutional guarantees are of secondary importance as long as the "social structure and political system do not change" (Ochieng', 97) and the people "remain in abject economic, cultural, technological, political, and intellectual thralldom." But, his remarks must be taken seriously if true freedom of expression is to be achieved.

NOTES

1. Kenya periodicals are abbreviated as follows: *The Weekly Review (WR), Daily Nation (DN), Sunday Nation (SN), Kenya Times (KT), Sunday Times (ST), Nairobi Law Monthly (NLM)*.

REFERENCES

Ainslie, Rosalynde. *The Press in Africa: Communications Past and Present*. New York: Walker and Company, 1966.

Alot, Magaga. *People and Communication in Kenya*. Nairobi: Kenya Literature Bureau, 1982.

Alot, Magaga. "Investigative Journalism and Social Responsibility." In *The Weekly Review* Feb. 1993: 31-32.

Altschull, J. Herbert. *Agents of Power: The Role of the News Media in Human Affairs*. New York: Longman, 1984.

Anderson, Benedict. *Imagined Communities*. London: Verso, 1991.

Ansah, Paul A.V. "The Right to Communicate: Implications for Development." *Media Development* 1, (1992): 53-56.

Barton, Frank. *The Press of Africa: Persecution & Perseverance*. New York: Africana Publishing Company, 1979

Bennett, W. Lance *News: The Politics of Illusion*. White Plains, NY: Longman, 1988.

Broadcasting Research Unit. *The Public Service Idea in British Broadcasting: Main Principles*. London: BBC, 1985.

Carter, F. "The Kenya Government and the Press 1906-60." *Hadith 2*, (1970): 243-259.

Curran, James and Jean Seaton. *Power Without Responsibility: The Press and Broadcasting in Britain*. London: Routledge, 1988.

Durrani, Shiraz. "Rural Information in Kenya."*Information Development* 1:3 (July 1985): 149-157.

Elderkin, Sarah. "The Prerogative of the Harlot." In *The Weekly Review* Sept. 11 1992: 21-23.

Ellul, Jacques. *Propaganda: the Formation of Men's Attitudes*. New

York: Vintage, 1965.

Gellner, Ernest. *Nations and Nationalism*. Ithaca: Cornell University Press, 1983.

Ghai, Y.P. and J.P.W.B. MacAuslan. *Public Law and Political Change in Kenya: a Study of the Legal Framework of Government from Colonial Times to the Present*. Nairobi: Oxford University Press, 1970.

Great Britain, Colonial Office. "Broadcasting Services in the Colonies: Interim Report of a Committee." *Colonial Office* No. 139. London: H.M Stationers Co, 1937.

Heath, Carla W. "Broadcasting in Kenya: Policy and Politics 1928-1984." Unpublished Ph.D. dissertation, University of Illinois, Urbana, 1986a.

Heath, Carla W. "Politics of Broadcasting in Kenya—Community Radio Suffers." *Media Development* 2, (1986b): 10-14.

Heath, Carla W. "Structural Changes in Kenya's Broadcasting System: A Manifestation of Presidential Authoritarianism." *Gazette* 37, (1992): 37-51.

Herman, Edward S. and Noam Chomsky. *Manufacturing Consent: the Political Economy of the Mass Media*. New York: Pantheon Books, 1988.

Hobsbawm, E.J. *Nations and Nationalism Since 1780*. New York: Cambridge University Press, 1990.

Imanyara, Gitobu. "Kenya: Indecent Exposure." In *Index on Censorship* 4 (1992): 21-22.

Jouet, Josianne. "Advertising and TNCs in Kenya." *Development and Change* 15 (1984): 435-456.

Karikari, Kwame. "The 'Anti-White press' Campaign: the Opposition of the African Press to the Establishment of the *Daily Graphic* by the British Mirror Newspaper Company in Ghana, 1950." Gazette (1992): 215-232.

Kenya. "African Socialism and its Application to Planning in Kenya," Sessional Paper No. 10 of 1963/65. Nairobi: Government Printing Office, 1965.

Kenya. *Development Plan 1989-1993*. Nairobi: Government Printing Office, 1989.

Kinuthia, Rumba and Charles Kariuik. "Press Freedom and Censorship." In *The Nairobi Law Monthly* May/June 1989

Lee, Chin-Chuan. ed. *Voices of China: The Interplay of Politics and Journalism*. New York: Guilford Press, 1990.

Lenin, V.I. "Where to Begin." In Lenin: About the Press. Prague: International Organization of Journalists, [1901] 1972.

Lerner, Daniel. *The Passing of Traditional Society: Modernizing the Middle East.*Glencoe, IL: The Free Press, 1958.

Moi, Daniel arap. Madaraka Day Speech. In *The Weekly Review* 6/4/93: 9-11.

Murungi, Kiraitu. "Legal Limits of Freedom of the Press in Kenya." In *The Nairobi Law Monthly* March 1988: 16.

Mwaura, Peter. *Communication Policies in Kenya.* Paris: UNESCO, 1980.

Mytton, Graham. *Mass Communication in Africa* London: Edward Arnold, 1983.

Ng'weno, Hilary. "The Situation and Perspectives of the Independent Press in Africa." In *The Weekly Review* May 3 1991: 15-18.

Nyang'oro, Julius E. "The Quest for Pluralist Democracy in Kenya." *Transafrica Forum* 7:3 (Fall 1990): 73-82.

Ochieng', Philip. *I Accuse the Press: An Insider's View of the Media and Politics in Africa.* Nairobi: Initiatives Publishers, 1992.

Parenti, Michael. *Inventing Reality: The Politics of the Mass Media.* New York: St. Martin's, 1986.

Pratt, Cranford. "Colonial Governments and the Transfer of Power in Africa." In *The Transfer of Power in Africa: Decolonization 1940-1960,* edited by Gifford Proser and Wm. Roger Louis. New Haven: Yale University Press, 1982.

Pye, Lucian. ed. *Communication and Political Development.* Princeton: Princeton University Press, 1963.

Schramm, Wilbur. *Mass Media and National Development.* Stanford: Stanford University Press, 1964.

Scotton, James F. "Kenya's Maligned African Press: Time for a Reassessment." *Journalism Quarterly* 52 (1975): 30-36.

Siebert, Fred S. "The Authoritarian Theory." In *Four Theories of the Press,* by Siebert, Peterson and Schramm. Urbana: University of Illinois Press, 1956a.

Siebert, Fred S. (1956b) "The Libertarian Theory." In *Four Theories of the Press,* by Siebert, Peterson and Schramm. Urbana: University of Illinois Press.

Smith, Anthony. *The Shadow in the Cave: The Broadcaster, his Audience, and the State.* Urbana: University of Illinois Press, 1973.

Swainson, Nicola. *The Development of Corporate Capitalism in Kenya 1918-1977.* London: Heinemann, 1980.

Widner, Jennifer A. "Kenya's Slow Progress toward Multiparty Politics." *Current History* May 1992: 214-218.

CHAPTER 3

INTERNAL AND EXTERNAL FACTORS AFFECTING PRESS FREEDOM IN NIGERIA

Festus Eribo

INTRODUCTION

This chapter examines the internal and external factors affecting press freedom in Africa's most populous country, Nigeria. The study focuses on the historical, cultural, political, and economic dynamics affecting the freedom of the press in the country. The effects of new technologies, international news flow, education, and media exposure on the press in Nigeria are examined.

Before the establishment of the first newspaper, *Iwe Ironhin,* in 1859, the people of the various empires, kingdoms, emirates and communities that were later forged by Europeans to constitute Nigeria had developed their own traditional means of public communication without foreign assistance. Endowed with originality and creativity, the people had developed their own local languages, folklore, religion, administration, military organizations, and economic activities without European influence. Various scholars including Oyediran (1979), Rodney (1981), Anise (1993) and Ekeh (1993) have argued that the European colonialists in Africa actually disrupted a natural evolutionary trend and replaced it with a Eurocentric developmental paradigm. In reality, the advent of Europeans brought along new communication technologies and philosophies that gradually overwhelmed the traditional mass media and cultures in many cities in Nigeria. The mass communication system in contemporary polyglot Nigeria is, therefore, an offshoot of both indigenous and foreign efforts. Subsequently, press freedom in Nigeria cannot be divorced from the internal and external factors which have influenced the mass media since 1859. Although press freedom in Nigeria has been malnourished and elusive, its liberating values are attractive to Nigerians that have placed a high premium on democracy, freedom of expression and a better life.

Press freedom is defined, in this study, as the availability of a free marketplace of ideas and information for all the citizenry without fear, favor, intimidation, or obstacles. The concept of press freedom abhors government control, censorship, interference, and undemocratic regulations aimed at abridging the freedom of opinion, expression, and transmission of information or ideas through the mass media and other channels of communication. Direct and indirect devices employed by governments, organizations, and individuals to impede the free flow of news, information, thought, and opinion in the media and society are considered infringements on the freedom of the press. Press freedom, which does not exist in a vacuum, is the cumulative result of a number of societal, economic, and political values. These values have been reflected over time by several factors within and beyond the local control, resulting in what has been identified in this essay as internal and external factors.

INTERNAL FACTORS AFFECTING PRESS FREEDOM

Since 1960, the press in Nigeria has operated under military dictatorships for more than two-thirds of the post-colonial years.

Like the press under the defunct communist dictatorships of Eastern Europe, the press under a military dictatorship or an authoritarian civilian administration cannot be free despite appearances. The vibrant press in Nigeria is largely sustained by the inner strength derived from a pristine communal tradition of free exchange of news and information in the marketplace, village meetings, festivals and other social gatherings. Since the health of a nation's mass communication system depends on the quality of its society, economy and political system, as well as the opportunity for a free exchange of ideas and information, the Nigerian press is confronted by several factors related to political and socio-economic forces. The following local factors (by no means exhaustive) will be examined: ethnicity, quality of journalists, ownership, and political system.

ETHNICITY AND PRESS FREEDOM

The role of ethnicity in the promotion of diversity and plurality of voices in Nigeria gives the country a unique heterogeneous press system. Nigeria is a conglomeration of about 250 ethnic groups which have painstakingly preserved their identities in a country of approximately 100 million people and 400 languages. Ethnic independence is a sensitive national issue. The powerful ethnic groups amalgamated by Lord Lugard to form the Nigerian nation state have continued to draw spiritual strength from the traditional rulers such as the local Oba, Oni, Alafin, Emir, and Obi. The mass communication system which is one of the media of political, cultural, and economic expression also draws some of its strength from the ethnic diversity and the geopolitical amalgamation of Nigeria.

Historically, each of the first three regions in the country (Western, Eastern and Northern regions) representing various ethnic groups had at least one newspaper published in English or the local language. The regions were so powerful that the Western region under Chief Obafemi Awolowo went ahead of the federal government in 1959 to establish the first television studio in black Africa in Ibadan, the capital of Western Nigeria (Agbaje, 1992).

At independence, Nigeria was ruled by a coalition government of the Northern People's Congress (which had supporters mainly from the Northern ethnic groups) and the National Council of Nigerian Citizens (which was nationally organized but particularly powerful in the East with the Ibos as the major actors). The Action Group under Chief Obafemi Awolowo with its main base in the West (largely Yoruba) was the leading opposition party. The West was, therefore, not influential at the Federal level and the Yorubas did not like the political imbalance of power. The political and developmental programs of the ethnic groups are vital to peace, unity and progress in the country. Therefore, the alienation of the Yorubas or other ethnic groups was politically unwise. During the ensuing crisis, some regional governments or political leaders banned the circulation of newspapers deemed as unfriendly to the region or ethnic group. The political conflict among the ethnic groups culminated in the first military coup on January 15, 1966.

The military take-over of government did not put an end to the ethnic dynamics in the country. The media were used to express the opinion of the ethnic group controlling them. For example the *Tribune* and the *Daily Sketch* tend to be sensitive to the issues affecting the Yorubas while the *New Nigerian,* based in Kaduna, has at different times orchestrated the northern opinion on national matters. The *Observer* is often alert to issues that affect the Edo people while the *Tide* and other papers in the Eastern part of the country cater largely to the interest of the Ibos and other ethnic groups in the region. Interestingly, the *Daily Times* which is based in Lagos pursues a deliberate policy of serving the whole country in the most objective reporting possible. Many of the private newspapers, irrespective of their location in the country, appear to be national in their coverage but are slanted in favor of the ethnic, economic and political interests of the owners (Mytton, 1983). This is particularly obvious when there is a national debate. The Yoruba area of Western Nigeria is the most media-rich territory in the country. Many of the print and electronic media are concentrated in Lagos and its environs, an area dominated by the Yorubas.

Table 1
Selected Dailies in Nigeria

Newspaper	Circulation	Location	Ownership
Daily Times	400,000	Lagos	Government/Private
National Concord	200,000	Lagos	Private
The Guardian	150,000	Lagos	Private
The Punch	150,000	Lagos	Private
The Observer	150,000	Benin City	Government
Nigerian Tribune	110,000	Ibadan	Private
Nigerian Standard	100,000	Jos	Government
Nigerian Chronicle	80,000	Calabar	Government
New Nigeria	80,000	Kaduna	Government
Daily Sketch	75,000	Ibadan	Government
Daily Star	75,000	Enugu	Government

Sources: *Europa World Year Book*, 1996: 2416. Ziegler, D. & Asante, M. K. (1992) Thunder and Silence: Mass Media in Africa. Trenton, NJ: Africa World Press, Inc. pp. 78-79. Agbaje, Adigun A. B. (1992) The Nigerian Press, Hegemony, And The Social Construction of Legitimacy, 1960-1983. New York: The Edwin Mellen Press. pp. 319-321.

Radio and television stations in Nigeria are located in all the regions of the country and are accessible to the major ethnic groups. There are now 30 states and the federal capital territory of Abuja representing the various ethnic groups. Each radio or television station is actively engaged in the gathering and dissemination of news within the state which controls it. These regional stations facilitate press freedom by providing regional and public access and a variety of opinions to the media. The stations place emphasis on the proximity and locality of news. The news broadcast is in English and the major local languages of the State that owns the station. English is the unifying language in all parts of the country. Local programs in English feature economic, cultural, and political activities at all levels. Some of the programs are so popular that they are considered for transmission on national radio and television. However, the use of local languages enhances the free flow of news and information to both the rural and urban population, literate or illiterate. Federal radio stations broadcast in Hausa, Yoruba, Igbo, Edo, Urhobo, Igala, Kanuri, Fulfulde, Nupe, Izon, Efik, and Tiv. Not all the 400 Nigerian languages are used in the electronic or print media.

Since the various media in Nigeria represent different voices based on ethnic or regional affiliation, there is an avalanche of diverse opinions on issues affecting the whole country or a part of the country. The people of Nigeria are the ultimate beneficiaries of this multiplicity of print and broadcast media because what may be under-reported or censored in one state may be the lead news in the federal media or the media in another state. When there is a civilian government, the bulk of the criticism of the federal government is found in various state and private media. When the soldiers are in power, the private media are more likely to challenge the military governments at the state and national levels while the government owned media are censored directly or indirectly by the military dictators. In spite of the covert or overt censorship, one can get a good idea of what is happening in the country if one listens to all the radio and television broadcasts as well as read all the dailies in the country. The voices of dissent are heard on all media and the elasticity of press freedom is constantly tested by the journalists. The federal radio and television networks which are slanted toward federal policies are broadcast nationwide. There are more than 20 million radio and about four million television receivers in the country (*Europa World Year Book*, 1996).

QUALITY OF JOURNALISTS AND PRESS FREEDOM

The journalists in Nigeria are as diverse as their ethnic background, national sense of duty, and education. Nigerian journalists are the products of various traditions in the pre-colonial communities that had no laws forbidding the dissemination of news. The traditional freedom of expression in the various communities has contributed to the resilience and lack of inhibition of the contemporary journalists in Nigeria.

The tradition of bravery among Nigerian journalists was

demonstrated in the early years of the nineteenth century press in Nigeria. For example, the motto of the *Lagos Times and Gold Coast Advertiser* was "Be Just and Fear Not." True to this motto, the paper wrote in its anti-colonialist editorial in 1881 that "we are not clambering for immediate independence, but it should be borne in mind that the present order of things will not last forever. A time will come when the colonies on the West Coast will be left to regulate their own internal and external affairs" (Kurian, 1982). Although censorship laws were introduced by the colonial administration, the journalists were bold and vitriolic in their attack on colonialism. In 1909, Nigeria had a seditious offenses bill. This was followed by Lord Lugard's press laws in 1917 when he framed the law giving himself the right to appoint a newspaper censor. That law referred to as the Federal Newspaper Ordinance of 1917 was followed by the Publications Ordinance of 1950.

In spite of colonial censorship, Nigerian journalists such as Herbert Macaulay, Ernest Ukoli, and Nnamdi Azikiwe were inspired by the bold tradition of Nigerian journalism. In 1937, Dr. Nnamdi Azikiwe established the *West African Pilot,* the forerunner of the early newspaper chains in Nigeria - the Associated Newspapers of Nigeria. Following the bold tradition, the chain challenged the colonial administration.

After attaining independence in October 1960, several attempts were made to muzzle the press. Decrees and regulations were introduced. Among the decrees were the newspaper (Amendment) Act of 1964, and the Sedition Law of 1964. In 1967, during the civil war, war-time Newspaper Decree 17 and Decree 24 were promulgated. Decree 24 in particular empowered the inspector general of police and the army chief of staff to detain without trial for an indefinite period anyone considered to be a security risk (Sobowale, 1985). The Nigerian Press Council was established in 1978 by military decree. The council, a self-regulatory body had powers to enforce a code of conduct and define the duties of journalists. Before the military handed over the reins of government to the politicians in 1979, a new constitution was drafted to give Nigeria a Presidential system of government similar to the one in the United States of

America but with a porous provision for freedom of expression. A democratically elected government which operated under the 1979 constitution was overthrown by the military in 1983. Other decrees intended to silence the press between 1983 and 1994 have been promulgated.

Peter Enahoro, Tom Borha, Neville Ukoli, Lateef Jakande, Sam Amuka, Sam Eguavoen, Dan Agbese, Michael Asaju, Ray Ekpu, Lade Bonuola, Iro Omorodion, and Wilson Uwaifo were among the first generation of Nigerian journalists to face a new type of censorship under military colonialism. In addition, a number of journalists have been arrested, detained, and jailed for reporting stories the government deems embarrassing. For example, Tunde Thompson and Ndika Irabor of the *Guardian* newspaper, Femi Akintunde of *Fame* magazine, Nosa Igiebor, Kola Ilori, Onome Osifo-Whiskey, and Ayodele Akinkuotu of *Tell* magazine were detained at different times for doing their reportorial duties as journalists. Despite the harassment, Nigerian journalists are undaunted in their belief in press freedom, social responsibility, democracy and the rule of law for every Nigerian. Nigerian journalists have not relented in demanding for accountability, probity, constructive development, and fairness in the government run by their compatriots in military uniform.

A fraternity between the press and the government in Nigeria is virtually impossible because of the traditional surveillance role of the press. The journalists, subjected to several types of military censorships, are now compulsorily skilled in journalistic maneuverability in search of press freedom. With each successive military dictator, the journalists try harder to uphold their major responsibilities to inform the people and seek accountability in government. Nigerian journalists who serve as government critics are, therefore, often reminded that arrests and imprisonment are the occupational hazards of every reporter and that journalists have the duty to publish the truth despite the reprisal from the government. The recalcitrant belief in press freedom by the professional journalists in Nigeria has caused unending schisms and crises between the press and the government during military and civilian administrations.

The task of promoting press freedom is formidable but not

insurmountable in Nigeria because of the calibre of journalists. According to Stevenson (1994) "Nigerian journalists face a daily struggle beyond the imagination of most Western journalists." Similarly, Ochs (1986) notes that Nigeria seems to have journalists who bounce back. Censorship, intimidation and repression continue just as journalists have continued to challenge the perennial authoritarianism of the military dictators.

OWNERSHIP AND PRESS FREEDOM

The ownership of the print media in Nigeria was private for more than a century after the establishment of *Iwe Ironhin* in 1859. The private newspapers were owned by both indigenous and foreign entrepreneurs. Many of these papers have died but the most widely known in their days were *Iwe Ironhin,* 1859, *Anglo-African,* 1863, *Lagos Times and Gold Coast Advertiser,* 1880, *Lagos Observer,* 1882, *The Eagle* and *Lagos Critic,* 1883, *Iwe Ironhin Eko,* 1888, *Lagos Weekly Times,* 1890, *Lagos Weekly Record,* 1891, *Lagos Spectator,* 1893, *Lagos Standard* 1894, and *Lagos Echo* 1894. The rapid growth of the print media in late nineteenth century Nigeria was motivated by the need to give expression to public opinion and growing nationalism which led to independence several decades later. The privately owned press was relatively free by the standards of the time.

The Nigerian press of the first half of the twentieth century was a bold political and economic agitator, privately owned and partly indigenous. The first successful daily was the *Daily News* which was established as a political party newspaper by Herbert Macaulay in 1925 to serve the National Democratic Party. The success of the *Daily News* was so resounding and alarming that European traders and the more conservative Africans came together and raised enough money to start a rival paper called the *Daily Times* on June 1, 1926. The *Daily Times* is the oldest, surviving newspaper in Nigeria today.

Dr. Nnamdi Azikiwe, trained in Columbia University in the United States, established the *West African Pilot* in 1937. The paper was so popular that it encouraged Zik to establish the

Associated Newspapers of Nigeria, the first newspaper chain in West Africa. This consortium had presses in Northern, Eastern and Western Nigeria and was truly national in nature. It was made up of the *Eastern Nigerian Guardian* based in Port Harcourt, the *Nigerian Spokesman* in Onitsha, the *Southern Nigerian Defender* in Warri, the *Comet* in Kano, and the *Advocate* in Jos. The colonial government was apprehensive of the demand for independence by the chain and described it as a "plague." The newsprint allocation to the chain was reduced. The papers survived the colonial period but were all dead within a decade after the attainment of political independence. Zik's papers failed in the post-colonial period partly because they had accomplished their mission to liberate Nigeria from colonialism. For example, *Eastern Sentinel* at Enugu failed in 1960 and the *Nigerian Monitor* at Uyo failed in 1962. Most of the dailies in the Zik group of newspapers survived until the late 1960s when they ceased publication because of the civil war (Edeani, 1985).

Other independent owners encouraged by economic and political considerations were Cecil King (Irish) of the Daily Mirror in London, Lord Roy Thomson of Fleet Street in London, and Chief Obafemi Awolowo, a Nigerian lawyer trained in England. Awolowo formed another newspaper chain, the Amalgamated Press of Nigeria. The chain included the *Daily Service, Nigerian Tribune, COR Advocate in Uyo, the Midwest Echo in* Benin City, the *Middle Belt Herald* in Jos, the *Northern Star in* Kano, and the *Eastern Observer* in Onitsha. In 1960, the Amalgamated Press of Nigeria collaborated with the Thomson Organization to publish the *Daily Express* and *Sunday Express*. The co-operation failed in 1965 (Edeani, 1985). The *Tribune* is the only surviving newspaper in the chain.

Private ownership of the press did not guarantee press freedom in Nigeria. The majority of the newspaper proprietors were actively involved in politics and power struggle. The private papers played advocacy role in the interest of their owners. According to Edeani (1985), Nigerian intellectuals, journalists and business community believe in governmental noninterference in the ownership and control of the mass media. Since independence in 1960, the ownership pattern has changed and now includes government and political parties.

The federal government ownership of the *Morning Post* in 1961 blazed the trail for government newspapers. The *Morning Post* was so tightly controlled that it lost credibility among its readers. After reporting in 1964 that workers had called off a general strike when they had not, the paper was on the decline. The blatant inaccuracy so crippled the *Post* that it was legislated out of existence in 1972 (Sobowale, 1985).

The electronic media and the News Agency of Nigeria (NAN) are government owned. Earlier attempts by Nnamdi Azikiwe to operate a wireless station in Nigeria in 1946 was unsuccessful. But this trend has been changing since 1993. Before 1993, the electronic media did not enjoy the diversity of ownership enjoyed by the print media. Radio and television stations in Nigeria were supervised by government appointed directors who coerced the journalists to submissiveness and co-operation. The introduction of privately owned electronic media may give new meaning to press freedom in Nigeria in the 1990s and the twenty-first century. Although the electronic media are widely used in both the northern and southern states, the South is clearly on the lead in the ownership of cable and satellite redistribution companies and television stations. Twelve of the 14 private television broadcasting companies approved in 1993 for operation are in the south (See Table 2).

In addition to the 14 television broadcast stations, the following eleven cable and satellite redistribution companies were assigned frequencies: ABG Communication System, MG Communication Systems, Satellite Network Systems, Osam Associates, Details Nigeria, Comfax Nigeria, Electronic Communications, Desmims Nigeria, Goldstein Satellite Network, Independent Communication, and DAAR Communications. Several private radio stations were licensed.

The diversity of ownership of the media in Nigeria has enriched the climate of press freedom in the country. But nagging problems of military coups and counter coups remain to be resolved. These coups are a plague that truly threaten the destiny of the whole nation. The concomitant political instability has created an inhospitable environment for development, press freedom, and democracy for about a quarter of a century.

Table 2
Private Television Broadcasting Companies

Company	Location
TDC Broadcasting Limited	Lagos
Degue Broadcasting Network (DBN)	Lagos
Clapperboard Television Limited	Lagos
Channels Incorporated Limited	Lagos
Prime Television Limited	Ikorodu
Murhi International Limited (Nigeria)	Otta
Galaxy Pictures Limited	Ibadan
IBW Enterprises (Nigeria) Limited	Benin City
Independent Broadcasting Network Limited	Warri
Triple Heritage Communications Limited	Abuja
Desmims Broadcasting (Nigeria) Limited	Kaduna
Vibrant Communications Limited	Aba
Triax company (Nigeria) Limited	Enugu
Minaj System Limited	Obosi

Source: Africa Communications. September/October 1993

THE POLITICAL SYSTEM AND FREEDOM OF THE PRESS

Nigeria has experienced three types of administrations since the introduction of the newspaper in 1859 — colonial, civilian, and military. Under all three administrative types, the role of the indigenous press has been to inform, entertain, educate and challenge. And under all three, there has been censorship of the press (Omu 1978, Oyediran 1979). When the cry for independence and the denunciation of colonialism were the dominant themes under foreign rule, the British colonial administration clamped down on the press. In 1945, the *Pilot* and the *Comet* were banned for six weeks and denied official advertising when they reappeared. Newsprint quota was another weapon of choice used by the colonialists to curb the growing strength and freedom of the press. Censorship by the colonialists was not always sanctioned by the Home Office in London and was, therefore, an illegal instrument. Britain was committed to the Libertarian press theory at home and was hesitant in approving gag laws for the colonies.

Ironically, the illegal gag laws introduced by the colonialists were later used by Nigerian politicians. The Nigerian politician is also known to have been intolerant of the press. During the political crisis of the mid 1960s, many newspapers were banned from being circulated in areas where the local politicians have been criticized by the papers. Censorship has continued since the attainment of independence and, in reality, degenerated into military dictatorship and the suppression of freedom of expression in both the press and society. The destiny of the Nigerian press under the control of the lackluster and abnormal militocracy and kleptocracy has been a sad experience for most Nigerians. Nigerian journalists still look forward to the day when they can practice in a democratic atmosphere of press freedom.

Table 3
Nigerian Rulers, 1960-1997

Ruler	Ethnicity	Government	Date
Sani Abacha	Kanuri	Military	1993-
Ernest Shonekan	Yoruba	Civilian	1993
Ibrahim Babangida	Nupe	Military	1985-1993
Muhammadu Buhari	Hausa	Military	1984-1985
Shehu Shagari	Hausa/Fulani	Civilian	1979-1983
Olusegun Obasanjo	Yoruba	Military	1976-1979
Murtala Muhammed	Hausa/Fulani	Military	1975-1976
Yakubu Gowon	Angas	Military	1966-1975
Aguiyi Ironsi	Ibo	Military	1966
Abubakar T. Balewa	Hausa	Civilian	1960-1966

In the history of the Nigerian press, the worst form of censorship is associated with the dictatorial maladministration of military officers who frequently stage coups and counter coups in order to grab power and control the government of Nigeria. Censorship was further tightened, expanded and promoted by the indigenous military dictators five years after the attainment of independence. At different times, the military governments banned or closed down newspapers and radio stations with or without reasons. For example, the *Nigerian Daily Standard* was banned for five years between 1970 and 1975 by the South-Eastern State government for criticizing government policy. In 1978, a popular magazine, *Newbreed*, was banned for two years and no reason was given for the action.

Four episodes of military clashes with the press reveal the nature of press freedom in Nigeria under the military. It is almost impossible to catalogue all the privations suffered by journalists since the beginning of military colonialism in Nigeria. Apart from several punitive imprisonment, detention, dismissal, demotion, transfer of journalists in the course of their legitimate duty, four landmark incidents have been documented here: the celebrated Amakiri case, the Thompson and Irabor imprisonment, the assassination of Dele Giwa, and the Nosa Igiebor Saga.

The Amakiri case: Minere Amakiri was a reporter in Port Harcourt, River Sate, for the *Nigerian Observer* based in Benin City, Bendel State. He covered a press conference of the Nigerian Union of Teachers, River State branch, on July, 27, 1973. The Union demanded better conditions for the teachers in the state and gave an ultimatum to stage an industrial action if the demands were not met. The Union's demand and ultimatum were published by the *Nigerian Observer* on July 30, 1973. The publication triggered the anger of some officials of the River State government who claimed that it was meant to embarrass the military governor, Commander Alfred Diete-Spiff, on his thirty-first birthday which coincided with the date of the publication. The reporter, Minere Amakiri, was arrested, taken to the governor's office and tortured — his hair was shaved from his head; he was given 24 lashes of the cane on his bare back; and he was locked up in a toilet for 27 hours. This incident was published by the *Nigerian Observer* on August 2, 1973. The journalists and members of the public were appalled and legal action was instituted. The trial judge condemned the torture and awarded 200 naira, the equivalent of 250 dollars at the time, for every stroke of the cane received by Amakiri (Ogbondah, 1994, p. 81). He was also awarded over 5,000 naira for his detention and the shaving of his hair.

The Thompson and Irabor imprisonment: Decree No. 4 of 1984 was an obnoxious gag law directly aimed at silencing the press in Nigeria under the military dictatorship of General Muhammadu Buhari. Two Nigerian journalists, Tunde Thompson and Ndika Irabor of the *Guardian* were victims of Decree No. 4 of 1984. The two journalists were jailed for two years each while their employers in the *Guardian* paid a fine of 10,000 naira. The decree provided for the jailing of journalists and the punishment of the their employers for any inaccurate publication found embarrassing to the government or any public officer. Specifically, the gag decree provided for imprisonment of journalists without the option of fine and the imposition of a fine of not less than 10,000 naira, the equivalent of about 20,000 dollars at the time, on the employers of the journalists found guilty by the decree. In addition, the employers could forfeit all or any of the equipment used by the journalists and their employers. Decree No. 4 was meant to censor the press and curb investigative journalism.

The assassination of Dele Giwa: The assassination of Dele Giwa, the editor in chief of *Newswatch* magazine, in 1986, was the first of its type in Nigeria. Dele Giwa was killed by a parcel bomb received in his home. It is widely rumored that the mail bomb was sent by the office of the president. Editor Giwa was a constant critic of the government. His assassination was, however, a shock to the Nigerian public which does not believe in the killing of journalists who disagree with military dictators. After the death of Dele Giwa, *Newswatch* was banned by the government for six months. The mysterious source of the bomb is still unknown in Nigeria.

The Nosa Igiebor Saga: In 1993 and 1994, Nosa Igiebor, editor in chief of *Tell* magazine and a former deputy general editor at *Newswatch,* suffered various forms of punishment from the military. He was imprisoned under the Babangida regime for calling for democratic civilian rule for Nigeria. On August 15,

1993, his magazine offices were searched by state security officials and the police. In the last four months of Babangida's dictatorship over 500,000 copies of *Tell* magazine were seized from printers, vendors, and distributors. The magazine and its staff were under surveillance by Nigerian security forces and the journalists were assaulted, harassed detained at different times. In 1994, 50,000 copies of *Tell* magazine were seized by five truckloads of soldiers who raided the offices of the magazine because of a story with the headline: "The Return of Tyranny: Abacha Bares His Fangs." Editor Nosa Igiebor received his journalism training in Nigeria, Ghana and the United States. His major offense is his objective reporting of the military government in Nigeria. Nosa Igiebor dodged an attempt to arrest him again in 1994.

After seizing power in November 1993, military dictator Sani Abacha banned all political activities and dissolved all democratically elected bodies, including the national assembly, senate, all 30 state assemblies, gubernatorial positions and 500 local government assemblies. By this singular action Abacha humiliated the will of the people to determine through universal suffrage who shall be their leaders. Furthermore, Abacha declared that all criticisms of his government be treated as treasonable offense.

By June 1994, arrests and detentions of journalists, politicians, and pro-democracy groups continued to dominate the machinery of repression under military dictatorship. Among those arrested for alleged treason in the summer of 1994 were Beko Ransome-Kuti, the leader of the Campaign for Democracy pressure group, Segun Osoba, a former editor and governor of Ogun State, and Chief Anthony Enahoro, a publisher and leading member of the group that fought and won independence for Nigeria in the colonial era. Also arrested were former state governors Bola Ige, Jonah Jang and Dan Suleiman. Ameh Ebute, president of the Senate dissolved by General Sani Abacha, and Senators Polycarp Nwite and O. A. Okoroafor were arrested for calling on the military dictators to step aside and reinstitute democracy in Nigeria. In addition, dozens of members of the National Democratic Coalition (NADECO) were hunted by the military. The Nigerian military dictator declared a nationwide search for his nemesis, Moshood Abiola, the man widely believed to have won the June 12 presidential election in 1993. The sum of $2,000 was offered for information leading to the arrest of Abiola for declaring himself the president on June 11, 1994, and re-instating all democratically elected governors, legislators and other officials. Abiola's arrest on June 23, 1994, by more than 600 police officers led to a series of street demonstrations in Lagos. Abiola's newspaper, the *Concord* remains closed by the military.

By early 1995, Abacha dissolved his cabinet and ran the country with a handful of loyal officers and a justice minister, an unprecedented monopoly of absolute power which led to an abortive coup in March 1995. The people and the press remain restive and resilient despite the closure of several newspapers such as *The Punch* and *The Guardian* and the introduction of absolute militocracy by General Abacha. However, General Abacha may return Nigeria to civilian rule by October 1998. This gesture is largely due to internal and external pressure.

EXTERNAL FACTORS AFFECTING PRESS FREEDOM

Foreign influence on the media in Nigeria has been treated with minimum enthusiasm partly because of the notion that local journalists have been the movers and shakers of their own communication system. Since there were traditional means of mass communication in one form or the other, the addition of the new European type of mass communication exemplified by the print and electronic media is seen as merely complementary to the traditional means of communication in Nigeria. However, foreign influence on the local media system has permeated the whole structure of indigenous oral and mass communications, resulting in an undeniably hybrid communication system. Fisher noted in 1985 that "powerful external forces—sometimes benign, sometimes disruptive—have influenced the media" and their audiences in this part of Africa. This influence is the result of centuries of economic, cultural and political relationships with Europe and later America. Although the media in Nigeria were influenced by British colonialism and Western philosophies, Afrocentric perspectives on mass communication and culture are strong (Uche, 1989 and Jimada, 1992). Nigeria strives to balance its internal dynamics against external factors to forge a creative synthesis. The historicity of these relationships is common knowledge. In this section, the external factors affecting press freedom in Nigeria such as new technologies, foreign ownership of the media, Western education and language and the spread of democracy are examined.

MEDIA TECHNOLOGY AND PRESS FREEDOM

The early infrastructure of the mass communication system in Nigeria bears some resemblance to today's infrastructural characteristics. Imported technology and infrastructure are vital parts of the mass communication system in Nigeria. The pattern of foreign technology, local contents and audiences continues even as we approach the twenty first century. For example, the introduction of Rediffusion which relayed radio programs to the local audiences through wired sets was initiated by the British but its contents were both foreign and local. The Rediffusion radio broadcasts carried BBC news and programs as well as local news and programs in indigenous languages. Elegalem (1985) notes that as early as 1933 when broadcasting in Europe and America was still in its early stage, the colonial Post and Telegraph department in Nigeria established a station to monitor the BBC and experiment with wired broadcasting. However, the Nigerian Broadcasting Service was not officially opened until June 16, 1952. The dissemination of local and foreign news, made possible by Western technology, has contributed to press freedom by diversifying news sources and amplifying the messages through new technologies.

International media such as foreign radio and television transmissions, films, records, video cassettes and recorders, fax, electronic mail and computers are available in Nigeria. These foreign technologies have demonopolized information since there is no mechanism to control all the media.

The establishment of the Nigerian Television Service in 1962 was accomplished through assistance of the National

Broadcasting Company International of the United States. The U.S. based NBC actually ran the new national television station in Nigeria for the first five years, thus transferring some skills in management, service, and technological know-how to the Nigerian station. The satellite communication system of the last two decades and the information superhighway of the 1990s were introduced in Nigeria by the developed countries. These new technologies have made it possible to provide news and information to more people in Nigeria in circumstances devoid of local censors. Although these foreign technologies engendered the free flow of news and information, they could not fully guarantee press freedom because of the repressive military governments that have plagued the nation.

FOREIGN OWNERSHIP AND PRESS FREEDOM

The foreign ownership of the first Nigerian newspaper blazed the trail for later ownership pattern of the means of mass communication in Nigeria. For example, the ownership of the press was in the hands of many foreigners and Nigerians before 1977. Although the Nigerian Enterprise Promotion decree of 1977 gave exclusive ownership of all media to Nigerians, book publishing and printing, publishing of periodicals and mass communication related business of pulp and paper were open to foreign participants. Many private and joint foreign ownership of publishing companies exist in Nigeria. Longman and Heinemann are some of the book publishing companies still contributing to the marketplace of ideas in Nigeria.

Foreign ownership guarantees press freedom in a rather unusual way. Foreign owned media allow criticisms of other interests except their own economic interests. Foreign owned media are usually better funded and the subsequent financial independence tends to encourage the journalists to report freely on issues and events. For example, the success of the *Daily Times* from its inception was due principally to the massive infusion of foreign capital. The objectivity of the *Daily Times* is an example of the influence foreign ownership has on press freedom. However, European legacy of press freedom is not all pervasive in the

Nigerian press in spite of the presence of foreign capital in the mass communication system.

Sometimes, foreign journalists are denied visas to the country or arrested and deported for interviewing people. For example, Geraldine Brooks, a staff reporter of the *Wall Street Journal* wrote an account of her arrest and deportation in Nigeria (on May 6) in 1994: "Another possible threat, in the government views, are foreign newspaper reporters. When I approached an army officer to ask for the military account of a violent incident, I was handed over to the secret police, held and deported "for security reasons." (*Wall Street Journal,* May 6, 1994.) Following her deportation from Nigeria, Brooks unleashed a series of true but subjective articles critical of Nigeria and Nigerians.

Foreign media used by Nigerians at home is usually free from government control. For example, the Voice of America and the BBC broadcasts to Nigeria and Africa in general are uninhibited by local politicians or dictators. The Nigerian audiences within and outside the country benefit immensely from such objective, fair, and accurate reporting of local events in foreign media. In addition to foreign radio broadcasts, the transmission and reception of foreign television news and programming from CNN and other international media organizations have increased the free flow of news and information beyond the control of local censorship. The availability of international electronic media has rendered futile the censorship instrument of banning the circulation of foreign print media which were found to be critical of the local policies and events. Also, the introduction of underground or off-shore radio station in Nigeria has added an uncensored voice to mass communication in the country.

WESTERN EDUCATION, LANGUAGE AND PRESS FREEDOM

The education of Nigerian journalists abroad has contributed to the fearless dispensation of the local mass communicators many of whom have themselves been exposed to Western education both at home and abroad. The influence of foreign training has facilitated press freedom in Nigeria. Ogbondah (1990) notes that beyond the shores of Nigeria, especially in the United States and Great Britain, several universities and research institutions have turned out handsome volumes of research work on Nigeria.

Nigerian journalists are the beneficiaries of several training programs organized by the International Press Institute, the BBC, the United States Information Agency, the United States Agency for International Development, Freedom Forum, and other organizations promoting press freedom worldwide. The cultural and developmental impacts of the training may have encouraged the unabated pursuit of press freedom in Nigeria. However, the practice of journalism geared toward the entrenchment of press freedom is the responsibility of the Nigerian mass communication practitioner as the actual agent of press freedom. However, Hawk (1992) points out that Americans must recognize Africans as the major agents of change in their country. Western education and language have been significant to the freedom of press in Nigeria but the trenches in which the battles are being fought are dominated by Nigerians. The journalists are armed with Western libertarian and social responsibility media theories in addition to indigenous values. The availability of Western mass communication literature and research is the bedrock of intellectual yearning for press freedom. The literature also serves as the source of inspiration for press freedom in Nigeria.

Although it is seldom emphasized, the English language has contributed to press freedom in Nigeria. Its wide use has made it possible for Nigerian journalists and the people to better communicate with each other and the world, thus promoting freedom of the press directly and indirectly. The English language has made it possible for Nigerian journalists and the public to receive news and information from uncensored international media sources.

The Spread of Democracy

The end of the Cold War and fall of communism have turned the tide of public opinion against authoritarianism and unabashed censorship swayed by ideological currents of the past. The subsequent liberation of the press in Eastern Europe resulted in the rise of several pro-democracy movements worldwide, including the National Democratic Coalition (NADECO) an alliance of politicians, retired military officers and pro-democracy groups in Nigeria. The activities of the Nigerian pro-democracy movement forced the Babangida military government, one of the most repressive military governments in the country, to surrender the reins of government to a short-lived and illegitimate civilian administration in 1993.

The spread of democracy has fueled the quest for press freedom in Nigeria by creating more awareness on the part of the Nigerians and the local journalists. The spread of democracy has made it possible to monitor press freedom more efficiently. International agencies such as Freedom House and the International Press Institute continue to monitor the violation of press freedom in Nigeria. Their efforts have yielded some results, including the release of journalists jailed by military dictators and the privatization of the electronic media. This new development is a sign of the changes that may check the abuse of press freedom in Nigeria. Although privatization of the media does not in itself guarantee press freedom in the Nigerian context, it takes away government monopoly of the electronic media, thereby mitigating the official inclination toward censorship. The post-Cold War era is witnessing the acceleration of free and open exchange of news and communication in the long march toward democracy for Nigeria.

CONCLUSIONS

The dynamic and bold press in Nigeria is the product of a combination of internal and external factors. Censorship of the press started in the colonial period and has continued even after colonialism. However, there is a vibrant press in Nigeria because of the plurality of voices, diversity of ownership, and a resilient press corp. Locally, the bold tradition of the Nigerian journalists has propelled the vitality of the press while the military dictators have constituted the major barriers to press freedom. Censorship of the press is essentially an internal phenomenon. The fragility and tenacity of press freedom in Nigeria have been tested under civilian and military administrations.

Foreign influence in the media is historically and practically evident. These external factors have been more positive than negative although censorship was introduced by colonial administrators. Western culture, capital, new technologies, and democracy have all contributed in no small measure to press freedom in Nigeria. Although the state of the press in Nigeria is predominantly a struggle between the people and their rulers, a coalition of indigenous and external forces cannot be ignored in any discourse of press freedom in Nigeria.

REFERENCES

Agbaje, Adigun A. B. *The Nigerian Press, Hegemony, And The Social Construction of Legitimacy,* 1960-1983. New York: The Edwin Mellen Press, 1992: 19-24.

Anise, Ladun. "Triple Imperatives of Contemporary African Governance: Debt, Democracy and Development, A Critical Perspective." In Eribo, Festus, Oyeleye Oyediran, Mulatu Wubneh, and Leo Zonn, eds. *Window On Africa: Democratization and Media Exposure.* Greenville, NC: Center for International Programs, East Carolina University, 1993: 77-96.

Edeani, David O. "Press Ownership and control in Nigeria." In Ugboajah, Frank O., ed. *Mass Communication, Culture and Society in West Africa.* New York: Hans Zolt Publishers, 1985: 44-62.

Ekeh, Peter. "Democratism Versus Democracy in Africa." In Eribo, Festus, Oyeleye Oyediran, Mulatu Wubneh, and Leo Zonn, eds. *Window On Africa: Democratization and Media Exposure.* Greenville, NC: Center for International Programs, East Carolina University, 1993: 51-76.

Elegalem, P. O. "Economic Factors in the Development of Mass Communication in Nigeria." In Ugboajah, Frank O., ed. *Mass Communication, Culture and Society in West Africa.* New York: Hans Zolt Publishers, 1985: 63-73.

Europa World Year Book, 1996: 730.

Fisher, Harold A. "International Cooperation in the Development of West African Mass Media." In Ugboajah, Frank O., ed. *Mass Communication, Culture and Society in West Africa.* New York: Hans Zolt Publishers, 1985: 74-84.

Hawk, Beverly G. *Africa's Media Image.* West Port: Praeger, 1992: 3-14.

Jimada, U. "Eurocentric Media Training in Nigeria: What Alternative? *Journal of Black Studies 22* 3 (1992): 366-379.

Kurian, George Thomas. *World Press Encyclopedia*. Vol. 2. New York: Facts on File, Inc., 1982: 687.

Mytton, Graham, *Mass Communication in Africa*. London: Edward Arnold Publishers, 1983: 117-126.

Ochs, Martin. *The African Press*. Cairo: The American University in Cairo Press, 1986: 67.

Ogbondah, Chris W. *The Press In Nigeria: An Annotated Bibliography*. New York: Greenwood Press, 1990: xi.

Ogbondah, Chris W. *Military Regimes and the Press in Nigeria, 1966-1993*. New York: University Press of America, 1994: 81.

Omu, F. I. A. Press and Politics In Nigeria, 1880-1937. New Jersey: Humanities Press Inc., 1978.

Oyediran, Oyeleye. *Nigerian Government and Politics Under Military Rule, 1966-79*. New York: St. Martin's Press, 1979.

Rodney, Walter. *How Europe Underdeveloped Africa*. Washington D.C.: Howard University Press, 1981.

Sobowale, Idowu A. "The Historical Development of Nigerian Press." In Ugboajah, Frank O., ed. *Mass Communication, Culture and Society in West Africa*. New York: Hans Zolt Publishers, 1985: 33.

Stevenson, Robert L. *Global Communication in the Twenty-First Century*. New York: Longman, 1994: 249.

Uche, Luke Uka. *Mass Media, People and Politics in Nigeria*. New Delhi: Concept, 1989: xxii- 225.

Wall Street Journal May 6 1994: 1.

Ziegler, Dhyana and Molefi K. Asante. *Thunder and Silence: Mass Media in Africa*. Trenton, NJ: Africa World Press, Inc., 1992: 78-79.

Chapter 4

New Media for the

New South Africa

C. Anthony Giffard

Arnold S. de Beer & Elanie Steyn

Introduction

On a continent swept by change, South Africa surely stands out as the nation where democratic reforms — including freedom of the press — have been the most far-reaching and the most unexpected. Just a few years ago leaders of black liberation movements were in jail or in exile; vocal critics of the government were banned or detained without trial, and the media were subject to strict censorship (De Beer, 1993; De Beer & Steyn, 1993:210; *IPI Report,* 1994:56-57; Steyn, 1994a). In 1994, after the first national elections in which all races could vote, three centuries of white rule were replaced by a multi-racial parliament and a black-led government of national unity. Now, says Nelson Mandela, the nation's new president, "for the first time, the future holds the promise of a brighter tomorrow."

There have been vast changes since February, 1990, when President F.W. de Klerk lifted the 30-year-old ban on the African National Congress, the Pan-Africanist Congress and the South African Communist Party, and freed Mandela and other black nationalist leaders from prison. The South African situation is unique in that it is probably the first time that a well-entrenched, militarily powerful ruling class has negotiated a revolution in the region (Accone, 1994; Commonwealth Observer Group, 1994:27). The ruling National Party, in full control of the state and undefeated in battle, agreed to abandon decades of apartheid and to enter into negotiations eventually leading to the democratic elections of 1994.

INTERIM CONSTITUTION

After the reforms of 1990, negotiations involving virtually every political constituency in the nation, from the Communist Party to the far-right Conservative Party (see MacLennan, 1994:4), resulted in agreement on an Interim Constitution that was approved by Parliament in December 1993. The agreement provided for a government of national unity, made up of parties winning at least 5 percent of the vote in universal elections that took place on April 27, 1994. The ANC, which won 62 percent of the votes in the elections, holds 252 of the 400 seats in the new National Assembly and 60 of the 90 seats in the Senate. Other parties represented are the National Party, 82 Assembly seats, the predominantly Zulu Inkatha Freedom Party 43, and the Democratic Party, 7. The new National Assembly and Senate will write a permanent constitution and rule the country until new elections in 1999.

BILL OF RIGHTS

A Bill of Rights, part of the new Interim Constitution, guarantees equal protection of all citizens under the law. Two provisions in the Bill of Rights are directly relevant to the media, providing constitutional guarantees of a free press for the first time in the nation's history (Grogan, 1993:51-53):

Every person shall have the right to freedom of speech and expression, which shall include freedom of the press and other media, and the freedom of artistic creativity and scientific work, and All media financed by or under the control of the state shall be regulated in a manner which insures impartiality and the expression of a diversity of opinion..

These political changes have already had far-reaching effects on print and broadcast media in South Africa, and more are certain to follow (e.g. see SABC, 1993; Louw, 1993; Cohen, 1994:10; *MISA Free Press,* 1994; SABC, 1994). Even before the 1994 elections, the media had operated in a climate of new freedom. The lifting of the ban on the liberation movements in 1990 made it possible for media to report their views for the first time in more than three decades (Mandela, 1994; Steyn, 1994a). New publications appeared to express the views of the formerly outlawed political groups. Stringent restrictions on print and TV journalists introduced during the State of Emergency in 1985 (see Giffard & Cohen, 1989) were repealed. The apartheid-era laws remaining on the statute books were seldom applied after 1991. The traditionally pro-National Party, state-controlled South African Broadcasting Corporation (SABC) began to provide a forum for dissident black voices (Gevisser, 1993:15; Qwelane, 1993:18; SABC, 1994).

During the campaign before the first all-race elections, an Independent Media Commission was established to ensure that there was fair treatment of all political parties on the broadcast services, and to monitor the political content of government publications (ACAG/Update, 1993a:8; *ACAG/Update,* 1993b:3). There was concern on the part of some parties that the SABC would, as in the past, favor the National Party. But, according to one international monitoring group, the SABC "undertook with enthusiasm a creative and highly constructive role in facilitating free political debate, promoting voter education, and encouraging democratic reforms" (Commonwealth Observer Group, 1994:26). The SABC also brought in a team of foreign experts — mainly from Australia and Canada — to train SABC staff for the election coverage, and to monitor their reporting.

Now, with the elections successfully completed and the new government in place, the media must help ease the transition to a truly post-apartheid society.

MEDIA IN THE NEW SOUTH AFRICA

President Mandela has said that he expects the media to support the new government's Reconstruction and Development Program, a socio-economic policy framework that "seeks to mobilize all our people and our country's resources toward the final eradication of apartheid and the building of a democratic, non-racial and non-sexist future" (Reconstruction and Development Program, 1994:1).

Among the main principles of the program are peace and security for all, including human rights and equality for all before the law; and nation-building, with the aim of developing the country's economic, political and social viability. The key programs the government intends to implement to achieve these goals are:

- Meeting basic needs — jobs, land, housing, water, electricity, telecommunications, nutrition and health care;
- Developing human resources, not only through education and training but also through arts, culture, sports and recreation;
- Building the economy, including cooperation with neighboring countries to create a large market offering stable employment; and
- Democratizing the state and society at every level.

All of these are predicated on involving people in the decision-making process. It is here that the media are expected to play a key role. Thus the program calls for "a democratic information system" to facilitate socio-economic development.

This task may be easier in South Africa than is the case in other African nations moving toward democracy, because the Republic already has the most highly developed telecommunications and media infrastructure on the continent (see Johnson, 1994).

OVERVIEW OF MEDIA
BROADCAST MEDIA

South Africa has a highly developed media system. There are already four television channels and more than 30 radio stations serving the nation's population of about 40 million people (for a discussion on the radio and television systems in South Africa, see De Villiers, 1993 and Mersham, 1993). The South African Broadcasting Corporation's 3 TV channels among them broadcast in seven languages, with efforts underway to broadcast in all of South Africa's 11 official languages, as well as some of the smaller non-official languages. M-Net, a subscription television channel owned by newspaper chains, covers the major population centers. Almost 10 million viewers watch one or more of these channels every day. Among white households, TV and radio usage is almost universal. It was estimated in 1993 that about 40 percent of black households in the country had television sets, while about 83 percent had radio receivers (Levy, 1994:5).

Seven of the SABC radio channels can be received from high-quality FM transmitters nationwide. Others serve ethnic and linguistic groups on a regional basis (see SABC, 1994). There are two independent, commercial radio services with nationwide coverage. These domestic radio services are estimated to have a daily audience of some 14 million people. Channel Africa, the SABC's external service, transmits programs to Africa and the Indian Ocean islands in seven languages.

PRINT MEDIA

South Africa has 17 daily newspapers and a dozen major Sunday or weekly papers. Fourteen of the dailies, with a combined circulation of about 1.1 million copies, are published in English. Three of the papers, with a combined circulation of about 230,000 copies, appear in Afrikaans. An English-language paper targeted at blacks, the Sowetan, has the biggest circulation in the country — some 210,000 copies a day. With the exception of one large Afrikaans Sunday paper and one in Zulu, all the major weeklies are in English. The two biggest Sunday papers are distributed nationally. Most of the dailies are local or regional. Newspaper circulation has been relatively stable over the past two decades, despite rapid increases in the size of the population and in literacy. Market penetration among the population as a whole is estimated at about 4 percent, which puts the Republic in the same league as countries like Peru and India. By contrast, there are about five radio listeners for each newspaper reader.

HISTORY OF THE PRESS

EARLY ENGLISH-LANGUAGE NEWSPAPERS

English-language newspapers date back to the early days of white settlement in South Africa. Although the Dutch East India Company founded a settlement at the Cape in 1652, there were no newspapers produced there for 150 years. The first local paper (and one of the first in Africa), the *Cape Town Gazette and Commercial Advertiser,* appeared in 1800 after the British took over the Cape. The arrival of a large party of British settlers in 1820 spurred the development of newspapers in Cape Town and on the eastern frontier, where the settlers were established. A long struggle over press freedom between printers in the Cape Colony and authoritarian colonial governors culminated in the press winning a large degree of freedom from government control as early as 1829 (see Diederichs & De Beer, 1993; De Beer & Steyn, 1993).

The press spread to the interior following the discovery of diamonds in the Northern Cape in 1869, and of gold on the Witwatersrand in the 1870s. By the turn of the century virtually every town of any size had its own newspaper. Most of the country's major English newspapers date back to this period: the *Eastern Province Herald* (1845), *Natal Witness* (1846), *Natal Mercury* (1852), *Daily News* (1854), *The Argus* (1857), *Daily Dispatch* (1872), *Cape Times* (1876), *Diamond Fields Advertiser* (1878) and *The Star* (1887). Several papers aimed at an African or Indian readership date to the latter part of this

80

period. They include *Imvo Zabantsundu (1884)*, *Illanga Lasa* (1904), and *Indian Opinion* (1904).

EARLY AFRIKAANS NEWSPAPERS

Several of the early newspapers at the Cape were bilingual — English and Dutch — reflecting the composition of the first settlers. The first purely Dutch newspapers at the Cape were founded, in part, as a reaction to the politics of the English papers, which from an early stage were identified with the humanitarian views of anti-slavery white liberals (see Muller, 1991). *Die Zuid Afrikaan* appeared in Cape Town in 1828 to fight, says one historian, against "the radicalism of the negrophilist philanthropolists" (Hachten & Giffard, 1984:29). These papers also promoted the use of Afrikaans, which was emerging as a separate language from its ancestral Dutch. The first Afrikaans newspaper, *Di Patriot,* appeared in 1876 (see Muller, 1991).

Hundreds of Dutch farming families, determined to escape British rule, left the Cape in the Great Trek of 1836 to found the Boer republics of the Orange Free State and the Transvaal in the interior. There they established papers like *De Staats Courant* (1857) and *De Volkstem* (1873), which promoted the Afrikaner point of view in the face of a huge influx of mainly English-speaking fortune seekers drawn to the diamond fields and goldfields.

Disputes between Britain and the Boer republics — exacerbated by the highly partisan press — culminated in the Anglo-Boer War of 1889-1902, a conflict that can be seen as the first major anti-colonial uprising in Africa. The peace that followed saw the Boer republics, the Cape Province and the province of Natal achieve a large degree of independence from Britain in 1910 as the Union of South Africa.

This was a period of consolidation for the press. English newspapers flourished in all the main cities, dominated as they were by English-speaking merchants and professionals. *The Rand Daily Mail* was founded in Johannesburg in 1902, and became the centerpiece of a chain of morning and Sunday newspapers known as the South African Associated Press (now Times

Media). The tendency toward group ownership continued with the rise of the Argus Printing and Publishing Company, which merged a group of mainly afternoon papers into the nation's largest press combine. Both groups had strong links to the powerful mining and financial houses that dominated the economy, and in turn were linked to British financial interests (Diederichs & De Beer, 1993).

A surge of Afrikaner nationalistic sentiment saw the founding of several new papers dedicated to supporting the political, cultural and economic interests of a people impoverished and suppressed after the Anglo-Boer War. Chief among these was *Die Burger,* which began publication in Cape Town in 1915. *Die Burger,* unlike the English papers, depended on the financial support of thousands of individual shareholders. It was closely linked to Afrikaner religious, political and self-help organizations (for a discussion on the relationship between the National Party and the Afrikaans press, see De Beer & Steyn, 1993). The paper is credited with playing a decisive role in the acceptance of Afrikaans as an official language in 1925, in the growth of the National Party, which came to power in 1948, and in South Africa's shaking off the last of its colonial ties and becoming a republic in 1961. *Die Burger* became the launching pad for the chief Afrikaans press group, Nasionale Pers, which spread from its base in Cape Town to the Free State and Transvaal, and now is the second-largest publishing concern in the Republic.

A second Afrikaans newspaper chain, Perskor, developed in the Transvaal with aims similar to that of Nasionale Pers: to promote Afrikaner culture and political power. Its flagship, Die Transvaler, founded in 1937 was the official organ of the National Party in the Transvaal. Like Nasionale Pers, Perskor owns magazines and regional newspapers in addition to its urban dailies.

NEWSPAPERS TODAY

The four major press groups previously discussed publish more than 90 percent of the dailies and weeklies sold in South Africa. They also own half of the nation's magazines. Together with the

SABC, they own the South African Press Association, the country's only wire service. The "Big Four" newspaper chains among them own M-Net (Mersham, 1993). This concentration of ownership is characteristic of the South African economy as a whole. One corporation alone, Anglo-American, is estimated to own 43 percent of the total share value on the Johannesburg Stock Exchange. The top six corporations own 87 percent (*Sunday Times,* 1994-05-08). These corporations also have held controlling interests in the newspaper chains, and through them, the highly profitable subscription channel. The two large English chains, Argus Newspapers and Times Media, were until 1994 closely linked through cross-ownership of shares (Klein, 1994:3).

The prospect of a new government led by the ANC, which had criticized monopolistic control of the media, spurred some major changes in the English newspaper groups just prior to the 1994 elections. Some of the criticisms referred directly to the newspaper chains. As Cyril Ramaphosa, secretary-general of the ANC put it, "the reality is that the media (are) by and large a white-owned and white-controlled business. Moreover, large sections of the media are in the hands of a few very powerful monopolies. This situation cannot lend itself to a truly independent media . . . media freedom must be underpined by an equitable distribution of media resources, development programs and a deliberate effort to engender the culture of open debate."

The ANC had hoped to start its own newspaper, but even a grant of some $3.5 million from the Italian government was not enough (Louw, 1994). However, the Argus Group transferred a controlling interest in its popular black daily, Sowetan, to a consortium of black businessmen. And Anglo-American, which through subsidiaries owned Argus Newspapers, sold off a controlling interest in the chain to an Irish-based media conglomerate, Independent Newspapers (Bruce, 1993:23). This company, in turn, eliminated the cross-ownership between Argus Newspapers and Times Media by purchasing one Times Media paper, the *Cape Times,* and buying out Times Media's shareholdings in three other Argus papers (Klein, 1994:3). As a result of these changes, the press structure as of 1994 was as follows:

THE ARGUS GROUP

Argus Newspapers alone accounts for 45 percent of all daily newspaper sales. Argus dailies in the major cities include its Johannesburg flagship, *The Star* (circulation 204,000), *The Argus* and the *Cape Times* (Cape Town); the *Daily News* and the *Natal Mercury* (Durban); and the *Pretoria News*. In addition, Argus Newspapers owns the Sunday Tribune (circulation 122,000), plus magazines and a stable of local papers. As noted above, the group is now controlled by an Irish publishing house, although Anglo-American retains some shares through various subsidiaries.

TIMES MEDIA

Times Media (formerly South African Associated Newspapers) is the second largest English-language newspaper chain. It owns several big-city dailies, among them *Business Day* (Johannesburg), and the *Eastern Province Herald* and the *Evening Post* (Port Elizabeth). The group's *Sunday Times* (538,000) is the biggest weekly paper. Times Media ultimately is controlled by the Anglo-American Corporation.

NASIONALE PERS

Nasionale Pers (Naspers) is the largest Afrikaans group. It owns three dailies, *Beeld* (Johannesburg), *Die Burger* (Cape Town) and *Die Volksblad* (Bloemfontein) and a 50 percent share in the national Sunday paper, Rapport (circ. 403,000). Nasionale Pers also owns *City Press* (250,000), a Sunday paper targeted at a black readership, and a large stable of magazines and regional newspapers. Nasionale Pers is unusual in that it has a large number of individual shareholders.

PERSKOR

Perskor, the second-largest Afrikaans group, has a 50 percent share in the Sunday paper, *Rapport,* and owns a politically conservative English daily, *The Citizen*. The group also owns various magazines. Perskor is controlled by a diversified conglomerate with the Rembrandt group as the main shareholder.

INDEPENDENTS

The *Sowetan,* formerly part of the Argus stable, targeted at black readers, now is controlled by a consortium of black business interests. It is the country's biggest daily (209,272). Other independents include the *Daily Dispatch* in East London, and the *Natal Witness* in Pietermaritzburg.

ALTERNATIVE NEWSPAPERS

Government censorship and restrictions on press ownership — and particularly the State of Emergency regulations after 1985 — limited the growth of an alternative press until the reforms of 1990 (see Mandela, 1994; Steyn, 1994a). Nevertheless, during the 1980s a number of left-wing papers began publication. Usually subsidized by foreign governments, religious, or political organizations, papers like the *Weekly Mail, Sunday Nation, Vrye Weekblad* and *South* supported democratic and liberation movements in the Republic. They provided a forum for views not commonly expressed in the mainstream press. Also included in this group were seven community newspapers and six magazines (also see Tomaselli & Louw, 1991 on the alternative press in South Africa).

The left-wing alternative press has been on the decline since the political reforms began, and more so since the advent of majority rule in 1994 undercut their reason for existence (Steyn, 1994b:11). Foreign funding has largely dried up. Today, most of the funding comes from the European Union, from grants supplied by the mainstream South African newspapers, and from the Dutch development aid organization, NOVIB (Emdon, 1994). Several of the publications have folded and others may follow (*MISA Free Press,* 1994). It seems possible, however, that the new government will establish a trust fund to support these publications.

To the far right of the political spectrum are *Die Afrikaner, Patriot and Sweepslag,* which support Afrikaner conservatives who reject the dismantling of apartheid and campaign for an independent white homeland (Diederichs & De Beer, 1993).

BROADCAST MEDIA

RADIO

The first radio programs in South Africa were broadcast in 1923. Today, a vast SABC network of TV and radio transmitters blankets the nation. There are more than 30 radio services, broadcasting over a network of 500 FM transmitters, linked by an Intelsat satellite. Some are national (Radio South Africa, Radio 5, Afrikaans Stereo, Radio Metro). Some are regional (Highveld Stereo, Radio Oranje, Radio Port Natal and Radio Algoa). Nine stations are aimed at particular groups in the vernacular (for example, Radio Sesotho, Radio Venda, Radio Swazi and Zulu Stereo). Programming on radio consists mainly of drama (some 800 plays and serials a year), music, talk shows, magazine programs, religion and sport. About 12 percent of air time is devoted to news (SABC, 1993; SABC, 1994).

In addition to the SABC services, there are two independent, commercial stations, Radio 702 and Capital Radio 604 (De Villiers, 1993). Several "pirate" stations, run by political groups, began operation before the elections in 1994, but the new Independent Broadcasting Authority (IBA) was instituted to deal, inter alia, with this problem as from 1994.

TELEVISION

The nation's first regular television service began in 1976, with a single channel broadcasting alternately in Afrikaans and English. Since then the service has expanded to three channels. TV1, the original channel, still broadcasts in Afrikaans and English to a daily audience of some 6 million viewers. CCV (Contemporary Community Values Television), carries programs in nine European, African and Asian languages. NNTV (National

Network Television) carries a high proportion of sports, but also a range of typically public-service programming (*Interkom, 1994a:8*). The SABC produces about 50 percent of its programs — and at present has a monopoly over TV news (SABC, 1994; *Screen Africa, 1994*). Other programs are imported, mainly from the United States and Europe. Imported series and movies shown on TV often are dubbed into local languages. In some cases, the original sound track is available in simulcast over radio transmitters (Mersham, 1993).

The SABC has an operating budget of about $340 million a year (SABC, 1994). Initially, the income was derived only from listener license fees. Advertising was introduced on a limited scale in 1978, but now accounts for more than three-quarters of the revenue. Television contributes two-thirds of the advertising income; radio the remainder. Income from license fees dropped off dramatically over the past few years as many black households in the townships refused to pay as a protest against apartheid. White right-wing groups then urged their followers not to pay either (*Die Patriot, 1994-02-11*). In 1993, it cost the SABC $22 million to collect $70 million in license fees. As a result, the licensing system has virtually broken down. There is no direct government subsidy, and with increasing competition from independent commercial radio and TV channels, the Independent Broadcasting Authority still had to decide on SABC's finances as a public broadcaster.

South Africa's first subscription TV channel, M-Net, began operation in 1986. It is owned by the four major newspaper companies, which were permitted to launch the channel to compensate for their losses in advertising revenue to SATV. The channel offers about 120 hours a week of entertainment programming, most of it imported. In 1993, M-Net had 815,000 subscribers in the Republic, and is also available via satellite to more than 30 other nations in Africa (Mersham, 1993).

Two international TV news channels — the British-based Sky News, and America's CNN — are available in South Africa. Sky News is broadcast over the TV1 transmitters when it ceases programming at around midnight, and continues until 6 a.m. CNN is broadcast at similar times over the NNTV transmitters

(The Daily News, 1994-01-13; *The Citizen,* 1994-02-19:15; *The Star Tonight,* 1994-01-14). Three international religious channels, Trinity Broadcasting Network, Christian Television and Good News Television use surplus capacity on SATV transmitters to reach South African viewers (Mersham, 1993).

Media Regulation

Government Control

South Africa has a dismal reputation for government restriction of the media — although some would argue that even in the past it had one of the freest media systems in Africa (Martin, 1991; Johnson, 1994). Particularly since the National Party came to power in 1948, journalists were prosecuted for publishing restricted matter, newspapers were closed down, and the broadcasting services made totally subservient to the government (Hachten & Giffard, 1984; De Beer, 1993). During the State of Emergency (1986-1990) the government enforced a near-total blackout on news of detentions, boycotts, protest actions and the activities of police in quelling unrest. Many of these restrictions applied to foreign as well as local journalists (Giffard & Cohen, 1989; Ecquid Novi, 10: 1&2).

President De Klerk repealed the emergency rules and other restrictions in his policy speech in February, 1990, in which he also lifted the ban on liberation movements like the ANC and the South African Communist Party and freed political prisoners. It was then possible for the press to report the views of even the most outspoken critics of apartheid. In addition, newspaper editors have worked with the government to remove many restrictive measures from the statute books (Cohen, 1994:10; Steyn, 1994a). The Internal Security Act was amended to reduce periods of detention without trial. Newspapers no longer need to pay a $10,000 fee to register. The government can no longer summarily ban newspapers. Curbs on reporting on police activities or prison conditions have been lifted (also see Burns, 1990; Grogan & Barker, 1993). Although a number of restrictive laws remain on the statute books, they are not being applied. Ken

Owen, editor of the *Sunday Times,* likens the situation to a "sort of Prague spring" (Owen, 1994).

POLITICAL CONTROL

Media policy in the new South Africa inevitably will be shaped by the new majority. As indicated above, a Bill of Rights now guarantees freedom of the press and of expression. Legislation that appears to contravene these guarantees can be challenged in the new Constitutional Court.

ANC MEDIA POLICY

The ANC's principal policy document, the Reconstruction and Development Program, has little to say about press freedom as such. However, the organization adopted a media charter in May 1992 which states that all people shall have the right to freely publish, broadcast or otherwise disseminate information and opinion (also see Louw, 1993). The policy calls for maximum openness on the part of government institutions, and for removal of all restrictions on free flow of information. According to Cyril Ramaphosa, the ANC "has always believed in the need for a vigorous and independent media... there can be no democracy... without an independent media, a media that is free to inform, to criticize, to probe." The ANC says it is committed to restructuring the SABC. It wants to maintain a public broadcasting service "to serve society as a whole and give voice to all sectors of the population" (SABC, 1994; Commonwealth Observer Group, 1994).

But the charter includes some clauses that may threaten media freedom, among them a proposal that "an accord of journalistic practice and the necessary mechanisms to ensure minimum bias and distortion be established" (Grogan, 1993). And it stipulates that press freedom must be supported by "equitable distribution of media resources and by development programs."

NATIONAL PARTY MEDIA POLICY

After many years of the National Party government's curbs on the media, the party itself realized the necessity of a free press in the post-February 1990 period. Roelf Meyer, at that time Minister of Communication, declared that the liberation of the media which has ensued since De Klerk's speech gave the party conclusive proof of the counterproductive nature of any restrictions on the media (1992:94).

> The National Party discovered that the market-place of ideas is much the same as any other market-place. The Party has learned that any artificial restriction on this market led to distortions. It is only in a free market that ideas can find their appropriate level.

Like democratic institutions elsewhere, the National Party came to realize that an open press serves the public by exposing shortcomings and malpractices on all sides. It has also placed much greater pressure on all participants in the national debate to communicate more effectively with the media, and hence with the public. The National Party welcomed the result that all major political and other players in society are now increasingly aware that certain practices and positions are unacceptable in the harsh light of media coverage and public opinion (Meyer, 1992; for a detailed review of the National Party's media policy, see De Beer & Steyn, 1993).

INKATHA POLICY

The Inkatha Freedom Party, the second largest black political party represented in the new parliament, takes a similar line. Chief Gatsha Buthelezi, head of the IFP, says that:

> ... broadcasting and media functions in a future South Africa must serve the public in such a way that the ideals of a democratic, non-racial, non-sexist and prosperous society are pursued to the fullest. This will of course require a fundamental change in the structure and the performance of broadcasting... Television and radio broadcasting in particular should be culturally diverse, reflecting and responding to the needs and interests of all audiences.

Pan Africanist Congress Policy

The Pan Africanist Congress (PAC) — which could not attain any seats in the 1994 Parliament — believes minority control of the media is the antithesis of freedom of expression, and control of the media must be freed from absolute monopoly (see De Lille, 1994). In its place, or side by side with it, an independent trust must be created to ensure the influence of people in the co-ownership of these enterprises. The PAC says there should be a limit to the number of papers owned by single companies to minimize the monopoly of news management. It argues that the state must assure the rights of minority alternative papers to exist through subsidies.

The PAC also proposes that there should be a press council to ensure proper standards in news dissemination, to safeguard the privacy of individuals, and to take action against any person who incites harassment of journalists. It wants a broadcasting corporation, independent of the state, and financed directly by listener fees.

Self-Regulation

Two voluntary, self-regulatory bodies — one for the print media, one for broadcasting — now exist in the republic. The Press Council of South Africa, founded by newspaper publishers and editors, is intended to uphold press freedom, encourage high professional standards, and receive and resolve complaints about published items (The Press Council of South Africa, 1993:1). The council has a full-time mediator who can resolve disputes, or refer them to a panel comprised of equal numbers of press and public representatives. The council has the power to require a correction or apology, or to levy fines against publications that contravene its code of conduct.

The Broadcasting Complaints Commission of South Africa also is an independent, self-regulatory body that adjudicates upon complaints against television and radio, in terms of its code of conduct (*ACAG/Update,* 1993a:7; BCCSA, 1994). Members of the National Association of Broadcasters are signatories to the code, which, like that of the Press Council, covers such issues as news reporting and commentary, obscenity, violence, sex and invasion of privacy. In the event a complaint is upheld, possible sanctions include a reprimand, an order calling on the broadcaster to carry a correction or an apology, or a fine. Members of the commission are appointed from nominations submitted by the public and the NAB.

INTIMIDATION

A serious constraint on free expression over the past few years — a period marked by much violence and disorder in South Africa — has been threats or actual physical attacks on journalists (see De Beer, 1993; *The Citizen*, 1992-11-21:4; *The Weekly Mail & Guardian,* 1994-05-06:11; *MISA Free Press,* 1994; Oosthuizen, 1994:1-4; Qwelane, 1994; Tholoe, 1994). A new breed of censors has appeared: township activists who use violence to intimidate media and prevent unfavorable publicity about their organizations. Black journalists covering violence in the townships are often seen as biased by members of the ANC, PAC or Inkatha, who sometimes subject them to verbal abuse and physical violence (Stander, 1993:14; Johnson, 1994:2). Several have lost their lives, dozens more have been injured. This has had an intimidating effect on journalists. For example, when the Sowetan endorsed the ANC and PAC in an editorial before the elections, its journalists complained to the editors that this had put their lives at risk from supporters of the Inkatha Freedom Party, which had not been endorsed (Tholoe, 1994b). In addition, white, anti-apartheid journalists have been threatened by right-wing vigilantes who regard them as traitors. One result has been a measure of self-censorship, and an unwillingness to ask "awkward questions" (Du Plessis, 1994:1; De Beer, 1993).

RESTRUCTURING THE BROADCASTING SYSTEM

The SABC dominates South African broadcasting virtually as a statutory monopoly. It was generally regarded as a product of the apartheid era, a propaganda arm of the National Party controlled by the white, Afrikaner establishment. Despite recent changes, this heritage is still reflected in its programming, channel structure, staffing and language policy (Currie, 1994a). Consequently, one of the first objectives of the liberation movements was to gain control of the SABC. The movement was led by the Campaign for Independent Broadcasting, which brought together more than 40 organizations, including political parties, labor unions, churches, educators and human rights organizations (*IPI Report,* 1993).

Under pressure from this powerful lobby, the government agreed in 1993 to appoint a new Board of Control that would enjoy the confidence and trust of the broad spectrum of South African society. After extensive consultations between the government and various political parties, a panel of jurists was named to appoint a new board (SABC, 1994:1). Much political infighting followed, but eventually a new board was installed, with a majority of black members and a black woman, Ivy Matsepe-Casaburri, who has close ties to the ANC, as chairwoman.

The board has since made several senior-level appointments to the SABC management, including the chief executive of radio services, Govin Reddy, and Zwelakhe Sisulu, who is likely to take over as the SABC's top executive. Sisulu, once imprisoned for two years for spreading "subversive propaganda," says he sees his involvement with the ANC as a strength: "If you are politically involved, you understand the dynamics of society better than someone who is not" (*Interkom,* 1994b:2-3). Reddy, who spent ten years in exile, once worked for the Third World news agency Inter Press Service, and served as head of current affairs for the Zimbabwe Broadcasting Corporation.

In addition, the new board, aware that "there are still perceptions that the SABC is inclined to give exposure to the pronouncements and activities of certain political groups only" (SABC, 1994:6), was to appoint an ombudsman to monitor the corporation's news services and field complaints. It is also taking active steps to improve the racial and gender balance of the staff through an affirmative action program, and to better use the SABC's extensive resources for education (SABC, 1994:6). By mid-1994 the employment rate was 2:1 in favor of Black applicants.

INDEPENDENT BROADCASTING AUTHORITY

The future of the SABC, and of other broadcasting services, will depend largely on policy decisions taken by the new Independent Broadcasting Authority (IBA). The IBA was created to administer the airwaves "at an arm's length from government" (*ACAG/Update,* 1993c:9). The enabling legislation, the IBA Act, recognizes three categories of broadcasters: public, private and community. It stipulates that the IBA should, among others, provide broadcasting services that cater to all language and cultural groups; promote the development of services that are responsive to the needs of the public, and protect a national and regional identity, culture and character (IBA Act, Section 2).

Its immediate tasks are to conduct inquiries into the future financing of public broadcasting, the imposition of limitations on cross-media ownership, and local content quotas (Markowicz, 1994). The most important inquiry is the investigation into the funding of the SABC. A viable private broadcasting sector probably will not be possible if the SABC continues to collect the bulk of radio and television advertising revenue. On the other hand, the SABC could not maintain anything like the level of service it offers now without those revenues (*The Star,* 1994-05-18), unless it is funded by the fiscus.

LOOKING AHEAD

No major changes on the short term seem likely in the newspaper field, after the rationalization that already has taken place. The remaining mainstream, commercial newspapers are well-established and, for the most part, profitable. Alternative, left-wing publications face a more problematic future. Most depended heavily on foreign subsidies. With the advent of majority rule, foreign funding agencies have cut back substantially on South African projects, and there is little local support (*The Star,* 1994-05-17).

It is in broadcasting that one can expect the most far-reaching reforms. Some argue that the SABC should continue to be the nation's public broadcaster, operating two national TV channels with windows for provincial news or other programs. It would also operate up to nine national radio services in the most commonly used languages. In addition, each of the nine provinces into which the republic has been divided could offer its own public broadcasting services. Funding could come from some combination of advertising, sponsorships, license fees, and state subsidy (Currie, 1994b).

Certainly there will be further changes in the SABC's programming. Sebiletso Mokone-Matabane, a black woman who is co-chair of the IBA, says that "the Broadcasting ethos in South Africa has to change. I want to see my people reflected on the TV screens, hear myself on the radio." Drawing on her experience as a member of the advisory council of a PBS station in Austin, Texas, she sees a system where cable stations and low-power community broadcasters provide channels for educational institutions as part of their license requirements (The Star, 1994-05-18).

Since the transition of power from the white minority to majority rule, the nation seems to have experienced a sense of relief, a glow of goodwill, a willingness to work together to promote the new policies of reconstruction and development. Oddly, however, this could have a chilling effect on press freedom. Despite restrictions, South African newspapers have in the past served a vital "watchdog" role, criticizing government policies and urging reforms (see De Klerk, 1994; Mandela, 1994). Now, with representatives of the political parties they support included in the government of national unity, they will be under pressure to tone down their criticisms and instead support national unity and the development process (Froneman & De Beer, 1994). To do otherwise could be regarded as unpatriotic, or worse. It will take a delicate balancing act to avoid substituting the watchdog role with that of a government lapdog.

References

ACAG/Update: July/August/ September, 5-8, July/August/September, 1993a.

ACAG/Update: April/May/June:3-5, 1993b.

ACAG/Update. The Kempton Park Acts, 1-12:
    July/August/September, 1993c.

Accone, D. "SABC-TV Captures the Spirit of the Election. Media Giants
    Miss Big Story."*The Star,* 29 April 1994.

African National Congress. *Reconstruction and Development
    Program.* Johannesburg: 1994.

Broadcasting Complaints Commission of South Africa: 1994.

Bruce, N. "The New South Africa in the New World Media Order."
    Rhodes Journalism Review December 1993: 18-24.

Burns, Y. *Media Law.* Durban: Butterworths, 1990.

Cohen, B. "A New Era, but Some Old Press Gags Live On."*The
    Weekly Mail & Guardian* 6 May 1994: 10.

Currie, W. Interview, Johannesburg, South Africa. 10 May 1994.

Currie, W. Options for Restructuring Public Broadcasting Services in a
    Democratic South Africa. Media and Broadcasting Consultants.
    Johannesburg, South Africa: April 1994b.

De Beer, A.S., ed. *Mass Media for the 90s. The South African
    Handbook of Mass Communication.* Pretoria: Van Schaik,
    1993.

De Beer, A.S. "The Censorship of Terror and the Struggle for Freedom:
    a South African Case Study." *Journal of Communication Inquiry*
    17. 2 (1993): 26-51.

De Beer, A.S. & Steyn, E.F. The National Party and the Media: a
    Special Kind of Symbiosis. *South African Media Policy, Debates
    of the 1990s.* By P.E. Louw. Bellville: Anthropos, 1993: 204-
    227.

De Klerk, F.W. Address to the 43rd Annual General Assembly of the
    International Press Institute, Cape Town, South Africa: February
    1994.

De Lille, P. The New South Africa. Address to the 43rd Annual General
    Assembly of the International Press Institute, Cape Town, South
    Africa: February 1994.

De Villiers, C. "Radio. Chameleon of the Ether." 1993. *Mass Media for
    the 90s - the South African Handbook of Mass
    Communication.* Ed. A.S. De Beer, Pretoria: Van Schaik, 1993.
    125-150.

"Swartes Betaal Nie TV-Lisensies Nie," *Die Patriot,* 11 Feb. 1994.

Diederichs, P & De Beer, A.S. "Newspapers. The Fourth Estate: a
    Cornerstone of Democracy." *Mass Media for the 90s-the South
    African Handbook of Mass Communication.* Ed. A.S. De Beer.
    Pretoria: Van Schaik, 1993. 71-100.

Du Plessis, T. Living with Intimidation and Violence. Address to the
    43rd Annual General Assembly of the International Press Institute:
    Cape Town, South Africa. February 1994.

Ecquid Novi. "Press Freedom in South Africa." *Ecquid Novi,* 10. 1&2. (1989)

Emdon, C. Director of the Independent Media Diversity Trust, Interview. Johannesburg, South Africa, 9 May 1994.

Froneman, J.D. & De Beer, A.S. "Calls for Nation Building in a 'New' South Africa: the Role of the Afrikaans Press." *Communicatie.* In press, 1994.

Gevisser, M. "Can the Leopard Really Change its Spots?" *Rhodes Journalism Review* 15 (July 1993.)

Giffard, C.A. & Cohen, L. "South African TV and Censorship: Does it Reduce Negative Coverage?" *Journalism Quarterly* (Spring 1989): 3-10.

Grogan, J. & Barker, G. "Media Law. To Tread Cautiously on Different Beats." *Mass Media for the 90s - the South African Handbook of Mass Communication.* Ed. A.S. De Beer. Pretoria: Van Schaik, 1993. 229-248.

Grogan, J. "Freedom of Speech and the New Constitution." *Rhodes Journalism Review* 7 (December 1993): 51-53.

Hachten, W. & Giffard, C.A. *Total Onslaught. The South African Press Under Attack.* Johannesburg: MacMillan, 1984.

Interkom. "Tot Siens TSS. Hartlik Welkom NNTV." Interkom 32 (Feb. 1994a): 8.

Interkom. "The New Faces at the Top." Interkom 32 (Feb. 1994b): 2-3.

IPI Report. World Press Freedom Review. South Africa. IPI Report 42. 12 (Dec. 1994): 56-57.

Johnson, S. *Living with Violence and Intimidation.* Panel discussion at the 43rd Annual General Assembly of the International Press Institute: Cape Town, South Africa. Feb. 1994.

Klein, M. "Board Conditionally Clears *Cape Times Deal.*" Business Day 5 May 1994: 3.

Levy, M. "Band-Aid Broadcasts Coming Unstuck." *Democracy in Action 8.* 1 (1994): 6.

Louw, P.E. *South African Media Policy, Debates of the 1990s.* Bellville: Anthropos, 1993.

Louw, R. Chairman, Independent Media Commission, Interview: Johannesburg, South Africa, 11 May 1994.

Mandela, N. Address to the 43rd Annual General Assembly of the International Press Institute: Cape Town, South Africa, Feb. 1994.

Markowicz, M. "Challenges Facing our New Broadcasting Supremos." *Media and Broadcasting Consultants.* Johannesburg. April 1994.

Martin, J. "Africa." *Global Journalism.* By J.C. Merrill. New York: Longman, 1991.

McLennan, J. "Reds on the March." *The Sunday Star,* 23 Jan. 1994: 4.

Mersham, G.M. "Television. A fascinating Window on an Unfolding World." *Mass Media for the 90s-the South African Handbook of Mass Ccommunication.* Ed. A.S. De Beer. Pretoria: Van Schaik, 1993: 173-200.

Meyer, R. "The Liberation of the Media." *Ecquid Novi* 13. 1 (1992): 93-98.

MISA Free Press. Three Titles Close. MISA Free Press 8. March 1994.

Muller, P. *Sonop in Die Suide.* Cape Town: Nasionale Boekhandel, 1991.

Oosthuizen, L. "The Safety of Journalists. South African dilemma." *Dialogus 1* 1 (Feb. 1994): 1-4.

Owen, K. Editor, *Sunday Times.* Interview, Johannesburg, South Africa, 11 May 1994.

Qwelane, J. "Our New 'Democrats' Need a Few Lessons." *Sunday Star* 19Dec. 1993: 18.

Qwelane, J. Living With Intimidation. Address to the 43rd Annual General Assembly of the International Press Institute, Cape Town, South Africa, Feb. 1994.

SABC. "This is the SABC in a Nutshell." *SABC Radio & TV 3* (1993): 52-55.

Screen Africa, SABC Stance on Local Production, March 1994.

Stander, K. "Targeting the Media." *Rhodes Journalism Review 6.* July 1993: 13-14.

Steyn, R. Address at the Opening Ceremony of the 43rd Annual General Assembly of the International Press Institute: Cape Town, South Africa, Feb. 1994a.

Steyn, R. "Newspapers Maligned." *Saturday Star,* 26 Feb. 1994: 11.

The Citizen. "Journalists Still Targeted: Union." 21 Nov. 1992: 4.

The Citizen, "M-Net Looking at Bop-TV Takeover." 9 Feb. 1994: 15.

The Daily News, "TV Stations Announce Changes to Operations." 13 Jan. 1994.

The Press Council of South Africa. *Consolidator's Report for January and February 1993.*

The Star Tonight. "Sky News Gets 14 Hours on SABC. 14 Jan. 1994.

The Star. "Magazine Forced to Close." 17 May 1994.

The Star. "IBA Officials Get Down to Business." 18 May 1994.

The Weekly Mail & Guardian. "Journalists Condemn Violence Against Them." 6 May 1994: 11.

Tholoe, J. Living with Intimidation and Violence. Address to the 43rd Annual General Assembly of the International Press Institute: Cape Town, South Africa, Feb. 1994a.

Tholoe, J. Deputy editor, *Sowetan.* Interview: Johannesburg, South

Africa, 11 May 1994b.
Tomaselli, K.G. & Louw, P.E. *Studies on the South African Media. The Alternative Press in South Africa.* Bellville: Anthropos, 1991.

ADDITIONAL READING LIST

Davis, D. "Who's Afraid of the Probing Press?" *Democracy in Action"* 8. 1 (1994): 18-19.

Du Preez, M. "Die Reg om te Weet, Ernstig Ondermyn." *Beeld* Dec. 1993: 9.

Haffajee, F. & Harvey, M. "How to Survive the SA Election Hazards." *The Weekly Mail & Guardian* 11 March 1994: 6.

Interkom. "What the IBA will Mean to the SABC." *Interkom* 34 (April 1994): 7.

Markinor.. *New Perspectives.* Randburg: Markinor House, March 1994.

MISA Free Press.. "Two More Media Workers Killed." *MISA Free Press.* March 1994: 3.

Prinsloo, J. & Criticos, C. *Media Matters in South Africa.* Durban: Media Resource Centre, 1991.

Raphaely, J. "The 1993 Freedom of the Press Lecture." *Rhodes Journalism Review* (July 1993): 48-51.

Sake-Beeld. "Uitsaaiwese Gaan Vanjaar 'n Gistingstyd Ondervind. Bykomende Betaalkanaal en Nuwe Amerikaanse TV-Diens in SA. *Sake-Beeld* 12 Jan. 1994.

Saturday Star. "Bunfight Predicted as Licence Applications Flood in. D-Day for Television." *Saturday Star* 12 Feb. 1994.

Screen Africa. "New broadcasters v the Old." March, April 1994.

The Citizen "IBA Faces Formidable Media Challenges." *The Citizen* 8 March 1994: 10.

The Citizen. "IBA Final List is Expected Today." *The Citizen* 9 March 1994: 4.

The Star. "De Klerk, a pioneer." *The Star* 3 May 1994" 10.

Tomaselli, K.G. "Who monitors the media monitors . . .?" *The Natal Mercury,* 27 April 1994.

Woods, M.J. "BBC World Service Deal Wrapped Up." *Saturday Star,* 22 Jan. 1994: 7.

Ziegler, D. & Asante, M.F. *Thunder and Silence. The Mass Media in Africa.* New Jersey: Africa World Press, 1992.

CHAPTER 5

CHANGING PERCEPTIONS OF PRESS FREEDOM IN TANZANIA

Paul Grosswiler

INTRODUCTION

Press freedom has progressed in Tanzania both in objective and subjective terms, with, objectively, the emergence of a half dozen privately owned newspapers since the late 1980s and, subjectively, the emergence of attitudes embracing press freedom and a private press by journalists who are experiencing this recent shift in press-government relations. Tanzania's experience of democratization demonstrates the close connection that can exist between a socialist country that attempted to achieve cultural autonomy since independence in 1961 and the pursuit of press freedom. Having severed the colonial ties with the West by nationalizing the press in the early 1970s and pursuing a development media model that emphasized horizontal communication and appropriate media technology by consciously choosing not to introduce television, Tanzania has built a self-reliant foundation that has enabled the emerging private press and the government to proceed gradually toward greater press freedom through a difficult but promising process.

The changing government-press philosophy toward the emerging private press and press freedom in Tanzania is the topic of a study conducted by the author among Tanzanian media workers, including 50 newspaper and radio journalists, journalism educators and students, government information officials, and members of a media women's association. The study, conducted in July and August, 1992, found that from the perspectives of Tanzania's media workers, the country's emerging private press and press freedom are viewed from a "third way," with a mixture of socialist, traditional, revolutionary and Western philosophies that are incompatible with authoritarian or development media philosophies devised by Western media researchers and applied to African media. (Grosswiler, 1993, 1996)

Unlike African nations that embraced colonial powers after attaining independence and followed a Western media model, and nations that fell into the Soviet-Communist influence and followed a totalitarian media model, Tanzania has developed a socialist media policy under longtime former President Julius Nyerere, designed to achieve cultural autonomy and minimize foreign cultural influences from both the West and the Soviet spheres. The mainland of Tanzania has not started a television system, although the island region of Zanzibar has a television and radio system, and the state runs Radio Tanzania. Like many African countries since the end of the Cold War, Tanzania is undergoing significant political and economic change viewed in the West as democratization. Economic and political liberalization has been taking place with accelerating speed since the late 1980s. Tanzania concurrently is undergoing an opening up of the media with the recent emergence of several indigenous private newspapers to compete with the government's *Daily News* and the Party of the Revolution's *Uhuru,* and relaxation of the monopoly distribution of Western news services formerly held by the state news agency, Shihata. Unlike the chaotic, often violent change that is characterizing similar political and economic changes in much of Africa, Tanzania's high degree of political stability since independence in 1961 has enabled the country to introduce democratic changes much more effectively and peacefully, albeit slowly.

Tanzania began introducing fundamental political changes with the July 1, 1992, launching of multipartyism. As of that date, opposition political parties were allowed to seek registration as the country moves to end decades of one-party rule. By the end of July, several parties had successfully registered. Also in 1992, two private newspapers published by a private company, *Express* in English and *Mwananchi* in Swahili, joined two private newspapers established in the late 1980s, the *Business Times* and *Family Mirror,* in English. It is in this climate of changing ownership patterns of the media, and changing civil and political rights, that the changing attitudes toward press freedom of media workers became central.

TANZANIA'S PRESS HISTORY

The press in colonial East Africa was largely a European creation. Editors of the white settler press remained focused on Britain and had little sympathy for anti-colonial movements. In Tanganyika, Erica Fiah's *Kwetu* appeared in 1937 to help foster claims of racial equality. His newspaper and others withstood continuous attempts by the colonial government to control the press. *Kwetu* appeared off and on until 1951 with some support from the British, who valued it because it reported many African grievances. During the 1950s, African-run newspapers reappeared after a decline in the postwar years. The government radio station started in 1951 (Haule, pp. 58-71).

The birth of the Tanganyika African National Union in 1954 marked the beginning of the nationalist movement that would spur an anti-colonial press. Nyerere started a small, duplicated paper, *Voice of TANU.* In 1957, to aid the campaign for "uhuru," or freedom, TANU started *Mwafrika,* which grew to a circulation of 20,000. Also in 1957, *Kiongozi* started publication as the official voice of the Catholic diocese. It too was anti-colonial. *Mwafrika* generated the first sedition charges in 1958 for calling the British "suckers of African blood." The second sedition charge was brought against Nyerere the same year. He was convicted and paid a fine, although he was not jailed (Haule, pp. 72-81).

Tanzania was built under Nyerere's presidency since 1962 on the concept of "ujamaa," or familyhood, a system of villages organized on traditional African and socialist principles. It was heralded in the Arusha Declaration of 1967, which also pointed toward nationalization of corporations and the media. This has been reflected in Tanzania's media policy decision not to introduce television. Instead, a video system has been used in rural areas for horizontal communication. Tanzania also has used radio in health campaigns and other adult education and mobilization projects (Hamelink, pp. 47-51).

Nyerere has promoted humanistic socialism placing people at the center of development. He disagreed with the Soviets' scientific socialism and its deterministic conclusions, and he wrote that ujamaa provided the unique framework relevant to Tanzania. Nyerere thought exploitation was not built into the African way of life. Village life emphasized the cohesion of communities and observed the principles of freedom, equality and unity. Nyerere charged that capitalism placed too much emphasis on the individual at the expense of the collective, while in communism the individual was lost in the collective. Traditional African values preserved democracy, self-reliance, sharing and work. The foundation of African socialism is the extended family (Akhahenda, p. 24).

At independence in 1961, Tanzania had four daily newspapers, two in English and two in Swahili. Lonrho, the British multinational whose acronym stands for London Rhodesian Mining and Land Co., owned the English-language *Standard, as* well as newspapers in Kenya and Uganda. Nyerere's party, TANU, owned *Uhuru,* a Swahili daily. A study by Condon (1967), however, found little difference between public and private newspapers in Tanzania. In 1970, Nyerere nationalized the *Standard.* It merged with the *Nationalist* to form the *Daily News* and was published by the government. Nyerere emphasized press freedom at that time, saying the newspaper would be:

> Free to join the debate for and against any particular proposal put forward for the consideration of the people, whether by the government, by TANU or other

> bodies. . . . It will be guided by the principle that free debate is an essential element of true socialism and it will strive to encourage and maintain a high standard of socialist discussion. The new Standard will be free to criticize any particular acts of individual TANU or government leaders and to publicize any failures in the community. . . . It will be free to criticize the implementation of agreed-upon policies. (Akhahenda, p. 8)

About the time of the Arusha Declaration, Nyerere equated media to educational mobilization, defining education as learning from books, radio, films, discussions and experience (Nyerere, 1973, p. 138). The Arusha Declaration itself identifies the news media as part of the means of production that should be owned by the government for the peasants:

> The major means of production and exchange are such things as: land, forests, minerals, water, oil and electricity, news media, communications, banks, insurance, import and export trade, wholesale trade, iron and steel, machine-tools, arms, motor-cars, cement, fertilizer and textile industries . . . . (Nyerere, 1968, p. 16)

Central to the freedom and responsibility of Tanzanian media were Nyerere's two essentials of democracy: (1) Everyone must be allowed to speak freely, but (2) once a decision is reached by the majority it must be obeyed (Coulson, p. 30).

Journalists both before and after the attainment of independence have had difficulty working freely in Tanzania. In 1972, a new editor of the *Daily News* who was appointed by Nyerere was dismissed by the president for criticizing the Sudan's practice of executing rebels. The reason given was "unacceptable criticism of a fellow African leader." In other instances since independence, a Reuters reporter was expelled in 1963; outgoing press dispatches were censored for three weeks in 1964; two Kenyan papers were banned and a British journalist was expelled at the same time. In 1973, a British journalist was tried secretly on spying charges and in 1974 another Briton from the BBC was expelled (Haule, p. 30).

Newspapers inside Tanzania also have been banned and editors detained. In 1967, the editor of *Ulimwengu* was detained and the weekly closed down for calling for a trial. Since then, a number of journalists have been detained. Generally, the press has practiced self-censorship. In 1966, Radio Tanzania broadcast nothing of Ghana President Kwame Nkrumah's overthrow until the government published a statement. In 1982, radio news reports ignored the hijacking of an Air Tanzania jet in London for many hours. Local journalists have been reminded of their obligation to follow the party line in seminars of the Mass Media Committee of the ruling party, Chama Cha Mapinduzi (CCM), or Party of the Revolution, which was formed in 1977 when TANU was dissolved. The media were warned by Nyerere in 1973 to "ensure that such factors did not tarnish the image of the nation nor undermine her objectives." Another official the same year warned the media against "unnecessary publicity to the country's setbacks which might demoralize the people." (Haule, p. 31)

One Tanzanian editor has identified the three most serious examples of censorship in Tanzania since the early 1980s. The first, a fire that destroyed the Bank of Tanzania in Dar es Salaam in 1984, was published on an inside page of the *Daily News* and the first government statement two years later was only that the fire was under investigation and further questions may "embarrass the government." No further comment has ever been made. The second, a gold mine accident in 1985 or 1986 that killed 30 people, was mistakenly reported by the government news agency, SHIHATA. The government, noting that such mining was banned, denied the accident had happened. The third, the police shooting of 20 people at a sugar factory strike in 1988, was turned over to a government commission whose results were kept secret (Maja-Pearce).

In other studies, Mytton (1968) found the main problems of Tanzania's newspapers to be illiteracy and poor distribution, the latter of which is still a major problem. Condon concluded that six years after the attainment of independence Tanzania's daily press was an urban press, with Dar es Salaam, the capital, consuming half the daily newspapers while accounting for 20 percent of the population. The literacy rate, according to a local account, has improved to as high as 80 percent (outside sources put the literacy rate at 46 percent), but newspapers have remained an urban phenomenon (Akhahenda, p. 14).

From Tanzania's leadership's point of view, the media have been controlled for political and educational reasons. In 1977, reviewing the Arusha Declaration, Nyerere wrote:

> The English language newspaper has been national-
> ized so that we could rely on it to report news accu-
> rately and to analyze events from a Tanzanian and
> socialist viewpoint, although in practice it has not been
> infallible on either count. And the radio has been used
> as an educational medium, for it reaches further and
> more quickly into our villages than any other form of
> communication. (Coulson, p. 55)

The winds of change, however, began blowing in Tanzania in the mid-1980s. Nyerere stepped down as president in 1985, succeeded by his vice president from Zanzibar, Ali Hassan Mwinyi. Political observers have written that the change was a way of allowing a new government to move toward an International Monetary Fund deal and away from "ujamaa." Tanzania and the IMF in 1986 reached a three-year agreement after a seven-year standoff between Nyerere and the lending institution over the IMF's austerity policies, including devaluation of the shilling by two-thirds. After becoming president, Mwinyi also campaigned to reduce corruption in the state apparatus. And the debate about television continued, with some predictions that the country may introduce it on the mainland by the early 1990s (*Africa Report,* November-December, 1986, p. 48; July-August, p. 51; May-June; and *Africa Confidential* pp. 3-4).

THE CHANGING TANZANIAN PRESS

The first private newspaper to be started since independence was a short-lived attempt in March 1987, when the first copies of a new weekly, *Africa Baraza,* were seized by the police within hours after they were printed (Hachten, p. 38). The newspaper contained a story criticizing corruption under Nyerere's presidency compared to the clean administration of Mwinyi (Puri, 1993). The next year, however, *Business Times* became the first privately owned English weekly, followed soon by the twice-monthly *Family Mirror,* now edited by Anthony Ngaiza, formerly head of the Tanzania School of Journalism. In February 1992, two more weekly newspapers began publication under the ownership of Media Holdings Ltd. in Dar es Salaam, the English-language Express and the Swahili-language *Mwananchi,* which means "Citizen." Both editors of these two newest papers have journalism experience from the days preceding nationalization of the press. Pascal Shija, editor of *Express,* worked on the *Standard* when it was published by Lonrho. Barnabus Maro, editor of *Mwananchi,* was a reporter for the Catholic newspaper *Kiongozi.* Shija, Maro and Ngaiza contributed many of the ideas about the private press's role in pursuing and securing press freedom that comprise the survey of opinions used in the study to be discussed below.

Within their first year, *Express* and *Mwananchi's* 30,000 and 40,000 weekly circulation challenged the government's *Sunday News* (circulation, 50,000) in English and *Mzalendo* (circulation, 110,000) in Swahili. Both new private weeklies had applied, along with *Business Times*, to begin daily publication, but so far the government has not registered any private daily newspapers (Puri, 1992).

In early 1993, two Swahili-language private papers, *Michapo* and *Cheka,* were banned by the government for violating media ethics. *Michapo* published a story about sex that the government said violated "norms and culture." The Minister of Information and Broadcasting, William Shija, who possesses a doctorate from Howard University in Washington, D.C., has warned private newspapers against unethical reporting that would incite religious and tribal conflicts. The ministry has drafted a plan, which was being discussed to set up a press council to regulate and register the private press. Journalists from the private press have spoken out against the banning of the two newspapers as an assault against press freedom (Puri, 1993), illustrating the close link between the emerging private press and press freedom in Tanzania, and the shift to political pluralism.

Coverage of Zanzibar, which was controversially united with Tanganyika in 1964 to create Tanzania, was carefully controlled by the government until the emergence of the private press and multipartyism. According to Maja-Pearce, the CCM's need to promote the harmony of the union contrasts with the views of Zanzibar's opposition movements. A Zanzibari leader, Seif Sharif Hamad, was fired as Zanzibar's chief minister in 1989 for criticizing the Chama Cha Mapinduzi and detained until late 1991. Even after his release he was not quoted in the government or party press. Only the emergence of the private press willing to risk censure and quote Hamad as a leader enabled the official media to cover his central role in the formation of one of the new opposition parties in mid-1992.

The movement toward multipartyism was initiated in February 1991 when Nyerere told a Chama Cha Mapinduzi conference that the days of the one-party state were passing: "Changes have become imperative and inevitably we must admit our previous mistakes and build afresh" (Maja-Pearce). Since 1990, about 50 new publications have been launched. With several opposition parties registered in 1992, elections were scheduled to be held in 1995, and the independent private press was seen as a way for various political parties' views to be expressed. The new private newspapers have published stories critical of the government's shortcomings and failures in issues such as management, theft and corruption, bringing calls from Minister Shija for the media to cooperate with government. As the private newspapers assert their independence, they are also gaining in circulation, sales and advertising compared to the official press (Puri, 1993). Some journalists express doubt that the official press will survive this trend toward privatization and new press freedom.

The growth of private media in Tanzania and their tolerance by the government reveal a dramatic shift in the government's thinking about the press, according to Walsh (1991, p. 10), who compares today's private press doing battle with the government and party press in its similarity to the liberation press that battled the imperialist colonial press in the 1950s. The exception to the comparison is that the government today has been unwilling to use the legal controls at its disposal to silence the private press; the colonial government was intolerant of the liberation press.

This new government tolerance of press freedom may have several causes. According to the *Business Times* editor, as Tanzania moves beyond the struggle to provide basic needs, it can afford to debate the "luxury" of more abstract issues like press freedom. Part of the credit also may be traced to Nyerere's 1989 call to debate the future of Tanzania's one-party state, a cue taken seriously by the *Family Mirror*. Other government leaders, including Zanzibar President Salmin Amour and Organization of African Unity Secretary General Salim Ahmed Salim, called for greater press freedom in the movement toward democratization in Africa. Another reason may be the government's need to accommodate Western donor countries that provide for much of Tanzania's economic existence (Walsh, p. 11).

While pushing the limits of press freedom, ethical excesses and abuses have routinely occurred, from stealing stories from other media to passing along dangerous health advice from columnists and convicting uncharged suspects in the newspaper (Walsh, p. 12). Careless and sensational news reporting has provided the leverage for the government to regulate the private media, although official media provide many of the incidents of unethical journalism. The proposed press council has been one government response, as has been the threat to ban or suspend offending newspapers. In 1992, the Tanzanian Journalists Association adopted a code of ethics as a further means of regulating the private press (Rules of Professional Conduct and Ethics).

Opportunism on both the part of some private newspapers and the government is cited by one observer as the greatest threat to press freedom and democracy in Tanzania (Maja-Pearce). The growth of papers that publish "dangerous lies, unfair comments and obscene reports," however, should not be equated with responsible newspapers dedicated to the emergence of democracy. Since its first issue after the call for the end of one-party rules, Family Mirror has fulfilled the primary function of a free press in a democracy by calling for the CCM to demilitarize, for the country's "illegal" laws, such as those allowing arrest without a warrant and detention without trial, to be repealed, and for neutral observers to oversee the transition from one-party to political pluralism.

> In other words, the *Family Mirror* fulfills the primary function of the independent press in a proper democracy, which is to monitor the role of the government in the process of governance, a function undertaken by its rivals *Business Times* and *Express*. The existence of such papers in Tanzania is the country's greatest hope that the elections due in 1995 will usher in the long-awaited democracy . . . . (Maja-Pearce)

MEDIA WORKERS AND PRESS FREEDOM: THE THIRD WAY

As the government and the new private media struggle in the process of furthering press freedom, journalists — including those who work for the private and the official media — negotiate the demands made by the government and the private press in forming their own belief systems. In 1991, only one percent of Tanzanian journalists cited press freedom as a source of job satisfaction, whereas 10 percent cited pressures and restrictions as a source of job dissatisfaction (Lederbogen, p. 34).

The author's study of media workers' attitudes toward press freedom and private press issues reveals that their media worldviews combine elements of socialist and Western media philosophies in a "third way" that juxtaposes and counterpoises journalistic and political values, transcending either global media system's way of thinking. The participants in the study represented both private and official media, men and women, with a wide range of education, experience and age. The major approaches, or composite attitude types, usually are given names in this research technique to add a more human dimension and help create an image of the ideas that the approach represents. The first approach is called the Competitive Populist because he or she has turned to the private press to carry out the development role of the media that the official press has failed to fulfill. This expresses both a continuation of past media practices and a break with past media structures.

The second approach, called the Status Quo Builder, wants to build up the status of journalists and confront the problem of the media's negative portrayal and hiring of women, but these professional and social changes are sought within the structures and functions of the media status quo of an official press that is government controlled.

The third approach, called the Development Promoter, uncritically supports a network of socialist development journalism roles and government controlled media structures by expanding rural media, positive news, youth issues and a populist approach. This factor also seeks development in journalism training, pay and investigative reporting, and wants to establish binding journalist qualifications.

The last, named the Critical Reformer, presents a deep distrust of government involvement in the media and a positive assessment of the impact of the emerging private press, but underlying this is a strong belief in popular media, the democratization of news and the New World Information Order, and criticism of the private press.

THE COMPETITIVE POPULIST

The Competitive Populist turns to the private press to carry out the development role of the media that the official press has failed to fulfill. Most of the respondents strongly believe the media should focus on processes and development issues and use a bottom-up approach. But he or she also thinks that people want to read about people, not about government leaders as in the past. This change is being brought about by competition from the private media. The competitive populist also thinks the media should report news which is critical of the government, which the official media have not been doing. To correct this problem, the government should have no control over the news or the media. This approach also places a premium on the need for journalism training by professionals, instead of teachers with no journalism experience, and the need for more journalism training throughout a journalist's career.

The Competitive Populist emphatically rejects a government-imposed journalism and self-censorship. The approach also believes in the viability of the private press by defending it against criticism of fanning ethnic conflict, sensationalism, deep societal opposition and insincerity. The denial of any role or redeeming qualities of the official press is reiterated by the rejection of the idea that it is free enough. The idea that the government press should be socialistic and free to debate proposals is also soundly rejected. The Competitive Populist, looking for alternatives, at the same time rejects Westernization of the press and the end of socialism but also rejects the use of Third World news agencies instead of Western news agencies for international news.

The media workers associated with this approach reflect this combination of socialist-official and capitalist-private media values. The media workers in this group are equally divided into two units, the public media workers and the private media workers. The focus on cultural issues is reflected by several media women's association members. But the most important members of this approach may be the key to the bridging of the past and future. Most members of this approach are journalism students, who are between one generation's ways of conceiving journalism under socialism and a new generation sensitive to changes in that system.

THE STATUS QUO BUILDER

The second approach's strongest opinions favor building up the resources, education and pay of journalists to do more investigative reporting, as well as dealing with the problem of the media's negative portrayal of women and poor record of hiring of women. These professional and social changes, however, are sought within the structures and functions of the status quo. The Status Quo Builder strongly believes that the media should adopt self-censorship to avoid conflict with government and that journalists should be held accountable for the news they report. They should also be disciplined for unethical conduct. The development model is strongly supported, as is the introduction of television, but freedom of the press is not an issue for the Status Quo Builder because the media by their nature are not free.

The Status Quo Builder also strongly defends the official press and trusts government, while he or she strongly disagrees with the idea that the private press has no problems and that the government should have no control of news. Defending the official press, the Status Quo Builder believes the official press will not die or become sensationalized in response to the private press. This approach also denies that the government has yielded to Western donor countries' demands for a free press, and denies that the news needs redefining in a national context that is not neo-colonial. Nyerere's socialist media policies are strongly defended, as is TAJA's code of ethics against charges of being forces of self-censorship. Also, the Status Quo Builder denies that media have to make leaders look good. Further in defense of the socialist status quo, the Builder rejects the idea that the media will become more Westernized.

This approach's allegiance to the current media system, and criticism of structural change, including the private press, are consistent with its membership of mostly official media workers who are older and have less education. But these otherwise conservative workers want to improve the quality of the media, showing a belief that the media system can be made to work for positive ends. Half the Ministry of Information media workers are among this factor's nine subjects, but only a minority of the public media workers. Also, only one of the six private media workers are on this factor. Although the approach is critical of the media's treatment of women and advocates hiring women media workers, a third of the group are women. Overall, the Status Quo Builder has less education and is older, with only one student among the group and no one under 30.

THE DEVELOPMENT PROMOTER

The third approach strongly favors opinions that promote development journalism roles by expanding rural media, positive news, youth issues and a populist approach. Three other statements seek development in journalism training, pay and investigative reporting, and one calls for establishing journalists' qualifications. In addition, the Development Promoter, thinks television should be brought to Tanzania, which is a belief firmly locked into a network of socialist media goals.

After asserting foremost the need for more journalism training, the Development Promoter calls upon the media to influence cultural norms and educate farmers and people in rural areas; to focus on processes and development; to initiate rural papers and local radio programs; to present positive news in an interesting way; to pay attention to youth issues; and to focus on people themselves using a bottom-up approach. In addition to journalist training, the Development Promoter strongly feels that the government should set journalistic qualifications before registering a newspaper and raise pay above the poverty level, while promoting investigative reporting.

The Development Promoter staunchly defends the official press, the socialist media and development journalism while criticizing the private media. The Development Promoter most strongly believes the official press will not die. Among related statements, the approach defends the media under Nyerere and the history of the official press, as well as the importance of the media's development role. The Development Promoter doubts that a private press would have helped Tanzania from the beginning, thus rejecting the idea of privatization of radio and that the private press has no problems. The Development Promoter does not dismiss freedom of the press, disagreeing that there is no press freedom in either a private or official press. The press, according to this approach, is not forced to make leaders look good, nor is the country bending to Western donors in promoting press freedom. TAJA's ethics code is supported, which matches the call for journalistic qualifications. The final two ideas suggest this approach is not critical of the official media system. The Promoter rejects statements that the media are insensitive to women and that television will present negative images of women in advertising. Aside from calling for higher pay and better training, the Development Promoter offers no criticism of the current system, and no alteration of its role for the media.

It is significant to the Development Promoter's strong support of the socialist roles of the media and journalistic training and pay, without any media criticism, that the media workers in this group are all from the public media or the journalism school. Although evenly representative of the range of education levels and ages, only two Development Promoters have more than 10 years of experience, and only one is over 40.

THE CRITICAL REFORMER

A deep distrust of government involvement in the media and a positive assessment of the impact of the emerging private press characterize the strongest beliefs of the Critical Reformer, but a contradictory part of this approach is an underlying but strong belief in popular media, the democratization of news and the New World Information Order, and development media roles. The Reformer also is critical of the private press.

Above all else, the Critical Reformer hates censorship. He or she would end the political appointment of media editors and stop all government control of news, news agencies and journalists. The private press now must do what the official media did not: Tell what the government is doing. The private media movement is helping change the government news agency, Shihata, by making it competitive and helping improve the prospects of journalists in terms of pay and freedom, as well as respect.

But this wave of freedom and private media should be used by the media to talk about people, not leaders, and focus on village news and issues, including government radio programs. Further, popular media of song, poetry and theater need to be emphasized by the mass media, and journalists should promote democratization of news and the New World Information Order. The Critical Reformer would completely overhaul the socialist media structures but retain the most socialistic of media functions.

The strong distrust of government is tempered by the acceptance of the country's socialist press history, the qualified defense and criticism of the private press, and a call for reform of the official media. The Critical Reformer strongly denies that the media should make leaders look good to mobilize the people, and that the media should censor themselves to avoid conflict with government. Indeed, the media-government relationship has been adversarial, and people do not want media to cooperate with government. The Critical Reformer defends the private press today against charges that it would stir up ethnic conflict, but in the next breath admits the private press has problems and the official press has had its benefits. In contrast to the past, the Critical Reformer believes that today the official press does not have enough freedom, although under Nyerere, the Critical Reformer argues, the media played a positive role, and Tanzania has shaken the colonial definition of news. Finally, the Critical Reformer rejects the idea that the media should follow development news and ignore politics, along with rejecting the idea that the private press will lead to the death of the official press.

The Critical Reformers are mainly journalists, but more of them are public media workers than private media workers, suggesting that the public media have the potential of change. However, none of the six Ministry of Information workers is a member of this group. The Critical Reformer also has a high level of education, with eight of 10 holding a post-secondary school journalism certificate or higher.

CONCLUSIONS

This study shows that the four attitude approaches have distinct and differing responses to questions about the emerging private media. It suggests neither a Western nor a communist approach to the media, but a third way that recombines ideas to fit Tanzania's form of socialism, placing the emerging private press in a Tanzanian context.

Regarding socialism and press freedom issues, most approaches strongly defend Nyerere's socialist media policies of the past, yet most factors strongly feel the government newspaper today should not be socialist. Further, all agree the media would not become more Westernized.

The private media, most approaches agree, should tell readers what the official press has not told them: how the government is operating. All agree that society does not oppose the private press and all defend the private press against charges of sensationalism. Yet all agree the private press has negative aspects and are unsure of both the benefits that journalists will derive from the private press and the impact of the importation of a private printing press. The quality of the private press journalists and the idea of the private newspapers banding together to fight government regulation also drew mixed responses.

On the official press, most approaches think it is a problem that many politicians want only good news coverage and knew they could get it in the official press, and most think the official press does not have enough freedom. Yet most believe the official press is not going to die.

Responding to the relationship between government and media, most groups agree the government-media partnership has been troublesome. Most also agree the government should stop appointing heads of the public media and three welcomed liberalizing changes in the government news agency. Yet there was deep disagreement about how much government should control news and how much the media should practice self-censorship.

In reaction to the Western media, most groups mildly believe television will create a cultural gap because of its cost and commercial nature, and most oppose foreign investment in the media. Most of the respondents also think the government's shift toward a free press is not designed for Western donor nations. Yet most factors think the media should not use more Third World news agencies.

Tanzanian media workers are involved in the process of creating a media system that reflects Tanzania's socialist history since independence with current openness and liberalization in the economic and political systems. Their attitudes may be seen as a selection of important elements from the ideas of the past, held strongly by the older media workers employed in public media. All respondents in the study perceive the media with ideas and structures of market economics and political pluralism as they are introduced, including an emerging private press. However, the underlying socialism persists and continues to provide a framework for the forces of change as Tanzania forges a "third way" in constructing press freedom.

REFERENCES:

Addison, Tony. "Adjusting to the IMF," *Africa* Report May-June 1986: 81-83.
Akhahenda, Elijah. *A Content Analysis of Zambian and Tanzanian*

Newspapers During the Period of Nationalization. Ph.D. Dissertation. Southern Illinois University:1984.

Coulson, Andrew, ed. *African Socialism in Practice: The Tanzanian Experience.* Nottingham: Russell Press Ltd., 1979.

Grosswiler, Paul. "Emergence of a Private Press in Socialist Tanzania: A Study of Media Worker Perceptions." *Association of Education in Journalism and Mass Communication,* International Communication Division, Kansas City, Mo. August 1993. "A Q-Methodology Study of Media Worker Attitiudes Toward Changing Roles of Media in Tanzania." Nov.1, 1996: 88-105

Hachten, William *The Growth of Media in the Third World: African Failures, Asian Successes.* Iowa State University Press, 1993.

Hamelink, Cees. *Cultural Autonomy in Global Communication.* New York: Longman, 1983.

Haule, John. *Press Controls in Colonial Tanganyika and Post-Colonial Tanzania: 1930-1967.* Ph.D. Dissertation. Southern Illinois University, 1984.

Lederbogen, Utz. *The African Journalist.* Bonn and Dar es Salaam: Friedrich, Ebert-Stiftung, 1991.

Maja-Pearce, Adewale. "The Press in East Africa: Tanzania." Index on Censorship. July-August 1992: 18-23.

Nyerere, Julius K. *Ujamaa: Essays on Socialism.* Oxford University Press. Dar es Salaam, Tanzania, 1968.

Nyerere, Julius K. *Freedom and Development.* Oxford University Press. Dar es Salaam, Tanzania, 1973.

Puri, Shamlal. "Independent Titles Dilute Former State Press Monopoly." *International Press Institute Report.* Sep. 1992: 21-22.

Puri, Shamlal "Shock as Two Private Papers Are Banned." *International Press Institute Report.* March 1993: 17-18.

"Tanzania and the IMF." *Africa Confidential* March 1987: 3-4.

Tanzania Journalists Association, "Rules of Professional Conduct and Ethics." June 1992.

"Tanzania: Prolonged Resistance Crumbles" *Africa Report* July-August, 1986, p. 51.

"Tanzania: Weak Party Support for Mwinyi," *Africa Report,* Nov-Dec 1986: 48.

Walsh, Patrick. "Press Freedom in Tanzania" Unpublished paper. Tanzania School of Journalism conference. Dec. 1991.

CHAPTER 6

PRESS FREEDOM IN UGANDA

Melinda B. Robins

INTRODUCTION

This chapter examines press freedom in Uganda and the changes
in the press under the Museveni government. Journalism in
Uganda has always been a dangerous business under various
administrations, including Idi Amin Dada's dictatorship and
Milton Obote's rule. However, the independent press under
President Museveni, who came to power in 1986, is vibrant
despite chronic financial problems. Still, Uganda's press is "free"
only in comparison to what has been in the past. Ugandan journalists are often detained incommunicado for sedition or defamation, and eventually released. Although there is no official
censorship, there are more subtle repression and self-censorship. The threat to press freedom is obvious since there is no constitutional provision for the protection of journalists.

UGANDA'S PRESS HISTORY AND FOREIGN INFLUENCE

Just as there is no way to separate Uganda's modern history from
its legacy of colonialism, Uganda's modern press is equally tied.

One still must turn to some of the authoritative Western texts of the past 30 years to learn the details of Uganda's press history, but with some caution. Media scholars looking at the Ugandan press in general have viewed it as an alien system forced on the country by the early missionaries or the colonial powers, and have believed that it has never quite lived up to its potential. Most of these texts were not written before the late 1950s, and for a very specific reason: In these years immediately before and after the attainment of independence of Uganda from colonialism, Western mass communication researchers looked to the press as a powerful index and agent of change. This modernization perspective accompanied the mainstream model of development that emphasized an ability to urbanize and industrialize along the lines of Western liberal democracies.

The Ugandan press system was and continues to be seen as in need of "development" and "modernization." This ideology of modernization has produced a way of seeing the press in Uganda as chronically backward, always failing when compared to Western ideals of a free press. Therefore, Uganda's press history is usually constructed so that it overlaps with Western press history, and seen in such dichotomies as free/not-free, developed/underdeveloped, always needing to "catch up" with what is available in the West, and often with Western inputs and expertise doing the job.

It also is of value to remember that Western texts by and large have ignored Uganda's indigenous media — the oral tradition, the transmission of culture and information in the marketplace, drumming, drama, song — or, when mentioned, they are implied to be somehow lesser forms of communication. "Modern" African-backed newspapers published with varying degrees of success throughout the early years also are given short shrift.

With those caveats in mind, one can turn to the usual texts to review the historical details of Uganda's press history. Its beginnings are to be found in late nineteenth century missionary publications, first meant as a medium of information for missionaries in the country and home on leave, and then published in indigenous languages to disseminate church-related information to the Ugandans. The first commercial paper, *Mengo Notes,* was an English-language daily, put out by the Anglican Church Missionary Society. The *Standard* started in 1902. Meanwhile, the Roman Catholics entered the newspaper industry in 1911 by publishing *Munno* in a local language. Various African-owned and operated newspapers were started in the 1920s, but all ceased publication due to lack of resources. In addition, British colonial government newspapers were published in English and several local languages in the 1950s.

In the mid-1950s, *The Uganda Argus* began publishing out of Kampala, joining the Uganda Herald, which succumbed not long after. *The Argus* belonged to the powerful East African newspaper group that included Kenya's *Standard,* started in 1902. *The Argus* opposed African political aspirations. Several nationalist publications were begun, but struggled against colonial government repression. Their editors and publishers often went to jail for sedition or illegal political activity.

In the 1960s, after attaining independence from Great Britain, Uganda's largest newspapers were the daily *Argus,* and *The People,* a weekly, both in English and catering to the educated elite. In addition, the Luganda language *Taifa Empya,* owned by the Nation group, had its base in Kenya. Other newspapers and periodicals came from outside the country and also were for the elite. Several vernacular papers were published by the government to fill the gap.

Isoba [1] notes a decline in Uganda's newspaper industry by the late 1960s, due to undercapitalization, and a lack of both machinery and trained staff. As if these weren't enough, Amin's repressions dealt a death blow to most publications after his rise to power in the early 1970s. Only now, under Museveni, does the Ugandan press seem to be progressing once again.

PRESS AND POLITICS IN UGANDA

To understand Uganda's press, it is necessary to understand something of its modern political history. Since its independence from Britain, the history of Uganda — once described by Winston Churchill as "the pearl of Africa" — is one of great human tragedy, political upheaval and economic deprivation. [2] Milton

Obote, a Northerner and the first head of state after the dissolution of the British protectorate in 1962, formed an uneasy and ultimately unsuccessful coalition with the southern Ganda people, who had been promoted in the colonial civil service. In 1971, Obote was overthrown by Idi Amin, a Nubian and a general in the military, who assumed dictatorial powers, terrorized the country and all but destroyed its economy until he was dislodged from power after invading northern Tanzania in 1978.

Journalism in Uganda is a precarious vocation. Idi Amin Dada jailed, tortured and killed journalists, including Nicholas Stroh of *The Washington Star*. Amin shut down all newspapers except the one he used as his own propaganda vehicle. Both before and after Amin, who ruled from 1971-1978, Milton Obote allowed some independent papers to survive, but their editors and journalists suffered constant harassment and prolonged imprisonment. [3]

Obote emerged the victor once again in an allegedly fraudulent election in 1980. His defense minister, Yoweri Museveni, fled into the bush to launch a guerrilla movement. Perhaps hundreds of thousands of Ganda people were tortured and killed by undisciplined government soldiers.

In 1985, Obote was overthrown by a faction within his army, and Tito Okello was named head of state. Although Okello made overtures to Museveni and his National Resistance Movement, the guerrillas continued to fight him. In 1986, the NRM ousted Okello and marched into the capital city of Kampala.

Since then, President Museveni has become one of the most powerful leaders in Ugandan history and is widely regarded as the most effective president since independence. He has gained great respect and support from the West for his attempts to restore civil order and turn around the economy, as shown by the nearly $1 billion in foreign aid that Uganda receives annually.

Censorship and Press Freedom under Museveni

Uganda's recent press history is nothing if not enigmatic, echoing the country's administration by President Yoweri Museveni and his National Resistance Movement (NRM), which took power in 1986. When historians — media and otherwise — look back at this chapter in Uganda's history, they no doubt will find it both intriguing and unique.

By the mid-1980s, civil war, economic adversity and government repression had almost killed the independent print media. But in early 1994, the once-barren media landscape was dotted with some 20 weekly newspapers in various languages, five dailies and one biweekly whose circulation after its first year of publication rivaled that of the leading daily. The diversity of ownership and range of topics covered — including rebel activity and human rights abuses by the army — seemed to speak well of official tolerance and openness both to an independent press and to the winds of democracy said to be blowing across the continent. In addition, two privately owned FM radio stations were to take to the airwaves in 1994, an uncommon occurrence at best in a continent where broadcasting virtually has been a government monopoly.

But the relationship between the media and government is still fraught with mistrust. Although new liberties have been allowed under Museveni, Uganda's journalists feel they have only just completed the first part of a long journey on the road to press freedom.

Journalists have found that a "watchdog" stance can only be pushed so far. Some 30 journalists have been arrested and detained during Museveni's rule, many of them repeatedly and for extended periods of time, resulting in great damage both to their personal and professional lives, and to their publications.[4]

The two charges generally brought against journalists in Uganda are publishing seditious material or false news, and criminal defamation. Authorities also can prosecute anyone publishing information regarded as being hostile to the armed forces, or with treason, which carries a mandatory death sentence. Over the years, a pattern of arrests has occurred in which the state imprisons or threatens with imprisonment those who criticize government policy or performance. However, a majority of the cases against journalists have been dropped or resulted in acquittal.

Besides the outright arrests and detentions, government pressures on the press are sometimes more subtle, but certainly damaging. In 1993, the government attempted to put the economic squeeze on the biweekly independent, *The Monitor,* by banning all government departments and state-owned companies from advertising on its pages. The ban was extended to all private newspapers in the country after some ministers of parliament argued that singling out *The Monitor* was discriminatory. This latter order eventually was rescinded, but not before some smaller papers were hit hard. *The Monitor's* relatively strong circulation figures (more than 30,000 per issue) kept the ban from hurting it too much. Following the ban, *the Monitor* reportedly gained an enhanced reputation as a publication independent of government. Perhaps because of this improved profile as a result of the ban, private businesses increased their advertising, resulting in more space sold to the private sector than had been sold before the ban to both the private and public sectors combined. As an ironic last note, not long after this the president granted *The Monitor* his first exclusive interview with a Ugandan newspaper in three years.

Museveni's relationship with the press has its other elements of humor, dark though they may be. On one day alone in October 1993, three journalists from two different papers were arrested for sedition, one concerning a story about nepotism by Museveni's in-laws, the other calling two Cabinet members "opportunists" who were misleading the president. The timing of their arrests on a late Friday afternoon after the courts had closed meant they were unable to post bail and had to be held in jail over the weekend without charge.

When later asked why his government continued to arrest journalists if conditions in the country had improved as much as he often claimed, Museveni replied that no one is above the law. Pressed to respond why the three were arrested on a Friday after the courts had closed for the day, Museveni said, tongue in cheek, "OK, OK. I will inform the police to arrest you on Mondays only." One journalist later wrote, "The president is not an easy man to match wits with. All the same, there was some comfort (with his joking response). Everyone heard it. The next time police officers come to arrest a journalist on any other day than Monday, they should be told they have come on a wrong day —

and be reminded to return next Monday. Jail-prone journalists may also do well to carry a toothbrush and a spare underwear to office on Mondays, just in case."[5]

But Museveni has not always used humor when addressing the media. He repeatedly has warned journalists that they will be locked up if they malign the good name of the national army. Journalism in Uganda continues to be considered a lowly profession, and Museveni has done nothing to dispel this public opinion. In informal remarks he made to East African journalists in 1989, he said there are two groups oppressing Uganda — journalists and common criminals. "They both think they are above the law," he said.[6]

Being on the president's good side or sharing his political ideals also has been no guarantee of immunity from arrest. In 1992, William Pike, the British editor-in-chief of the state-owned daily newspaper — who had been with Museveni in the bush during the guerrilla war — and one of his reporters were charged with sedition for a front-page story critical of the justice system. Again in 1993, a newspaper editor who supported the National Resistance Movement (NRM) was arrested for publishing seditious material about nepotism in public office.

Now the independent press under Museveni is alive, but it's not necessarily well. Uganda's press is "free" only compared to the past. Amin murdered journalists; now they are detained and eventually released, often after losing their personal property, or their publications have folded. A question that must be asked daily by each journalist is "How far can I go?"

PROBLEMS AND SOLUTIONS

Lively though it may be, Uganda's press has more than its share of problems. After past years of state repression, most of the publications are immature quality-wise when compared with those in the West, carrying poorly written and researched articles and uneven layout and use of artwork. Economically, they are rarely in the black, have inadequate and antiquated facilities, and face a chronic newsprint shortage.

Ethically, some journalists are corrupt, with coverage bought and sold like tomatoes in Uganda's markets. The "little brown envelopes" (government stationery) that contain bribes are essential to supplement meager editorial salaries. Stories routinely are withheld to appease advertisers or government officials.

Getting information is a long and arduous process. Civil servants are not bound to speak to reporters, nor must government hand over any information about its business, or allow reporters to cover meetings. As a result, attribution of information is very difficult in the Ugandan context. It's hard enough getting information let alone attribution. Logistically, it's difficult to get an appointment with a news source even if he or she has agreed to an interview. Telephones may not be working; civil servants may not be at their desks.

Uganda's colonial history is evident in many ways, with the media a prime example. At independence, the British handed over the control of the country and its mass communications system catering to the educated and elite. Since then, Uganda has not been able to effectively broaden the system to include the majority of the people living in rural areas.[7] It has been almost as if the 80 percent of Uganda's population of some 20 million people who live in the countryside don't exist. There are few resources to employ correspondents, and travel from the capital is expensive, exhausting and time-consuming. Government-run radio remains the most effective vehicle of mass communication reaching the countryside, but its newscasts are a string of official releases, many of them starting with the phrase, "President Yoweri Museveni said today," and with many references to "positive development."

There are many counts against a viable commercial press in Uganda, including a need for more literacy and basic formal education for its rural inhabitants. The number and diversity of local languages also is a constraint, with English, the official language, used by less than one percent of the population. With apparently small potential for a substantial mass market, there is only small incentive for large-scale private investment in the media. An advertising base is still in its infancy.

An effective distribution system also is lacking, with electricity-dependent printing facilities located in the capital city. The time, cost and effort to transport newspapers to the rural areas via a crumbling infrastructure also severely restricts their economic feasibility. Newspapers are not affordable to the average person, with a month's supply of newspapers costing perhaps twice as much as the average monthly wage.

Independent Uganda's press has rarely if ever been used for development purposes — that is, to enhance literacy and disseminate health, agricultural and other useful information. The country has no official media policy. President Museveni's semi-annual progress reports do not mention the media at all. However, he has made many public remarks concerning the media. "Our cause is to use the press as a tool to education and enlightenment," he said in a 1989 speech. But, he continued, "our first duty is to obey the law and not use the press as a camouflage for certain selfish interests."[8]

A former director of information for the Ministry of Information and Broadcasting in 1989 said that the media are not a priority for the Museveni government. "I don't expect us to be able to improve things considerably for the media in the coming years due to the state of the economy . . . . We're looking to private concerns to do the job of informing, educating and entertaining."[9] However, there is an official interest in building media structures and in reaching more than the educated elite. American Fulbright assistance was sought and received in the late 1980s to create a journalism program at Makerere University, the country's premier institution of higher education, thus addressing a lack of training for the country's journalists. And in 1991 and 1993, the government-owned daily New Vision began to publish limited-circulation weekly editions in local languages for three rural areas. A Ugandan diplomat [10] said he presumed the papers would help people feel like they belonged to Uganda — the elusive "nation-building" ideal sought by most leaders of former colonies whose borders were drawn by the imperial powers— and that they were not being ignored by government.

However, he noted that "These (new papers) may contain some information that would be useful to literacy and farming, but mostly they need to contain local exciting news, or why would anyone read them?" His point is well taken, and worth examining when considering "press freedom," words which conjure up certain ideals not found in existence anywhere in the world. Capitalistic venture is at the core of Uganda's emerging independent press. As the press builds a general readership and an advertising base to survive, it is subscribing less to an educative and informative role and more to one of entertainment. As in the West, if it is not successful as a business, it cannot do any job promoting democracy and informing the electorate.

Many of the problems facing the independent Ugandan press are not unfamiliar across Africa. However, the Ugandan situation is enigmatic due to the diversity of ownership by political parties, broadly associated with ethnic groups, which were ordered to suspend all activities when Museveni took power. These parties were not outlawed, however, and they continue to function on an unofficial basis. They also may publish newspapers, which in turn is often the justification for muzzling them. Government claims these restrictions on political activity are compensated for by the parties' ability to speak out on the pages of their publications.

After years of civil war, Ugandan "development" has been superseded first by the need for survival and then for recovery. Museveni has chosen to pursue a mixed economy and embrace the harsh conditionalities of the World Bank's structural adjustment program, including the adoption of a single exchange rate determined by market prices; liberalization of imports; and reform of the public sector, including massive layoffs and a reduction in the number of government ministries.

Although there has been some progress made in reducing inflation and increasing agricultural production, the country faces an acute balance of payments problem due to low world prices for coffee, its only major cash crop. Uganda is now more dependent than ever on foreign aid to purchase essential imports like oil, and to service its foreign debt, about $3 billion since 1993, an increase of nearly 90 percent since the NRM assumed power.[11]

Although the West has given Museveni firm support, officials have said they are concerned about the slow pace of political and economic reform, and are beginning to measure Uganda against more liberal African states rather than contrasting it with its own former governments.[12] Museveni seems committed to democracy, but he makes it very clear that "democracy" doesn't necessarily mean "multipartyism." Instead, he advocates a "no-party democracy" he claims would eliminate the divisiveness of political inter-fighting based on ethnic group and religion. Such a system is seen as more appropriate until the country is economically developed.[13]

Museveni's broad-based system — which he claims would be an amalgam of political doctrines representative of national thought — is designed as a bridge that eventually would lead to a multiparty democracy after the parties stop polarizing themselves along sectarian lines. However, Museveni's history as head of state since 1986 has led some observers to be concerned that a monolithic system could continue despite his promises otherwise. When he took power, Museveni promised a return to civilian rule in four years. In 1990, he extended his term in office for another five years.

However, his drive to pass a "no-party" constitution prior to 1996's direct presidential elections has gained some credibility for the first time in African politics, perhaps because of Museveni's successes as head of state and his seldom-questioned personal integrity. Still, public calls for a formalized multiparty system are building, and strong cultural forces provide underlying support for the old political parties.

Before 1995, a constitutional commission recommended suspending party activity for at least another seven years, after which time a referendum would be held on the issue. The current political system is paternalistic, with the ruling NRM selecting a few people from the suspended parties for ministerial and other political posts, a setup that has brought a measure of political coherence and stability unknown in the country for over two decades. In the May 1996 election, Museveni won 72 per cent of the vote.

Despite the new liberties under Museveni, Uganda's new draft constitution is little different from the old one as concerns the media. Asked to make proposals to the constitutional review commission in the early 1990s, journalists' associations presented a list of principles they wanted to see enshrined in the new document, including freedom of information; the scrapping of an official secrets act; the abolishing of criminal libel and sedition; and recognition of the idea of comment in the public interest. However, press freedom appears only once in the draft constitution, one of a long list of other freedoms such as of opinion and of association.

CONCLUSIONS

Today, one can only speculate as to why Museveni has allowed considerable press freedoms, tenuous though they may be. He seems genuinely committed to democracy, despite the many questions raised by his "no-party democracy" plan. Perhaps he agrees that the establishment, maintenance and fostering of an independent, pluralistic African press is essential to economic development, as stated in Article 19 of the Universal Declaration of Human Rights.

It is said that a gauge of a country's transition to democracy is its treatment of the press. It is too soon to tell whether press freedoms will prevail in Uganda.

As in other African countries moving toward pluralism, the press in Uganda is still walking a tightrope, its independence and even its very existence threatened by various government repressions as well as the economics of running a viable business in an unfavorable climate. Uganda's press freedom continues to be fragile, although the tightrope that its journalists walk is perhaps thicker than in some other African countries.[14]

REFERENCES

Africa Confidential. "Uganda: A Long March to Democracy." 34. 2 (Jan. 22, 1993): 1-2.

Ainslie, Rosalynde. *The Press in Africa: Communications Past and Present.* London: Gollancz, 1966.

Article 19. *World Report.* London: Longman, 1992.

Barton, Frank. *The Press in Africa: Persecution and Perseverance.* New York: Africana, 1979.

Drost, H., *World's News Media.* Essex: Longman, 1991: 518-519.

Economist Intelligence Unit. *Country Reports: Uganda, Rwanda,*

Burundi. London: 1993.

Encyclopedia of the Third World. New York: Facts on File. 1992: 2001-2016.

Freedom House. *Freedom in the World: The Annual Survey of Political Rights and Civil Liberties*. New York. 1993: 506-508.

Hachten, William. *Muffled Drums: The News Media In Africa*. Ames: Iowa State University Press, 1971.

Hansen, H, and Twaddle, M., eds. *Uganda Now: Between Decay and Development*. Athens, Ohio: Ohio University Press, 1988.

Hansen, H, and Twaddle, M., eds. *Changing Uganda*. Athens, Ohio: Ohio University Press, 1991.

IPI Report. *World Press Freedom Review* Dec. 1992: 40.

Isoba, John C.G. "The Rise and Fall of Uganda's Newspaper Industry, 1900-1976," *Journalism Quarterly* 57. 2 (Summer 1980): 225-233.

Katana, Francis. Personal telephone conversation with the *charge d'affaires* for the Ugandan Embassy in Washington, D.C. Nov. 10, 1992.

Kurian, G., ed. *World Press Encyclopedia*. New York: Facts on File. 1982: 893-899.

Matovu, Jacob. *In Search of Mass Communication Strategies to Facilitate National Unity in Uganda*. Dissertation. University of Michigan, Ann Arbor, 1984.

Matovu, Jacob. "Mass Media as Agencies of Socialization in Uganda," *Journal of Black Studies* 20. 3. (March 1990): 342-361.

Meldrum, A. "The Fragile Freedom." *Africa Report* Sept./Oct. 1993: 54-57.

Museveni, Yoweri. Speech to journalists at the inauguration of the Federation of East African Journalists Association. Kampala, Uganda, May 22 1989.

Nieman Reports. "The African Media in a Changing Africa." Fall, 1993: 30-61.

Novicki, M. "Uganda's Man of Vision." *Africa Report* July/Aug. 1993: 23-25.

Okullo-Mura, J. Personal conversation with the director of information for the Ugandan Ministry of Information and Broadcasting. Kampala, Uganda, June 2, 1989.

Onyango-Obbo, Charles. "Ear to the Ground," *The Monitor,* Kampala, Uganda Nov. 2-5 1993: 8.

Ouma, D., and C. Watson, "Uganda." *The Africa Review*. London, 1992: 214-217.

Shelby, B. "The Measure of Freedom." *Africa Report* May/June 1993: 60-63.

NOTES

1. Isoba, p. 232.
2. Several sources offer a good overview of Uganda's situation since colonialism. See for example Hansen and Twaddle 1988 and 1991, Ouma and Watson, and *Encyclopedia of the Third World*.
3. For a history of Uganda's press, see for example Kurian and Drost.
4. There are various regularly updated sources monitoring the world's press, often including that of Uganda. For example, see Article 19, Freedom House, and *IPI Report*.
5. From the biweekly column by editor Charles Onyango-Obbo of *The Monitor*.
6. Museveni spoke at the 1989 inauguration of the Federation of East African Journalists Association in Kampala.
7. See Matovu, 1984 and 1990.
8. Also from Museveni's speech to East African journalists in 1989.
9. From a personal conversation with J. Okullo-Mura in Kampala in 1989.
10. From a personal telephone conversation with F. Katana, *charge d'affaires,* in 1992.
11. See the Economic Intelligence Unit quarterly publications for updates on Uganda's political and economic situation.
12. See *Africa Confidential*.
13. For his personal description of the "no-party democracy" concept, see Museveni's interview with Margaret Novicki in *Africa Report*.
14. For overviews of Africa's current press situation, see *Nieman Reports,* Meldrum, and Shelby.

CHAPTER 7

PRESS FREEDOM IN ZAMBIA

Francis P. Kasoma

INTRODUCTION

Zambia attracted world attention in 1991 when it became the first country in Africa to change from a long-standing despotic government to a democratic one through the ballot box. President Kenneth Kaunda, who had ruled with an iron fist for 27 years, was defeated by the younger and more democratic Frederick Chiluba. Chiluba's accession to power through the Movement for Multiparty Democracy (MMD) also marked the beginning of the liberalization of the Zambian press which Kaunda had muzzled in order to hoodwink public opinion.

This chapter discusses developments of the Zambian press in the 1990's. The chapter discusses both the newspapers and broadcasting. The underlying principle is that a government-controlled press cannot be as free as an independent one if freedom of the press is defined narrowly as the ability of journalists to report news and comment without extra-legal interference from people wielding political, economic, religious or other powers.

In Africa, and Zambia in particular, where governments have been known to control the press almost completely, freedom of the press has come to be identified with lack of government interference in the running of the press. Broadly, however, freedom of the press means more than just the ability of journalists to report news and views as they see fit without any interference. It also means the accessibility of the people to the press to express their views without being curtailed by journalists or those who control the media. In addition, it means the availability of newspapers and other media to the people when they need them. The author will extend the discussion of the freedom of the press in Zambia to this wider context.

This chapter discusses in perspective developments in freedom of the Zambian press since the MMD government came into power in 1991. The discussion is based on public pronouncements of those in government as well as the responses journalists make to such pronouncements, particularly in the way they practice journalism. The chapter also focuses on the future of press freedom in Zambia, based on the government policy derived from the MMD manifesto.

Before the Press Reform

Zambia attained independence from Britain in 1964 when Kaunda and his United National Independence Party (UNIP) took effective control of the government. The country's press then, including broadcasting, was partly government and partly privately-owned. But as the Kaunda government entrenched itself into power by virtually eliminating all political opposition, the press was increasingly usurped by the regime.

Kaunda saw the press as a tool for propagating his philosophy of humanism which he effectively used to silence all opposition and criticism. He maintained:

> that the journalistic profession, in all its ramifications and specifications, must develop as an integral part of the humanist transformation of Zambia just as those who practice it are an integral part of its people. (Kaunda, 1989)

By 1972 when Kaunda, at the pinnacle of his power, declared

Zambia a one-party state, the press had almost totally been taken under the control of the government. What followed was a period of almost total subjugation of the country's media, although journalists did not give in without putting up a serious fight. The struggles of Zambian journalists against total subjugation by the Kaunda regime have been documented in other studies of the press in Zambia (See Kasoma, 1986).

By the time Kaunda was defeated at the polls, the Zambian press had become known as the "Kaunda's press," publishing mostly news and views which Kaunda and his henchmen wanted and excluding any information which they would frown upon.

Turok (1992) best described the Zambian press under Kaunda. He wrote:

> While Kaunda's regime was not as vicious as many in Africa, the need to keep one's mouth shut and opinions to oneself was substantial. Individuals might speak out here and there, only to be met with public threats from the President himself if the individual was prominent enough. Zambia became a society of gossip and speculation based on rumor . . . "Meeting at night in private houses" was one of the most serious allegations that could be made. Yet permission to meet openly was refused and it was near impossible to publish a dissident newsletter or journal. (Turock, 1992, p.15)

Kaunda even appointed and fired editors-in-chief of the country's two daily newspapers: the *Times of Zambia* and the *Zambia Daily Mail*. He wanted the Zambian press to parrot the party's programs and his personal philosophy of humanism. He did not want the press to be critical of his government's policies and actions maintaining that the press had to be a partner in development instead of behaving like an opposition to the government.

Because of Kaunda's excessive control of the press, Chiluba's Movement for Multiparty Democracy, as part of the manifesto for getting into power, promised to restore freedom of the press. The MMD said it believed that freedom of expression and the right to information were basic human rights.

As such journalists will have to play an important role in promoting democracy and development in an MMD-led government. All bona fide journalists, both local and foreign, will be accredited to perform their duties without hindrance. (MMD, 1990)

The MMD promised that individuals and organizations would have a right to own and operate their own press and electronic media facilities. But even the MMD government would not abandon the control of government-owned media. It merely promised that such media would serve as vehicles to promote national unity, reconstruction, development and international co-operation.

PRESS REFORMS

Since it came to power in November 1991, the Movement for Multiparty Democracy (MMD) government has been rather indecisive in implementing its media policies. As a sign of this indecision, the government kept changing its Ministers of Information and Broadcasting. Within a short period of less than two years, up to the beginning of 1994, the ministry saw four ministers. The first was Stan Kristofor who nearly reversed the MMD's policy of encouraging freedom of the press. His ministerial style was full of threats to reporters who did not toe his misconceived press policy.

The eccentric Kristafor banned Zairean musician Tshala Muana's musical shows on television because he claimed they were immoral. Such dictatorial behavior made him unpopular among not only the journalists, but also the public, both of whom breathed a sigh of relief when he was suddenly removed after being in office for only a few months.

Kristafor was succeeded by Dipak Patel who tried to put in motion MMD's policy for a free press. He initiated and supported the formation of a Mass Media Reform Committee following a widely attended consultative meeting of journalists, academics, lawyers, politicians and other concerned people which was called to discuss "The Media and Democracy—the way forward."

The Media Reform Committee—after a year of consultations and deliberations—submitted to the government wide-ranging measures that would ensure press freedom in the country. The proposals included:

- Freedom of the press to be specially provided for in the Constitution of Zambia as a fundamental right to freedom of expression and government to be prevented by the Constitution from making any laws or regulations which would restrict freedom of the press.
- The repealing or amending of laws which hinder freedom of the press.
- The removal of the Zambia National Broadcasting Corporation from government control. The opening up of broadcasting to private enterprise.
- Privatizing of newspapers and newspaper printing companies which the government owns and controls.
- The practice of responsible journalism to be a subject of self-regulation by journalists and not subject to statutory regulation (Media Reform Committee, 1993, pp. 5-6).

By early 1994, these proposals were still under active consideration by the government. Patel was certainly more progressive than his predecessor, judging by some of his public pronouncements and actions. His pledge that government would open the airwaves to private broadcasting was being implemented at the beginning of 1994 when the government advertised for those who wanted to start private radio and television stations to come forward and obtain licenses. Patel also promised to privatize at least one of the two daily newspapers owned by government as soon as a special study jointly commissioned by his Ministry and the Zambia Privatization Agency had been completed and the modalities worked out. He publicly supported the idea that journalists should be left to operate on their own without any interference from politicians.

But just when things looked like moving in the right direction as far as freedom of the press was concerned, Patel was removed from the ministry and replaced by Remmy Mushota. Mushota had rather unorthodox ideas of freedom of the press. He constantly kept referring to the government "tolerating" some of the "irresponsible" independent newspapers as if freedom of the press was a special favor bestowed on journalists by the government rather than a constitutional right. Mushota maintained that the independent newspapers had misused their freedom and laws had to be put in place to prevent further abuse of this freedom, (Frank Talk, February 6, 1994). In line with this thinking, Mushota prepared a policy document which proposed the setting up of a Press Council and a Licensing Board for journalists by the Ministry, clearly sending signals that the ministry should still wield influence over not only who practices as a journalist but also how he or she practices journalism.

The fourth minister was Kelly Walubita, who took over the ministry in February 1994 and whose immediate task was to finalize the "Zambia Media Policy" document initiated by Patel. The document, which was to be a blueprint of the country's general approach to media, particularly their relationship with government, was put together in 1994.

If outspokenness against government is a yardstick to how free a press is in a given country then the Zambian press, particularly the independent one, is really free by any standards. Zambian newspapers have definitely moved away from the practice of personality cult that they gave Kaunda to a stage where everything the post-Kaunda president does is put under the microscope and criticized. By 1994, there was practically nothing against the Head of State that Zambian journalists could not broadcast or publish in the newspapers. The press had taken its watchdog role against allegations that were published against it through lengthy press advertisements.

The *Weekly Post* in particular had led the onslaught against President Chiluba and his government. The newspaper consistently portrayed the MMD Government as an incompetent, corrupt and crime-prone administration that was incapable of ruling the country. As far as the newspaper was concerned, Chiluba and his ministers had been making one mistake after another and did not do anything right. Chiluba himself was painted by the *Post* as an incompetent and weak-willed president who at one time was shown as not being in full control of government and at another as displaying dictatorial tendencies.

The *Weekly Post* never failed to come up with front page sensational leads of an alleged drug trafficking, promiscuous, corrupt, immoral or sheerly incompetent government minister. The newspaper's columns were full of anti-government and anti-MMD diatribes. The biweekly had literally become the newspaper for all those who had an ax to grind against Chiluba and his MMD government. It never said anything good about Chiluba and the government.

In a rare critical letter against the newspaper by a John Muzoka of Lusaka entitled "Please, give MMD government a break," the writer stated that he had been stunned and in total disbelief at the amount of hatred and biased reporting against the MMD government by the newspaper.

> Your total aim seems to be to embarrass and ridicule selected MMD leaders namely President Chiluba, Sata, Nakatindi Wina and recently Vernon Mwaanga, you have never printed anything good to praise MMD— your reports have always been negative—bordering on inciting your readership against the MMD government especially against our president. Why, sir, why? Is this what you call responsible journalism? Thank God we have a democratic and tolerant government otherwise your *Post* should have been posted for good and in limbo. (Weekly Post, Friday November 5 1993)

Less outspoken but still very critical of government was the church-owned *National Mirror* which also often came up with anti-government and anti-MMD lead stories. *The Mirror* in an editorial once criticized President Chiluba for calling on Catholic bishops to come up with tangible solutions to the economic hardships the poor Zambians were facing because of the structural adjustment programme instead of merely criticizing his administration. Referring to the president's statement as "uncalled for," the *Mirror* asked:

> Why should the bishops be expected to do the work of the government anyway? (*National Mirror*, August 2–8 1993)

Reacting against the firing of the short-lived Mannaseh Phiri as Director-General of Zambia National Broadcasting Corporation (ZNBC), the newspaper said:

> If the MMD is to be credible as a transparent and accountable government then they should desist from the underhand methods of the Second Republic where the media were perceived as instruments of the government. (*National Mirror*, September 6–12 1993)

Another privately-owned weekly, *The Sun,* had also not been left behind in criticizing government both in its news reports and comment. Front page headlines such as "State House to Get Luxury Vehicles" (*The Sun*, October 25-31 1993). "Guns Saga: Police Tortured Woman" (*The Sun*, November 8-14 1993) and "Minister Grabs Vehicle" (*The Sun*, February 7-13 1994) were but a few examples.

In a realistic editorial partly castigating the MMD government for its ills and partly praising it for its strong points, *The Sun* chided the MMD government leadership for taking to affluence which was not commensurable with leaders of a poor country. It said the Zambian people have had to bear the consequences of the social adjustment program, adding, "There are more unemployed people today than two years ago . . . . There are more beggars today on the streets than two years ago" (*The Sun*, November 1-7. 1993, p.3).

The Sun, which started in August 1993, has promised Zambians popular journalism reminiscent of its British namesake. In its inaugural issue, the newspaper, however, promised to actively participate in society's efforts to nurture, guard and consolidate Zambia's young democracy. It declared:

> We will not hesitate to blow the whistle when corruption rears its ugly head, when selfish interests are put before duty, when the poor cry out and the establishment ignores them. (*The Sun,* August 30-September 5 1993, p.3)

The newspaper has so far done just that.

Another tabloid, the *Weekly Standard,* was, by 1994, less

vocal against government and the MMD probably because the proprietor, Richard Sakala, was none other than President Chiluba's special assistant for press and official State House spokesman. Unlike other independent tabloids, the newspaper went out of its way to defend government against attacks. One such deference was contained in an editorial in which the newspaper said the cacophony of corruption charges against government was a matter of grave concern. It said the tendency where corruption had become a buzz word for politicians was a dangerous development which impinged on the political integrity of the country.

> We fully agree with the sentiments expressed by the Movement for Democratic Process that it is irresponsible for politicians to make claims which they can not substantiate. (*Weekly Standard,* September 13-19 1993, p. 8)

But even the *Weekly Standard* occasionally came up with some mild criticism of government policies. It, for instance, disapproved of the structural adjustment programme which government had been using to revamp the battered economy. "Whether one likes it or not, the Structural Adjustment Programme (SAP) has brought a lot of misery to the common man in Zambia," the newspaper concluded in an editorial (*Weekly Standard,* August 23-29 1993, p.8).

The government-owned *Times of Zambia* and *Zambia Daily Mail,* had in the early 1990s become almost totally pro-government both in their news columns and editorials. Very rarely did one see in them any semblance of critical reporting against government. One such rare moment was when the *Sunday Times of Zambia,* the *Times of Zambia's* sister newspaper, took a swipe at the red-tape that had always dogged government and led to delays in implementing recommendations of past commissions of inquiry (*Sunday Times of Zambia*, December 5 1993, p. 3). For the most part these newspapers took the position of projecting the government and MMD viewpoint and defending them whenever they were under attack from the independent media.

Since the two newspapers were the country's only dailies, the impression their pro-government stance gave was that Zambia's press was pro-government since one had to wait until Monday (*The Sun*), Tuesday (*Weekly Post* and *National Mirror*) and Friday (*Weekly Post*) to read news and views critical of the government.

Apart from the freedom to be outspoken against the government which was exercised mainly by the independent newspapers, the Zambian press had, in the early 1990s, become rather permissive in its publication of sexually-related material, particularly of women. During the time of Kaunda, this was the cause of castigation of the press by the administration who incited the general public to demonstrate against newspapers publishing this type of material. In one incident, the *Sunday Times of Zambia* published a picture of a nude white couple embracing each other to illustrate a feature on sex education. Strong protests came immediately from the government, accompanied by demands by UNIP that the newspaper be banned. Minster of Information Sikota Wina warned that the government would take the "most extreme" measures against the *Sunday Times* if it continued to publish pictures of nude men and women under the "false guise" of sex education. He said not only was the general public disgusted at the sex series, but that its publication violated the law prohibiting publication, possession or redistribution of obscene literature (Kasoma, 1986: 100).

The material which the *Sunday Times of Zambia* or any of the newspapers published during the Kaunda days, however, was nothing compared to the literature and pictures that the independent newspapers are carrying in the 1990s. Pictures of Zambian girls dressed only in underpants have been published regularly in a number of independent newspapers such as *The Sun,* with hardly any protest from the government and the general public in spite of the same law prohibiting publication of obscene material which Wina referred to being still in force. There can be no doubt that the Zambian press has become more permissive during the 1990s than it has ever been before.

Other features illustrating the freedom enjoyed by the Zambian press include the political advertisements which often took the form of diatribes against another party. MMD started the tradition in 1990 when it launched a series of offensives against UNIP in the independent newspapers and on the broadcast media which were effectively used to discredit the ruling party. By early 1994, the tradition had intensified—this time with MMD as the governing party at the receiving end from the opposition parties, particularly the National Party (NP). The NP never failed to place its nearly half page advertisements in the *Weekly Post* and *The Sun* discrediting the MMD government. A disturbing aspect of these advertisements was the fact that they were often not identified as advertisements with the result that the gullible readers regarded them as editorial material from the reporting staff whom they often accused of being biased against the party being discredited.

BROADCASTING

At the time of writing this chapter, Zambia had only one state-owned broadcasting station, the Zambia National Broadcasting Corporation (ZNBC), which transmitted both radio and television programs to a greater part of the country's population. The radio broadcasting section of ZNBC was originally started as an African service by the colonial government in 1941. Television broadcasting was started by a private company, the London Rhodesia Company (Lonrho), in Kitwe in 1961 but was purchased by the new Zambian government at independence in 1964 and incorporated into the state broadcasting system. As was the case during the colonial time, the government has over the years used ZNBC to propagate its policies and information as well as provide educational services to the people.

With the advent of multiparty politics in the 1990s, the MMD government looked determined to hold on to the station as a government utility while inviting private entrepreneurs to open their own stations. Early in 1994, the government had advertised to members of the public who wished to start private radio and television station to apply for licenses. Only a restricted number of channels were made available, namely, five frequencies per town for Frequency Modulation (FM) and one frequency per town for Medium Wave (MW) in radio broadcasting. For television, three frequencies per town were made available for Ultra-High Frequency (UHF), frequency band 70-582 MH2 and two frequencies per town for frequency band 580-960 MH2 also in UHF.

During the 27 year one-party rule of Kaunda, radio and television were extensively used for government propaganda and no dissenting views or news were allowed to be broadcast. In 1990 when campaigning for the multiparty elections was just beginning, Kaunda's government even denied opposition parties the right to advertise their election campaigns on radio and television. They were only allowed after a successful court injunction by MMD. The very first MMD election advertisement which was screened was preceded by an announcement to viewers that ZNBC was screening it to comply with a court order, suggesting that without the High Court's intervention the state facility was not going to be made available to advertisements from the opposition.

In the early 1990s with multipartyism in place, ZNBC became more accommodating to opposition party views by giving considerable airtime to news and views about the other parties. Opposition party leaders were even allowed to address the nation on radio and television in special programs. In spite of this liberalization, there were still complaints from the opposition that not enough of their news and views were being broadcast. There were also complaints from some ZNBC staff that government officials often interfered with their reporting.

In the run-up to the 1991 general elections, the Press Association of Zambia (PAZA) sought an injunction against the Director-General of the Zambia National Broadcasting Corporation (ZNBC), Steven Moyo, for being biased against the MMD and other opposition parties in his organization's coverage of the build up to the general elections. PAZA was asking the court to temporarily remove Moyo (as well as the Managing Editor of the *Times of Zambia,* Bwendo Mulengela) from their posts until after the elections, contending that a continuation of their biased coverage would contribute to the elections not being free and fair. The court obliged and a protracted legal battle ensued during which the two media heads were effectively kept out of office.

Moyo was many times involved in editing television footage concerning Kaunda's addresses and tours to give what was screened the maximum "public relations" effect. The little news that was published about the opposition, particularly MMD, was always slanted to give it the effect that these parties were not serious enough and did not have people who would form an alternative government. The mammoth rallies that Chiluba and other MMD leaders addressed were made, through the distortion of the camera, to look as if they were only attended by a few people. On the other hand, the comparatively poorly attended public meetings of Kaunda were doctored to give the impression on the television screen that they were attended by thousands of people. The best cameras and other television field equipment were exclusively reserved for him leaving the equipment-depleted ZNBC with hardly anything for outside coverage.

These incidents reveal the extent the country's only radio and television broadcasting station went in pleasing its master, Kaunda, and the UNIP government. Indeed Kaunda used ZNBC as a personal megaphone through which he often addressed the nation. Lengthy rallies and addresses to party cadres were beamed live on radio and television and then repeated, often without editing, several hours later. He appointed and fired the director-general of ZNBC who had to owe personal allegiance to him. Discussion programmes which tended to be critical of the government were ordered off the air.

One such occasion involved the author in 1986 when Kaunda caused his Minister of Information and Broadcasting Services to remove a University of Zambia distance education weekly radio program called "University of the Air." The occasion was the critical remarks one lecturer made concerning Kaunda's philosophy of humanism. The programme, which was used to teach the university's extra-mural students and was produced by this writer, was never brought back.

Both radio and television broadcasts were used by the UNIP government to discredit the opposition through a smear campaign. Most of this smear campaign was conducted through editorials which originated from the so-called Department of National Guidance which was run by Kaunda's boot-lickers. The

MMD was portrayed through these editorials as a party of criminals and drug-traffickers which would plunge the country into tribal bloodshed if voted into power. The editorials were supplemented by spot advertisements at peak listening and viewing times, which UNIP never paid for, consisting of rather empty slogans such as "UNIP is power" or "UNIP means progress" or "UNIP means peace and stability."

After the fall of the UNIP government the broadcast media in the early 1990s became more accommodating, although government still wielded a lot of control over them as portrayed by the activities of some ministers of information such as Kristafor referred to above. TVZ is not able to broadcast sometimes live, lengthy interviews of leaders of the opposition political parties making scathing attacks on President Chiluba and his government. Opposition leaders such as UNIP's Kebby Musokotwane, are now able to address the nation on both radio and television on any matter they would like to share with fellow Zambians.

Perhaps the most interesting development in broadcasting in Zambia is the opening of the airwaves to private broadcasting. ZNBC would no longer hold the monopoly of broadcasting in the country. The introduction of independent radio and television stations would result in divergent news and views being broadcast to the Zambian people in the same way plural and independent newspapers have brought this about. The government-owned station would have to justify its existence to the Zambian public which is likely to switch to other stations providing better programs. Advertisers, too, are likely to channel most of their big advertisements to the most popular broadcasting stations.

A matter that is likely to be controversial is the prospect of political parties applying for broadcasting licenses. An announcement by Moyo in late 1993 that UNIP intended to apply for a broadcast license was received with downright opposition by Minister of Information and Broadcasting Services, Mushota. Mushota made it clear that the MMD government would not grant any broadcasting license to any political party.

Another development in Zambian broadcasting in the early 1990s had been the removal of presidential speeches from programming which used to bore Zambians ad nauseum during the

Kaunda days. Chiluba's speeches, except for the short, occasional presidential addresses to the people on special national days, were rarely beamed live and in full on radio and television, let alone re-broadcast either in full or edited versions. The abandonment of the broadcasting of presidential speeches left more airtime for more representative views in broadcast programmes. Discussion programmes on controversial cross-party topics were broadcast on both radio and television. The participants were not always sympathetic to the government and the ruling party.

ZNBC in the 1990s also discontinued the hierarchical arrangement of news in which the broadcast news line-up was arranged according to the seniority of the news makers in government rather than the news value of what they said. During the days of Kaunda, his news invariably always came first regardless of the news value of what he was saying or doing. There were ridiculous situations when both television and radio started off as the main headline of their news bulletins with Kaunda playing golf or viewing a game in a game park and then much later in the bulletin reported some earth-shattering news of an airline disaster.

A new feature in broadcasting in Zambia which surfaced during the multiparty political era was the phone-in radio or television programme fondly referred to as "Face-the-Nation." In this live program, a person in public office was interviewed by a conveyor and the public was invited to ask him or her questions by telephone. Among the people who had appeared on this programme was President Chiluba who was asked piercing and sometimes embarrassing questions. Some of the people telephoning merely made critical comments rather than ask questions. It had become clear from the outspokenness of the questioners that they meant to use their freedom of expression and of the press to maximum.

The advent of independent radio and television broadcasting would, no doubt, bring an even more liberalized atmosphere in the country's broadcasting. But in order to make this freedom a reality, it would be necessary to repeal or at least substantially amend the Broadcast Act to remove the vast powers vested in the Ministry of Information and Broadcasting Services to control broadcasting.

Impediments to a Free and Democratic Press

Events in the media since the election of President Chiluba show that freedom of the press does, to a very large extent, exist in Zambia. But this freedom is, however, relative. There may never be a situation where the press is absolutely free to do whatever it wants. A few limits ought to be imposed on press freedom which should emanate from (1) the law of the land and (2) journalistic ethical limitations.

Even after it is reformed to bring it in line with the country's democratic aspirations, the law in Zambia would continue to have a limiting effect on just how much information the press can gather and publish as well as how far it can comment on issues and events without overstepping on other equally important human freedoms and rights. Laws such as those against defamation of a person's character would still be there albeit in a more accommodating way for journalists than the present one.

The amount of freedom, however, which the law would take away from the press would depend on how much pressure journalists continue to exert against government and law makers in the parliament. In the early 1990s it was the feeling of many Zambian journalists, for example, that the constitutional provision on freedom of expression, which as we have seen above, had been extended to include the press, fell far short of allowing a truly free expression. The constitutional provision gave freedom of expression in one breath and almost wiped it out through a series of exceptions whose interpretation by the politicians in government and sometimes the law courts made freedom of expression almost non-existent.

The Constitution of Zambia, as amended in 1991, did not have a specific clause protecting freedom of the press. It merely mentioned in passing in Section 20 under Paragraph (2) that:

> Subject to the provisions of this Constitution no law shall make any provision that derogates from freedom of the press

The Clause, however, in Paragraph (3) made some sweeping exceptions under which freedom of expression and, presumably, of the press, could be curtailed. These included:

a) In the interests of deference, public safety, public order, public morality or public health

b) For the purposes of protecting the reputations, rights and freedoms of other persons concerned in legal proceedings, preventing the disclosure of information received in confidence, maintaining the authority and independence of the courts, regulating educational institutions in the interests of persons receiving instruction therein, or the registration of persons receiving instruction therein, or the registration of, or regulating the technical administration or the technical operation of newspapers and other publications, telephony, telegraphy, posts, wireless broadcasting or television.

c) Restrictions on public servants.

It has to be admitted that this long list of exceptions—the interpretation of which was often biased against the press—is restrictive of freedom of expression and of the press.

Moreover, the Preservation of Public Security Act (Chapter 106) gave the president sweeping powers to prohibit the publication and dissemination of matter which he thought was prejudicial to public security, and to regulate and control the production, publishing, sale, supply, distribution and possession of publications. Given a president who would want to apply this law to the letter, freedom of the press in Zambia would be completely wiped out. As if these restrictions were not enough, the Penal Code contained more than ten pieces of legislation which tended to restrict freedom of the press by making journalists liable for indictment for contravening them.

To these legal restrictions must be added extra-legal ones which African governments often exert on the press and for which the MMD government has been guilty to an extent. Reporters and editors in the government-owned media, including ZNBC, have complained of receiving calls from senior officials threatening their livelihood over critical stories they have run or which are being written. Those detained include *Weekly Post* Managing Director Fred M'Membe who was briefly detained for questioning following a story linking a cabinet minister to drug-trafficking (*Weekly Post,* February 18, 1994).

Journalists in Zambia had to put up a serious fight to remove laws that unduly and severely limited their freedom as well as prevent new unfair ones from being enacted. This fight cannot be waged successfully unless journalists are well organized as a professional body. Unfortunately, journalists in Zambia have been poorly organized. The Press Association of Zambia (PAZA) has been largely dormant save for a few flashes to life such as the court injunction against Moyo and Mulengela of ZNBC and Times Newspapers respectively referred to above. The other journalists' organization, The Zambia Union of Journalists (ZUJ)—which in early 1990s was just beginning—was too new to be effective, having been severely weakened until the beginning of 1994 by the conspicuous absence in it of journalists employed by the government who constituted the majority of all the journalists in the country. These journalists were obliged to belong to the Civil Servants Union of Zambia in line with the thinking that journalists employed by the government media were civil servants. Due to the weakness of ZUJ, the pay and other conditions of service remained very poor, providing no motivation for journalists to fight for freedom of the press.

ACCESS TO THE PRESS

The other meanings of freedom of the press as defined at the beginning of this chapter: of availing accessibility to the people to express their views in the press as well as making the media available (through circulation) to the people when they need them, have been equally problematic.

As the above discussion on broadcasting demonstrates, the government-owned media have a limit to just how much freedom of expression they can allow the general public, particularly those who hold opposing views. Media managers were constantly called upon to explain to individual government ministers why certain views were published or broadcast. When such complaints are repeatedly made by very high officials in government, the pressure on journalists can be unbearable. Even more frightening was the fact that people whose views displeased those in the Kaunda government were often tracked down by security people from the Office of the President who harassed them in every possible way. It was not just the government media which were subject to threats by the Kaunda government for allowing the people to speak freely, the non-government media received such threats too. The Church-owned *National Mirror* was repeatedly snubbed by Kaunda for publishing news and views from the so-called dissidents. Kaunda, who sarcastically referred to the newspaper as "The Little Mirror," even ordered the state-owned parastatal companies in the country not to advertise in the newspaper. The order, however, made the *Mirror* even more popular to both the public and the private companies who gave it moral and advertising support.

It was not only in the media that the people of Zambia were not allowed by their own government to voice freely views and news which the government did not like. In public places, Kaunda's men were everywhere listening in to conversations, including private ones, and whisking the offenders away for interrogation which was often accompanied by torture. People instinctively learnt to speak in whispers having first looked over their shoulders to see if anyone was within ear-shot. Some instinctively conferred in small corners when they wanted to speak about matters that concerned them but which the government did not like to hear. These were the so-called "dark-corner meetings" which Kaunda so often condemned.

With the arrival of multiparty politics in the 1990s, "dark-corner" meetings completely disappeared in Zambia. People spoke very freely both in public and private places criticizing their government, particularly the president. The press too, especially the independent newspapers, as we have seen above, very often reflected views critical of the MMD government and the president. Zambians wrote letters to both private and government newspapers criticizing the president and his government whenever they felt like doing so. In broadcasting, the same spirit of free speech was noticeable during discussion programs. Indeed it can be said that the Zambian press—from the point of view of this aspect of press freedom—has been very free since the beginning of the 1990s.

However, the media in which the Zambian public express themselves so freely, are not made available to many people. The Zambian newspapers are essentially a town press. They hardly circulate in rural areas. But even in towns where they circulate, few people can afford to buy them. One newspaper costs 200 Kwacha which amounts to K6000 per month if one were to buy one newspaper every day. That amount of money is almost a month's salary for many workers who fall below the poverty line category. Very few people in Zambia, therefore, can afford to buy newspapers constantly even if they want to. Then there is also the problem of the illiteracy rate which was estimated at 24 percent in 1994. This means that for approximately two and a half million people in this country of more than nine million people, newspapers are useless as a mass medium.

For broadcasting, although transmitter coverage spreads very widely—about 75 percent for radio and with television covering all the provincial centers and the main urban areas—the actual coverage is far less due to various factors such as the unavailability of workable receiver sets and electricity or batteries (Kasoma, 1988, p. 25 and Unesco, 1989, pp. 50-53). Most Zambians are, therefore, left without being given a chance to follow what the broadcast media are saying so that they can participate in the debate as free citizens. In such a situation, a free press becomes meaningless since most people are unable to enjoy its effects. Zambia's press has a very long way to go before it can reach every citizen.

CONCLUSION

The Zambian press of the 1990s set off the country's multiparty democracy to a very good start and looked likely to ensure its success provided it remained as vigilant and outspoken against bad governance as it had been initially. The continuation of its outspokenness, however, depended upon how much fight for their rights journalists put up. Freedom of the press is never given on a silver plate but is won through the struggle that journalists have to wage against government's efforts to suppress them. The moment journalists relax this fight, press freedom starts diminishing until very little or nothing is left.

Governments all over the world have never been known to be darlings of the press, particularly the independent one. They believe the press is out to destroy them and it should, therefore, be watched and controlled to some extent. Governments in Africa, due to their short democratic tradition resulting in instability, are even more prone to try to subjugate the press. Only when the press fights back can there be a semblance of press freedom.

The future of the freedom of the press in Zambia can only be bright when the momentum for this fight is kept, or better still, increased. Now that the democratic process is in place to protect and support them, Zambian journalists should not allow the government to bully them into submission. If they do that, freedom of the press will disappear and perhaps never come back for many generations.

REFERENCES

Constitution of the Republic of Zambia. Lusaka: Government Printer, Amended in 1991.

"Frank Talk." A weekly Television Zambia discussion programme, Feb. 6 1994.

Kasoma, Francis P. *The Press in Zambia.* Lusaka: Multimedia Publications, 1986.

Kasoma, Francis P. "The State of the Media in Angola, Botswana, Lesotho, Mozambique, Swaziland, Tanzania, Zambia, and Zimbabwe." Nordic/ASDCC Media Seminar Proceedings, Harare, Zimbabwe Tampere: University of Tampere, Department of Journalism and Mass Communication, (16-19, Sep. 1986): 17-33.

Kaunda, Kenneth. "Speech by His Excellency The President, Comrade Dr. Kenneth D. Kaunda on, the Occasion of the Commissioning of the Zambia Institute of Mass Communication Buildings on Wednesday 25 October." 1989.

Movement for Multiparty Democracy (MMD) Manifesto. 1990.

National Mirror, Aug. 2-8, 1993.

National Mirror, Sep. 6-12, 1993.

Penal Code, Chapter 146 of the Laws of Zambia.

Preservation of Public Security Act, Chapter 106 of the Laws of Zambia.

Sun, the, Aug. 30-Sep. 5 1993.

Sun, The, Feb. 7-13 1994.

Sunday Times of Zambia, Dec. 5, 1993.

Turok, Ben. "Preparing the Ground for the Future." *Index on Censorship* 21.4 (April 1992).

Unesco. *Broadcasting for Development in Zambia* 2 pp. (1989): 50-53.

Weekly Post, The, Feb. 18 1994.

Weekly Standard, The, Aug. 23-29 1993.

Weekly Standard, The, Sep. 13-19 1993.

CHAPTER 8

PRESS FREEDOM IN ZIMBABWE

Tendayi S. Kumbula

INTRODUCTION

Press freedom has had a long, tenuous existence in what today is known as Zimbabwe. The governments in power have often professed their commitment to press freedom. In reality, however, the communications media have suffered from contradictory tendencies, as political self-interest has too often ridden roughshod over the public's right to free and unfettered news and information. In the turbulent days before and during the illegitimate Ian Smith regime, pre-publication censorship was commonplace. Since Rhodesia became the independent Zimbabwe on April 18, 1980, there has been no direct censorship. But there has been government control of the print and broadcast media. Editors have also engaged in self-censorship as a modus operandi for survival.

PRESS, POLITICS AND GUERRILLA FORCES

The Lancaster House Constitution of December 1979 became Zimbabwe's constitution when the country became independent from Britain in 1980. It is a Westminister-type document designed to promote multi-party democracy. The Declaration of Rights comes under Chapter 111 of the constitution. This section deals with the basic rights and freedoms of the individual, regardless of race, color, sex, political opinion or place of origin. This includes the right to life, liberty, security of the person and protection under the law, protection of the privacy of the home and other property.[1] These rights are, however, subject to restrictions, such as when a person dies during a war, the police power to arrest or the execution of a sentence for a convicted person.

Section 20 of the constitution guarantees freedom of expression, the right to receive, impart and hold ideas and information without interference and freedom from interference with peoples' correspondence.[2] It is this part of the constitution which protects freedom of the mass media. Under normal circumstances, this provision seems to be a straightforward guarantee that Zimbabweans can receive, read, discuss and share ideas, news and information freely, without government control or interference. But this is not an unqualified right.

Conditions have been attached. Thus, for example, restrictions may be placed on the media, citizens or on what is generally called civil society *per se,* in the interests of defense, public safety, the economic interests of the state, public health, public morality, public order or to protect the rights, freedoms and reputations of other people or the private rights of persons involved in legal proceedings. Restrictions may also apply to protect or prevent the disclosure of confidential information or to maintain the authority and independence of the judicial system (courts, tribunals) or the House of Assembly. A state of emergency, imposed in 1965 by the rebel Smith regime, did not lapse until July 25, 1990. It gave Prime Minister Robert Mugabe's postcolonial government and its organs unlimited power to control the media and the citizens. It freely violated human rights. Government could, if it wanted, control what was published or broadcast. There was no appeal against such actions, which left the media largely cowed and controlled. Certain laws on the books, some inherited from the minority Smith regime, such as the Law and Order (Maintenance) Act, also gave the government unlimited power over the media. Such laws gave the Zimbabwe police the power to allow or permit meetings or rallies. In reality, meetings of the ruling Zimbabwe African National Union-Patriotic Front (ZANU-PF) were always allowed. Opposition meetings were hardly ever permitted, thus violating the spirit of the constitution, which guaranteed freedom of assembly and association.

Section 21 of the constitution also guarantees Zimbabweans freedom of assembly and association, including the right to form or belong to political or trade union associations with other people. Again there are also restrictions or exceptions, including protection of defense, public safety, public order, public morality or public health and protection of the rights or freedoms of other persons.[3] The constitution also states that any person who thinks any of these provisions and freedoms, enshrined within the Declaration of Rights, have been violated can apply to the Appellate Division for redress.

However, the story of the media in Zimbabwe cannot be separated from the history of the troubled country. When, on November 11, 1965, Smith and his white minority Rhodesian Front party unilaterally declared the country independent (UDI). This was the culmination of a struggle—which had started in the late 1800s when white settlers arrived in this part of Africa—to impose permanent white minority rule. UDI was a calculated attempt to ensure perpetual white control at the expense of the Black majority. Ironically, this would accelerate the advent of Black majority government.

Formal white control began in the late 1880s when Cecil John Rhodes, the British adventurer after whom the country was at one time named, sent emissaries north from South Africa. Rhodes became a politician and mining magnate in South Africa. His people sought mining rights from local chiefs. They succeeded in tricking King Lobengula of Matabeleland to sign the Rudd Concession, which gave Rhodes exclusive mineral rights[4] to an area that, according to their interpretation, covered Zambia and Zimbabwe (formerly Northern Rhodesia and Southern Rhodesia). This concession eventually was used to make the area part of the British Empire.

On October 29, 1889, Rhodes received a British royal charter authorizing his British South Africa Company to "acquire by any concession, agreement, grant or treaty, all or any rights, interests, authorities, jurisdiction and powers of any kind or nature whatever, including powers necessary for the purpose of government and the preservation of public order."[5]

On September 12, 1890, a so-called pioneer column that had been moving north from South Africa, hoisted the British flag on what it called Fort Salisbury. This would become Salisbury, the capital of Southern Rhodesia. After the attainment of independence it was renamed Harare, the capital of Zimbabwe. Rebellions by the indigenous African majority were ruthlessly suppressed in 1896-97, establishing a pattern where force would repeatedly be used to oppress and suppress the African majority.

In 1922, there was a white referendum, which rejected union with South Africa.[6] In 1923, British South Africa Company rule over the country ended. It was replaced by internal self-government for the white minority. Again, Africans were not consulted. Whites controlled the country and could do what they wanted, without consulting the disenfranchised black majority. However, Britain retained control over foreign affairs and matters dealing with African affairs. In theory, Britain could veto any legislation passed by the Rhodesian Legislative Assembly if it was unfair to the African majority but this power was never exercised. When successive Rhodesian legislatures steadily whittled away African rights, on land and other issues, there was no British veto.

In the 1960s, the Southern Rhodesian whites pushed for independence which would retain control in white hands. But, under mounting pressure by African nationalists, the British backed off. It was under these conditions that Smith undertook UDI, which placed the country under virtual international ostracism, led to economic sanctions and eventually forced the country's African nationalists to opt for guerrilla warfare as the only way to end minority rule. During this time, the country's media systems suffered unparalleled restrictions, including outright censorship. More than 30,000 people, mostly blacks, would die before Zimbabwe's birth.

Zimbabwe, with about 11 million people spread over 150,318 square miles, is a landlocked country in Southern Africa. It is bordered by Zambia in the north, Mozambique in the east, Botswana in the west and South Africa in the south. Many of its economic and transportation links are with these countries. Lack of its own ports and harbors forces Zimbabwe to rely on Mozambican and South African facilities. Thus, its economy and politics have also been subject to ripple effects from its neighbors, especially South Africa and Mozambique. Outside South Africa, Zimbabwe boasts one of the most highly developed industrial infrastructures in sub-Saharan Africa.

Zimbabwe also has some of the oldest newspapers in Africa. In June 1891, the *Mashonaland* and *Zambesian Times*, a hand-written paper described by one journalist as a "crude but readable cyclostyled sheet" [7] was published. On October 20, 1892, *The Rhodesia Herald* replaced the *Mashonaland* and *Zambesian Times* as the country's major daily newspaper. The paper, since renamed *The Herald*, survives today as the country's oldest and biggest daily newspaper. But it has changed over the years. It was started by the Argus Company of South Africa. On October 12, 1894, the Argus Company chose to start a second newspaper, the *Bulawayo Chronicle* in Bulawayo, the country 's second largest city. Today, these papers are the oldest in the country. The two papers supported the British South Africa Company in its quest to continue ruling Rhodesia.[8]

The two Argus papers also adopted an anti-African policy. After the Salisbury Chamber of Mines demanded in 1903 that there should be restrictions on attempts to Christianize Africans, *The Rhodesia Herald* declared that, "The Black peril will become a reality when the results of our misguided system of education have taken root, and when a veneer of European civilization struggles with the innate savage nature."[9] The media in Rhodesia catered to the needs of the white settlers by ignoring news of interest to the African majority. Much of the early news was about events occurring in the metropolis—from politics to sports, while events on the African continent were ignored. The needs, aspirations and hopes of the Africans were never published. However, news about crime by blacks was prominently covered. The media had not changed much by the time the country achieved its independence. They were still geared mainly toward white readers and advertisers. This was not surprising since all top Rhodesian Printing and Publishing newspaper executives in Rhodesia were white, as were all the editors, copy editors, almost all of the reporters and most of the advertising and circulation executives. This had important implications for the media at independence.

Incoming Prime Minister Mugabe and his colleagues had learned the importance of information and propaganda during their exile years as African guerrillas battled the Rhodesian army and air force. From Ethiopia, Mozambique, Zambia, Tanzania and elsewhere, the guerrilla forces had clandestinely broadcast sometimes inflammatory news and information to the country's African majority. Although it was illegal to listen to such broadcasts or to receive literature from banned political organizations, the broadcasts from exile became the main source of news and information about the struggle to remove the Smith regime. The broadcasts boosted the morale of the guerrillas and the African masses. They provided an alternative source of vital information from what the Rhodesian Broadcasting Corporation was transmitting. As Julie Frederikse noted in her *None But Ourselves,* the struggle for Rhodesia was not just a military one. It also had important political and psychological components, including the struggle for the minds and allegiance of the African majority.

MANY FACES OF CENSORSHIP

The media have sometimes been described as agenda setters because when they focus on an issue, that brings it to the forefront. It becomes the main source of discussion and attention. This has been demonstrated repeatedly in the United States where, in January 1994, the case involving Lorena Bobbitt's slicing of her husband's male organ and sexual molestation allegations against entertainer Michael Jackson for a while dominated newspaper, television, radio and magazine reports, talk shows, tabloid newspapers and tabloid television shows.

The media are important because they inform, educate and

entertain. They also foster a common culture or propagate the ideas and theories of the country's political, economic, educated, ruling, cultural and social elites. They open a window into the thinking of such people. They also allow those in power to control what the media report or what the masses will or will not know. Under ideal conditions, they can also provide two-way communication between rulers and their subjects.

Thus, it seemed almost inevitable that the new Mugabe government would move fast and decisively to acquire the means to control the electronic and print media. It was easy to take over the electronic media because under Rhodesian laws the broadcast outlets were already under *de facto* government control. The Smith regime had been appointing the board of governors which oversaw the broadcast authority. Although in theory the electronic media were autonomous, in reality the Smith regime exercised effective political control, including guidelines that required that the African opposition be denied on-air access. News reports about the guerrillas were to be negative. The guerrilla fighters and their leaders were to be referred to as "terrorists." Radio and television became part of the propaganda onslaught against the guerrillas. There could be no positive news or information programs on radio or television about the guerrillas. The Rhodesia Broadcasting Corporation (RBC) was part of the Smith regime's propaganda machinery. It was subject to regular political pressure. It banned news and views unpopular with the Smith regime.[10] Stories that might pressure the regime were unwelcome. After UDI, legislation was passed by the Rhodesian parliament imposing a fine of up to $1,500 or two years in prison for anyone who permitted any hostile broadcast to be heard in public. Pro-apartheid Radio South Africa replaced the British Broadcasting Corporation as the main source of external news. Smith himself admitted that radio was one of the most powerful tools in the ongoing "war for men's minds."

In a related development, Julie Frederikse found a confidential RBC memo, dated August 28, 1978, signed by T. W. Louw, RBC's director of news, which listed a number of organizations that could not be mentioned by Rhodesian radio and television staff. These included the Patriotic Front (an alliance of ZAPU and

ZANU), ZAPU (Zimbabwe African People's Union), ZANU, the Zimbabwe African National Liberation Army (ZANU's guerrilla wing), the Zimbabwe People's Liberation Army (ZAPU's military wing) and the Zimbabwe People's Army. Louw's memo, in part, said:

> Let me emphasize that there is to be no mention of these bodies nor any reference which might serve to identify any of these groups. In addition, there is to be no reference to any leader or office bearer or member of these groups.
>
> I must point out that the most severe penalties will follow any transgression of this directive. There may well be circumstances in which it would be in the National interest for the type of materials specified to be broadcast. Any such suggestion must be referred to me or, in my absence, to the Assistant Director. In no circumstances will any other member of the staff contravene the terms of this directive.[11]

This directive was religiously followed, as were other directives to demonize Mugabe and ZAPU president Joshua Nkomo, by referring to them as "terrorist leaders" or "leaders of terrorist organizations." Their political parties were similarly referred to as "terrorist" movements and their followers, especially the guerrilla fighters, were called "terrorists." Ironically, after attaining independence, the Mugabe government used similar tactics, by referring to dissident opponents, then operating in Matabeleland, as "bandits."

The Mugabe government quickly appointed its own board of governors to oversee the renamed Zimbabwe Broadcasting Corporation (ZBC). American-educated Tirivafi Kangai, who had been ZANU-PF's California-based U. S. representative, became ZBC's first Black director-general. It was a political appointment because he had no media background.

Many of the others appointed to top policy-making or programming positions at ZBC also had political backgrounds, from the party's exile days in Mozambique, Zambia and Tanzania.

Those without such credentials from the guerrilla war days often found themselves, despite their qualifications, shunted to lower-echelon positions within the new ZBC hierarchy.

Today ZBC runs the country's two television and four radio stations. Government funding from the Ministry of Information subsidizes the electronic media, which also depend on annual license fees which must be paid by all Zimbabwe residents who own or rent radio and television sets. The Mugabe government also established the Zimbabwe Mass Media Trust (ZMMT) to set long and short-range policy for all the Zimbabwe media. Initially the board set to oversee the ZMMT was a cross-section of Zimbabweans of all political and economic stripes. Over the years, however, the board has become increasingly political. It is now dominated by those with strong ZANU-PF connections.

According to the *UNESCO Statistical Yearbook,* the number of radio receivers in Zimbabwe has increased from 750,000 in 1987 to 775,000 in 1988 and about 801,000 in 1989.[12] Radio has more reach in Zimbabwe than any other medium. Even areas without electricity still listen to radio, because of the availability of battery-powered sets. At growth points, areas designated by the government to promote rural development, people often gather to listen to radio or, sometimes, to watch battery-operated television sets.

Zimbabwe has four radio channels. Radio 1, broadcasting in English, is a general station that covers news and music, while Radio 2 and Radio 3 are geared more toward African listeners. They also provide a mixture of music, news and other entertainment. Radio 4 is the most innovative. It is also the educational channel. With support and technical assistance from the German Friedrich-Ebert Foundation, Radio 4 is making its mark. In February 1992, the Germans handed it over to their Zimbabwean counterparts. It broadcasts 12 hours daily on FM transmitters scattered across the country. Four hours a day are for education, from grade one to the sixth year of high school. It has replaced scarce school materials in some areas to become the main source for learning.[13] It has also been creative in seeking listener feedback. Radio 4 personnel venture into rural areas, armed with recorders, to tape and then broadcast listener response to their programs.

This is important in a country with a shortage of phones, even in the urban areas.

Soon after attaining independence, the new government set about designing a strategy to take over control of the country's main daily and weekly newspapers from their South African parent. Mugabe said it was unthinkable that the country's main print media outlets should retain their connection with a company based in racist South Africa. With the help of a $5 million grant from Nigeria, the Mugabe government (through ZMMT) acquired a controlling interest in Rhodesian Printing and Publishing, which was renamed Zimbabwe Newspapers (Zimpapers) Ltd. Dr. Davison Sadza, a physician with no newspaper background, became the chairman of the separate ZMMT and Zimpapers boards.

At the time of the takeover, Zimpapers controlled *The Herald,* the country's main daily newspaper, published in the capital Harare, and *The Bulawayo Chronicle,* published in Bulawayo, the country's second largest city. Its other properties were *The Sunday Mail,* the country's largest circulating newspaper, based in Harare; *The Sunday Mail,* is the weekly sister to *The Herald.* Both are headquartered in Herald House. They share the same managerial, advertising and circulation staff, fleet of vehicles and drivers, but are located on different floors, compete editorially and have different editors, reporters and photographers. *The Chronicle* and *The Sunday Times* also share the same building, advertising and circulation staff, managers, but also have competing editorial staffs. The fifth member brought into this Zimpapers stable was *The Mutare* (now *Manica) Post*, published in Mutare, the country's largest eastern city. All these papers, which dominate the country's print outlets, are in English, Zimbabwe's official language. However, the company has also started *Kwaedza/Umthunya,* published in Shona and Ndebele, the country's main African languages.

Then Minister of Information and Tourism Nathan Shamuyarira, himself a former journalist, called the acquisition by ZMMT of controlling shares in Zimpapers the beginning of many changes to reshape the country's image and identity. He told a Harare news conference, as reported on the front page of *The Herald* on January 5, 1981, "We will continue to take any measures that will reassert the interests of Zimbabwean society in its totality." Shamuyarira also declared that the non-profit ZMMT was prepared to plow its share of profits back into Zimpapers.

Although he said there would be no significant management changes in the papers' structures, he also made it clear that African editors were to be appointed and that these would be people with a background in African politics. He stated that ZMMT would be

> "autonomous and independent" and not subject to government interference, a position that has not always been followed. Shamuyarira said under the Mugabe government the press' duty would be the basic media one—"to inform, educate and entertain" all Zimbabweans. He said ZMMT's takeover of the newspapers had been designed to eliminate South African influence and to reorient the papers toward the country's often ignored African majority.

In the same issue of *The Herald,* George Capon, the white chairman and managing director of Zimpapers, said, "A long and valued association with the Argus Group has been broken, but there can be few, if any, among the staff who cannot honestly say that in the present circumstances the break was inevitable."

However, comments in The *Herald,* from opponents of the Mugabe government were not so charitable. Nkomo, then president of the opposition Patriotic Front-Zimbabwe African People's Union (PF-ZAPU) but now one of Zimbabwe's two vice-presidents under Mugabe, declared:

> It is a complete tragedy that the Government has taken such a step, because it is vital to have some independent opinion from somewhere when one is in power, lest one be misled by self-created blinkers that one is right all the time. This step is worse than what the Rhodesian Front did during its abominable time in office. I really find it difficult to believe that such a step was necessary, because if the government did

not like South African presence in the news media, it should have asked the Zimbabwean public to buy the South African-held shares of the group.

Nkomo also said:

> I am surprised that Nigeria, a country with probably the freest Press in Africa, could lend money to ZANU (PF) to muzzle the Press in Zimbabwe. This is probably the last free statement through our newspapers here, where the radio and television are already under the heel of ZANU (PF). One would have thought radio and television were enough propaganda tools.

Before the increasingly tight government control over the newspapers, *The Herald* felt free to publish Nkomo's statement criticizing the Mugabe government. In later years, there was little criticism of the government to be found in the Zimpapers and ZBC outlets.

The takeover was condemned by the British National Union of Journalists but it was blessed by the Union of Zimbabwe Journalists (ZUJ), which said the union was not concerned about ownership—as long as freedom of the press existed. A ZUJ statement to *The Herald* said, in part, "It is the union's sincere hope that the government will uphold its declared intention not to interfere with the freedom of the press."

Meanwhile, another opposition leader, the Rev. Ndabaningi Sithole, former leader of Mugabe's party, questioned the rationale behind the government's action. He said it appeared to be a government attempt to control what the people read, saw and heard.

His statement in *The Herald* said:

> I was shocked this morning. It came so suddenly. Already the government is controlling television and radio and only one party is projected—that is ZANU (PF). One really suspects that only ZANU (PF) will be projected in the press that will be government controlled.
>
> My own fears, which I have always felt, are being jus-

tified now. Once the government controls the media, that means we have had it, unless they stick to their promise that they will not interfere with the press.

Nkomo's and Sithole's fears were soon realized when government functionaries began to interfere with the media. Editors who did not toe the government line were called on the carpet or, on at least three occasions, fired.

Immediately after the attainment of independence the government had also taken other measures to have more control over news and information. On August 27, 1980, barely five months after coming to power, Shamuyarira announced that the government would establish a national news agency. At that time the Inter-African News Agency (IANA), founded in 1964 as a subsidiary of the South African Press Association, was the domestic news-gathering and dissemination outlet. In 1980, it was replaced by the Zimbabwe Inter-African News Agency (ZIANA)[14], whose job is to gather and distribute news to all media outlets. ZIANA also has the additional task of determining what foreign news will reach the Zimbabwe media. In the past the Zimbabwe media subscribed directly to Associated Press, United Press International, Reuters and Agence France Presse. Once ZIANA came into existence, all foreign news entering the country had to be routed through it. ZIANA editors then decide what news and information to forward to their subscribers. That way they actually determine what *The Herald, The Sunday Mail* , ZBC and the other media get.

Farai Munyuki, a former newsman in Zambia who also attended an American university, became *The Herald's* first black editor. After two and a half years he was removed from the paper and sent over to edit ZIANA. In an interview before leaving *The Herald,* he declared that ZIANA's job was to give an ideological lead to the country's newspapers. It is worth quoting here what he said:

> I believe ZIANA should formally be structured both organizationally and in substance, and in this way the government will be able to achieve uniformity of ideology . . . . I believe that the achievement of national

integration and transformation is a function of a society's use of the media, to enhance the values, customs and objectives of the people . . . Certainly our emphasis should be different from those of the Western media, although the general means of communication are similar.

I also believe that ZIANA should be able to contribute to the development of a Zimbabwean society and to promote national unity by ensuring a balanced presentation of views from all parts of the country.[15]

Despite the wishes pronounced by Munyuki, who has since left ZIANA, the domestic news agency has been viewed by many journalists as a government agency. This is not surprising because of its founding and leadership. Its current editor is Henry Muradzikwa, a former editor of *The Sunday Mail*. Muradzikwa was fired from *The Sunday Mail* after the paper published a story reporting that Zimbabwean students had been deported from Cuba because they had AIDS.[16]

The story came out at an embarrassing moment, when a high Cuban official was visiting Zimbabwe. Mugabe reportedly said that he was going to deal with Muradzikwa. The firing followed soon after that. Fortunately for Muradzikwa, he reportedly apologized, was rehabilitated and eventually sent to ZIANA. But he was not the only Zimbabwe editor to be fired.

One of the most celebrated cases was that of Willie Dzawanda Musarurwa, his predecessor at *The Sunday Mail*. Musarurwa was easily the country's most venerated journalist. He had also been a politician. As a member of Nkomo's PF-ZAPU, he spent 10 years in detention, without trial, during the days of Smith's UDI. He became the only editor chosen from PF-ZAPU ranks. Once he became editor, however, he ceased all political activities on behalf of PF-ZAPU, although he was regarded suspiciously by ZANU (PF) adherents, who thought his paper was not sufficiently pro-government

Musarurwa, the first African to edit *The Sunday Mail,* was fired in July 1985 by Elias T. Rusike, the first African managing director and chief executive officer of Zimpapers. Musarurwa said he was asked to resign and was promised government help in getting another job—if he left quietly. True to his principles, Musarurwa refused to cooperate. Rusike sacked him. In his book, Rusike later claimed that he was acting as the government's "hatchet man" in writing dismissal letters to Musarurwa, Muradzikwa and Geoffrey Nyarota. Rusike said he acted against Musarurwa after repeated pressure from the Ministry of Information which found Musarurwa's independence embarrassing. Musarurwa was also accused of using his paper to publish the views of opposition parties.

In a six-page single-spaced letter to Rusike, which Musarurwa showed to the author, a former colleague of Musarurwa and news editor at the *Sunday Mail* from 1982 to 1983, behind closed doors in his office, he rebutted the accusations against him. He denied he had ever been anti-government or that he was using the paper to promote opposition to ZANU (PF). He argued he was merely doing what any good editor should do, by opening up his paper to all shades of opinion in Zimbabwe. He argued that being editor did not mean he had to be slavishly pro-government. He was the first editor fired. He would not be the last.

He died suddenly of a stroke on April 3, 1990. Ironically, the Mugabe government which had fired him, proclaimed him a "national hero" to be buried at Heroes' Acre near Harare. This burial site is set aside for Zimbabweans who have made singular contributions to the country or to its struggle for independence. He became the first journalist at Heroes' Acre, something he would have found amusing. Now, there is a Willie Musarurwa Memorial Trust. On January 22, 1993, a seminar on press freedom in Zimbabwe was held by the trust, which hopes to immortalize Musarurwa's memory by fighting for a free press. A booklet titled *Press Freedom in Zimbabwe* was published out of its proceedings.

The third editor to be fired was Nyarota. Zimpapers publications have never been known for enterprise or investigative reporting—with one notable exception. Zimbabwe has suffered from a shortage of motor vehicle and spare parts. There are long waiting lists for those wishing to purchase motor vehicles.

Many of the cars, brought into the country as kits, are assembled at Willowvale, outside Harare. Through the help of Obert Mpofu, a member of parliament who received a misdirected check, *The Chronicle* uncovered a major scandal, which showed that government ministers and other high officials were abusing their positions.

Government price controls limited how much dealers could charge for new cars. However, *The Chronicle,* then edited by Nyarota, with Davison Maruziva as assistant editor, discovered that these high government officials were buying cars and re-selling them at exorbitant prices, in violation of the government's own price controls. Despite government pressure and threats, Nyarota and Maruziva exposed the scandal which became known as "Willowgate." *The Chronicle* became so popular in October 1988 that people were queuing to buy it, sometimes ignoring *The Herald,* so they could find out the latest details in the unfolding scandal.

As a result of these exposures, Maurice Nyagumbo, a senior cabinet minister for political affairs, committed suicide. Minister of Defense Enos Nkala, who had publicly threatened to arrest the offending editors, resigned in disgrace, as did Minister of Higher Education Dzingai Mutumbuka, Minister of Industry and Technology Callistus Ndlovu, Political Affairs Minister Frederick Shava and provincial governor Jacob Mudenda. It was the first time in the country's history that a newspaper had done that.

Mugabe, who had earlier dismissed the stories as not worth much of anything, was forced to appoint a commission of inquiry to look into the matter. Its March 1989 *Report of the Commission of Inquiry into the Distribution of Motor Vehicles* verified what the newspaper had reported. However, none of the culprits really suffered. Shava, who had been convicted of perjury, was pardoned and never went to prison. He's now making a political comeback. None of the other officials was ever charged or tried.

However, Nyarota found himself booted upstairs. He was "promoted" to a newly-created position, as a public relations executive with a high salary but no editorial duties, at Zimpapers' Harare headquarters. He later followed Rusike to *The Financial*

Gazette. After a falling-out over editorial control, Nyarota also left that paper. His deputy, Maruziva, was brought back to Harare and made assistant editor of *The Herald,* which is under tighter government control because it is in the capital, where it is seen and read daily (except Sundays) by Mugabe, his cabinet, other government officials and also by diplomats and business leaders. Some critics have referred derisively to *The Herald* as the "government gazette," because of its perceived pro-government slant.

The 102-year-old *Herald,* with a circulation of 134,000, is edited by Tommy Sithole, who is also editor-in-chief of all Zimpapers publications. *The Herald* and the 100-year-old *Chronicle,* with a circulation of 74,032[17] (*The Europa Yearbook 1993*) are both published in English. They are the largest daily newspapers in the country. *Editor and Publisher International Year Book 1993,* lists the circulations as 129,830 and 65,512 respectively. Zimpapers' other publications, *The Sunday Mail* in Harare, circulation 135,000, edited by Charles Chikerema, and *The Sunday News* circulation, 66,372, edited by L. Chikuwira in Bulawayo, are the largest Sunday papers. They are also both in English. The two Harare publications are regular broad sheet newspapers, while their Bulawayo counterparts are tabloids. Because of new equipment acquired in the early 1980s, the Harare papers publish in color. The machinery is capable of printing up to 60,000 copies per hour.

Buffeted by falling advertising revenue and internal scandals for the first time, Zimpapers is facing serious competition, despite increasing circulation. *The Herald's* circulation increased from 75,837 copies in 1979 to 136,108 copies in 1990, before beginning to fall because of newsprint shortages. *The Sunday Mail* rose from 90,300 copies to 137,021 copies during the same period. Other Zimpapers publications also showed similar trends, with *The Chronicle* going from 36,322 copies in 1979 to 66,405 copies in 1990, while *The Sunday News* rose from 30,000 copies in 1979 to 66,720 copies in 1990. *The Manica Post*, a weekly, went from 3,699 copies in 1979 to 17,464 in 1990. *Kwaedza/Umthunya,* the only Zimpapers African language publication, started in 1985 with a circulation of 18,427 copies, rose to 93,013 copies in 1989 and then dropped to 62,365 in 1990. These circulation figures are from a book by Rusike, former managing director of Zimbabwe Newspapers. They showed impressive circulation gains, compared to those from the 1975 edition of UNESCO's *World Communications,* which showed Rhodesia with four daily and 10 non-daily newspapers and a total circulation of 83,000, which worked out at 15 copies per 1,000 people.[18] By 1988 those figures had jumped to two daily newspapers with a circulation of 214,000 copies for almost 11 million people. In passing, it should be noted that the circulation figures differ somewhat depending on whether The *Europa Yearbook, Editor and Publisher International Year Book or The Politics of the Mass Media* is the source.

THE BOLD PRESS OF THE 1990S

The Financial Gazette (sometimes also called the "Pink Paper" because of the color of its newsprint) is published by Modus Publications, whose managing director is the same Rusike mentioned above. He and other African businessmen bought *The Gazette* from its white owners. Soon after the purchase, Rusike resigned from Zimpapers to run Modus. *The Gazette* has a circulation of about 25,000 weekly. But its influence far exceeds its numbers. It is very popular among white businessmen. Usually it has 24 to 32 pages, often bulging with business ads. It has also picked up readership among Africans, who saw it as an alternative to the government-controlled Zimpapers publications. *The Gazette* publishes stories, some of them quite critical of the Mugabe government. Despite threats and attacks by government officials, it has usually spoken out. In January 1994, for example, it editorially attacked Mugabe for pardoning a ZANU (PF) youth leader and a Zimbabwe counter-intelligence official who had been convicted in the shooting and wounding of Patrick Kombayi, an opposition Zimbabwe Unity candidate in the 1990 Zimbabwe elections. Almost immediately after the two men had lost their appeals to Zimbabwe's highest court, Mugabe used a presidential pardon to free them from their jail sentences. This is not the first time that Mugabe has pardoned people convicted of serious criminal offenses.

On January 23, 1992, *The Gazette* published a long three-column article titled "Only Free Press Can Save our Country from Manipulation." It was written by Jonathan Moyo, then a lecturer at the University of Zimbabwe, who was also considered one of Mugabe's most articulate critics. Moyo was frequently quoted in the international media challenging the Mugabe government. Moyo's comments were in response to Mugabe's criticism of weekly newspapers, magazines and some individuals whom he accused of yellow journalism. The Mugabe government has sometimes been frustrated by criticism of its policies. It sees any such criticism as the work of opposition parties and foreign-supported "opposition" newspapers bent on propaganda. Wrote Moyo:

> There is something morally crushing about giving us, as the official press is fond of doing, national character to the prejudices of a leader of a particularly idiosyncratic ruling party just because the leader also happens to be the head of state. In a multi-party democracy, which this country is supposed to be, at least constitutionally, the media should draw a sharp line between party and national affairs.
>
> But this is where the government-controlled media fails the nation. Their brief, whether decreed from above or self-imposed, is to report ZANU (PF) affairs as if the ruling party is greater than the nation. This docility sometimes takes on disgusting proportions when the government-controlled media reports whatever Mr. Mugabe says and wherever he says it, without analyzing its contents. Presumably, this is in keeping with the ZANU (PF) doctrine of presidential infallibility.

Such questioning of Mugabe and his party is rare within the Zimbabwe media. It has never surfaced within the government-controlled electronic media. Neither has it been seen on the pages of the daily papers. Apart from the days when Musarurwa edited *The Sunday Mail* or when *The Chronicle* was investigating the Willowgate scandal, the Zimbabwe government has been immune from media criticism.

In another forum, Moyo argued that when there is no press freedom, other freedoms would also not exist. He said there is no press freedom in Zimbabwe because the media are government-controlled and that the media failed to distinguish between Mugabe and the national interest. Said Moyo:

> It is a matter of public record, Mr. Chairman, that over the last 12 years of independence, *The Herald, The Chronicle* and ZBC, to name a few government mouthpieces, have never criticized Mr. Mugabe. Not even once. The desired subliminal effect of this miscarriage of journalism is that readers and listeners are supposed to believe that Mr. Mugabe is infallible. Of course, that is nonsense, Mr. Chairman. You and I know that everyone makes mistakes and that Mr. Mugabe has made a lot of mistakes. But the mistakes have not been covered by the government-controlled media because of the "dear leader" mentality, which has served as a major political impediment to freedom of the press in this country.[19]

That has changed somewhat lately, with the emergence of *The Daily Gazette*, a tabloid whose front-page slogan is "Zimbabwe's only independent daily newspaper." The *Daily Gazette*, a stablemate of *The Financial Gazette*, has been challenging *The Herald* for readership. Its front-page stories have often been different from those in *The Herald*. Since its founding in 1992, it has particularly delighted in publishing stories critical of the government. Its August 9, 1993, story for example (which was not carried in the rival *Herald*) was headlined, "Poaching: Army, ZRP (Zimbawe police) Implicated." The decks dealt with an alleged cover up and the obligatory government denial. Many Zimbabweans who want to be kept informed buy both papers daily.

In 1993 Modus Publications took another step toward becoming a chain that can compete with Zimpapers by starting another paper, called *The Sunday Gazette*. Like its sisters, this is a colorful tabloid that is engaged in head-to-head competition with *The Sunday Mail*. *The Sunday Gazette* offers its reader a diet of hard news, features, entertainment, business, finance and sports stories. It remains to be seen how successful Modus' newest papers will be. But they seem to have been well received so far.

Before launching its Sunday and daily papers, Modus had been involved in the publication of the *Sunday Times,* which was started in October 1991. Herbert Munangatire, an African businessman started the *Sunday Times* using some reporters and editors formerly with Zimpapers. But after some financial problems, the *Sunday Times*, whose circulation at one time had reached 40,000, was back on the street, competing with *The Sunday Mail* and *The Sunday Gazette*. For the first time in years, Zimbabweans can choose from rival daily and Sunday newspapers.

The *Sunday Times* has also not been afraid to challenge the Mugabe government and the ruling party, although like *The Sunday Gazette,* it has not sided with any political organization. Beginning October 1991 it vigorously pursued the story of Rashiwe Guzha, a young woman who disappeared and is feared dead. Guzha was involved with Eddison Shrihuru, a senior official of the Central Intelligence Organization (CIO), a group that used to send shivers down the spines of some Zimbabweans. The paper published regular stories about Guzha and even an editorial demanding justice in her case. Shirihuru died in August 1993.

At his funeral services Mugabe said the case was closed. Not so, argued the *Sunday Times,* as it continued to demand a full accounting in the case. The paper has given its readers a mix of hard and soft stories, entertainment, religious, national and international news, plus a good dose of sports news.

Other Zimbabwe publications worth noting include *Moto,* published in Gweru, with a circulation of 27,000. *Moto* is a monthly that often carries caustic political analyses and comment. *Moto* was once banned by the Smith regime for its support of the forces that were fighting for Black majority rule. Now it is under attack from the Mugabe government, which it once supported, because it has dared to question the government's human rights policies. It would be ironic if *Moto,* became the first publication to have been banned by the colonial and post-colonial governments.

Parade magazine, whose circulation is about 100,000, is one of the oldest monthlies in the country. It started out as a strictly entertainment magazine, but has changed to add more news about sports, especially soccer. It has also carried a series of tough, often insightful articles about politics and the Mugabe government. Its August 1991 cover story, for example, was on Edgar Tekere, a former Mugabe lieutenant, who now heads the opposition ZUM. Inside were two full pages devoted to Tekere. Other features included a critical analysis of the budget, exploitation of domestic servants, prostitutes, AIDS, and killer dogs. This magazine, under editor Mark Chavunduka, has not been afraid to take on the government or to question the powerful in Zimbabwe politics.

Parade, which describes itself as "Zimbabwe's most widely read news magazine," lately has been challenged for readers by *Horizon,* edited by Andrew (Andy) Moyse, a former *Herald* copy editor. Later, he became *Parade* editor, before starting *Horizon,* part of whose funding came from Scandinavian sources. Moyse is one of the few whites to edit a magazine most of whose readers are Black. His magazine has also distinguished itself by publishing regular entertainment, features and other such fare, and also by its willingness to publish hard-hitting stories, some of which have not been welcomed by the Mugabe government.

In summary, press freedom is making a comeback in Zimbabwe. During the days of UDI, in the 60s and 70s, the freedom flame had almost been extinguished by the Smith regime. It used the state of emergency, other pieces of draconian legislation, censorship, banning of publications, and the arrest, detention or deportation as weapons in its war against press freedom. Additionally, the Smith regime also used its control over the Rhodesian Broadcasting Corporation to ensure that only its voice was heard. Opponents were denied access to the airwaves, which were regularly used as a propaganda tool in the unsuccessful attempt to destroy the guerrilla forces and other anti-UDI opponents.

When the Mugabe government came to power in 1980 it

publicly proclaimed its support for press freedom. Chapter 111 of the Zimbabwe constitution, which is the Declaration of Rights section, guarantees fundamental rights to the country's citizens. These include freedom of expression, freedom of assembly and association , personal liberty, freedom from arbitrary search and entry and the right to life. Despite these protections in the constitution, however, there are also provisions under which they may be abrogated or suspended in the interests of national security or under a state of emergency.

For most of the 80s the press in Zimbabwe was largely cowed, except, sometimes, for *The Financial Gazette.* Aside from Willowgate and a few other situations, the government was pleased with its control over the media. Editors met frequently with and were briefed by cabinet ministers and even by Mugabe himself. However, much of what is learned during such sessions could not be passed on to readers, listeners and viewers. Because of the government's control over radio and television and its control over Zimpapers through its controlling shares in the Zimbabwe Mass Media Trust, there was a lot of self-censorship by editors. The government hardly ever had to use all the resources at its disposal. Editors were conscious that the government could have them demoted, fired or transferred. At one time this author was summoned to a meeting with the minister of information and his subordinates and questioned for having allowed *The Sunday Mail* to publish a story quoting foreign journalists who disagreed with the Kadoma Declaration.

Frontline governments in Southern Africa, including Zimbabwe, had complained repeatedly that South African-based Western correspondents wrote biased stories about their countries. To correct this, foreign ministers from the involved countries, which included Botswana, Angola, Mozambique and Zambia, had agreed during a meeting in Kadoma, Zimbabwe, that they would no longer allow South African-based correspondents into their countries. Few of these countries, except Zimbabwe, ever honored the declaration. Needless to say, it was unpopular among foreign correspondents who saw it as being violative of press freedom. The author was forced to explain to the minister why he had allowed the story to run since it challenged a government policy.

Since the 1990s, however, the pendulum has swung in the other direction. Independent, though not necessarily free, newspapers and magazines have become more common in Zimbabwe. On any given day or issue, it is now possible to get several viewpoints from the media, although the large Zimpapers publications continue to follow the government line and to give more publicity and favorable story placement to the government. During the 1990s elections, for example, Zimpapers would announce ZANU (PF) rallies and publish, usually on the front page, speeches by senior ZANU (PF) officials—while ignoring opposition parties. The trend was even more pronounced on radio and television, which seemed to have become the ruling party's cheerleaders.

The 1995 general elections was a good indicator of what's happening in the media. A number of opposition parties were prepared for that campaign against ZANU (PF). For the first time there were independent daily and Sunday papers, which allowed opposition candidates to get their messages out to the masses. However, it seems unlikely that the government will relinquish its control over the electronic media. Since some of Zimbabwe's voters are illiterate, it was difficult to reach those of them who live in rural areas or in remote parts of the country, which radio reaches but not newspapers. The continued presence of independent newspapers may, however, help level the playing field in the urban areas where more people can read. In a study of the media in the 1990 elections, one author said, "The access of the various political parties to the media in Zimbabwe is definitely far from fair. There is no doubt that the ruling party enjoys a lion's share of publicity in the state-controlled media in. In 1996, Mugabe won another six-year term as president.

Not only do the minority parties receive scant coverage, but the little coverage they do get is extremely negative while the vast coverage enjoyed by the ruling party is quite positive. In fact, the national media, particularly certain newspapers, are now carrying out the ruling party's public relations—this in addition to the party-owned media."[20]

Notes

1. Zimbabwe Constitution, Chapter 111, p. 11.
2. Ibid: 24.
3. Ibid: 24.
4. Mtshali, Vulindlela B., *Rhodesia: Background to Politics,* 1967:
5. Ibid: 37.
6. Bowman, Larry W., *Politics in Rhodesia,* 1973: 7.
7. Barton, Frank, *The Press of Africa,* 1979: 218.
8. Ibid: 219
9. Ibid.
10. Ainslie, Rosalynde, *The Press in Africa,* 1967. 166.
11. Frederikse, Julie, *None But Ourselves, Masses Vs. the Media in the Making of Zimbabwe,* 1982: 266.
12. *UNESCO Statistical Yearbook.*
13. *Slippery Roads in Africa: Radio 4—a Project History,* 1992: 7.
14. *World Communications,* UNESCO, 1975: 98.
15. *The Rhodesia Herald,*
16. Index on Censorship, 21.4 (April 1992): 46. Also Rusike, E.T.M., *The Politics of the Mass Media,* 1990: 87.
17. *The Europa Year Book* 1993, Vol. 11.
18. *World Communications:* 96
19. *Press Freedom in Zimbabwe,* 1993: 13
20. Mandaza, Ibbo, and Lloyd Sachikonye, eds., *The One Party State and Democracy,* 1991: 148-9

Selected Bibliography

Atkinson, Norman, *Teaching Rhodesian.* London: Longman, 1972.

Austin, Reginald, *Racism and Apartheid in Southern Africa:* Rhodesia, Paris: The UNESCO Press, 1975.

Faringer, Gunilla L., *Press Freedom in Africa,* New York: Praeger, 1991.

Freedom in the World 1989-1990, New York: Freedom House, 1990.

Good, Robert C., *U.D.I. The International Politics of the Rhodesian Rebellion,* Princeton University Press, 1973.

Hachten, William A., *Muffled Drums: The News Media in Africa,* The Iowa State University Press, 1971.

Herbst, Jeffrey, *State Politics in Zimbabwe.* Berkeley: University of California Press, 1990.

Liebenow, J. Gus, *African Politics: Crises and Challenges,* Bloomington: Indiana University Press, 1986.

Martin, Phyllis M., and Patrick O'Meara eds., *Africa,* Bloomington:

Indiana University Press, 1986.

Merrill, John C., *Global Journalism: A Survey of the World's News Media,* New York: Longman, 1991.

Murphree, M.W. ed., G. Cheater, B. J. Dorsey and B.D. Mothobi, *Education, Race and Employment in Rhodesia,* Harare: Mardon Printers, 1975.

Muzorewa, Abel T., *Rise Up & Walk,* Nashville: Abingdon, 1978.

Mytton, Graham, *Mass Communication in Africa,* London: Edward Arnold, , 1983.

Nordenstreng, Kaarle, and Lauri Hannikainen, *The Mass Media Declaration of UNESCO,* Norwood, New Jersey: Ablex Publishing Corp., 1984.

Ochs, Martin, *The African Press,* The American University in Cairo, 1986.

Stevenson, Robert L., *Communication, Development and the Third World,* New York : Longman, 1988.

Truth From Below—The Emergent Press in Africa, XIX Article 19 Censorship Report, London: 1991.

Ungar, Sanford J., *Africa,* New York: Simon and Schuster, 1985.

Zimbabwe: Wages of War, New York: The Lawyers Committee for Human Rights, 1986.

Wiseman, John A., *Democracy in Black Africa,* New York: Paragon House Publishers, 1990.

NEWSPAPERS AND MAGAZINES

Africa Report Magazine
The Boston Globe
The Bulawayo Chronicle
Christian Science Monitor
The Daily Gazette
The Financial Gazette
The Guardian
The Herald
Horizon Magazine
The London Times

The Los Angeles Times
Moto
The New York Times
Parade Magazine
The Sunday Gazette
The Sunday Mail
The Sunday News
Sunday Times
The Washington Post

PART 2

ARABIC SPEAKING

CHAPTER 9

PRESS FREEDOM IN EGYPT

James J. Napoli

Hussein Y. Amin

The first newspaper in Egypt was started under Napoleon Bonaparte in 1798, and was intended primarily for the use of his occupying troops. The implied authoritarian control of the press was consistent with the authoritarian structure of government that prevailed both under the Ottoman and later, under Egyptian administrations. Agitation for a free press, democracy, and independence from British control continued up until the overthrow of King Farouk and the establishment of a socialist government. This chapter traces the censorship of the press in Egypt over time, the subsequent subjugation of the media under Nasser and the evolution toward greater press freedom under Sadat and Mubarak.

AN OVERVIEW OF EGYPT

The Arab Republic of Egypt is located in northeast Africa, facing the Mediterranean Sea on the north. It is bounded on the south by the Sudan, on the west by Libya and on the east by the Red Sea and Israel. Cairo is the largest city and the capital of the country. Alexandria is the second largest city. There are numerous smaller cities and villages scattered along the Nile River, with the population mostly engaged in agriculture. Most people are Muslim, though a substantial minority, about 15 percent, are Coptic Christians. The official language is Arabic. Egypt has been subject to many different colonial powers, including the Turks, French and English. In 1952, the Egyptian Revolution took place, and Egypt was ruled by an Egyptian president for the first time in its history.

The per capita income in Egypt is $710 per annum (*Europa World Year Book* 1996, 1105). One of the most serious threats to Egypt's economy is its exploding population, which is currently 63.5 million. The population is expected to reach 90 million by the year 2025. The country is also beset by a high rate of illiteracy, which is estimated to be 50 percent, and by problems in sanitation and health care.

Under the Permanent Constitution of 1971, Egypt adopted the name Arab Republic of Egypt, declaring a democratic socialist state based on the alliance of the people's working forces and guaranteeing the rights of individuals. The Constitution defines the structure and functions of the state, the basic components of society, public liberties, rights and obligations, the supremacy of the law, and the system of government.

The Executive: The president, nominated for a term of six years and eligible for unlimited renomination, is chief of state, head of government and supreme commander of the armed forces. The president appoints one or more vice-presidents, the prime minister, deputy prime ministers and state ministers, as well as important civil, military and diplomatic officers.

The Legislature: Over the last decade, Egypt has made steady progress toward becoming a multi-party democracy. The legislature is bicameral, consisting of the Shura Council and the People's Assembly. A minimum of 350 members of the People's Assembly, at least 50 percent of whom must be either workers or farmers, are elected for five-year terms by direct secret ballot on the basis of universal adult suffrage. Thirty additional seats are reserved for female representatives. The president may appoint, in addition, up to 10 members. While the president determines the main policy of the state and the cabinet supervises its implementation, ministerial responsibility to the Legislature is constitutionally defined. Established in 1980, the Shura Council is an advisory body of 210 members. Members are elected to the council, except for 70 members chosen by the president.

The five main political parties are the ruling National Democratic Party, the New Wafd, the Socialist Workers Party, the Liberal Socialist Party, and the Unionist Progressive Party (Amin 1986, 12).

The Judiciary: Egypt's legal system has been influenced not only by Islamic teaching, but also by the Napoleonic code. Sharia, or Islamic law, is the main source of legislation. The Constitution guarantees the independence of the Judiciary; legal decisions are the mandate of judges, as there is no jury system.

A Supreme Council, presided over by the president, supervises the affairs of the judicial organizations, although the highest judicial authority, with the power to determine the constitutionality of laws and regulations, is the Supreme Constitutional Court or the Court of Cassation.

Religious courts were abolished in 1956, and their functions were subsequently transferred to the unified national court system under the Council of State. Cases involving security are heard by the Supreme State Security Court, but members of the armed forces are subject to military law (Amin 1986, 13).

The press, which includes opposition newspapers, is described as free by the Mubarak government, but it is characterized by great ambivalence that expresses itself in a fawning semi-official press, licensed and handicapped. There are signs of tightening of the press laws. The broadcast media are entirely owned and controlled by government. Although some limited discussion of issues by government opponents is aired occasionally, both radio and TV remain essentially government propaganda mouthpieces. Rhetorical claims to free press lack credibility among the general public.

PRINT MEDIA

Egypt had no press, either figuratively or literally, until Napoleon Bonaparte invaded the country in 1798 in an attempt to disrupt the British Empire, and possibly to lay the groundwork for an attack against British India. Egypt was still loosely attached to the Ottoman Empire, an attachment that began in the early 16th century and was to extend to the outbreak of World War I. But the French invasion marked the beginning of a pronounced European influence synchronous with the modern era of Egyptian history. The newspaper started by Napoleon, *Courier de L'Egypte,* was deliberately propagandistic; it was to inform, instruct and sustain the morale of the French expeditionary force. Since Egypt had no printing presses, Napoleon brought his own to publish the *Courier* and a second newspaper in French (Rugh 1979, 6, 170). The next year, Napoleon ordered the fashioning of Arabic type, but it was never used for newspapers, and by 1801 the French were forced to evacuate Egypt after suffering heavy losses against Turkish-British forces. The rivalry between the French and British for predominant influence in Egypt continued, however, even to the present day in current jockeying for position by advocates of French and English languages in the Egyptian media.

It was not until 1828 that an indigenous Egyptian newspaper in Arabic was published by Egypt's modernizing ruler, Muhammad Ali, who also was the officially designated representative of the Ottoman government. He had direct control over everything published. In fact, as early as 1824, — after establishing the Bulaq Press as the government publisher — he had issued a decree prohibiting its printing of anything without his permission (Almaney 1974, 136). Although the first Arabic papers contained news and entertainment, they were intended from the start as official government publications that gave guidance to civil servants and provided authorized editorials to the literate public. This use of newspapers as official organs was not only consistent with the precedent established by the French in Egypt, but with the prevailing authoritarian political structures throughout the Arab world. The press began as a state, rather than a private, enterprise — in part because there was no tradition in the Middle East for routine discussion of political affairs in print. The division between the government and the governed was profound, and the role of the public was simply to obey their rulers, whose role was to act in the best interests of the community (Ayalon 1992, 266-267).

The great watershed for the Egyptian press as an independent player in Egypt's political life was the 1870s. During that period, for instance, what is now Egypt's semi-official newspaper and one of the Arab world's most important publications, *al-Ahram,* was established. A successor of Muhammad Ali who had been given the title of khedive by the Ottomans, Ismail Pasha, actively encouraged the founding of private and independent newspapers in the 1860s and 1870s — in part to secure public support for his efforts to gain greater political independence from Turkey and greater financial autonomy from the European powers (Vatikiotis 1992, 183). He watched the press carefully, however, and suppressed voices he deemed too critical of himself. The nationalistic and intellectual ferment of the press nevertheless helped provoke the deposition of Khedive Ismail in 1879 and the Egyptian army revolt of 1881, which was crushed by the British. Although the Ottomans remained the nominal rulers of Egypt for more than three decades to come, the occupying British maintained actual control from 1882 until the 1952 revolution. The British made many promises over the years to withdraw their troops, and in 1922 gave Egypt token independence, but it was 1956 before the last British soldier left the country.

The first legislation passed in Egypt specifically to control the press was the Publications and Newspapers Act of 1881, which provided prior government authorization of publishing and stipulated that each newspaper provide financial security. The law also formalized government authority to suspend or confiscate publications to safeguard order, public morality and religion, and it empowered the Minister of Interior to forbid the entry of foreign publications (State Information Service 1985, 8).

The virulent attacks against the British subsided for a short period — about a half dozen years — after 1882. Many journalists who had played an important part in the momentous events of the preceding years were for a time imprisoned or deported. But the focus of the newspapers, which was somewhat dispersed in Ismail's time, became sharper in subsequent years. After the accession of Khedive Abbas Hilmi in 1892, in particular, journalists attended to the critical question of the British occupation — both pro and con. The nationalist sentiment was best encapsulated by the slogan "Egypt for the Egyptians" (Kelidar 1993, 8). The khedive encouraged the anti-British campaign, which degenerated to a degree of vituperation characteristic of the gutter press. But the British, confident in the strength of their military presence and solicitous about the pro-British papers, generally refrained from taking action. The 1881 law was not applied harshly, though it continued to rankle the nationalists.

The press was used by such nationalists as Mustafa Kamel and Saad Zaghlul to keep up the pressure on the British, who suppressed a popular revolt in 1919. The British did grant limited independence to Egypt in 1922, and the 1923 constitution provided for press freedom, ensuring there would be no censorship or confiscation of newspapers by mere administrative acts. However, the clause guaranteed press freedom only "within the law," and its provisions could be suspended "in the interest of the social system." The 1936 constitution, which was in effect until 1952, retained the same ambiguous wording, "The press is free within the law," giving the party in power considerable leeway in controlling the press (Almaney 1974, 137). Press censorship was, for example, in effect during World War II and, again, for several years following the 1947 war with Israel. Nevertheless, during the reign of King Farouk, immediately before the revolution, the press operated with considerable freedom in criticizing government policies and attacking corruption, so long as it did not upset the uneasy triangle of power among the British, the palace and the liberal opposition Wafd Party. "In the time of (the) Farouk regime," observed the venerable journalist Mustafa Amin in a personal interview (Oct. 26 1992), "freedom of the press was better than we have now." It was also more competitive. Just before the revolution, there were 18 dailies in Cairo and 14 in Alexandria at a time when the populations were a fifth of what they are today (McFadden 1953, 18).

The development of the Egyptian press under the king, as well as its progress toward more fully realized freedom, came to an end, however, with the deposition of Farouk in 1952. At first, the new military government was in an unstable relationship with the press, with censorship being imposed and lifted a number of times. On March 7, 1954, Nasser lifted censorship for a month before clamping down again to stifle criticism of military controls by the Cairo press, which had launched a campaign for restoration of political freedoms (Dabbous 1993, 102). In subsequent years, Nasser consolidated his power and in 1960 nationalized the press, which thereby fell, along with other Egyptian institutions, under direct government control. Ownership of publishing houses, including Al-Ahram, Rose Al-Youssef, Al-Hilal and Akhbar Al-Yom, went to the Arab Socialist Union, initially called the National Union. But even before nationalization, Nasser had successfully purged the press of his worst critics, and — with the arguable exception of *al-Ahram* editor and Nasser confidant Mohamed Hassanein Heikal — independent voices in Egypt were silenced. By 1959, the International Press Institute could report, "There no longer exists in the Egyptian press a single newspaper which could really constitute a menace to the new regime, and one can go so far as to say that all of the press has become an instrument of propaganda for the regime" (Walker 1983, 173).

Besides imposing state ownership, centralization and censorship on the press, Nasser tapped into deep national tendencies that continued to shape the press to the present day. One was a mistrust of the West, which was seen as hostile to Arab nationalism, and of the Western media, which were viewed as an instrument of imperialism. He also exploited the assumption, which prevailed in the Arab world prior to and after Napoleon, that information control was a government prerogative. In his efforts to use the press for national mobilization and development, he also reasserted the authoritarian premise that government should maintain a monopoly over information and parcel it out as it deems appropriate. Sometimes what was parceled out was misinformation (Nasser 1990, 10). But President Nasser's tremendous personal popularity in Egypt and the Arab world seemed to overcome any dissatisfaction the public might have felt for the way the mass media were being used.

Nasser's successor, Anwar Sadat, generally expressed a more open attitude toward the press, as he did toward the economy and political opposition. But his affirmation of press freedom always came with a caveat. "I believe in a free press," he said, "but it must be a responsible press" (Ochs 1986, 131). In practice, Sadat's policy toward the press was ambivalent. In 1974, he removed censorship and other press restrictions, but retained state control of the media. When he authorized opposition parties, he also gave them the right to issue newspapers, but he constantly pulled them in and out of business. He personally liked and rewarded some journalists, but uncooperative journalists exasperated him and, in September 1981, he imprisoned hundreds of them and closed the opposition papers (Dabbous 1985, 8; Nasser 1990, 10-19; Ochs 1986, 131). His "free-press" policy effectively devolved to a situation in which the media were again viewed mainly as an instrument for managing public opinion. Sadat was killed in October 1981 by religious extremists.

Shortly after he became president, Hosni Mubarak veered toward democracy by releasing imprisoned opposition party leaders and lifting the ban on opposition papers. "I admire the Egyptian press," the president said in a speech before the People's Assembly on June 6, 1983. "I respect its writers. I am merely requesting that we appeal to reason and logic. Thank God there is no censorship and no restrictions" (State Information Service 1985, 19). Certainly there is little question that the press under Mubarak operates far more freely than under the two previous regimes and more freely than in most other Arab and African nations. Newspapers and magazines publish a wide range of views on many subjects, including criticism of public officials and even the president himself. The national and opposition press "vary in editorial policy and there are differences in political persuasion from one paper to another, in some cases considerable," observed one political scientist. "Make no mistake, the Egyptian daily and weekly newspapers presently (advocate) a spectrum of political opinion. On some controversial issues it can be very broad indeed" (Hill 1991, 3).

Nevertheless, the president retains sweeping powers to control the press, particularly under the emergency law of 1981 — a chronic subject of criticism in the opposition press. Further, Mubarak's public adherence to the principle of a free press remains a thin veneer for practices that continually vacillate between tolerance and repression, an aspect of what journalist Salah El Din Hafez (1993) called the "crisis" of the Egyptian press.

CONTEMPORARY PRESS CONTROLS

The press operates under the Egyptian Constitution of 1971, which prohibits censorship, and Law 148 of 1980, which states that the press "is an independent popular authority performing its mission freely in the service of the community" (Appendix B, Chapter I, Article 1). In theory, there is no press censorship, but in fact censorship permeates every aspect of expression in Egypt — not just newspapers, but broadcasting, theater, movies, magazines and books. The principal censoring organization is the Office of Censorship in the Ministry of Culture, but other organizations that exercise censoring authority include the Ministry of Interior, Ministry of Information, Al Azhar University's Publications Department (primarily over religious books), the State Information Service, the Office of the President for Information, the Egyptian Post Office and the Ministry of Transportation, Communications and Shipping (Ammar 1990, 66-68). Legislators have interpreted constitutional provisions regarding free expression in such a way as to impose severe restrictions on communication, including the press. In the view of the Egyptian Organization on Human Rights (EOHR), they have "invented a series of means and procedures that turn... press censorship (into) a stable and deep rooted fact that makes the continued recourse to a press censor or to emergency law unnecessary" (EOHR 1990, 5). If invoked in the interests of state security, however, the emergency law authorizes everything from pre-publication censorship to confiscation of publications to the closing down of publishing houses. In addition, the Egyptian Penal Code has a chapter, with 31 articles, on "crimes of the press." Under the code, journalists can be fined or imprisoned for insulting the

Egyptian president, the president of a foreign country, government officials, the armed forces or parliament. Bans on press coverage of certain sensitive topics, especially if they involve high government officials, and threats of confiscation are relatively commonplace. Many foreign publications, including Western and other Arab news magazines and newspapers, are generally available, but are stopped on occasion if they contain something government officials find objectionable.

Though not nearly as severe as under the Nasser and Sadat regimes, arrests and abuse of journalists also continue to take place under President Mubarak. From 1988 to 1990, for example, the EOHR (1990) reported that the homes of two reporters were raided by police, and their professional papers and books confiscated. Thirteen were assaulted by police while doing their jobs, and 23 others were detained in police stations or jails for periods ranging from 48 hours to seven months. Ten journalists were tortured.

Not to be discounted, either, are non-governmental sources of intimidation of journalists. The resurgence of radical Islamic groups in Egypt has been accompanied by a wave of terrorist attacks against police, government officials, members of the Coptic Christian minority and foreign tourists — which at least puts government human rights abuses in some perspective. Outspoken journalists viewed as unsympathetic to the extremists also have been threatened and targeted. The assassination of the prominent secularist writer and journalist Farag Fouda by religious extremists in 1992, in particular, brought to the surface concerns that other liberal-minded journalists could be in danger for their writings (Anis 1992, 6).

But the threat of violence by government or anyone else is not the primary controlling mechanism. The most effective limits on the press are far more subtle, since they are inherent in the organizational structure of the mass media. The national press — owned by government through the Consultative (Shura) Council — dominates the publishing scene. State authority over the press is exercised through the Higher Press Council, one third of whose members are appointed by the President; the ruling National Democratic Party effectively controls the elected membership. As a result, there is no need for direct censorship of the national press, since the Higher Press Council appoints the chief editors and the heads of the boards of directors of the national newspapers, who can ensure a compliant editorial policy. Except for a few luminaries in the profession, such as Mustafa Amin and Ahmed Baha al-Din, journalists are at the mercy of editors who retain their positions, and the many perquisites of those positions, by supporting the president. The council also oversees the Egyptian Press Syndicate, membership in which is required for anyone who wants to work as a professional journalist. And the board has the power to interrogate journalists or refer them to the state prosecutor, to grant them licenses to work with foreign newspapers and to approve requests for issuing new newspapers.

The most widely read national dailies are *al-Ahram (The Pyramids)* and *al-Akhbar (The News),* and the most widely read weekly is *Akhbar al-Yom (Today's News).* These and other government papers, which can take advantage of substantial financial and technical resources belonging to the state, maintain a virtual monopoly on the press. The state owns not only the principal publishing houses, but the sole Egyptian news service, the Middle East News Agency. In the abstract, private ownership of newspapers is allowed, but the legally required financial preconditions for starting a paper, as well as the difficulty in obtaining a license, are so onerous that no private newspaper has been established. For example, the law requires that a proposed daily newspaper maintain a level of capital at L.E. 250,000 (nearly $75,000), but that no individual or family member possess more than L.E. 500 (about $150) of the paper's capital.

The opposition press, which began publishing in 1976, consists of one major daily, *al-Wafd (The Delegates),* published by the liberal Wafd party. The other three major opposition parties are El Tagamo'a El Watani, a leftist party; El Ahrar, the socialist party; and El Am'al Alashtraki, the socialist labor party with Islamic influences. The most important of the opposition party weeklies are El Am'al's *al-Shaab (The People)* and El Tagamo'a El Watani's *al-Ahali (The Natives).* Other small party newspapers are published on an irregular basis, and there are some important political magazines, such as the muckraking *Rose al-Youssef.* The number of publications in Egypt has increased substantially since 1981, when there were only 77 licensed publications. Since then, another 285 publications of all types have been licensed, including general and special interest magazines, as well as magazines for hospitals, airports, companies, the military and various trades (Napoli and Amin, 1994).

The opposition press is dependent on government for newsprint and distribution. It has poor facilities and extremely limited financial resources, in part because the most important advertisers are in the public sector and use most of their advertising budget on government media. Further, the opposition press has restricted access to government information sources, which — together with a generally weak commitment to "objective" and substantiated reporting — has eroded its credibility among the public. Robert Springborg (1989) maintains that government has deliberately adopted "a strategy of seeking to discredit the opposition press by inducing it to commit excesses" (194). In fairness, however, neither the opposition nor the government press can be credited with balanced reportage, and some journalists on national newspapers also work for the opposition press. Mohamed Hassanein Heikal, in a personal interview on Dec. 14, 1992, observed that however desirable press freedom was, competent reporting by the Egyptian press would be "enough to keep me happy." What is the point, he asked, of allowing the press to express opinions "without telling me what's happening?"

Unlike his two predecessors, President Mubarak does not directly intervene in the operation of the press, though editors and leading columnists say they occasionally receive phone calls from the president responding to articles or just discussing issues. A Press Bureau connected with the Ministry of Information also conveys information and suggested guidelines to editors in the national press on a regular basis, and even opposition editors are kept in close contact with the government line. To keep the most vociferous critics from pushing too hard, especially since 1986 (the year of a widespread revolt among military conscripts), Mubarak and the minister of information also have launched scathing public attacks against what they consider press "excesses," effectively keeping the opposition press and annoying columnists off balance (Springborg, 1989, 194).

Further destabilizing the media environment is the ambivalence of government policy, which professes to support a free press, but unpredictably exerts pressure to control the flow of information. It can be argued — and we do in fact argue — that the futility of censorship is becoming ever more apparent as the number of information sources grows in an expanding and increasingly available global and domestic media network. But the Egyptian government persists in efforts to manage the media, including the press, in a manner more consistent with its Nasserist, authoritarian roots than with current realities.

Recent history provides numerous examples that suggest government confusion in handling both its Arabic and foreign-language media. One occurred in October 1993, when President Mubarak, in a referendum the government promoted domestically and internationally as democratic, "won" a third six-year term with nearly a 95 percent approval rating. The government indeed seemed to have internalized its democratic rhetoric by tolerating a pre-election front-page article in *al-Wafd* opposing the referendum. Almost simultaneous with the election results, however, Labor Party leader Helmi Murad and two journalists for *al-Shaab* were arrested for articles published in the paper bitterly critical of the president. The party secretary-general, Adel Hussein, and the paper's chief editor, Magdi Hussein, were questioned. The crackdown raised such an outraged reaction among members of the Press Syndicate that even Ibrahim Nafie, head of the Syndicate and editor of *al-Ahram,* had to express his "grave concern."

Syndicate members also reacted strongly to proposed legislation — proposed by whom was never made clear — that would have given the government still more control over the organization. It would have tightened admission to the Syndicate, made it tougher for free-lancers to write for publication, stacked the organization with generally pro-government radio and television workers and prescribed a range of punishments for journalists who attacked government officials or who violated "honor" (Proposal 1993). Mubarak distanced himself from that proposal, as he did from an earlier proposal to stiffen libel laws (Negus, 1993).

Foreign journalists, who had already been complaining about

government harassment, also were quick to report the retraction under government pressure of the November 1993 issue of an English-language magazine, *Cairo Today,* because of an article about human rights in Egypt. Another English-language publication based in Cairo, the weekly *Middle East Times,* also had several issues banned in 1993. Among the offending stories were one that referred to a report of an alleged car thief who was reported to have been injected with human excrement by police and another on government efforts to remove politics from the classroom. The editors, who were told they should produce more positive stories to help counteract negative publicity about terrorist shootings and bombings, which had had a devastating effect on tourism, eventually agreed to submit sensitive articles to the appropriate ministries before publication. Among the stories the newspaper did not receive approval to print was an account of the *Cairo Today* censorship case (Napoli, 1994, 49).

BROADCAST MEDIA

Radio: Radio broadcasting was started in Egypt in the early 1920s by amateurs, such as Ahmed Sadek El Gawahergi, who began wireless stations (Al Wakaea 1926, 8). Reportedly over 100 amateur wireless stations began operations during this period, including Radio Farouk, Radio Abou El Holle (Sphinx) and Radio Sabou (ASBU 1971, 17). But broadcasting was in confusion because the new medium was proliferating more quickly than regulations could be developed (El Halwani 1982, 70). In 1931, the government decreed that all stations be closed.

The number of receivers at that time did not exceed 4,000. Most radio set owners were foreigners and Egyptians in the highest socioeconomic class. The announcements and programs were in Arabic, English and French (El Sayed 1981, 61).

On July 15, 1932, Tawfik Dous, the minister of telecommunications, proposed to the Council of Ministers that the Marconi Co. be given responsibility for the construction and operation of a State Radio Service. A week later the Council approved, and government signed a 10-year renewable contract with Marconi (El Halwani and El Abed 1987, 305).

The radio service started broadcasting on May 31, 1934, reaching the Delta, Suez and some parts of Upper Egypt. The company was not concerned about wide coverage, since the receivers were concentrated in urban areas where people could afford the high cost of radio sets and where electricity was available (El Sayed 1981, 64).

The contract with Marconi was renewed in 1943, but it required a more active role for Egyptians. It specified that 75 percent of monthly paid employees and 90 percent of hourly paid employees had to be Egyptians. However, this contract was terminated on March 4, 1947, two years before its expiration date, partly in response to the nationalist movement after World War II (El Sayed 1981, 65). That year the Ministry of Social Affairs took over the service from Marconi, while the Ministry of Telecommunications was given responsibility for its technical facilities.

On July 23, 1949, the service was given independent status under a 13-member board headed by the prime minister. The law stipulated that the service would be impartial and prohibited it from propagating the principles of any political party or getting involved in partisan disputes unless reporting parliamentary debates. A news department was formed and correspondents were assigned to cover local and international news. This was a step forward in Egyptianization since the service was no longer dependent entirely on newspapers and foreign news agencies (Boyd 1993, 19). The 1949 law remained in effect until the 1952 Revolution (El Halwani and El Abed 1987, 322).

Radio remained under the control of government, but it was reorganized to increase its effectiveness by the Free Officers, who recognized its potential importance to the revolution. It could be used to directly reach the people with the new regime's messages, such as the news that the kingdom had become a republic. Radio became the "voice of the revolution" (Boyd 1993, 120).

Nasser quickly realized that radio could be used as an arm of government not only in Egypt, but throughout the Arab world. The medium came under the ownership and tight control of the government, which used it to bypass the literacy barrier to reach the public (Rugh 1979, 166). Radio stations were expanded and new services established, including the General Program, the National

European program, the Sudan Program, the Foreign Language and Beamed Services, the Voice of the Arabs, the Alexandria Local Service, the Palestine Broadcast, the Second Program, the People's Program, the Middle East Program, the Holy Koran Broadcast, the Musical Program and the Youth Broadcast.

The General Program, previously called the Main Program, was known as Radio Cairo in other Arab countries. Its main goal was "the supportive maintenance of the morale of the audience to stay ready and alert for battle against Israel and awareness of the facts, dimensions, goals, and means of psychological warfare, and strengthening the relationship between the masses and the active army front" (Boyd 1993, 21).

The National European program, which also existed before the revolution, was broadcast in Italian, Greek, and German, in addition to English and French, after 1952 (ERTU 1992, 86).

The intent of establishing the Sudan Program, or service, was to strengthen relations between Egypt and the Sudan (ERTU 1992, 88). And the Foreign Language and Beamed Service started broadcasting in 1953 in 34 languages to reach other areas of the world that President Nasser wanted to address (ERTU 1992, 86).

The Voice of the Arabs was first broadcast on July 4, 1953, transmitting daily for 30 minutes. The broadcast was expanded in 1954 to seven hours per day. The main goal of the broadcast was to represent Arab unity. It was the best known and most widely listened to broadcast in the Arab world, although its effectiveness suffered because of its misleading coverage of the 1967 war. The incident not only damaged the service and Egyptian Radio in general, but by eroding people's trust in the truth of its broadcasts, it instilled in the public a preference for foreign services, such as the British Broadcasting Corporation (Boyd 1993, 29).

The Alexandria Local Service started on July 26, 1954. The service, which broadcast eight hours daily, was the first Egyptian service to originate outside Cairo. It was intended to reflect the character of the region (ERTU 1992, 78).

The Palestine Broadcast Service, established to promote the Palestinian cause, was first broadcast as an independent service on Oct. 29, 1960, with a daily 30-minute broadcast. It was later expanded to six hours transmitted in three periods (ERTU 1992, 88).

The Second Program began broadcasting on May 5, 1957, for three and a half hours every day.

The People's Program was first broadcast on July 29, 1959, intendedly to combine the different specialized programs that were included in the General Program before and after the revolution. The service's programs were aimed at promoting national development (El Halwani 1981, 81).

The Middle East Program began on May 31, 1964. It was a commercial station, since it allowed paid commercial advertising (El Halwani 1982, 82). The Holy Koran broadcast, which had its first transmission March 29, 1964, included recitations of the Holy Koran and religious discussions. The Musical Program was first broadcast in March 1968. And the Youth Broadcast service, begun in 1975, was broadcast in the afternoon to reach students with educational, political, and social messages designed for that age group (El Halwani 1982, 82).

Unlike his early relationship with the print media, Nasser's attitude toward radio broadcasting was clear. The revolutionary government realized the power and influence of the medium on public opinion and attitude formation, and immediately opted for censorship, propaganda and more stringent government controls. Most radio services and programs were politicized, promoting a favorable image of the president (Head 1974, 20).

Under Sadat, too, government maintained tight control over the medium, particularly after a 1971 incident when Vice-President Ali Sabry attempted a coup by trying to wrest control of the radio and television building. The rebellious group surrounded the building with police, who had orders to keep Sadat from entering. Several top broadcast officials who were involved were immediately replaced when the coup failed (Head 1974, 20).

In 1971, the Egyptian Radio and Television Union (ERTU) was formed. According to Law No. 13, issued in 1979 and modified by Law No. 223 in 1989, ERTU has the sole authority to establish and own radio and television stations in Egypt (ERTU 1994). ERTU exercises complete control over any material broadcast by radio or television.

On April 1, 1981, the broadcasting network concept was introduced. Egyptian Radio comprises seven networks: the main network, the regional network, the educational network, the religious network, the commercial network, the Arab network, and the beamed service network.

Television: The first proposal to create a television broadcasting service in Egypt came in 1951. The proposal, made by a French radio and television company, was not taken seriously by government, however, and the idea was not implemented (Omar 1964, 55).

Nasser became interested in establishing television in Egypt in 1954, two years after the revolution. He wanted it as a medium for mass propaganda, but this proposal was not immediately implemented (Page 1977, 43).

Egyptian Television started broadcasting on July 21, 1960, the eighth anniversary of the 1952 revolution. The broadcast began with verses from the Holy Koran followed by a speech from Nasser on the celebration. Initially, it broadcast five hours a day, but the period was reduced to three and a half hours after the celebration (Khamis 1989, 17).

From the very beginning, the most important source of programming for Egyptian Television was films, encompassing romance, slapstick comedy and politics. News was also broadcast, solely in Arabic at the beginning but later in English and French as well. Foreign programs, including British and American programs, were also used by Egyptian Television until the 1967 war.

After Egypt's defeat, the number of foreign programs broadcast over Egyptian Television decreased substantially, since diplomatic relations between Egypt and Great Britain, as well as between Egypt and the United States, were broken. Programs from the Soviet Union were substituted. This situation continued until the 1973 war. Television then reoriented itself toward the West to reflect the government's changing international political orientation.

*Channel 1:*Television service began with one channel, which broadcast three hours daily. The channel was a comprehensive service, which included news, variety programs, children's programs, sports, serials and films. The channel was also known as the Main Program and the First Program. It covered the Nile Delta and the Nile Valley as far as Assiut. It also covered Aswan, Port Said and Suez. By January 1977, the service covered all of the populated areas of the country.

Channel 2: The Second Channel, also known as the Second Program, began broadcasting one year after the first channel in 1962. Broadcasting soon increased to 13 hours a day, 10 hours on the first channel and three on the second channel. The channel was designed specifically for urban areas, featuring programs that would appeal to a sophisticated, educated audience (Amin 1986). By 1977, the Second Channel reached 70 percent of the populated area and covered all of it before the end of 1978.

Both channels One and Two are local networks, the only local networks in Egypt. Initially programmed separately, since 1976 the schedules have been coordinated to reduce duplication.

Channel 3: Established in October 1962, Channel Three was designed mainly for the foreign community. Most programs were imported films and tapes. Channel Three was closed after the 1967 war, and its programs were transferred to channels One and Two. The channel was reopened and then closed again after Nasser's death for a period of one year. After reopening again, the channel was later closed for economic and political reasons.

The current Channel Three began broadcasting on Oct. 6, 1985, for two hours daily. The addition of this channel increased the number of overall broadcast hours of the three channels to 25. Channel Three's broadcast was later increased to five hours. The channel, whose transmission only reaches Cairo, is noted for its discussion programs on the problems of average Egyptians.

Channel 4: Channel 4 is a local station that reaches Ismailia, Port Said and Suez. It began its trial broadcast in October 1988 in Ismailia, and its first official broadcast was at the end of May 1989 (Gouili 1993, 5).

Channel 5: Channel 5 is another local station. It began broadcasting in December 1990, currently for five hours daily. The channel's broadcasts reach Alexandria and surrounding areas only (Gouili 1993, 4).

The Egyptian Space Network: The Egyptian Space Network (SpaceNet) started broadcasting Dec. 12, 1990, and averages 13 hours of programming a day. Programs include news, sports, entertainment, religion, education and culture. Transmissions reach Arab countries as well as some areas in Africa, Europe and Asia. Egypt uses the ARABSAT to transmit its programs (Amin 1992, 15-20).

CENSORSHIP AND BROADCASTING

The first law defining the function of the Office of Censorship was issued in 1975, although the Office of Censorship itself was established in 1911. The law stated that every cinematic, theatrical or musical work must pass through the censor for licensing prior to being broadcast. According to this law, if a film was produced before being issued a license, both the producer and director could face imprisonment for a period of not less than one month and not more than six months, as well as a fine of not less than L.E. 200 (Saad 1970, 287-302).

Under the law, the censor should exercise his authority by ordering the removal of any scene that conflicts with religions, national security or official government positions on issues, such as economic policy or foreign relations, and social ethics and traditional norms. During the 1960s, when the Egyptian government nationalized most production companies, the law became irrelevant.

On August 17, 1983, the Board of Trustees of ERTU issued a number of rules and regulations defining the role of the Central Administration for Revision and Scripts. ERTU stated that all materials and programs must be revised by the censors before they are broadcast, thereby ensuring compliance with the country's general policy and national goals. It also said the censors could revise the artistic, moral, and social content of scripts, as well as the form of narration and the broadcast content. ERTU documents indicated that scripts must be revised by the censorship authority to ensure conformity to the general order, general ethics, and the society's religious and spiritual values, to protect youth from "deviation" and to prevent negative statements about religions or religious beliefs (ERTU 1983, 119). Any materials that might have a negative effect on work or workers and/or encourage "deviation" or lead to frustration would be prohibited. ERTU also asserted that broadcasting of any material that encouraged the use of violence, aided in spreading crime or was sexually provocative must be avoided. These rules were altered later to form the ERTU Code of Ethics.

Criticism of the government's handling of film and radio and television broadcasts, particularly over the question of creativity, has been continuous. Egyptian producers and directors argue that censorship kills the spirit of creativity. It has become a problem that they face in every stage of preparing the movie. Monieb El Shafie, head of the Chamber of Cinema Production, has commented that censorship has become a monster that "rips films up under the false justification of protecting the public. Also, members of the censorship unit are not specialists and know nothing about art. In the end, the real victim is the quality of Egyptian cinema" (Akhbar al-Yom 1993, 8).

Tawfik Saleh, an Egyptian producer, observed that in the 1960s there was much more freedom of expression than there is now. In addition, the censorship unit operated differently. Today, he said, each censor makes up his own standards and implements them without the other censors' knowledge (Akhbar al-Yom 1993, 8).

Scriptwriter Waheed Hamid said the censor was "a conscience, not an authority. I recall that one of the censors at the Radio and Television Union refused an advertisement for a foreign film because the heroine tells one of her neighbors, 'I am pregnant.' The censor said that 'pregnant' is an obscene word that implied sex and taboo. They refuse this, but allow the other ads that depict the Egyptian women in an insulting image. When I write, I don't keep the censor in mind. I am already bound by my own standards" (Akhbar al-Yom 1993, 8).

Coverage in Egyptian newspapers of the controversy over censorship ended with the government's response: more censorship. The government formed the Higher Council for Censorship (Akhbar al-Yom 1994, 1).

NEWS: DOMESTIC CONFRONTATION, INTERNATIONAL COMPETITION

ERTU news departments have faced a good deal of criticism for their weaknesses in gathering and presenting news for radio and television. The weaknesses stem from the fact that, as government departments, they are bound by government rules, codes and procedures in reporting news involving the Egyptian government. These restrictions — imposed by government to ensure control — have driven audiences away from the national service (Boyd and Amin 1993, 77-87). Because of the question of credibility and the failure of domestic radio to cover news objectively, many Egyptian listeners have tuned in to foreign radio broadcasts, especially in times of crisis. Foreign radio services that have programs in Arabic, such as the British Broadcasting Corporation (BBC), the Voice of America (VOA), and Radio Monte Carlo, have developed a broad listenership in Egypt (Rugh 1979, 149).

The first domestic challenge in television broadcasting that ERTU had to face was Cable News Egypt (CNE), a joint venture with ERTU to receive and re-transmit Cable News Network International (CNNI). Many professionals envisioned ERTU pulling the plug on any controversial report on the Middle East or on any report with material not conforming to the nation's perceived cultural norms (Foote and Amin 1992, 18). Fathi El Bayoumi, chairman of ERTU, acknowledged that there would be times when CNN reports would clash sharply with the government party line and that Egyptian Television would immediately respond. No CNN broadcast has been censored partly because it is technically impossible to censor on the air, but also because the licensing agreement explicitly prohibits censorship (Foote and Amin 1992, 18-19).

The second challenge facing ERTU was the granting of permission for direct broadcast satellite dishes to be brought into the country. Since then, many Egyptians, especially from the upper middle and upper class, have bought or leased satellite dishes that allow them to receive foreign news, information and opinion through a large number of international television channels (Boyd and Amin 1993, 2). One of the most popular channels in Egypt is the Turkish channel, because it broadcasts semi-nudity on some of its programs. This situation prompted the governor of Damietta to ban satellite dishes in public places. Access to international television also raised many questions about opposition parties' access to electronic media to express their political opinions and represent their viewpoints on Egyptian current affairs programs. Unlike Nasser and Sadat, who never granted opposition parties access to broadcast media, Mubarak has begun to extend to them limited access.

CONCLUSION

Egypt rightly considers itself the media center of the Arab world. It produces films, television programs, radio broadcasts, newspapers, books and magazines that are widely distributed throughout the region. But Egypt also is a recipient of a vast amount of information and entertainment from the rest of the world, and it is becoming increasingly difficult for government to maintain the level of control over information it once enjoyed. A story banned in the national press may still turn up in the opposition press or in other Arabic and English newspapers and news magazines that make their way into the country. If it is important enough, it will be aired on foreign radio and television broadcasts, which, unlike foreign print media, cannot be stopped at the border.

The practiced socialist impulse to manage information is becoming not only more ineffective, but more damaging to government in a period of expanding global communications. As in 1967, when the Voice of the Arabs was caught in a blatant lie, government credibility continually suffers every time its media try to repress information that is readily available from many other sources. The long-term impact of losing credibility can be debilitating to government's professed efforts toward a more fully democratic political system, and even toward maintaining its own stability.

Egypt has several reasonable options for the future, but they all imply liberating the media from the days when they were considered mere propaganda tools for government. It can relax controls on the national print and broadcast media to enable it to report on public affairs with more balance, objectivity and thoroughness. That option needs to be taken, in any case, to prevent the media from becoming increasingly marginalized by their competition with the opposition press and, more significantly, the expanding foreign media. Further, it can move toward privatization of the media to multiply the number of domestic sources of news and information without pre-defining them as "opposition." But the government first must abandon the idea that it has the power to control the public by controlling the press, and that a free press will invariably work against its interests.

REFERENCES

Akhbar al-Yom. (27 November 1993): 8.
Akhbar al-Yom. A Higher Council of Censorship, (15 January 1994): 1.
Almaney, A. Government Control of the Press in the United Arab
    Republic. in Alan Wells, ed. *Mass Communications, a World
    View*. Palo Alto: Mayfield Publishing Co., 1974: 135-148.
Al Wakaea El Misria. Unheadlined news item. 1. 8. 1926.
Ammar, S. *Censorship of English-language Books in Egypt*.
    Unpublished master's thesis. Cairo: The American University in
    Cairo, 1990.
Amin, H. *An Egypt-Based Model for the Use of Television in
    National Development*. Unpublished doctoral dissertation.
    Columbus: The Ohio State University, 1986.
Amin, H. The Development of SpaceNet and Its Impact. in Ray E.
    Weisenborn, ed. *Media in the Midst of War: From Cairo to the
    Global Village*. Cairo: Adham Center Press, 1992: 15-20.
Anis, M. Death by extremism. *Al-Ahram Weekly* 11-17 June 1992, 6.
Arab States Broadcasting Union.*The United Arab Republic: TV*. Cairo:
    Arab States Broadcasting Union, 1971.
Ayalon, A. *Sihafa:* The Arab Experiment in Journalism. *Middle Eastern
    Studies* 28. 2, 1992: 258-280.
Boyd, D. *Broadcasting in the Arab World: A Survey of the Electronic
    Media in the Middle East*. Ames: Iowa State University Press,
    1993.
Boyd, D. and H. Amin. The Development of Direct Broadcast Television
    to and within the Middle East. Conference Paper. Kansas City:
    The Association for Education in Journalism and Mass
    Communication, 1993.
Boyd, D. and H. Amin. The Impact of Video Cassette Recorders on
    Egyptian Film and Television Consumption Patterns. *The
    European Journal of Communication* 18. 1, 1993: 77-87.
Dabbous, S. The Role of the Press in Egypt's Democratic Experiment.
    Conference paper. New Orleans: Middle East Studies Association,
    Nov. 1985.
Dabbous, S. Nasser and the Egyptian Press. in Charles Tripp, ed.
    Contemporary Egypt: Through Egyptian Eyes. London:
    Routledge, 1993: 100-121.

Egyptian Organization for Human Rights. *Freedom of Opinion and Expression in Egypt.* Report. Cairo: Egyptian Organization for Human Rights, 1990.

Egyptian Radio and Television Union. *Egyptian Radio and Television Yearbook.* Cairo: Egyptian Radio and Television Union, 1992.

El Halwani, M. *El Izaat El Arabiah (Arab Broadcasting).* Cairo: Dar El Fiker El Arabi, 1982.

El Halwani, M. and Atef El Abed. *Anzemat El Izaat El Arabiah (Arab World Broadcasting Systems).* Cairo: The Arab Publication House, 1987.

El Sayed, S.M. *Policy-Making in the Egyptian Broadcasting System: A Case Study Analysis.* Unpublished doctoral dissertation. Madison: University of Wisconsin Press, 1981.

Europa World Year Book. Europa Publications 1, 1996: 1105.

Foote, J.S. and H. Amin. Global Television News in Developing Countries: CNN's Expansion to Egypt. Conference paper. Montreal: The Association for Education in Journalism and Mass Communication, Aug. 1992.

Gouili, S.A. *Agenda Setting and Local Issues on Egyptian Regional Television Broadcasting.* Unpublished master's thesis. Cairo: The American University in Cairo, 1993.

Hafez, S. *Ahzan Horriet El Sahafa (Anguish of Press Freedom).* Cairo: Al-Ahram Center for Translation and Publishing, 1993.

Head, S.W. *Broadcasting in Africa — a Continental Survey of Radio and Television.* Philadelphia: Temple University Press, 1974.

Hill, E. Politics and the Popular Press of Egypt. Conference paper. Washington: Middle East Studies Association, Nov. 1991.

Kelidar, A. The Political Press in Egypt, 1882-1914. in Charles Tripp, ed. *Contemporary Egypt: Through Egyptian Eyes.* London: Routledge, 1993: 1-21.

Khamis, S. *A Comparative Study on the News Credibility of Egyptian Television and Newspapers.* Unpublished master's thesis. Cairo: The American University in Cairo, 1989.

McFadden, T.J. *Daily Journalism in the Arab States.* Columbus: Ohio State University Press, 1953.

Napoli, J. Journalists in Egypt Fear Return to "Bad Old Days" of Strict Censorship. *Washington Report on Middle East Affairs,* Jan. 1994: 49.

Napoli, J. and H. Amin, The Specialized Magazine Trend in Egypt: Development and Consequences. Conference paper. Miami: University of Miami Eleventh Annual Intercultural and International Communication Conference, Feb. 1994.

Nasser, M.K. Egyptian Mass Media Under Nasser and Sadat. *Journalism Monographs* 124. Columbia, S.C.: Association for

Education in Journalism and Mass Communication, Dec. 1990.

Negus, S. Government Backs Down on Libel Law. *Middle East Times,* Egypt Edition, 14-20 Sep. 1993: 2.

Ochs, M. The African Press. Cairo: The American University in Cairo Press, 1986.

Omar, F. *El Television Fi El Goumhouria El Arabiah El Motahedeh wa El Alam (Television in the United Arab Republic and the World).* Cairo: The National House for Printing and Publication, 1964.

Page, D.C. *A Comparative Analysis of Television and Broadcast Systems.* Unpublished doctoral dissertation. Ann Arbor: The University of Michigan, 1977.

Proposal: Press Syndicate Law. Cairo: Egyptian Press Syndicate, 1993. (unpublished).

Rugh, W.A. *The Arab Press. Syracuse: Syracuse* University Press, 1979.

Saad, A.M. *Tarekh El Cinema El Mesriah (The History of the Egyptian Cinema).* Cairo: Al-Ahram Publishing House, 1970.

Springborg, R. *Mubarak's Egypt, Fragmentation of the Political Order.* Boulder & London: Westview Press, 1989.

State Information Service. The Egyptian Press: Laws and Regulations. Conference paper. Cairo: International Press Institute, Mar. 1985.

Vatikiotis, P.J. *The History of Modern Egypt.* London: Weidenfeld and Nicolson, 1991.

Walker, M. *Powers of the Press.* New York: Adama Books, 1983.

CHAPTER 10

PRESS CONTROLS AND THE POST-COLONIAL SUDANESE PRESS

Mohammed Galander

William J. Starosta

On 1 January 1956 Sudan emerged as the first independent African state south of the Sahara. Under the 1956 Transitional Constitution, the country adopted a "Westminster" type of parliamentary democracy, and granted press freedom which should be "observed within the limit of the law" (Salih, M.A., 1975, p. 32). Under the post-colonial liberal system, the number and variety of newspapers and magazines published within the Sudan was, by all standards, remarkable. In 1951, a country with a literacy rate of only five percent published seven daily and 14 weekly Arabic newspapers, a daily and a weekly in English, and a weekly Greek paper (Sterling, 1972). On the eve of independence, the country produced nine daily and seven weekly "intensely partisan" newspapers (Rugh, 1979, p. 58).

The "intensely partisan" post-colonial press leaned toward political parties and functioned as "party-affiliated" newspapers. The existence of party-affiliated newspapers has since become a feature of Sudanese media, and has affected much of their objectivity. The press of the post-colonial democratic period consisted of three types: the party-owned, the non-party, and the party-affiliated. There were six non-party newspapers, five party-owned papers, and three party affiliated papers. Several weekly tabloids also existed, but these appeared irregularly due to financial difficulties (Salih, M.A., 1975). Of these *al-Akhbar* (the News), *al-Nas* (People), *al-Sabah al-Jadid* (New Morning), and *Anba' al-Sudan* (Sudan News) are noteworthy.

The party-affiliated group consisted of privately owned newspapers and magazines which were not owned by political parties but were constantly expressing distinctively partisan views on behalf of the political party of their choice. *Al-Sahara* was one of these papers which some scholars referred to as "a cautious advocate of Marxism" (Sid Ahmed, 1984, p. 51). Another party-affiliated newspaper was *Sawt al-Mara'ah* (Voice of Woman), the first female magazine which addressed the social issues of Sudanese women. Under the editorship of Fatima Ahmed Ibrahim, a famous communist, Sawt al-Mara'ah gained a wide reputation as another pro-Communist party-affiliated magazine (Salih, M.A., 1975; Sid Ahmed, 1984).

The National Government's Attitude Toward the Press

Because the press had contributed remarkably toward independence, it earned high public admiration in the post-colonial era. Journalists, especially veterans of the nationalism movement, garnered public respect and became celebrities (Sid Ahmed, 1984). The press, in such a positive atmosphere, flourished and became a tool of public education, and a true reflector of public opinion. The post-colonial national governments treated the press in accordance with this status and, as a result, few confrontations, if any, occurred between the government and the press during this period.

The only instance of confrontation happened when the government of Abdalla Khallil, in 1958, advised the press to refrain from publishing "statements that might restrain relations with Egypt" (Cookson et al., 1964, p. 200), at a time when the government was preparing to negotiate highly controversial trade and irrigation agreements with Egypt. A highly self-confident press rebuffed such advice and the president of the Press Association bluntly rejected the request, and threatened to defend the constitutional rights of the press (Cookson et al., 1964).

ATTITUDE OF THE PRESS TOWARD THE GOVERNMENT

As a free press of a nation taking its first steps on the democratic road, not only did the post-colonial press inform, educate, and entertain, but it also advised, guided, and helped to maintain national unity and to foster nation-building. The generation of post-colonial journalists handled such responsibility well (Babiker, 1985; Sa'id, 1989; Salih, M.A., 1975; Salih, M.M., 1971). Sa'id (1989) summarized the achievements of the press as follows:

> The press played a remarkable role in helping political parties translate freedom into a better life quality for the people. It critically addressed the inadequacies of the government, revealed the wrong and corrupt practices, and steadfastly stood against all malicious abuse of power. The press was a true inspirer of the people toward the achievement of progress in the country. (p. 6)

Assessing the performance and role of the press in the post-colonial era, Mohammed Ali Salih (1975) also spoke well of the non-party press. Based on the analysis of Salih and Sa'id, the authors drew the following conclusions about the performance of the three categories of the press:

1. *The Party-owned press:* Such papers largely reflected political bickering and posturing. They "leaned toward sensationalism and were overwhelmed in their coverage by political rivalry, accusations, undermining of opponents, and defending leaders and parties" (Sa'id, 1989, p. 7). In the party-owned press the ethi-

cal standards of the press "were jeopardized . . . Discussion of political differences sometime led to personal accusations and counter accusations and, in a country where the press was both informative and educational, the impact on the readers was considerable" (Salih, M.A., 1975, p. 45).

2. *Party-affiliated newspapers:* These reflected the same coverage style of the party-owned press. *Al-Saraha's* incessant attacks on the Ansar sect and on its leader in 1957 provide a good example of such party bickering in the party-affiliated press. *Al-Saraha's* anti-Ansar attitude led some members of the sect to attack the editor of the paper, Abdalla Rajab, and to literally break his arm (Salih, M.A., 1975).

3. *Non-Party newspapers:* The non-party papers were generally what scholars have come to consider the "objective" newspapers (Sa'id, 1989, p. 6; Salih, M.A., 1975, pp. 43-44). The non-party press focused mainly on major issues such as "national unity and development" (Salih, M.A., 1975, p. 45). Political crises received due attention from the non-party press, which stressed the need for a rational approach to sensitive political and social issues and the need to preserve independence, national unity, and democracy (Salih, M.A., 1975). Total respect for political, social, and religious leaders prevailed in the press, which saw in these leaders symbols of social cohesion and unity.

ABBOUD'S MILITARY REGIME: INDEPENDENT PRESS COMES UNDER CONTROL

Political instability, civil war, and political bigotry overwhelmed the post-colonial parliamentary period of 1956-58 and, eventually, led to a military takeover in November of 1958. The new regime banned political parties and suspended the party-owned newspapers; but it allowed the private press to resume publishing after a brief suspension (Sa'id, 1989). Party newspapers including *al-Nil* of the Umma party, *al-Alam* of the NUP, *Sawt al-Sudan* of the PDP, *al-Midan* of the Communist party, *al-Akhwan al-Muslimon* of the Muslim Brothers party, and *al-Istiglal* (Independence) of the Socialist Republican party ceased to exist (Salih, M.A., 1975). The non-party newspapers of *al-*

Ayam, al-Ra'i al-Am, and *al-Sudan al-Jadid* continued to publish as dailies, and *al-Akhbab, al-Nas, Anba al-Sudan,* and *al-Saraha* as weeklies.

Although General Abboud's regime enjoyed relative stability, it faced opposition from a broad spectrum of the population as it curtailed freedom of association and expression, and took several steps toward limiting press freedom. Despite such increased repression, the era witnessed both qualitative and quantitative improvements in Sudanese journalism. In an effort to strengthen its propaganda, the government improved the national radio station's transmission power and opened, in 1962, a television station, one of the few of its kind in Africa at the time. The military regime established the first government-owned daily newspaper *al-Thawra* (the Revolution) which was unpopular but qualitatively unmatched by any of the independent papers because of the unlimited resources available to it through the government. As to training, the government's foreign policy enabled many journalists to receive, for the first time, proper professional and academic training abroad (Salih, M.A., 1975). Even within the independent press, major improvements occurred. In 1961, Abdel Rahman Mukhtar launched *al-Sahafa* (the Press). The paper introduced Sudanese readers to a new kind of format, "Colored headlines, wireless photo services, and a degree of sensationalism" (Salih, M.A., 1975). A variety of weekly and monthly literary, political, and sports magazines also flourished during this period: *al-Sabah al-Jadid* (the New Morning), *al-Quissa* (the Story), *al-Shabab wa al Riada* (Youth and Sports), and a host of specialized tabloids, magazines, and journals turned newsstand kiosks into a flourishing business in the country.

THE MILITARY REGIME'S ATTITUDE TOWARD THE PRESS

The regime began to curb press freedom three days after its inception, when General Abboud told the Sudanese press that "the press is free, but we will not allow you to criticize the government. We want to serve the people sincerely, so let us work quietly, without any disturbance" (Salih, M.A., 1975, p. 49). This statement from the new military authority summarized the thinking of the new military regime and exemplified the way in which the new authority conceptualized the role of the press.

The independent newspapers resumed publishing under clearly defined conditions which included "refraining from publishing what may defame, debase, or undermine public confidence in the regime; incite public contempt and threaten security and order; or insult foreign friendly countries and leaders" (Sa'id, 1989, p. 6).

A year later the government amended the Press Act of 1930 so as to allow the administration the opportunity to deal with the press from a security perspective. The amendment gave the Minister of Interior the upper hand in issuing licenses and appointing journalists to a committee that advised him on the press (Salih, M.A., 1975). The government, under a new provision of the Act, began to routinely send "top secret" letters to the editors advising them not to publish certain types of news (for example, student strikes), sometimes even ordering them to fire journalists (Salih, M.A., 1975, p. 35).

Closing down newspapers for violation of the law became more commonplace under Abboud's military regime. During a six-year period, the government twice closed *al-Ayam* for six months in 1959 for criticizing the trial of trade union members in front of military courts, and for a year in 1962 for criticizing foreign diplomats. The government also closed *al-Sahafa* twice; for six months in 1962 for alleging the existence of slave trade, and for a year in 1963, for demanding the restoration of democracy (Salih, M.A., 1975). *Al-Sudan al-Jadid* newspaper, and *al-Sabah al-Jadid* magazine also experienced suspension for shorter periods in the early years of the military regime.

Growing opposition in 1961 led the military to contemplate nationalizing the press. Following the return of General Abboud from Egypt (whose press was nationalized the previous year) a proposition appeared for the nationalization of the press in Sudan. "The Sudanese press fought back with commendable courage" (Nile Enigma, 1960-1961, p. 2) against this proposition, and the issue eventually faded away.

The regime also established the first government-owned newspaper under a national government in 1960. The Ministry of Information and Labor published the regime's daily newspaper, *al-Thawra,* first under the editorship of a government public relations officer, Gaily Ahmed Omer, until two famous journalists, Mohammed al-Khalifa al-Rifi and Abdalla Rajab, became its editor at separate times. In addition to the Arabic *al-Thawra,* the government published an English daily, *Sudan News,* with the purpose of competing against Beshir Mohammed Sa'id's independent daily *Morning News.* Sa'id — regarded by the government as an opposition element —was also the president of the Sudan Journalist Union (SUJU), and remained a staunch defender of democracy.

ATTITUDE OF THE PRESS TOWARD THE MILITARY REGIME.

Born under a democratic environment a decade earlier, the independent press remained relentlessly opposed to the military regime's curbs on press freedom. On the organizational level, although the Sudan Journalist Union became an illegal organization, the Union's president, Beshir Mohammed Sa'id, in 1961 co-signed a memorandum demanding the "military's return to barracks" (Nile Enigma, 1960-1961, p. 2). Beshir received a brief jail sentence for that act. and later left the country for New York, where he joined the UN Information Office (Nile Enigma, 1960-1961, p. 2).

On the editorial level, some newspapers published several editorials critical of the military regime. *Al-Ayam* published two such articles, one against the trial of civilians before military courts, the other against the conduct of some foreign diplomats. This led the government to close the paper indefinitely. *Al-Sahafa* received suspension for publishing an editorial demanding the return to democracy (Salih, M.A., 1975). The press also fought back against the government when a proposition for nationalizing the press received public discussion (Nile Enigma, 1960-1961).

The Second Democratic Period:
Return of the Party-Owned Press

The civilian uprising against the military regime in October of 1964 forced General Abboud to step down, and restored parliamentary democracy after six years of authoritarian rule. With the reemergence of parliamentary politics, party-owned press came once more to life, this time with a variety reflecting the social and structural changes that had taken place in society.

Of the primary traditional parties, both the Umma and NUP suffered splits from within and, as a result, two wings of the Umma party emerged, the Al-Hadi wing, whose official organ became the *al-Nil* newspaper, and the Al-Sadig wing with *al-Umma* as its official newspaper. Since the NUP had split into two parties prior to the 1958 coup, *Al-Alam* remained the political organ of the NUP, whereas *Sawt al-Sudan* became the official organ of the PDP. An additional factional split in the NUP produced another paper, *October* (the name referred to the month in which the civilian revolt deposed General Abboud), as the political voice of the NUP dissidents. The Communist Party, whose relentless opposition to the military regime brought it more popularity and support, restored *al-Midan* as the party's official organ, and instituted several weeklies to serve as the party's "satellites." These papers included *Advance,* an English weekly edited by Joseph Garang; *al-Dia'a* (the Light), published by al-Tahir Abdel Rahman; and Awad Birair's *Akhbar al-Usbou'* (News of the Week), which became a "rostrum for Communists" when the party and its paper became illegal in 1967 (Salih, M.A., 1975, p. 65). The Muslim Brothers published *Al-Akhwan al-Muslimon* but later, when they widened their political platform to accommodate other Islamic groups, they changed the name of both the party and the newspaper to *al-Mithaq al-Islami* (the Islamic Charter).

During this period several party-owned and non-party English newspapers appeared for the first time. This new development stemmed from the structural political changes which admitted the south as an integral force in Sudanese politics. Several "southern" political parties appeared and launched their papers in

English, whereas many of the national parties started English editions of their papers, or published English ones to address the
English-speaking southern élite. During this period, eight independent, government and party-owned newspapers were published in English. Famous among these were *Morning News* of
the Al-Ayam publishing house and the *Vigilant* of the Southern
Front party.

THE 1984 INTERIM GOVERNMENT:
SUPPRESSION UNDER DEMOCRACY

A largely leftist caretaker government took over from the military regime as a prelude to a multiparty system. Accordingly, the
government embarked on (revolutionary) policies aimed at
undermining the influence of traditional forces of society, and at
purging those who collaborated with Abboud's regime
(Bechthold, 1976).

Under the political motto "al-tat-hir" (purification), the interim
government began a policy of "purification" of the political life
within which it purged all public servants who collaborated with
the military regime. Some newspapers fell victims to these purification policies; the interim government suppressed six of the
non-party newspapers because they allegedly "received subsidies from the military government" (Henderson, 1965, p. 214).
A major daily among the six was *al-Sahafa,* whose editor and
publisher admitted publicly to having received two thousand
Sudanese pounds "'to have fun with' the regime's Information
Minister" (Salih, M.A., 1975, p. 55). The policy of press suppression did not last long, however, for the traditionalists soon
challenged the interim government, forced it out of office, and
formed a more moderate one (Bechthold, 1976).

THE POST-ABBOUD DEMOCRACY AND THE PRESS.

Despite the liberal atmosphere of the post-Abboud parliamentary
period of 1964-69, the government manifested an authoritarian
attitude toward the press. The suppression of *al-Sahafa* and the
other five papers during the interim period reflected such an atti-

tude and set a precedent; not even under the military regime was such a number of newspapers, individually or collectively, suppressed.

In another incident, the elected government of Prime Minister Mahjoub confiscated, in 1965, an edition of the daily *al Ra'i al-Aam* due to an editorial critical of the Minister of Interior. The incident resulted in the joint strike of the Sudanese press in protest of the confiscation, causing the Minister of Information to diffuse the situation by means of an apology to the journalists (Salih, M.A., 1975).

The government also resorted to the use of Penal Code articles against one of the English papers when it indicted the editor of the *Vigilant,* the organ of the Southern Front, for publishing an article which the government considered liable to stir "feelings of hatred and contempt" against it (Salih, M.A., 1975, p. 64).

The government was so intolerant to press criticism that it tried publishing its own daily paper, *al-Jamhouria* (the Republic). But this venture did not succeed, for the other press met the decision with stern criticism, and accused the government of "stabbing press freedom in the back" (Salih, M.A., 1975, p. 66). The government-owned paper soon proved a failure and, within a short period, the government stopped its publication.

ATTITUDE OF THE PRESS TOWARD THE DEMOCRATIC GOVERNMENT.

The second democratic period witnessed the continuation of the pre-Abboud type of bickering which resulted in the "total neglect of major national problems" (Bechthold, 1976, p. 256) facing the country. Continuous inter- and intra-party conflicts crippled the successive coalition governments which fell one after the other and, eventually, led to public discontent and frustration.

The party-owned press became overwhelmingly drowned in political bickering, "repeated the pre-military era of ultra-partisanship, and helped spread feelings of animosity and hatred in the political atmosphere" (Salih, M.A., 1975, p. 69). Political feuds among rival parties, and rival members of the same party found their way to the pages of the party-owned press; whereas the newspapers, being partisan, carried on their own side-battles too (Salih, M.A., 1975).

The non-party press reflected the public mood of discontent and frustration with the political situation. Articles and editorials in the leading papers criticized the parties and politicians, calling for changes in attitude and performance of the parties. Under the title "Hiwar Ma'a al-Safwa" (Dialogue with the Elite), a series of articles in *al-Ayam* received much fame. In the articles, the writer, a famous Sudanese intellectual who later became Minister of Foreign Affairs in the succeeding military government of Nimeiri, critically analyzed the political scene, and concluded the Sudanese intelligentsia must face its responsibilities by stepping in and taking over from the traditional leadership. *Al-Sahafa* also ran a series of articles which posited that the seat of the educated élite was vacant in the political arena, and called upon the élite to occupy that "vacant seat" (Salih, M.A., 1975, p. 70).

MAY 25 REGIME: INCEPTION OF SUDAN'S "MOBILIZATION PRESS"

Many scholars consider the May 25, 1969, military coup by General Nimeiri one of the most important political phases in the history of Sudan. Not only did the regime pursue a political path different from that of the previous civilian and military governments, but it also reshaped the country's power structure, and laid the foundations of a new social and political order. As a social institution, the press was one of the targets of the new authorities' radical restructuring.

THE FIRST YEAR: THE INDEPENDENT AND "REVOLUTIONARY" PRESS.

As all military coups do, the Nimeiri regime banned all political parties and suppressed their newspapers. Although the regime suspended the non-party newspapers for a short period, it soon issued new licenses for some of them and, eventually, four non-party dailies and five weeklies resumed publishing (Sa'id, 1989).

Although the military government did not introduce new press laws during the first year, it did not hesitate to flex its muscles with respect to the press. Apart from the call for the press to become a true voice of the "May 25 Socialist Revolution," the regime instituted the harshest censorship ever to Sudanese journalism (Rugh, 1979; Sa'id, 1989; Salih, M.A., 1975). Military and security officers exercised censorship by scanning the pages of all the dailies every night to safeguard against the publication of anti-revolutionary materials (Sa'id, 1989; Salih, M.A., 1975).

Contrary to what Rugh reported in his book (Rugh, 1979), the "May 25 Revolution" established two government-owned newspapers. In 1970, the Ministry of National Guidance published *al-Ahrar* (the Liberals) as a daily newspaper which continued until the nationalization and "reorganization" of the press in August of 1971 (Ministry of Education, 1971). In 1970, the army also began publishing a weekly political newspaper which addressed broad issues rather than military ones. The nature of *al-Quat al-Musallaha* (the Armed Forces) as the organ of a newly effective political force—the armed forces—and its closeness to members of the Revolutionary Command Council (RCC) as the highest political authority, quickly raised the paper to the level of a semi-official organ, and a dependable source of political information.

PRESS NATIONALIZATION.

The press did not enjoy its new role as a "revolutionary" press, with restricted freedom, for long. On 26 August 1970 General Nimeiri, in accordance with the socialist policies of the regime, announced the nationalization of the press and, thereby, brought an end to half a century of the institution of an independent press in the Sudan. The regime justified press nationalization on the grounds that the press "had been founded to serve the purposes of British imperialism," and that some of the newspapers had become "stooges of foreign powers" (Legum, 1971, p. B51).

According to the nationalization decrees, the press was organized under the General Press and Publishing Corporation to which Mahjoub Mohammed Salih, an able veteran journalist and editor, and co-owner of *al-Ayam* daily newspaper, became the director. The new organization established two publishing houses, Dar al-Ayam and Dar al-Ra'i al-Am. The Corporation gave Dar al-Ayam the duties of publishing a daily (*al-Ayam*), a weekly (*al-Sudan al-Jadid*), a provincial (*Kordofan*), and a woman's journal. Dar al-Ra'i al-Am had the responsibility of publishing a daily (*al-Sahafa*), another English daily, a weekly (*al-Ra'i al-Am*), and a monthly magazine (*al-Khartoum*). Except for publishing two dailies, *al-Ayam* and *al-Sahafa,* the two publishing houses accomplished few other publishing tasks.

With the press as a public property, the senior posts in the newly-established newspapers became political posts to which General Nimeiri appointed the occupants. Except for Mahjoub Mohammed Salih, the director of the Press Corporation, appointments to the most senior posts of the newly-organized press went to politicians and bureaucrats who had little knowledge of the profession. Following the nationalization and reorganization of the press, an ambassador and a famous literary writer and novelist, Jamal Mohammed Ahmed, assumed the responsibilities of director and editor of the nationalized *al-Sahafa*. *Al-Ayam's* most senior post went to a politician, Musa al-Mubarek, who came to the daily newspaper from the post of Minister of Industry. The two papers had several non-journalist politicians as their editors and directors before the posts finally reverted to professional journalists. From 1970, when the press was nationalized, to 1983, ministers, politicians, university professors, army officers, diplomats and, lastly, professional journalists assumed the senior posts in the two publishing houses. At two points in time, two professional journalists simultaneously assumed the highest editorial post and managerial post of the two newspapers. In 1972, Al Fatih al-Tijani, the editor of the previous non-party al *Ra'i Al-Am,* became the chairman and editor of *al-Ayam,* whereas Mohammed al-Hassan Ahmed, the previous owner and editor of *al-Adwa'a,* became the chairman and editor of *al-Sahafa.* Ten years later, two journalists, Fadlalla Mohammed and Hassan Satti, assumed the highest posts in *al-Sahafa* and *al-Ayam* respectively. Except for these two brief periods in which journalists held the top editorial and executive posts of the newspapers, a continuous separation was maintained between the editorial and executive posts. The obvious aim of political appointments to the press was to ensure the loyalty of the press through the positioning of politicians at the top of each paper, entrusting these politicians with the duties of internal censor (Gallab, personal communication, January 1992).

Under the new organization of the press, the issue of who directed the press became a source of confusion for both the journalists and the government. In a 15-year period, the nationalized press fell under the supervision of several political and governmental departments, some of which had no connection with the formulation or implementation of communication policies. The two newspapers during this period came under the supervision of the General Press and Publishing Corporation in 1970, the Minister of Information in 1971, the Revolutionary Command Council in mid-1971, the Ombudsman in 1972, then back to the Minister of Information that same year, and, finally the Sudan Socialist Union (SSU) in 1973, where they became organs of the political organization.

Editorial posts, both junior and senior, likewise became subject to political decisions of the government. At first the Chief Editor became the highest administrative and editorial position to which the editor of the daily newspaper remained subordinate (Legum, 1971). But later, the post of Chief Editor disappeared and the Chairman of the Board of Directors assumed the highest administrative post. Under this new conception, the post of Editor of the daily newspaper became subordinate to the Chairman. Because the post of Editor was a political one, the president of the SSU (President Nimeiri) appointed and relieved the editors of the two daily newspapers. At a later stage, the two editors became members of the Central Committee of the ruling SSU (Sudan Party Games, 1983). Appointing and changing editors followed the same pattern of appointing and shuffling cabinet ministers during the May regime; as a result, the editorial leadership of the two newspapers changed approximately eight times during this period.

TIGHTENING THE GRIP OVER THE PRESS

The press reorganization under the Press and Publication Corporation did not target the print media alone. As press nationalization included news agencies, the Press Corporation grouped all private-owned news agencies under one government owned Sudan News Agency (SUNA). The corporation also established an agency monopolizing the distribution of local and foreign publications, a governmental advertising agency, and an agency for the registration of journalists, printing presses, and publications. Later, when the government dissolved the Press Corporation, the Distribution House and the Press and Publication Committee remained as autonomous departments under the Ministry of Information. The nationalization of the press and news agencies, together with the monopoly over publishing and distributing printed materials, provided the government with the ultimate control over the whole communication process in the country. As radio and TV remained under government control, the government completely seized Sudan's communications media.

THE PRESS AND PUBLICATION ACT OF 1973.

The May 25 regime promulgated a new press law in 1973 to replace the 1930 Press Act of the British Administration. The new act consolidated the regime's power over communication activity, and established the legal basis for the SUU's ownership of the press. The new Press and Publication Act (1973) provided for the following:

1. The absolute ownership of the press by the SSU.
2. The assignment of the Minister of Information as responsible for "the daily and direct supervision of the newspapers, to ensure conformity with the general information policy."
3. The establishment of the Press and Publication Council, whose function it was to watch over press activity to ensure compliance with "what the political power ascribes," to register and issue licenses for journalists, and to advise on the issuance of licenses for newspapers and printing presses.

4. The empowerment of the Attorney General to prohibit, confiscate, or stop importation and circulation of any newspaper or printed material seen as endangering "public order, security, morals," or interfering "with the authority of the State or the Socialist Republican system."

5. The penalization for the possession of unlicensed printing presses, the publishing of unlicensed newspapers, and the unauthorized importation of printed materials (Press and Publication Act, 1973).

RESTRICTIONS ON THE ENTRY TO THE PROFESSION.

To accomplish its duties of licensing and registering journalists, the Press Corporation established the "Press and Publication Council," and entrusted it with the duties of licensing and registering journalists. A three-member standing committee handled these duties and, as of 1973, newspapers needed to obtain the approval of this committee before hiring any journalist. With a security officer as one of its members, the committee carried out an extensive political check on potential journalists to ensure the appointment of journalists loyal to the regime (Gallab, personal communication, January 1992).

PERFORMANCE AND ROLE OF THE PRESS.

The SSU National Charter stated that "the press is a public ownership under the administration of the SSU" (Sudan Socialist Union, 1972, p. 6); whereas the Permanent Constitution of 1973 stated that "the press is free within limits of the law, and is an instrument for public education and enlightenment" (Sudan Government Gazette, 1973). A great deal of the political literature of Nimeiri's regime spoke to the role and duties of the press under the "Revolution of May." The press, under the "May 25 Socialist Revolution," constituted "a platform for guidance, criticism, and rectification;" "an effective instrument for presenting public opinion and linking people to government;" and a "revolutionary instrument for arousing public interest in the revolutionary achievements and in development" (Sudan Socialist

Union, 1972, pp. 6-8). With restrictive laws, censorship, security checks, and political pressure surrounding it, the press became part of the political machinery and functioned as the basic propaganda tool of the regime. The two papers became billboards of the SSU and the president, with almost all the utterances of President Nimeiri and his SSU, no matter how long, receiving full coverage. In an atmosphere that commended non-critical journalism as a sign of political loyalty, journalists became conformists and chose to take no initiative on their part. As a result, the leading papers relied heavily on the sole government news agency to supply the daily news and activities of the government and they, together with the government-owned radio and TV, reproduced what the news agency produced becoming, thus, daily replicas of each other (Looking at the Structure, 1979). With the introduction of a program of national development, following the peace agreement in the South in 1973, "development journalism" became the prevailing norm for journalistic activities through which the newspapers — and the other mass media—maintained a central position in the propaganda machinery of the regime.

Public confidence in the two government dailies sank low. El-Tayeb Hag Attya, professor of mass communication in Khartoum University, in 1979 described *al-Ayam and al-Sahafa* as being "identical" in political coverage, "dependent on SUNA for news provision," and as resembling "government handouts whose editorial content the SSU determined" (Looking at the Structure, 1979, p. 21).

The journalists themselves showed dissatisfaction with the state of their newspapers. In an interview with *Sudanow,* the monthly government magazine, the editors of the two papers talked at length about what they thought were reasons for their papers' weakness. Hassan Satti, *al-Ayam's* editor, cited "the absence of trained and professional journalists, and lack of proper training" as reasons for the absence of criticism in his paper (Looking at the Structure, 1979, p. 22). Fadlalla Mohammed, editor of *al-Sahafa,* attributed the problem to what he called "lack of access to inside information," and called for legislation that would provide journalists access to non-classified information (Looking at the Structure, 1979, p. 24). The sole political organization in the country showed discontent with its own press as well. President Nimeiri occasionally issued public criticism of his party's press, and many SSU conventions and conferences discussed and widely debated the state of the press, and passed many resolutions to remedy the situation (Full Court Press, 1983; Looking at the Structure, 1979; Problems of the Press, 1978). Al-Fatih al-Tijani, a previous editor of *al-Ayam* who served for a brief period as the Party official in charge of the media, expressed the government's disillusionment with its own press when he attributed the inadequacies of the newspapers to the failure of the journalists to do any serious work, and called journalists "only civil servants" (Full Court Press, 1983, p. 13).

The inability of the May regime's press to satisfy the readers resulted in the popularity of privately-owned sports magazines and newspapers, and in the increase of popularity of foreign Arab newspapers and magazines. The circulation figures of the two newspapers reflected a quantitative drop. *Sudanow* reported that in 1983, in a six-month period, the total circulation of *al-Ayam* reached 37,000 copies (Full Court Press, 1983). The last available data for *al-Ayam* before its nationalization showed the paper as having a circulation of 45,000 copies (Ministry of Information, 1971). Although the economic situation may have effected such regression, the low journalistic quality of the newspaper had a lot to do with such a drop (Full Court Press, 1983; Sa'id, 1989).

ATTITUDE OF THE PRESS TOWARD THE GOVERNMENT.

Under a nationalized press in which the journalists became government employees, little chance existed for the press to engage in any watchdog activity. Journalists gave in to government pressure and, eventually, a "mobilization" type of press (Rugh, 1979) prevailed. Under Nimeiri's regime, the Sudanese press typified the case of a press falling under the authoritarian power of a regime. Even the SSU, which enjoyed considerable power and prestige under previous regimes, played little or no role. Dissolved after the inception of the May regime in 1969, the

Union returned to life several years later under the regime's watchful eye; but professional and political differences crippled it at the expense of its positive role in the enhancement of the profession (Journalists Disunited, 1979).

THE ENGLISH JOURNALS: AN OASIS OF FREE EXPRESSION.

The era of Nimeiri witnessed a brief peaceful solution for the civil war in the south. As a result, the Southern Region became an important force in the political arena. According to the peace agreement signed between the central government and the Southern politicians, the South was to enjoy a relatively more liberal political life than the North. Because social and political institutions related to the south enjoyed a greater degree of freedom in organization, expression, and criticism, the English magazines and newspapers, which Southern Sudanese published, became more objective and critical than the Arabic ones. Of these *Sudanow* was, by far, the one that foreign scholars and writers on Sudanese affairs admired the most (Voll, 1990). Established in 1976 by Bona Malwal, a Southern politician, journalist and, at the time, State Minister for Education, the monthly magazine quickly became a reliable source on Sudanese current affairs much respected and admired for its objective and unbiased reporting of local affairs.

Nile Mirror, another south-oriented English newspaper with reasonable editorial freedom, appeared in 1971 as a publication of the Ministry of Southern Affairs in Khartoum. The weekly newspaper became a forum for the English-speaking southern Sudanese in which they debated and discussed the issues of the region. After the 1972 Addis Ababa Agreement, by which the South became a separate regional entity, *Nile Mirror* became the official organ of the Southern Sudan Government, though political differences between the elements of the successive regional governments and economic hardships troubled the newspaper until the final days of the May regime.

Sudanow survived and continues, to this day, as an important source of information about current affairs in Sudan. The fact that the magazine served a useful purpose for the regime, by providing a liberal face to the critical international community, explains the magazine's ability to criticize and publish materials other government newspapers could not publish.

When Nimeiri's regime fell to civilian pressure in April of 1985, the press was the absolute property of the SSU and, except for several sports weeklies and fortnightlies, the government exercised ultimate monopoly over the communication media in the country. Sixteen years of press control profoundly influenced the subsequent liberal press of the 1985-89 parliamentary phase. Not only had most of the journalists become socialized to an authoritarian press system, but also a generation of readers became socialized to a conformist type of journalism in which criticism became synonymous with cynicism. Under the liberal atmosphere of the post-Nimeiri era journalists — long stigmatized as mouthpieces of Nimeiri's system — joined the new free press and attempted to cope with a new atmosphere of freedom with which many of them had little or no experience.

THE PRESS OF THE THIRD DEMOCRATIC ERA

On 6 April 1985 another civilian revolution brought down Nimeiri's authoritarian rule and, as a result, a transitional civilian-military type of government succeeded the longest regime in modern Sudanese history. The new government dissolved all of Nimeiri's institutions, and passed a new provisional constitution under which the press regained freedom. With the restoration of press freedom, a barrage of daily, weekly, and biweekly newspapers and magazines came to life. Some of these newspapers revived previous ones which existed before Nimeiri's regime, whereas others were new ventures. An unprecedented number of newspapers and magazines appeared during the four-year period of 1985-89. In these four years, the number of applications for newspaper licenses reached a peak of 134. Out of this number, 91 daily, weekly, biweekly, and monthly non-party and party-owned papers were published during the four years, with varying degrees of regularity in circulation.

The Government's Attitude Toward the Press.

Although it restored press freedom, the transitional government continued to maintain the two daily newspapers of Nimeiri's era as official newspapers until the end of the transition period. For a short while, the succeeding parliamentary government of Sadig al-Mahdi maintained the two papers as government-owned mavericks in a sea of independent press; but eventually it suspended the two papers and returned the names of *al-Ayam* and *al-Sahafa* to the original owners (Sussman, 1989). The owners of *al-Ayam* resumed publishing it as a private paper, and continued until the end of the parliamentary period. *Al-Sahafa's* original owner, Abdul-Rahman Mukhtar, retained its name as his property, but for unknown reasons did not resume publication of the paper.

The transitional government abolished the "1973 Press and Publication Act" and substituted instead a new "1985 Press and Publication Act" (Sussman, 1989). The Act, though couched in liberal terms suited to the prevailing democratic spirit, retained some of the articles of the 1973 Press Law of the previous regime, thus partially curbing press freedom.

The country's deteriorating economic conditions adversely affected the newly-born independent press. Scarcity of newsprint and other publishing materials drove prices beyond the reach of many newspapers. The few printing outlets in the country limited further the amount any newspaper could print, and the general decline of business made advertising an undependable source of revenue for these papers. Under this situation, many newspapers could not sustain publishing; some began to appear irregularly, whereas others chose to close down altogether. Out of 91 papers which appeared in the country after April of 1989, twenty-five were irregularly circulated, and twenty, unable to withstand unfavorable conditions, died.

The adverse economic conditions made some newspapers vulnerable to various partisan, government, and even foreign pressure (Hizb al-Ummah, 1991; Sa'id, 1989). The senior author is aware of one incident in which the owner and editor of a weekly paper (which later died) conveyed that he had received, several times, money from two embassies in Khartoum for publishing articles in favor of their countries. Many of the newspapers became accustomed to publishing full-pages of "congratulatory messages" on the national days of several Arab and Islamic countries. Although the papers published this material as advertisement, suspicion of attempts of some countries to influence the papers continued to trouble political leaders and concerned journalists (Sa'id, 1989; Hizb al-Ummah, 1991).

The government and the political parties exercised different kinds of pressure on the press. Article 19 (1991) gave two examples of such pressures: the confinement of government advertising to certain dailies and weeklies, and the hoarding of newsprint practiced by some politically active businesspersons. Sussman (1989) mentioned another: "The backdoor policy of monetary controls which prevented newspapers access to foreign currency" (p. 175). The several governments of the period made frequent attempts to impose direct control over the press. The transitional government abolished the 1973 Press Law, but replaced it with a new "1985 Press Law." It also imposed restrictions on military news, and had several confrontations with the press during its one-year rule (Kilongson, 1986). Compared to previous parliamentary governments, the three coalition governments of the 1986-89 period had the worst record for curbing press freedom. During this period, the government made three attempts to pass a new press law with restrictive articles. The imposition of a State of Emergency in August of 1987 gave the government a powerful hand over the press, and enabled it to close down some newspapers (News from Africa Watch, August 1990; Sussman, 1989). In a period of two years (1987-1989) the government closed down *al-Syassa, al-Ra'i,* and *al-Watan,* and detained two editors for some time (News From Africa Watch, 1990).

THE RISE OF THE PARTY-AFFILIATED PRESS.

Although partisan affiliation of the independent press has become a constant feature of Sudanese journalism, the trend appeared more pervasive during the 1986-89 period. Previously, some non-party newspapers expressed party opinions and functioned as voices of those parties. During the 1986-89 period, the trend became more of political parties establishing "independent" newspapers (Puri, September, 1989). Many documents consider the NIF the most active political group in this activity, and assign to it two dailies, *al-Sudani and al-Usba,* a triweekly, *Alwan,* and a weekly, *Sawt al-Jamahir* (Article 19, 1991; News From Africa Watch, 1990; Puri, September, 1989).

While most documents do not discuss the involvement of other parties in the acquisition of newspapers, indications of political linkages between some non-party newspapers and certain parties existed. *Al-Watan* was one of these newspapers. Established by the former editor of the Umma Party newspaper, *al-Watan* showed signs of subtle connections with the Umma Party. In at least one instance the Umma Party leader, Prime Minister Sadig al-Mahdi, acknowledged his involvement in the newspaper's editorial policy (Puri, 1989). The Minister of Information at that time, Tom Mohammed Tom, told the senior author that a leading Umma minister sent a personal letter requesting the Information Minister to grant a license for the paper (Tom M. Tom, personal communication, February, 1992).

Some documents also refer to *al-Ashiga's* magazine as a party-affiliated one (Puri, 1989). The magazine's proprietor, al-Baghir Ahmed Abdalla, held the position of information advisor to the leader of the NUP, a fact that explains these documents' categorization of the magazine as party-affiliated. Toward the end of the democratic period, *al-Tilagraph* started publishing with resources and a staff that made many suspect Ba'athist influence (The Ba'ath is a pro-Iraq political party). Four dailies and semi-dailies, and one weekly magazine, constituted the party-affiliated newspapers. Compared to the total number of non-party dailies (four newspapers), the party-owned and party-affiliated papers constituted more than 69 percent (nine newspapers) of the newspapers available to the public. Because Sudanese are inclined to read party-owned papers less, these papers generally have the lowest circulation. Instead, party-affiliated papers became more important for conveying party views to the public. Although most of the available circulation data reflect approximate figures, they report the average circulation of the pro-NIF daily and semi-daily newspapers as 90,000 copies (Article 19, April 1991); whereas the total circulation of the four non-party newspapers (*al-Ayam, al-Khartoum, ay-Syassa, and Sudan Times*) was 72,000 copies.

ATTITUDE OF THE PRESS TOWARD THE GOVERNMENT.

After sixteen years of suppression, many weaknesses character-ized the returning independent press. Newspapers which existed before the May 25 regime came back economically weak, and had to depend on a staff much less experienced than the one they had sixteen years earlier. The newly-established papers had prob-lems of their own; the editors of these papers—despite their lack of any journalism background—appointed themselves editors and added more to the professional weakness of their papers (Sa'id, 1989). An increase in demand in the job market for jour-nalists made some of the papers employ unqualified persons as journalists, and some of these soon rose to top editorial posts. These factors had a tremendous impact on the quality of the press. In the words of a highly-respected journalist and ex-editor of the *al-Ayam* daily newspaper, some of the papers "reckoned to sensationalism, and attempted to stir calamities, and under-mine society" (Sa'id, 1989, p. 10). Muhie al-Deen Titawi, the edi-tor of one of the two government-owned daily newspapers and ex-co-owner of *al-Usbu'*, evaluated the press of the 1986-89 par-liamentary period as having "played a very dangerous role in inflaming hatred, debasing national unity and state sovereignty, and questioning the Afro-Arabic identity of the country" (Titawi, 1991, p. 3). To Titawi, the Salvation Revolution had "to destroy those forums that stood for disunity and advocated the country's subservience to polarization and hegemony." Mahjoub Irwa, the editor of *al-Sudani,* a daily newspaper from the third democra-tic era, described the performance of some newspapers as hav-ing ushered in "an era of decadence in Sudanese journalism" (Irwa, 1988, p. 8).

THE "IRRITANT" PRESS.

A remarkable feature of some of the press of the democratic period was the attempt of some newspapers to practice a crude form of "muckraking" by attacking every aspect of the public and personal lives of several politicians and senior government officials. This unprecedented trend of debasing public personalities introduced a new kind of journalistic coverage to a conservative society which socially disdains public discussion of private life and personal behavior of others. Although the newspapers claimed to be practicing their watchdog role, evidence of subjectivity and political bias in their muckraking existed. In most cases these papers provided no substantiating evidence for their accusations, used intimations and innuendoes and, in most cases, failed to quote sources regarding their allegations against the public figures. The party-affiliated papers directed their muckraking only against members of parties they opposed; whereas members of the parties they identified with received no critical coverage. Instead, these papers refuted accusations against these members, and dismissed the allegations and rumors (Tuhmat al-Jahil, December 2 1988).

The three newspapers most active in this muckraking were *Alwan, al-Watan,* and *al-Ra'i. Alwan* started as a sports tabloid sometime toward the end of the May 25 regime, but switched to a political weekly immediately after the downfall of the regime. Little is known about its proprietor and editor, Hussein Khogali, as a journalist, though he was an NIF member who unsuccessfully contested in the parliamentary elections of 1985. Although many of the documents on Sudan's press consider *Alwan* the second official organ of the NIF, the senior author did not find any evidence of the party's ownership of the paper. The pro-NIF editorial policy of the paper, and the fact that the proprietor ran in the elections as an NIF member, caused the authors to accept *Alwan as* party-affiliated.

The previous editor of the Umma Party newspaper, *Sawt al-Umma,* established *al-Watan in* 1988 as a non-party paper. Two facts attest to the party-affiliated nature of *al-Watan:* the involvement of Sadig al-Mahdi in some of the editorial decisions of the paper (Puri, 1989), and the admission by a former information minister that a leading Umma Party minister endorsed the paper (Al-Tom, A.M., personal communication, February 1992).

Al-Ra'i appeared in 1988 as a non-party newspaper. An army ex-officer, Mohammed Medani Tawfig, owned and presided over the editorial staff of the paper. Before he left the army, Tawfig started writing critically about the politicians of the interim period in *al-Quat al-Mussalha,* the army's newspaper, and gained much fame for these articles. After leaving the army, Tawfig established the paper and devoted it to vitriolic criticism of the army command, and to the way it conducted the war in the South. The government also received considerable irritating criticism from *al-Ra'i.* Tawfig's newspaper most irritated the army commanders because it started accusing them of betraying their soldiers in the South and engaging in corruption, and because it began to touch on what the army command saw as confidential matters.

Public and official criticism of the press increased. Al-Sadig al-Mahdi, the Prime Minister of the period, on more than one occasion referred to what he saw as the adversarial role of the press, and "in several occasions he condemned them as antidemocratic" (Sussman, 1989, p. 323). During his term as Prime Minister, he made similar remarks about the press in front of the Constituent Assembly, where he remarked:

> Elements of the Sudanese media, in cooperation with the foreign media have been attempting to create an impression that there is religious and racial conflict in Sudan. (News From Africa Watch, August 1990, p. 7).

An Africa Watch newsletter on the status of information in Sudan during the third parliamentary phase pointed to the following as signs of bias in the coverage of the period: characterization of the Prime Minister, other ministers, and officials as corrupt, incompetent, and treacherous; the calls for Jihad (holy war) and the resurrection of the spirit of confrontation and resistance; and publication of materials implicitly condoning the attempts of the deposed ex-President Nimeiri to return to power (News From Africa Watch, August, 1990).

The government acted against two of these irritant newspapers. It detained for some time the editors of both *al-Ra'i and al-Watan,* and closed their newspapers (Article 19, April 1991). *Alwan*, the most outspoken of the three, did not receive any suspension, though many politicians and individuals raised civil cases against it. *Al-Ra'i* remained closed for much of its three years, and many of these times the authorities detained the editor for "publishing materials detrimental to security and the performance of the armed forces" (Article 19, April 1991, p. 11). The government closed *al-Watan a* week before the military takeover of 1989, and detained its editor, Sid Ahmed Khalifa, for publishing an interview with the former President, Ja'afer Nimeiri, who claimed in the interview that he would soon be back in power (Article 19, April 1991).

When the "National Salvation Union" took over on 30 June 1989 the two editors of *al-Watan* and *al-Ra'i* were still under detention. The new regime released these editors, but suspended the non-party press and allowed only the army newspaper to publish for a brief period. Since then, the government launched two daily newspapers, *al-Ingaz al-Watani* (the National Salvation) and *al-Sudan al-Hadeeth* (the New Sudan). Sudanow resumed publishing after a brief suspension, and some government magazines appeared from time to time. Several sports weeklies which fill the newsstands invite comparison with the press of the Nimeiri's era.

CONCLUSION

This chapter summarized the political history of the Sudanese press from the period of independence to the end of the 1986-89 parliamentary period. The chapter outlined the role of the press in political life, its impact on Sudanese nationalism, its attitude toward the government at each of several periods, and the controls exerted by the government of the same periods over the press. The chapter outlined three types of ownership during this period, discussed the effect of press rivalries on press performance, and categorized the press as party-owned, party-affiliated, and non-party. The demise in the quality of Sudanese journalism is correlated with the rise of the party-affiliated and party-owned press. Finally, the chapter assessed the effect of the 1969-85 May regime's press nationalization on the performance and role of the Sudanese press.

REFERENCES

Babiker, M. *Press and Politics in the Sudan.* Khartoum: Khartoum University Press, 1985.

Bechthold, P. *Politics in Sudan: Parliamentary and Military Rule in an Emerging African Nation.* New York: Praeger, 1976.

Cookson, J.A., John, H.J., MacArthur, A.G., McEwen, J., MacGaffet, W. & Vreeland, M.C. *US Area Handbook for the Republic of Sudan.* Washington, DC: US Government Printing Office, 1960.

Full Court Press. *Sudanow,* 1983.

Gallab. Personal communication, 1992.

Henderson, K. *Sudan Republic.* New York: Praeger, 1965.

Hizb al-Umma [Umma Party]. *Al-dimoqratiah fil Sudan.* [Democracy in Sudan?]. Author. 1990.

Journalists Disunited. *Sudanow,* Feb. 1979: 23.

Kilongson, M. Reports of Famine are Prohibited. *Index on Censorship* 15. 20, (1986): 10.

Legum, C. The Mass Media—Institutions of the African Political Systems. In O. Stokke, ed. *Reporting Africa.* New York: Africana Publishing Corporation, 1971.

Looking at the Structure. *Sudanow,* Feb. 1979: 21-23.

Ministry of Information [Sudan]. *Sudan Today.* Nairobi: University Press of Africa, 1971.

Nile enigma. *Africa 24,* (Dec. 2 1960-1961: 1-3.

Press and Publication Act of 1973. Act No. 6. Sudan Government, 1973.

Puri, S. Sudanese Press Takes a Hammering. *IPI Report 39.* 9. (Sep. 1989): 1,9.

Rugh, W. *The Arab Press.* Syracuse: Syracuse University Press, 1979.

Sa'id, B.M. Araa' hawl mustaqbal al-sahafa al-Sudanya. [Opinions on the Press of Sudan]. Unpublished manuscript, 1989.

Salih. M.A. *The Press in Sudan During Three Periods.* Unpublished master's thesis. Indiana University, 1975.

Salih, M.M. *Al-sahafa al-Sudanya fi nisf quarn* [Half a century of the Sudanese press]. Khartoum: Khartoum University Press, 1971.

Sid Ahmed, A. *Mass Media and Development in Sudan.* Unpublished doctoral dissertation. Pennsylvania State University, 1984.

Sterling, C. *International Propaganda and Communications.* New

York: Arno Press, 1972.

Sudan Government Gazette. *Democratic Republic of Sudan, The Permanent Constitution of 1973*, 1973.

Sudan Party Games. *Africa Confidential 24*. 9. (Apr. 27 1983): 4-5.

Sudan Socialist Union. *The National Action Charter*. Khartoum: Sudan Socialist Union Publications, 1972.

Sussman, L. *Power, the Press and the Technology of Freedom.* New York: Freedom House, 1989.

Tom M. Tom, personal communication, Feb. 1992.

Voll, J. Sudan: State and Society in Crisis. *Middle East Journal 44.* 1990: 575-578.

PART 3

FRANCOPHONE

CHAPTER 11

REINVENTING THE
DEMOCRATIC PRESS OF BENIN

Allen W. Palmer

INTRODUCTION

Multi-party elections were conducted in Benin in 1991, marking the collapse of the Marxist regime of Mathieu Kérékou which had ruled the People's Republic of Benin since 1972. Predictably, there was a rush to fill the information vacuum as democracy struggled to take root. As many as 40 to 50 newspapers rushed into print, filling the street kiosks with a wide array of ideas and opinions. Freedom of the press in this small West African nation injected new life into the private press, and it also raised new public criticisms that many of the newspapers were engaging in a kind of tabloid journalism that had never been experienced before.

In a sense, Benin's journalism is a stepchild of the country's turbulent political life. Life in Benin had not been easy, even before the Kérékou dictatorship. Marxism did not provide the solution. Under Kérékou, economic conditions steadily deteriorated and many observers thought political change was inevitable. The only question unanswered was whether there would be a peaceful or violent transition. With rare exceptions, since its independence from France, Benin has had a history of bloodless government takeovers. After attaining independence in 1960, there was a bewildering succession of coups, mutinies and counter coups, arguably more than any other state in sub-Saharan Africa. Even though Kérékou's regime was the most stable in the nation's recent history, it became virtually impossible for outsiders to track the succession of challenges to the country's political leadership.

Many of the challenges to Benin's political authority were organized around powerful personalities rather than ideologies. Behind those personalities, however, are deep-seated, traditional loyalties and rivalries. The Beninois have learned to expect frequent change. Perhaps the need for competent journalism is even more keen in an African nation like this, where each morning brings important information about the latest events.

Benin's press has tried valiantly to meet the challenges of public dialogue, particularly with the inauguration of multi-party elections, but the structural problems are deep and not easily resolved.

With the advent of free elections, hopes soared among many Beninois who had waited patiently for political and economic reform. Some dissidents fled the nation's political and economic chaos of the 1970s and 1980s for refuge elsewhere in Africa or Europe. With the fall of the Marxist government in the 1990s, at last the Beninois would be free to pursue a democratic path. Traveling that path, however, proved to be difficult.

Although political policy was liberalized in 1991, long-standing social and economic problems have never been so apparent. The nation inherited an intractable set of economic problems. In a region of perennially poor nations, Benin is one of Africa's poorest. There is a persistently low GNP, meager natural resources, high population density and diverse ethnic and political fractures. Benin, like many of its sub-Saharan neighbors, is confronted with serious handicaps in competing with serious impediments in a shrinking, competitive, and interdependent world.

The economic reality in Benin — already strained to the

breaking point under Marxist rule — has required its citizens to adapt to the austere economic policies of the World Bank and International Monetary Fund to forestall the kind of social and political calamity experienced by several other undeveloped African nations. "Economic restructuring" has become a code word for privation.

What role could the newly unleashed press play in such turmoil? Amid all its challenges, those who make up Benin's journalism community retain hope that democracy is the answer to the country's problems, and democracy will go only so far as its roots in the nation's press. How such a press can fulfill those aspirations, or even survive, in the face of political and economic distress is uncertain. To understand Benin's press, however, is to understand its roots in the country's history, particularly the last century.

Benin had four distinct phases of journalism. The first period was based on French colonial journalism through the first half of the 20th Century. The second period was a decade of post-colonial journalism after independence from France in 1960. The third period was Marxist-Leninist journalism from 1972 to 1991. The fourth period began with the inauguration of an uninhibited, open press from 1991 to the present day. Never has the press been as free as in the last phase, but the challenges are nearly as daunting as ever.

The historical challenges to the press in Benin betray a deeper sense of the profound uncertainty about the role of democracy, and its institutions, in the unstable political, economic and social life of this nation. In spite of a tendency to privilege the political dimension, this nation's problems are not uniquely political, nor economic. In a real sense, Benin is a victim of its own history, a history fraught with contradictions.

BENIN'S PRESS IN PERSPECTIVE

With a population of approximately 6 million in one of Africa's smallest and most densely populated states, Benin struggles to feed and clothe its own people. As one observer put it, the nation produces few commodities that it consumes, imports most of what it consumes, and produces few goods to export. Investment capital is scarce; the business climate is not well adapted to supporting a private, commercially-based press. A thriving black market meets the demands of the people for most basic goods, most of which flow across the loosely guarded frontier with Nigeria. By default, most of the support of the nation's private press arises from political personalities and causes, injecting a political tone into virtually everything that is published.

The colonial borders of Benin, like much of West Africa, are made up of north-south lines whereas the geographical terrain tends to flow along an east-west direction. As a result, informal and cultural loyalties are confounded. For example, because of colonial borders the Ewe tribe was divided between three separate countries: Benin, Ghana and Togo.[1] It is not surprising, therefore, that informal commerce has always existed to bypass the ill-fitted international boundaries in West Africa.

Notwithstanding its boundaries, the reasons for the persistent underdevelopment of Benin have been blamed variously on the failure of Benin's people to grasp the promise of modernity, its unfavorable weather conditions, and even the profound shock precipitated by the slave trade of the 17th and 18th centuries which ruptured the social fabric of this land.[2]

Some 46 ethnic groups, several of which originated from outside the present boundaries of Benin, live within Benin's borders. The most prominent ethnic peoples are the Fon, Adja, Yoruba and Bariba. Known prior to 1974 as Dahomey, this land was historically recognized among Europeans for its somewhat eclectic history, namely for its elite women warriors, the Amazons, a thriving slave port and its distinctive animist cults, known collectively as vodun or vodoo.[3]

A French protectorate was established in Benin when Dahomey's leaders refused to abolish the lucrative slave trade in the 1860s. Missionary schools in Ouidah, Porto Nova and Agoué — established in the late 19th Century — engendered one of French Africa's more advanced educational systems. Once established in the south, education spread somewhat more slowly to the north.

The last king left the Dahomean throne in 1900, replaced

by French colonial authority. Once colonial rule was in place, it dominated official activities and commerce. Nearly every phase of Dahomean public life, including the press, operated under strict colonial rule. West Africa was administered by a long series of colonial governors by appointment from France.

French colonialism constituted a highly centralized structure, centered on Paris. It did not envision the self governance of colonies, but rather the organic unity between France and its overseas possessions. The French had little use for traditional African culture as such, intending to replace it with French language and culture through assimilation.[4]

Colonialism was described in these words: "In Africa the aim is assimilation. Native institutions are to be used for utilitarian reasons where desirable, but strictly in subordination to the objective of frenchification and not because they have any inherent value in themselves. The aim is to make the African a black Frenchman, and to make the colonies not self-governing Dominions but so many *departments* of France."[5]

This process of assimilation was only marginally successful, but Dahomey became widely known as the "Latin Quarter of West Africa." Its people were recognized for their educated elite who were employed by both the French and Senegalese as advisers to government officials throughout West Africa. Over time, these elites began to sense the value of their position and, through their new-found intellectual prowess, began to resist assimilation in favor of equality, a cause which the French might have understood historically, but not culturally.

THE DAHOMEAN PRESS

The people of Dahomey who were colonized found their voice in their newspapers as early as the 1880s. The tradition of journalism in Benin extends back to the colonial law of July 29, 1881 which extended press privileges to the French possessions. Consistent with the French colonial system, the law specified that all colonial publications must operate under the charge of French nationals. Several subsequent laws of the 1920s tightened the control in terms of prohibiting the publication of any material contrary to French authority.

The journalists who published, even with restraint, did so at the discretion of French censors. Still, Dahomey's literate began to appreciate the potential power of the press. The existence of a thriving family of political journals after the turn of the 20th Century was due in no small part to a strong core of political and intellectual elites who began to assert themselves.[6]

The nation's best known author and editor was Paul Hazoumé, a descendant of Dahomian nobility who edited the newspaper *Le Messager du Dahomey* during World War I while he worked in the Musée de l'Homme in Paris. He later published two famous books, *Le Pact du Sang au Dahomey* (1937) and *Doguicimi* (1938), which are still widely cited in Benin.

One of the leading journalist-dissidents was Louis Hunkanrin who spent much of his life in prison or in exile in France, Mauritania and Mali. He founded an early Dahomean branch of the League for Human Rights and was a thorn in the side of French administrators for decades. At different stages in his life, he wrote for *Le Messager du Dahomey, La Voix du Dahomey and L'Eveil du Benin.* He later served as special consultant to Benin's post-colonial presidencies.

Journalistic efforts also engendered a small, but growing body of Dahomean literature dedicated to the life and culture within the identity of the colony.[7] Such writers as Paulin Joachim, a journalist and poet, became important sources of inspiration and example to young scholars. Joachim was a native of Cotonou who went to France to study law, but was directed instead into a journalism career in Paris, eventually becoming political editor of *France-Soir* and editor of *Bingo and Décennie 2.*

Even without formal journalistic training, many of Dahomey's colonial-era writers and editors learned to resist the authoritarian control of the French. According to Bellarmin Codo, professor of history at the University of Benin, the lessons learned by Dahomey's earliest journalists was to oppose "the wall of silence" and to use the ideological power of the press to mobilize public opinion against colonial oppression.

"In spite of their lack of training and other handicaps, our earliest journalists brought to their work a sense of conscience of their role and their mission, but also the fragile nature of their enterprise," explained Codo. "Could the colonized journals change the order of things? It was evident they could not. The press didn't know how to stop the politics of oppression and exploitation."[8]

However, the journalism of Dahomey opened the door to an "oppositional model" of journalism, an approach which privileged the political dimension of news and spoke at different levels: one was directed on behalf of the vested interests of publisher or sponsor, the other to the Dahomeans. One of the largest obstacles for journalists was the matter of language. Their work was accomplished in French, a language for which few except the privileged and educated in Dahomey were fluent. The many native languages, including those spoken among the powerful Yoruba and Fon, were virtually ignored in French colonial journalism.

ASPIRATIONS OF BENINOIS JOURNALISM

Perhaps the best-known colonial newspaper in Dahomey was *La Voix du Dahomey* which published most of the first half of the century. The vision which *La Voix du Dahomey* held up was as "an organ to defend the general interest of the lands of the African federation" through what it called "combat journalism." It set about to hear the desires and grievances of the Dahomian proletariat"; to be a spokesperson both for the elite and the common people."[8]

As defined by another newspaper, *La Presse Porto-Novienne,* this colonial vision of journalism saw the ideal journalist as a "a soldier who fights not with a rifle, but with ideas . . a patriot who ardently defends just causes, liberty, rights, a public advocate, a cultivator of light, a savior of the homeland . . . (and is) the great enemy unleashed on those who commit injustice. The journalist is militant, a politician who offers his life to defend the interests of the people . . . ."[9]

From the mid-1930s there were at least 10 other newspapers in Dahomey, including *Le Phare du Dahomey, L'Eveil Togo-Dahoméen, Le Courrier du Golfe du Bénin, L'Etoile du*

Dahomey, L'Echo des Cercles, Les Cloches du Dahomey, La Tribune Sociale du Dahomey, Vers la Supreme Sagesse and *Le Coeur du Dahomey.*[10]

Many of the newspapers served special-interest audiences. For instance, *Le Phare du Dahomey* was an important weekly published in Cotonou between 1929 and 1949 by Augustin Nicoué primarily for the Brazilian readership. *Le Phare* was active in attacking the abuses of colonialism, carrying articles by many of the colony's intellectuals and nationalists.

After attaining independence from France on August 1, 1960, Dahomey's political leadership was united for a short time in a single party — The Union Progressiste Dahoméenne — but internal conflicts polarized allegiances into three ethnic/regional movements. In the southeast, the Goun and Yoruba peoples in the Porto Novo region were led by Sourou Migan Apithy, the nation's most experienced political leader. In the coastal-central region, the Fon and Adja areas were led by Justin Ahomadégbé, a descendant from a royal Dahomean family. In the north, Hubert Maga, a Natitingou schoolteacher who launched a career in politics, became the leader of northern interests, including the powerful Bariba people. Much of the political infighting which occurred in Dahomey beginning in the 1960s revolved around these three political movements. None was able to unite in a stable coalition, nor able to purge the others.

Apithy had been the leading territorial leader after World War II, but his reputation was marred by the corruption and ineptness of his administration. Maga and Ahomadégbé formed a compact to lead the new post-colonial government, but Apithy survived to become vice president in 1960.

As president, Maga faced the prospect of the forced return of hundreds of Dahomeans who had been in colonial service throughout the French colonies in Africa. Their obligatory return to their homeland destabilized the small nation, which became ripe for a military takeover three years later. In the ensuing nine years, there were six successful coups, nine changes of government and five changes of constitution.

The rapid changes in government were reflected in a passage by writer Jean Pliya in a popular satirical comedy in 1970: "Ah!

Misery! The more the situation changes, the more the common people suffer . . . . We, common people, we know all about patience. We know that taste by taste, the palm wine fills the gourd. But will our wait never end? Whether whites or blacks are our rulers, must we always be badly led?"[11]

Instead of fulfilling the promises of independence, the post-colonial period in Dahomey was one of turmoil and struggle. According to one observer, the sad truth was that Dahomey retained a sense of colonial dependence even after attaining independence, but there was no decisive power to fill the void of leadership.

The Kérékou Legacy

In recent history, the benchmark of change is measured against the coup d'etat of October 26, 1972 which established Kérékou as the military leader of the nation. Prior to Kérékou's Marxist government there had been 10 presidents of Dahomey in 15 years. Even after attaining independence, French support continued to prop up the economic and educational system.

It wasn't until Kérékou revealed his intentions to adopt Marxist doctrine in 1974 that the absence of intellectual and press freedom became an issue for Dahomeans. The nation's leaders formed a revolutionary government and renamed the radio station, formerly known as "Radio Dahomey" as "the Voice of the Revolution." Television broadcasts were initiated in 1978. The radio-TV station broadcast in French, Fon, Yoruba, Bariba, Mina, Fulai, Dendi and several other dialects.

Widespread changes in the military, legal and educational systems were coupled with the adoption of a new name — Benin, a new constitution and the election of a National Revolutionary Assembly. The name "Benin," was from Nigeria, an identity borrowed from the Edo ethnic group further south in Nigeria populated heavily by the Binis (Benin City is located in Nigeria, not Benin). With the establishment of the People's Republic of Benin, the National University became a center of ideological and political agitation. Eventually Kérékou closed all schools and the university in 1985, purging many academic and intellectual leaders.

Enfilade by radicals and anti-colonial sentiments boiled over into mob action resulting in attacks on the French Cultural Center and other foreign-owned interests. Kérékou embarked on a plan to nationalize some private enterprises, set up collective farms with production goals and ordered students to devote part-time labor to farm work. He formed a single trade union and strengthened the military.

These measures, however, made little difference in the already-strained economy and the condition of the common people steadily worsened. There had been remarkably little economic progress through the entire first half of the 20th Century. The nation was exporting the same amount of palm products in the 1960s as it was in the mid-1800s, in spite of a steadily rising population.[12]

Once Marxist, Benin was aligned with the East and began to receive an infusion of capital and technical assistance from Eastern Europe and China. Outside aid from socialist countries, however, did not achieve the purposes Kérékou intended. Economic conditions did not significantly improve. In the end, Marxism was unable to resolve the country's many dilemmas.

One well-known episode in January 1977 captured the sense of frustration prevalent in Benin. Under the code name "Force Omega," outside interests sponsored an invasion of Cotonou with armed mercenaries. Airplanes landed in Cotonou airport and soldiers stormed to the center of town. Despite having the advantage of complete surprise and little resistance, the mercenaries abandoned their adventure after several hours and returned to the airport to escape. There were a dozen casualties and some $28 million in damage in Cotonou. Beninois leaders later accused France, Gabon and Morocco with knowing about or supporting the plot and demanded remuneration, without success.

Benin was on the verge of bankruptcy and civil disorder in 1990 when Kérékou called for a new constitution. Dissidents took control of the constitutional conference and deposed the former leader, forming a new cabinet in a multi-party system with Nicéphore Soglo, a former dissident and World Bank official, as national president. Kérékou was granted a military retirement and allowed to move into private status. He continues to live in Benin.

Kérékou's ousting was relatively peaceful, but the problems which provoked public dissatisfaction over his government would not be resolved easily. One of the foremost issues, and one which even a free press has struggled to understand, is the extent of corruption in Benin's public and private sectors.

REINVENTING THE BENINOIS PRESS

After Kérékou was deposed, the nation witnessed an explosion of publishing of all types. Under President Soglo in the early attempts at peaceful, multi-party democracy, the Beninois press flourished in volume, if not always in quality. A few career journalists who survived the Marxist years continued to contribute to a non-adversarial, pro-development state newspaper. Others moved to positions in the private sector.

The great growth was immediately obvious in the private press. At times, the new newspapers engaged in freewheeling speculation and government leaders were provoked to call for press reform. The private press, however, was much less willing than before to submit to the political will of Benin's leaders.

An incident after the 1991 elections demonstrated such intransigence. There was considerable official concern expressed over a description of the president's wife as an "ugly witch" in two newspapers, *Le Soleil and Tam Tam Express*.[13] Such transgressions, among others, were understood by presidential aides simply as indicative of the state of the "rotten journalism" and efforts were made to improve the quality of journalism training available to aspiring reporters and editors. Journalists were encouraged to pursue formal training. A country's professional guild placed new emphasis on professional ethics and standards.

Press seminars were organized to explore press ethics and train journalists. A workshop on ethics was sponsored by the Friedrich Naumann Foundation. Another series of seminars on economic and political reporting was hosted by the U.S. Information Agency (USIA) and U.S. Aid for International Development (USAID). Benin's journalists also were invited to participate in journalism training programs in Europe and North America.

The entanglement of the press with political power continued to pose obstacles for the journalists of Benin. The director of *L'Observateur,* was prosecuted for libelous comments and was sentenced to six months in prison. The case raised a new focus by the nation's journalists on the problems of libel and the potential for a "chilling effect" because of expensive and exhausting legal battles.

Beninois journalists also accommodate some unique dimensions arising from the paradigm of development journalism in the less-developed nations. For one, Benin legal statutes offer a legal right of reply to any party offended by the press. The law states that all legal publications must insert a free notice in the next available publication explaining any corrections of errors in order to set the record straight. The response must appear in the same place, printed in the same type as the contested article. The fine for failure to accommodate the right of reply can range from the U.S. dollar equivalent of $400 to $4,000.

Some observers continue to doubt the motives of journalists, speculating about political behaviors of sponsors and the financial backing of publishers. The entanglements are rife. At least one newspaper in Cotonou has been widely rumored to receive financial support from Libya.

ASSESSING THE PROBLEMS

Thomas Megnassan, editorial director of *La Récade* and one of the nation's veteran journalists, identifies one of the key weakness of the Beninois press in how it uniformly treats politics over economic and social dimensions of life. He believes that until the press learns to deal dispassionately with issues, without vexing political and government leaders, it will continue to face such problems.

The roots of the difficulties for journalism in Benin run even deeper, however, into the question of the structure of the press' popular support and financing. Most of the nation's publications are affiliated, directly or indirectly, with political figures, parties or causes and depend on them for a revenue stream. There is little advertising support for most publications because of a serious lack of formal commercial activity to sustain an advertising base. Until there is more national economic activity, there will be only a meager advertising platform from which the press can operate. In the meantime, the few newspapers which survive will be compromised by special interests of benefactors and sponsors, or the government.

Megnassan believes the nation must come to grips with the necessary role of the press in a democracy, no longer the exclusive voice of the elite or the state. "It must become the press of the masses. No one can say, 'the state, that's me.' It is a press for all, with a power which can say it is truly the Fourth Estate. Until this happens, it will not speak the voice of reason, but of instinct and privilege."

He recognizes that the promise of democracy for Benin will go no further than the freedom and independence of its mass media. Until the press gains commercial independence, it must find the financial means to support itself, to pay promising young journalists adequate salaries to justify staying in the profession, and to defend itself from expensive legal entanglements.

The intersection of political life and responsible journalism is of interest, as well, to Joseph Gnonlonfoun, a magistrate at the National Assembly. Gnonlonfoun observed that the press and political power are mutually self-sustaining and self-contradictory. "The press needs a certain kind of political power, without which it cannot survive because people won't take it seriously. On the other hand, the politically powerful are persuaded that the press must relay its actions, or they detest the strength of the press. This is a self-contradictory friendship."[14]

For their part, journalists must be circumspect about their role in society because the power they hold in their hands is an extremely dangerous instrument when badly used. Part of the problem, as analyzed by Gnonlonfoun, is the confusion between freedom of the press and independence of the press. "Freedom should never signify independence." The dependence of press freedom on commercial support is a key example of such a relationship. Commerce will sustain a responsible press, but the support will disappear the moment the press abuses its power irresponsibly.

Similarly, Charles Moumouni, an editor of *L'Horizon* pointed to the problem of material resources as perhaps the most critical obstacle facing development of a democratic press in Benin. In order for the press to become and stay independent, it cannot be the outlet for any particular political ideology. "We must recognize everything that occurs in society, without the kind of partiality that poisons open discussion," said Moumouni. Yet, the influence of government on the information which is available to the public is keen. Official government sources are tight-lipped, unless there is a perceived advantage to them to release information.

Léon Brathier, an editor of *La Nation,* also an officer of the Benin journalists' association, expressed concern about the state of professionalism which is needed to raise the credibility of the press. "Because good journalists don't speak for particular interests, they court all the possible risks of offending them. We can't ignore the responsibility we have to our society as a whole and the necessity to show solidarity in the defense of journalism."

Many of the obstacles to a free and independent press in Benin arise from the weakness in the economy. Besides the difficulty of providing press facilities to publish the few newspapers, there is often a shortage of newsprint. Further, many publications are at the mercy of local distributors who exercise considerable control over which publications are promoted on the streets. Distributors have found that sensationalized headlines are much more profitable, even if they exact a heavy price in terms of press credibility.

Beyond the questions of press economics, many Beninois journalists wonder if there is sufficient courage for the local press corps to be the heart of a democratic reform. Even though Marxist influence has been overthrown, many of the old ways of thinking persist.

In a wide-ranging discussion among more than two dozen leading Beninois journalists, there was general recognition of the constraints on the local reporters and editors. Routine influence by government officials is a continuing source of concern for broadcast journalists in particular. Many have been challenged for straying from the demands of government policy.

Annick Balley, a television anchorwoman for ORTB, the Benin broadcasting organization, pointed out that the control on the government information system demands a "service" model of the democratic media. "It is not our role to attack the evils around us. The press is required to be neutral, informative, educational," she explained. "We simply can't compare West Africa's media system with the media of North America which is more mature," said Balley.

In another sense, at least part of the resistance to an independent press arises from the ambiguity of whose interests are at stake in social and economic issues. "The stakes are high because interests are entrenched and, if threatened, powerful people will defend their advantages," said one veteran journalist. "We are learning that we must have tangible proof to support claims against corruption. But we aren't yet expert enough at doing the things journalists should do."

Many journalists can relate tales of greed and corruption in some government and business sectors in Benin. Claude Agossou, a radio reporter, recounted how he tried to pursue a case of corruption in the office of a public retirement fund, tracing responsibility to the highest levels of the agency. Once his inquiries became known, he was warned to stop the investigation with personal threats.

The narrow, selfish interests of corrupt people, public or private, notwithstanding, is raising consciousness of the value of the new public discourse in Benin. No longer can the nation consider itself an enclave. Benin's contact with the rest of the world is destined to increase, and soon. The government tourist authority has already begun an initiative to attract more foreign visitors—and their foreign capital—with the international promotion of the legacy of the slave trade. Visitors will be taken along the ancestral footpaths, known as La Route de l'Esclave, used by slavers to transport captives from the interior regions to ocean ports. Receiving special attention will be the contributions to the spread of African religious practices in Brazil, Cuba, Haiti and the United States.

While tourism will not provide the kind of capital necessary to rescue Benin's economy, it will begin to introduce the nation's people to the importance of universal values, or aspirations, and of development.

FUTURE PRESS DEVELOPMENT

While few people in Benin's small journalism community dare predict what the future might hold for their nation, or themselves, they remain optimistic. Many younger journalists are looking ahead to a long, if not entirely prosperous, career in the mass media. Among them are those who have the strength of will, if they can only find the means, to support their professional commitments. They sense the importance of their profession to the long-term development of their nation.

The kind of people who are attracted to journalism will make a difference in the kind of leadership it is able to provide for democratic processes. Among the brightest hopes for the Benin press are people like Abraham Voglozin, a writer for *Le Monde des Affaires* in Cotonou. Voglozin holds two doctoral degrees from European and Canadian universities—one in social psychology and another in chemistry. He decided to launch yet another career in journalism because of the need he observed in Benin for leadership in public communication and education. "The Benin press must always inform, liberally and objectively," observed Voglozin. "It must struggle for its freedom which it has not yet really found here." The obstacles which limit press performance include access to good sources of information, both official and private, and the lack of adequate training about what the role of a democratic press might be."

As the nation's journalists begin to realize the possibilities of democracy in their fragile land, they sense the importance of their role in its development. One American embassy official observed that the people at work in establishing democracy in Benin in the 1990s are the rough equivalent of the colonial leaders in the early history of the United States, and in other democratic nations. Observing the Beninois' struggle for democracy offers new insights into the tremendous risks and opportunities taken elsewhere as people struggle to achieve authentic self government.

REFERENCES

Adissoda, M.A. *La Presse au Dahomey (1890-1939)*. Mémoire de maîtrise d'Histoire. Université de Dakar, 1973.

Allen, Chris, Michael Radu, Keith Somerville, Joan Baxter & Keith Somerville, eds. *Benin, The Congo, Burkina Faso: Economics, Politics and Society*. London: Pinter Publishers, 1989.

Argyle, W.J. *The Fon of Dahomey*. Oxford, Clarendon Press, 1966.

Betts, R.F. *Assimilation and Association in French Colonial Theory* New York: Columbia University Press, 1961.

Bradbury, R.E. *Benin Studies*. London: Oxford University Press, 1973.

Codo, Bellarmin. "*La Presse Dahoménne Face aux Aspirations des Evolués; La Voix du Dahomey (1927-1957)*. Thése de doctorat. Université de Paris VII, Département d'Histoire, 1978.

Codo, Bellarmin. "Ethique et Deontologie Dans la Presse Dahomeenne Sous la Colonisation: Apercu Sur L'example de *La Voix du Dahomey.*"

Cornevin, Robert. *Histoire du Dahomey*. Paris: Éditions Berger-LeVrault, 1962.

Decalo, Samuel. *Historical Dictionary of Benin*. London: Scarecrow Press, Inc., 1987.

Gnonlonfoun, J., "Rapports Presse/Pouvoir Politique au Benin," *La Presse Beninoise Face aux Exigences d'Ethique et de Déontologie*. Cotonou: La Nation/Fondation Friedrich Naumann, 1993: 11-13.

Huannou, Adrien. *La Litterature Beninoise de Langue Francaise* Paris, A.C.C.T., 1984: 179-180.

Hughes, John. *The New Face of Africa South of the Sahara*. New York: Longman, Green and Co. 1961.

Huannou, Adrien. *La Littérature Béninoise de Langue Française* Paris: Éditions Karthala, 1984.

La Presse Porto-Novienne, August 1934.

La Voix du Dahomey, Aug. 1, 1934.

Lokossou, C.K. *La Presse au Dahomey: 1894-1960. Évolution et Réaction Face a l'Administration Coloniale*. Thése pour le doctorat. École des Hautes Études en Science Sociales. Paris, 1976.

Manning, Patrick. *Slavery, Colonialism and Economic Growth in Dahomey, 1640-1960* London: Cambridge University Press, 1982.

Shelby, Barry. "The Measure of Freedom," *Africa Report*, May/June 1993: 63.

Wallbank, T.Walter. *Documents on Modern Africa*. New York: D. Van Nostrand Co., Inc., 1964.

NOTES

1. John Hughes, The New Face of Africa South of the Sahara, New York: Longman, Green and Co. 1961: 68.

2. See Chris Allen, et. al. eds. *Benin, The Congo, Burkina Faso: Economics, Politics and Society,* London, Pinter Publishers, 1989: 82; Manning, P. *Slavery, Colonialism and Economic Growth in Dahomey, 1640-1960,* London: Cambridge University Press, 1982: 286.

3. Benin has a distinctive tie to Haiti because much of Haiti's population originally was transplanted to the New World by slave trade. Rituals and fetish practices in Haiti have been traced to southern Benin, as well as names, clothing and oral traditions. See W. J. Argyle. *The Fon of Dahomey,* Oxford, Clarendon Press, 1966; and Robert Cornevin. Histoire du Dahomey, Paris: Éditions Berger-LeVrault, 1962.

4. R.F. Betts. *Assimilation and Association in French Colonial Theory,* New York: Columbia University Press, 1961.

5. T.Walter Wallbank. *Documents on Modern Africa,* New York: D. Van Nostrand Co., Inc., 1964: 48-49.

6. The history of the Benin press has been documented in several academic projects. See, for example: M.A. Adissoda. *La presse au Dahomey (1890-1939).* Mémoire de maîtrise d'Histoire. Université de Dakar, 1973; C.K. Lokossou. *"La Presse au Dahomey: 1894-1960. Évolution et réaction face a l'administration coloniale."* Thése pour le doctorat. École des Hautes Études en Science Sociales. Paris, 1976; Bellarmin Codo. *La Presse dahoménne face aux aspirations des "évolués"; "La Voix du Dahomey" (1927-1957).* Thése de doctorat. Université de Paris VII, Département d'Histoire, 1978.

7. Adrien Huannou. *La Littérature Béninoise de Langue Française,* Paris: Éditions Karthala, 1984: 26.

8. *La Voix du Dahomey,* Aug. 1, 1934.

9. *La Presse Porto-Novienne,* August 1934.

10. See Bellarmin Codo. "Ethique et Deontologie Dans la Presse Dahomeenne Sous la Colonisation: Apercu Sur L'example de *La Voix du Dahomey,"* 4-5.

11. As quoted in Adrien Huannou, *La Litterature Beninoise de Langue Francaise,* Paris, A.C.C.T., 1984: 179-180.

12. Samuel Decalo. *Historical Dictionary of Benin,* London: Scarecrow Press, Inc., 1987.

13. It should be underscored that Benin's preoccupation with vodun suggested a special emphasis on witchcraft in such an epithet. The incident described is from Barry Shelby, "The Measure of

Freedom," Africa Report, May/June 1993: 63.

14. Magistrat J. Gnonlonfoun. "Rapports Presse/Pouvoir Politique au Benin," *La Presse Beninoise Face Aux Exigences d'éthique et de Déontologie,* Cotonou: La Nation/Fondation Friedrich Naumann, 1993, pp. 11-13.

Chapter 12

Deconstructing the Dialectics of Press Freedom in Cameroon

MacDonald Ndombo Kale, II

Introduction

Some three decades ago, Marshall McLuhan predicted that the world would slowly transform into a global village. Today, that global village, albeit with its imperfections, has become a reality. Few of us will deny the fact that we are now experiencing the emergence of an information society which places a heavy premium on the production, processing, and distribution of information.

With this emphasis on information, the media around the world are now taking on additional importance and responsibilities. This in turn has generated an intense interest in our quest to better understand the functioning of the media. This quest is even more urgent in the developing world where communication requirements are immense and the resources available to fulfill those requirements are limited.

In Africa for example, the imperatives of this information age society, coupled with the exigencies of a changing global geo-political landscape, have produced an intense socio-political consciousness among the masses. This consciousness is not unlike the one experienced in the decades of the 1950s and 1960s when most African nations were embroiled in the struggle for independence from colonial imperialism. The role of the mass media of information in fomenting this change has necessitated an examination of the concept of free speech and press in Africa.

While freedom of the press in Africa has been the subject of a number of studies, the authors of most of these studies have always made the assumption that the notion of liberty of thought and expression is of universal validity. This paradigm is not only based on a universalistic view of press freedoms as well as other fundamental human rights but is also largely a Eurocentric construct. It is therefore not surprising that these scholars invariably conclude that by and large the media in Africa are not free or at best enjoy only minimal freedoms in certain African nations.

It is our contention that this approach is short-sighted and fails to paint an accurate picture of the media in Africa. Accordingly, using Cameroon as a case study, it will be argued in this chapter that such a Eurocentric approach is inadequate in understanding the nature of the African media in general, and Cameroon's in particular, because it fails to take into consideration certain socio-political exigencies that impinge on govern-ment\society\press relationships.

These exigencies are not unique to Cameroon or Africa for that matter. For one thing, even in the United States of America where a broad right to speak and publish exists and there is a categorical prohibition against governmental interference, the freedom to speak and publish is not absolute. For instance, the courts have recognized the right of government to bar dissemination of expression that threatens national security interests or public safety. Thus, it is clear from this example that this right to speak and publish, which has had its fullest development in America, is grounded in the socio-political, cultural, and economic realities of the nation.

It is now generally understood that media systems are closely related to the kinds of government in which they operate. In essence, they are products of the political systems which create them. Thus, the "hegemonic hypothesis" of press-society interaction posits that although the natures of social structures and mass media systems vary among nations, the ultimate function of the press remains constant across societies. The press ultimately supports the status quo hierarchy regardless of the nature of either the press system or social power structure.

Clearly then, whether press freedom exists in any country can only be ascertained through an investigation of the government-press relationship within the context of the political, cultural, and economic realities of that country. Every nation operates with a clear set of codes governing the media. These codes reflect the political ideology of the nation. Thus, it is clear that no meaningful discussion of any media system can be addressed without reference to the political ideology of the nation. The point here is that generalizations about press freedoms cannot be made outside of the specificities of time, place, and level of socioeconomic development.

It is within this framework that we propose to examine the dialectics of press freedom in Cameroon. It will involve an investigation of the role of the press and the nature of the relationship between the press and the government. It will be argued that a better understanding of the nature of press freedom in Cameroon can only be achieved by looking at how the political, cultural, and economic realities of the country impinge on this freedom.

Because of these imperatives, it is necessary for us to view and define press freedom in Cameroon differently from how it is understood in the West. The major objective here is to revitalize the discourse on press freedom by situating it within a socioeconomic and cultural milieu. By so doing, the author will try to peel away at the loaded language that has been employed in discourses on press freedom in Africa.

The chapter begins with a brief overview of the political history of Cameroon and then examines the development of the press through the colonial era to the present. Though rather cursory, the discussion here is intended to provide a contextual framework to understand current media policy in Cameroon.

BACKGROUND AND DEVELOPMENT OF THE PRESS

The Republic of Cameroon covers an area of almost 179,000 square miles, and is geographically situated in what is generally referred to as the hinge of the African continent. Cameroon stands out as an African country which went through three different colonial experiences: German, French, and British.

The country's first colonial experience as a German colony lasted from 1884 - 1910. This period witnessed the development of a political, economic, and social framework that was to constitute the trappings of the later day Cameroon nation. With Germany's defeat at the end of World War I, Cameroon became a mandated territory of the League of Nations and, later, a Trust Territory of the United Nations. Under this political arrangement, the country was split into two parts with one half being administered by Britain and the other by France as Trust Territories of the United Nations. After attaining independence in 1961 and 1960 respectively, the two territories reunited and became the Federal Republic of Cameroon.

In spite of this unusual colonial heritage, very few scholars have undertaken an extensive study of the mass media in Cameroon. Though the media of mass communication are comparatively underdeveloped, Cameroon like most other nations professes a policy toward the media that insures liberty of speech and the press. However, unlike the industrialized nations of the West, Cameroon must constantly strive to balance the inherent tension between the government's need to ensure free speech and press rights, and its perception of the media as agents of development. This indeed is what constitutes the dialectics of press freedom.

Cameroon's checkered colonial history has had a major influence in the development of the country's press regime. Modern channels of mass communication were established in Cameroon in 1903. This date marks the first time a newspaper was established and circulated in the country. Like elsewhere on the continent, it was the missionaries who were at the forefront of this experiment to establish a mass media system. In the case of Cameroon, it was the German Protestant missionaries.

Though the German missionaries established printing presses in Cameroon, the early newspapers that appeared in the country were actually printed in Germany.[1] The first newspaper to be published and circulated in Cameroon by the Protestant missionaries was *Das Evangelische Monablatt* (The Evangelical Newsletter). It was first circulated in 1903 and was meant to serve as an evangelizing platform for converting Cameroonians to Christianity.

Besides *Das Evangelische,* other newspapers were also published by the Protestant missionaries. Noteworthy among these, was *Elolombe ya Kamerun.* Appearing in 1908, *Elolombe ya Kamerun* was published in Duala, an indigenous Cameroon language.[2] In addition to being published in a local language, the paper also stood out as one of the first newspapers in Equatorial Africa to be edited by an African.[3]

Two other newspapers circulating in Cameroon during this early part of her colonial history were the *Official Gazette* and the *Kamerun Post.*[4] Both were published in the German language and were intended for the colonial administrators and settlers. Thus, these early publications were endeavors carried out by both missionaries and colonial administrators.

The trend established by the German colonialists and missionaries was continued by their French and English counterparts. In the British-administered sector of the country, the colonial government published the *News Sheet;* and the Presbyterian missionaries, *The Cameroons Chronicle.*[5] Like the *Official Gazette, the News Sheet* contained information that was only pertinent to the activities of the colonial administrators. In much the same way, *The Cameroons Chronicle* like — *Das Evangelische* — was used by the missionaries for proselytizing. The *News Sheet* first appeared in 1930 and *The Cameroons Chronicle* in 1940.

The French colonialists and missionaries also established a number of publications. Among them were *L'Eveil des Camerounais, L'Echo du Cameroun,* and *Nieb be Krissten.*

The first two publications were founded by French settlers, while the third was a missionary endeavor. *L'Eveil des Camerounais* first appeared in 1919 and the others in the mid 1930s. It must be noted here that generally, French colonial policy discouraged the establishment of an indigenous press. However, because of Cameroon's special status as a Trust Territory of the United Nations, this policy was somewhat relaxed there.

This brief historical account of the development of the press bears some significance to our understanding of the nature of press freedom in Cameroon. It is clear that the press and for that matter modern mass media arrived in Cameroon with the colonizers. As such, some of the characteristics exhibited by the press today are reflective of the colonial era. For instance, newspaper ownership in Cameroon today continues to be an enterprise in which both government and private interests participate actively as proprietors.

Besides ownership, the system of regulations and controls of the press in force today is largely based on the French colonial model introduced in Cameroon some fifty years ago. Like the colonialists before them, Cameroon policy makers have set in place laws and regulations that tend to favor the government owned media.

Another characteristic holdover from the colonial era is the ideological slant of the press. During the colonial era, the government publications sought to express the views of the administration while the private publications were designed to complement the evangelical efforts of their various missionary owners. In Cameroon today, private publications tend to be partisan, espousing the political views of one party or the other. The government publication — like its colonial counterpart — continues to propagate the official administration line.

Since the two Trust Territories were administered separately by Britain and France, there were differences between the press policies in British Cameroons and French Cameroons. Though fewer
than their French counterparts, the English speaking publications in Cameroon even today tend to be more critical of the government than the French speaking press.

PRESS - GOVERNMENT RELATIONSHIP

Does freedom of the press exist in Cameroon? The answer to this question depends on a number of factors. Foremost among these factors is one's conceptualization of the concept of press freedom. If by freedom of the press we mean the unrestrained communication of thoughts or opinions as understood in the traditional libertarian sense, the likely answer to this question is "no." On the other hand, if we mean the presence of a written constitutional commitment to press freedom and/or the existence of a special legal regime for the press, we may answer this question with a "yes."

Though both lines of inquiry examine legitimate issues involving press freedom, they nevertheless fail to give us an accurate picture of the situation in Cameroon. In the first place, the search for understanding press freedom in Cameroon cannot focus exclusively on forms of regulation. It has to transcend the forms of regulation and inquire into the socio-political and economic exigencies that underpin the system of regulation.[6]

In the second place, it must be understood that normative constitutional commitments to press freedom do not necessarily guarantee the existence of an unfettered press. Like forms of regulation, normative constitutional commitments are also reflective of the political ideology of the state. In other words, while any number of nations may have a constitutional guarantee of press freedom, the form of its implementation is determined by the political theories that the state espouses.

Thus, an attempt to understand the nature of press freedom in Cameroon must not only take into consideration normative constitutional commitments and/or forms of regulation, but more importantly the whole socio-political and economic framework in which the media operate. Because the press is perceived as playing an integral role in the nation's development, it is this framework that can be used as a point of reference for determining press freedom.

Cameroon is one of the few African States that has succeeded in maintaining stability and continuity of its polity for a protracted period after it gained constitutional independence.

This success is partially attributed to a pursuit by the political leaders of two fundamental policies of economic development and national unity. Another factor is experimentation with various forms of political arrangements without upsetting the delicate patchwork of national unity.

The attention given to the media of mass communication in Cameroon and the conceptualization of press freedom in that polity is determined by how media affect the fundamental policies of the nation.[7] The twin goals of economic development and national unity are seen as achievable only through a collective effort involving the media. As Paul Biya, the Head of State, put it:

> National development — which is the purpose of our action — is based on national unity. Given this fact and the immense task that we still have to accomplish, it is our duty to denounce and fight all that is likely to destroy what we have built, what we are building and what we want to build.[8]

Given this perspective, it is not surprising that policymakers view the press as an agent of development and expect journalists to emphasize both political and economic activities in their coverage of events.[9]

The media of mass communications have long been regarded as having potential to facilitate development.[10] Policymakers in Cameroon view the media as a national resource in much the same way as they view agricultural, industrial, and mineral resources. Since the latter resources are state controlled for the benefit of its citizens, it would seem appropriate to expect the state to also exert some control over the media of mass communications.

Because national unity and economic development have been identified as fundamental policy goals, policymakers in Cameroon naturally look at the mass media, because of their potential to reach a broad cross-section of the population, as instruments for achieving those goals.[11] Thus, viewing the media of mass communication as agents of development and thereby exercising control over them as a means to facilitate development programs is neither inconsistent with the fundamental policies of the state nor of conventional wisdom of the role of the media. For instance, Ralph Barney has observed that:

> Unless significant and systematic quantities of development stimulating information are available to a broad cross-section of the people, minimal development activity will occur.[12]

Hence, in the battle for economic survival and political stability information — which is the product of the mass media of communications — should be seen in the context of Cameroonian realities; reflecting the level of its collective spirit and development. As Ahidjo, a former Cameroonian Head of State, put it:

> . . . information is the hyphen enabling the collective will of the nation to be translated into reality . . . Without information, there is no participation, still less any genuine adhesion to national targets, no mobilization and no effective representation.[13]

In sum, Cameroon policymakers view the press as having a political, economic, and cultural role. In addition, the press is perceived as taking on an educational role as well. As the former Head of State, Ahmadou Ahidjo, pointed out, the government's concept of the role of the mass media is to, "Inform and educate at home, explain and persuade abroad."[14] Consequently, policymakers see a nexus between the economic, political, and educational role of the media. Again, Ahidjo tells us that:

> Lack of information leads to passivity and alienation of the masses. This passivity and alienation cannot be permitted at this stage of nation-building. Information can increase a citizen's thoughts and knowledge, elevate his thinking, stimulate his intellectual curiosity. He will become conscious of Cameroonian realities, . . . (and) will understand the role he has to play in the economic and political life of the country.[15]

In his belief that a well-informed citizen is "more aware of the major stakes in national development, more conversant in his behavior, and more capable of performing his duties to the nation,"[16] Paul Biya appears to underscore Ahidjo's point.

Because national unity and economic development constitute the central pillars of state ideology in Cameroon, and because of a realization of the role of the media in forging this ideology, the press is assigned a special status within the state. It is regarded as an irreplaceable vehicle of information that must not only inform the citizens on development projects, but must also educate them on how to carry out those projects.[17] Journalists are assigned the role of not only stimulating, orienting, and controlling all development projects,[18] but also the imperative duty to ensure that development projects are accomplished.[19]

To make sure that they function as expected, journalists are trained to assume the role of development agents who must exercise discretion in the practice of their profession for the collective good of the nation as a whole. Commenting on the curriculum of the journalism institute in Cameroon, a former director of the school, Herve Bourges, had this to say:

> . . (the curriculum) is a symbiosis between abstracts and technical teaching. The students learn to adapt the media to the needs of their countries and face the realities of their day-to-day jobs. We teach them how to explain the news to the public because there is currently a barrier between what the journalists print or broadcast and what the population understands.[20]

Obviously, this concept of development journalism is what underpins any discussion of press freedom in Cameroon. Thus, it should be confined to whether or not the press is free to operate within the parameters defined by the nation's fundamental policies of economic development and national unity.

Based on this understanding, the role expected of a journalist in Cameroon is somewhat different from that of his/her counterpart in the West. As Faringer has observed, "the concept of development journalism implies a news philosophy significantly different from that promoted in Western industrialized countries."[21] It is clear from this context that the luxury of a "free press" as defined by Western standards undoubtedly cannot exist in Cameroon.

CONSTITUTIONAL COMMITMENTS
AND FORMS OF REGULATION

The government of Cameroon professes a system that guarantees freedom of speech and the press. There is a provision in the Constitution of the Republic of Cameroon guaranteeing the right of individual expression and freedom of the press. In addition, there are a number of ordinances, decrees, and laws that regulate the press. Thus, freedom of the press is based on a constitutional commitment and the existence of a special legal regime for the press.[22]

The law that governs the press and other media of mass communication was promulgated on December 21 1966. This law, the basic press law, was modeled after the 1881 and 1893 French press laws which were applied to Cameroon after the departure of the Germans.[23] The law has been amended five times since its passage, with the most recent amendment being that of 1990. The basic press law provides the framework for fulfilling the rights of individual expression and freedom of the press guaranteed by the Constitution. Following the French model, the statute basically proclaims that the freedoms of the press and expression guaranteed by the Constitution are exercised under conditions provided by the law.[24] In addition to providing the framework for exercising freedom of expression, the law also defines which organs of the media it applies to and how the profession of journalism is to be practiced in Cameroon.[25]

Notwithstanding the provision in Article 6, chapter 1 of the press law guaranteeing a free press, this freedom does not appear to be absolute. While the law facilitates the creation of newspapers, there are a number of restrictions imposed on the press in Section III. For example, all editors are required to submit copies of their papers respectively to the Procurator General of the Republic, the Governors Office in the province of publication and to the Ministry of Territorial Administration for censorship purposes.[26]

Violations of this and other provisions could result in the confiscation of the newspaper and payment of a fine. In extreme cases, editors might be jailed and the paper shut down.

In effect the new law institutionalizes censorship with its provision for a priori administrative censorship. Draconian as these
measures may appear, the government believes it is justified in
imposing them if responsible journalism is to be encouraged.
Nevertheless, it also recognizes the potential chilling effect of
such restrictions. However, given the priorities of the nation's
development objectives, the chilling effect is seen as a necessary
evil. As one government minister summed it up, the press
"should be a pillar of the New Deal government and not a forum
of conflict of interest and personalities."[27]

The chilling effect of the censorship provision seems to be
mitigated through a provision of the law that states that appeals
against censorship decisions, suspensions and bans can be made
to the law courts. Unfortunately, recourse to the law courts and
the maximum period of 30 days for the disposal of conflicts arising from censorship is far from reassuring to those who prefer
to see the press function in absolute freedom. In addition,
because no indication is given as to who is a competent judge to
hear these appeals, more often than not bureaucrats tend to
usurp these functions.

How can one reconcile the explicit guarantee of press freedom and liberty of expression found in the Constitution with the
existence of a legal regime that appears to circumscribe these liberties? To answer this question one needs to understand why
these laws have been passed, how they operate in practice, and
what role the press is seen to play in society. In other words, one
needs to look at the dialectics of press freedom in Cameroon.

THE DIALECTICS OF PRESS FREEDOM

The dialectics of press freedom in Cameroon are characterized
by the nature of the relationship between the press and the government. The nature of press/government relationship clearly
demonstrates a tension between the government's need to carry
out its political and economic objectives and its need to ensure
freedom of the press. This tension is not unique to Cameroon.

For Cameroon policymakers the controlling issue involved in
this tension is determining who has the right to inform. Realizing

that an unfettered and irresponsible press could compromise national unity and socioeconomic development, the government has made it clear that its political and economic agenda takes precedence over uncontrolled press freedom and has called on the press to take on an active role in promoting this agenda. To this effect, the government has implemented legal and extralegal controls to guide press activity in Cameroon.

To an observer of press activity in Cameroon, this relationship — characterized as it is by laws and regulations — seems to take on the form of control and censorship by the government. In essence, the conclusion can be drawn that under such conditions the press cannot operate freely. The press, in other words, cannot perform its duty as the veritable barometer of the socioeconomic and political pressure of the nation.

That the press in Cameroon does not operate as the "fourth estate" of the realm is unquestionable. However, to conclude that this precludes the press from operating freely or that the inability of the press to act as government watchdog is simply a factor of governmental controls, is in many respects unwarranted. It is unwarranted because such a conclusion is based on a framework of media analysis that is clearly biased by European and American media theories.

Faringer underscores the point by emphasizing the risks inherent in this approach of media analysis in the Third World that takes a Eurocentric framework as a point of departure. Such an approach in her words "disregards the unique history and context of the Third World in which these media function."[28] Commenting on the mass media in Africa, Ziegler and Asante also note that "these Eurocentric formulations . . . grossly skew the nature of the media institutions to the European model."[29]

Because there are few universally objective standards by which any press system can be judged,[30] it would seem that a better understanding of press activity in Cameroon requires a framework of analysis other than the Eurocentric formulations that many observers of the media environment in Africa are quick to apply. Ziegler and Asante appear to have provided such a framework. Ziegler and Asante advocate a formulation of the media as either (1) unrestrained, (2) restrained or (3) directed.[31]

They describe an unrestrained media as one that operates "according to their own values, norms and objectives."[32] A restrained press on the other hand is controlled by the government. In contrast, the directed press "operates under the influence of the government's stated objectives for national development."[33] This third formulation, directed media, provides the best framework for analyzing press activity in Cameroon.

Though the 1972 Constitution guarantees freedom of the press, the system of controls imposed on the press appears to infringe on this freedom. However, since the media in Cameroon are directed, a certain degree of press control is necessary to ensure that the government's stated objectives for national development are realized.

In its role as spokesperson, moderator, conscience, informant, educator and entertainer, the press is indispensable in shaping national opinion. Such power brings with it responsibilities and without necessary safeguards this power could be abused. It is this realization that leads government officials to be of the opinion that misinformation in the press could undermine efforts at forging national unity and derail development plans. Thus, the officials find it necessary to implement regulations that safeguard against the dissemination of rumors, false, or critical information that can have an adverse effect on government policy. While this may appear as blatant censorship, there is reason for the government to be concerned. In a society with a low level of literacy, news based on rumors may not only undermine the government's development policies but could also have a negative impact on the credibility of the press.

In addition, the manner in which Cameroonian journalists, particularly in the private press, identify and articulate their mission lends credence to the government's fears. As one observer points out, newspaper proprietors and journalists have a tendency to:

> consider information as a commercial product and ignore the rigorous imperatives of information as a service to the community. Information is sacrificed for

escapism and distraction in order to win readers for advertisers.[34]

The net effect is that journalists tend to be more interested in sensational reporting as opposed to investigative journalism. A cursory glance at some of the stories and news reported in the daily papers will confirm this observation. For example, it is common to see headlines like: "Talking Boar Chases Woman; Seizes Dress," "Panic Dead Woman Awakes," or "Man Jailed for Sucking Blood."[35] More often than not accounts of these and other crime stories are from people who did not witness the events.

Preoccupation with such noncritical, sensational, yellow journalism is motivated by the desire of editors to gain larger audiences and to increase the circulation of their newspapers. Consequently, such a competition for readership has seriously affected the watchdog role of the press because it has led to a further fragmentation of a limited and heterogeneous readership. This has in turn led to a further corrosion of the press' credibility as information seeker and giver. As a former Cameroon journalist has noted, the press "increasingly panders to smaller audiences" thereby "minimizing its role as a national player."[36]

Beyond the regulations imposed by the government, the effectiveness of the press in disseminating information to the masses is hampered by the proliferation of press organs. These publications — usually sponsored by the various political parties and editors — are more interested in promoting the ideas of their sponsors rather than in reporting the news accurately. This has led to the development of a dangerous fanaticism in the press.

Even though most of the publications of the private press are sponsored by political parties, they still experience financial difficulties. This lack of a sound financial base has also affected the publication of these newspapers. Most privately owned newspapers do not honor their periodicity and publication tends to occur at the convenience of the publishers. Thus, the quality and durability of a privately owned newspaper depends on the effort of one individual. It is common for a publisher to combine the duties of editor, business manager, reporter and copywriter in order to stay in business.[37]

Beset by financial, managerial and sometimes regulatory problems, the coverage of the privately owned newspapers is not only limited to the immediate vicinity where publication occurs, but the content of the papers tends to be limited as well. As a result, the effectiveness of the private press as national players is further mitigated. Given the above conditions, it is not surprising that the government would see fit to establish regulations designed to alleviate these problems.

Imponderables of Press Freedom

How can there be a free press in a system that promulgates regulations designed to control this freedom? What effect has the legal regime of the press in Cameroon on press freedom? Can the press in Cameroon be both free and guided? These are the questions that must be answered in order to unravel the dialectics of press freedom in Cameroon.

The institution of a legal regime for the press in Cameroon does not necessarily preclude it from operating freely. The literature on media studies appears to agree that media institutions are products of the political systems which create them.[38] Thus political ideology determines not only journalistic paradigms, but control of media institutions as well. Even in the United States where the emphasis is on media professionalism, "this media professionalism is consonant with the dominant ideology."[39]

Again, it is necessary to emphasize that any meaningful discussion about press activity in Cameroon cannot be done without reference to the political ideology of the state. Clearly then, whether the press operates freely in Cameroon becomes a question of determining what role is defined for it by the state and whether it operates freely in that role and within the parameters of state ideology.

As pointed out earlier, state ideology in Cameroon is premised on the need to attain national unity and socioeconomic development. Socioeconomic development is understood to mean the development of basic socioeconomic and industrial infrastructures such as to improve the material well-being of all Cameroonians. Because these goals benefit society at large, Cameroon policymakers expect the media to play an active role in their realization.

Such a role as expected of the press will preclude it from being an adversary of the government in the sense understood in industrialized democracies. The press cannot therefore — as contended by the former President Ahidjo — claim the sort of luxuries as is the case in the West.[40] Indeed, the press is seen more as being in partnership with the government. In many ways, it is an extension of the government rather than the fourth estate of the realm.

This government/press partnership has inevitably resulted in limitations being set on the press. In a speech to the private press, a former Minister of Information and Culture underscored some of these limitations. Extolling the virtues of Cameroon's democratic institutions, he nevertheless pointed out that:

> . . . democracy does not allow journalists to publish without discernment the most whimsical and uncontrolled information. It also means, in a democratic regime, it is not always advisable to expose the public to information that could disturb public order or compromise the security of the state.[41]

In addition, the press has been advised to discard any information that is disruptive because it compromises national unity and deters realization of national goals.[42] Statements such as these, are addressed to the press in general and underscore the government's policy regarding the parameters of press freedom. There are times, however, when editors or publishers of newspapers who appear to ignore the message are singled out and told to toe the line. For example, a former Minister of Territorial Administration told the publisher of one of the more critical and controversial newspapers, *Le Messager,* to disseminate "healthy, dispassionate, and less controversial information."[43]

Journalistic restraint for the sake of social tranquillity is a doctrine that has found adherents besides government policymakers. The limitations placed on the press are not only justified by government officials, but by journalists as well. A *Cameroon Times* editorial concurred with the government that the press should eschew:

> the freedom to express destructive opinions which create rancor in a society which strives to promote political harmony and peaceful co-existence.[44]

Another prominent Cameroonian journalist justified the need to control the sort of information provided by the press on the grounds that journalists — like other human beings — are fallible.

> And since human beings are, after all, fallible, Government thought it should reduce the chances of our misjudgments by providing for a final checking prior to publication . . . When our obligation to inform, educate, explain and persuade collides with other fundamental goals or interests of the State which might escape us, someone who knows has to intervene so that we do not appear to have cross-purposes.[45]

Clearly then, it would appear that both the government and the press community see a need for a guided press.

As pointed out earlier, this need for a guided press is based on a state ideology that regards social and political stability as prerequisites to economic progress and national development. This ideology demands that press policy be made relevant to the political needs of the nation. In this mode of thinking, all resources available to the nation must be mobilized toward the realization of its goals. It is, therefore, not surprising that the press cannot take on the traditional role of fourth estate of the realm as understood in the West. The roles assigned to the press and for that matter the media, are closely aligned with government policies which are often presented as serving the collective good of the nation.

However, within the parameters of state ideology, some questions can be raised as to whether the press in Cameroon operates freely. In light of the socio-political and economic needs of the country, the operative concept in Cameroon's press paradigm is development journalism. Basic to this concept is the notion that the press corps must operate as development agents and actively participate in disseminating information and educating the masses about the government's development activities and goals. In this role, the press is not only required to practice some self-censorship but must rely on the government for most of the information that it is supposed to pass on to the masses. It is in this area, taking the particularities of the Cameroonian context into consideration, that one can assess the freedom with which the press operates.

Notwithstanding recent political developments that have led to the lifting of restrictions on multiparty politics in the country, the government and the political system in Cameroon continue to operate in secrecy. Cameroonian and foreign journalists have often expressed great frustration in their attempts to obtain information from government officials regarding the activities of the state. It is this frustration in accessing news sources that perhaps accounts for the greatest limitation on press freedom within the context of Cameroon. To function effectively as development agents, journalists must have the freedom to access information. Difficulties in reaching government ministers and the reluctance of senior officials to comment on government projects greatly restrict this access. Recent efforts taken by the government to remedy this situation by instituting ministerial press conferences have met with little success.

The main objective of these press conferences is to establish dialogue between the government and the people, with the press as the intermediary. Ministers are supposed to inform the press on developments in their ministries and answer questions. Though providing a very important potential source of information to journalists, the press conferences in practice tend to be inefficient. For one thing, ministers tend to be afraid to say things that might annoy the President.[46] For another, journalists themselves tend to be afraid to ask probing questions, either out of concern for their political and financial security or because they are incompetent.

Another remedy introduced by the government to facilitate news flow is the employment of public relations officers in the various ministries. However, like the press conferences, this has not improved matters. For one thing, the public relations officers are, as Wete observed "the last to be informed of what is happening in their ministries."[47] For another, like their bosses, these public relations officers — even when they have an idea of what is going on in their ministries — tend to be afraid of releasing information for fear of annoying someone.

This state of affairs has resulted in a situation in which journalists are not only frustrated by the lack of news sources, but also the inability to determine what is or is not publishable. More often than not they have to resort to unofficial sources and personal relationships to get information.[48] Because the reliability of these sources often prove to be questionable the press ends up reporting very little political news other than accounts of official ceremonies. This of course is contrary to the objectives of the government since its press policy is one that emphasizes the reporting of political and economic news, albeit from the perspective of policymakers.

In light of the above situation, it may be fair to conclude that journalists lack the freedom to operate within the prescribed parameters of state ideology. After all, they are expected to convey to the masses news about government development programs and yet are not able to freely access the sources of this information.

The above notwithstanding, some journalists have developed innovative ways to circumvent the system. For instance, official versions of news stories are sometimes reported in coded language to indicate to the audience that those accounts should be consumed with a grain of salt. As Chinje states:

> Before the advent of democratic change in Cameroon, for instance, the media would preface every government-imposed editorial opinion with a quote from one of the Head of State's many speeches, signalling that the message should be consumed with care.[49]

Thus, this coded language could take the form of an obvious omission or insertion of a particular word or words in the newspaper or a wink on television.

Journalists, especially those working for the government-owned media, have also developed a strategy for criticizing government in which the criticism is couched in the form of hopes for improvement, while at the same time applauding the achievements of the government. In addition, as part of this strategy, some journalists have also developed a habit of writing in a language that can be understood only by the educated minority. A noted Cameroonian journalist and priest once stated that he had been advised to write his articles with "big words" so that most Cameroonians would not understand them.[50]

Satire is another strategy employed by the news media, particularly the anglophone press, to criticize the government. Often columns like "Ako Aya" in *Cameroon Outlook,* "King for Toli" in *Le Courrier Sportif,* and "Mola Fako" in *Fako Magazine* are written in Pidgin English with an abundant use of innuendoes to criticize the government.[51] Other columns like "Ngumba's Diary" and "Matters Arising" both in *Cameroon Life* are written in English. The use of political and social satire to advocate reform and criticize the government would seem to indicate that Cameroon journalists appear to have learnt to make the best of the information they can report.

But it will be wrong to conclude that all criticisms of the government by the press are through satire. The recent mushrooming of political parties, with each trying to carve a niche in the press, has resulted in the expression of diversified opinions. Thus each political party either owns a newspaper or receives support for its platform from one of the private publications. This state of events has led to a bolder and more forthright stance taken by the press in their criticism of the government.

For instance, one of the more celebrated cases of open criticism of the government was the so called "Monga Affair." This case was about an Open Letter written by the editor of *Le Messager,* Celestin Monga. In this letter, Monga not only ridiculed the president and his government, calling on them to resign, but also charged that the Head of State and his wife were involved in the failing of the Societe Camerounaise de Banque. These statements led not only to the confiscation of that edition of *Le Messager* by the police, but also to the arrest of its editor and closing of the offices of the newspaper.[52]

Within the context of press freedom in Cameroon, this *cause celebre* is remarkable in a number of ways. In the first case, the "Monga Affair" tested the legal limits of journalistic freedom under the revised 1990 Press Law. Celestin Monga and the proprietor of the newspaper Pius Njawe were accused of having slandered the Head of State, the National Assembly and the Judiciary. In a very highly publicized trial which attracted both national and international attention, both Njawe and Monga were set free and the ban on *Le Messager* was lifted. Thus, this case, to a certain extent, demonstrates that journalists can find relief in the Press Law.

Another effect of this case on press freedom was that it more clearly defined how far the press could go in their criticism of the government and its policies. While outright criticism of the government didn't necessarily begin with the publication of Monga's "Open Letter to President Paul Biya," it certainly emboldened journalists in their attack of the system. Now, it is not unusual to see articles ranging from those questioning the legitimacy of the Head of State and his government to the plight of the rural and forgotten masses.[53] Neither is it uncommon to see headlines like "Fraud at INTELCAM: Biya's Cousin in 800m. Francs Scandal"[54] or "Military Terror in Bamenda."[55]

It would seem from the above discussion that lack of access to government news sources notwithstanding, Cameroon journalists have found means to maximize and make the best of the information they can report. Furthermore, journalists, particularly in the private press, are increasingly testing the limits of their freedom by publishing articles critical of the government and the Head of State.

CONCLUSION

In deconstructing the dialectics of press freedom in Cameroon, I have attempted to peel away at the loaded language that has been employed in discourses on press freedom in Africa. These dialectics involve two competing paradigms: a universalist view of press freedoms as well as other fundamental human rights, versus a relativist vision of these same freedoms. The objective here is to relativize press freedom by situating it within a socioeconomic and cultural milieu.

Using Cameroon as a case study, the author argued that generalizations about press freedoms cannot be made outside of the specificities of time, place, and level of socioeconomic development, and that these considerations are central to any analysis of press freedom in Cameroon. In other words, in contemplating the issues of press freedom in Cameroon, the suggestion is made here that we need to suspend our understanding of this concept as applied in the West.

Cameroon is one of the countries in Africa that allows the existence of a private press alongside government owned media. This, and the fact that policymakers regard socioeconomic development and national unity as primary goals, has led not only to the enlisting of the press as partners in achieving these goals, but also in establishing certain guidelines under which the press operates. The parameters of press freedom in Cameroon are, therefore, defined by the political, social and economic exigencies of the state. Considerations of national interests provide the context for press freedom and journalists are expected to operate with these obligations in mind.

While the legal regime does not specify the kind of information that is unpublishable, it is clear that indications of the limits of press freedoms are contained in speeches by the Head of State and other senior government officials. This strategy of dispensing counsels underscores the government objective of dealing with the media through persuasion rather than coercion. It is this that leads us to conclude that the press in Cameroon, though guided, given the exigencies of the situation, is relatively free.

SELECTED BIBLIOGRAPHY

Aboaba, Doyin. "The Nigerian Press Under Military Rule." Unpublished doctoral dissertation. Buffalo: State University of New York, 1979.

Ahidjo, Ahmadou. *The Political Thought of Ahmadou Ahidjo.* Monaco, 1968.

Biya, Paul. *The New Deal Message.* Yaounde: Sopecam Publications, 1984.

Bourdon-Higbee. "The Besieged Media of Cameroon." *Monatana Journalism Review*. 19, 1976.

Bourges, Herve. *Reflexion sur la Role de la Presse en Afrique*. Paris: Institut Francais de Presse, 1973.

Cameroon Life. vol. iii, No. 6, July 1992.

Cameroon Post. Sept. 6-13 1991.

Cameroon Times. Sept. 25 1984: 8.

Cameroon Tribune. July 18 1984: 8-9.

Chinje, E. "The Media in Emerging African Democracies: Power, Politics and the Role of the Press." *The Fletcher Forum of World Affairs*. vol. 17, 1993.

Curry, J.L. and Joan Dassin. *Press Control Around the World*. New York: Praeger Publishers, 1982.

Hachten, W.A. *The Growth of Media in the Third World: African Failures, Asian Successes*. Ames: Iowa State University Press.

Kale, MacDonald N. "The Role of Public Address in the Search for National Integration in *Africa: A Rhetorical Investigation of the Cameroon Nationalist Movement*." Unpublished doctoral dissertation. Bloomington: Indiana University, Bloomington, 1985.

Keane, J. *The Media and Democracy*. Cambridge: Policy Press, 1991.

Lahav, P. *Press Law in Modern Democracies*. New York: Longman Inc., 1985.

Lerner, D. and Wilbur Schramm. eds. *Communication and Change in Developing Countries*. Honolulu: East-West Center, 1967.

Man Chan, Joseph and Chin-Chuan Lee. *Mass Media and Political Transition: The Hong Kong Press in China's Orbit*. New York: The Guildford Press, 1991.

Martin, R. "Building Independent Mass Media in Africa." *The Journal of Modern African Studies*. 30, 1992.

Momoh, P.T. "The Press and Nation-Building." *Africa Report* 32, 1987.

Mytton, G. *Mass Communication in Africa*. London: Edward Arnold, 1983.

Ugboajah, F.O., ed. *Mass Communication, Culture and Society in West Africa*. Oxford: Hans Zell.

Sumner, W.G. *Folkways: A Study in the Sociological Importance of Usages, Manners, Customs, Mores and Morals*. Boston: Ginn, Athanaeum, 1911.

Udoakah, N. "Press freedom, the West and Africa." Africa, 154:35, June 1984.

Wete, Francis. *Development Journalism: Philosophy and Practice in Cameroon*. Unpublished doctoral dissertation. Columbia: University of Missouri, Columbia, 1986.

Ziegler, Dhyana and Molefi Asante. *Thunder and Silence: The Mass Media in Africa.* Trenton, New Jersey: Africa World Press, Inc., 1992.

NOTES

1. Francis Wete, "Development Journalism: Philosophy and Practice in Cameroon," (Unpublished Ph.D. dissertation, University of Missouri, Columbia, 1986): 94
2. Wete: 95
3. Ibid
4. Ibid
5. National Archives, Buea, Republic of Cameroon.
6. Pnina Lahav, "An Outline for a General Theory of Press Law in Democracy," in P. Lahav, ed. *Press Law in Modern Democracies.* New York: Longman Inc., 1985: 354.
7. Wete, op. cit., p. 137.
8. Paul Biya, *The New Deal Message.* Yaounde, Cameroon: Sopecam Publications, 1984: 525.
9. Wete: 138.
10. Ralph B. Barney, "Mass Media Roles in Development: A Descriptive Study from Four Developing Countries." *Gazette* 19. 4: 223; Lucien W. Pye, "Communication, Institution Building, and the Reach of Authority," in Daniel Lerner and Wilbur Schramm, eds. *Communication and Change in Developing Countries* Honolulu: East-West Center, 1967: 37.
11. Wete: 141.
12. Barney: 223.
13. Ahmadou Ahidjo, *The Political Thought of Ahmadou Ahidjo.* Monaco, 1968: 58.
14. Ahmadou Ahidjo, General Policy Statement, Cameroon National Union party congress, Garoua, March, 1969.
15. Ibid.
16. Paul Biya, *New Deal Message.* Yaounde, Cameroon: Sopecam, 1986: 22.
17. Cameroon Tribune July 18 1984: 8-9.
18. Ibid: 8-9.
19. Ahmadou Ahidjo, Speech at Inauguration of National Station of Radio Cameroon, Yaounde, Jan. 20 1980.
20. Herve Bourges, *Reflexion sur la Role de la Presse en Afrique* Paris: Institut Francais de Presse, 1973: 8-9.
21. Gunilla Faringer, *Press Freedom in Africa.* New York: Praeger, 1991: 127.

22. *Constitution of the Republic of Cameroon*, 1972, Article 20.
23. Wete, *op. cit.*: 162.
24. Article I, Loi No. 90/052 du 19 Dec. 1990.
25. Ibid., Titre I, Art. 2.
26. Ibid., section III, Art. 4.
27. *Cameroon Tribune* Sept. 25 1984: 8.
28. Faringer, op. cit.: 108
29. Dhyana Ziegler and Molefi Asante, *Thunder and Silence: The Mass Media in Africa*. Trenton, New Jersey: Africa World Press, Inc., 1992: 104.
30. Doyin Aboaba, *The Nigerian Press Under Military Rule,* Unpublished doctoral dissertation, State University of New York, Buffalo, 1979: 105.
31. Ziegler and Asante: 104.
32. Ibid: 104.
33. Ibid.
34. Wete, *op. cit.*.: 146.
35. Cameroon Times, Sept. 21 1974: 1.
36. Eric Chinje, "The Media in Emerging African Democracies: Power, Politics and the Role of the Press," *The Fletcher Forum of World Affairs* 17, Winter 1993: 62.
37. Wete: 176.
38. See for example, Aboaba, op. cit.: 102.
39. Joseph Man Chan and Chin-Chuan Lee, *Mass Media and Political Transition: The Hong Kong Press in China's Orbit*. New York: The Guildford Press, 1991: 30.
40. *Cameroon Tribune* July 1 1974: 1.
41. Sengat Kuo, Address to Private Press, quoted in Wete, op. cit.: 154.
42. Wete: 157.
43. Ibid: 157.
44. *Cameroon Times* Aug. 7 1976: 72.
45. Wete: 166.
46. Wete, op. cit.: 170.
47. Wete: 170.
48. Bourdon-Higbee, "The Besieged Media of Cameroon," *Montana Journalism Review* 19, Montana School of Journalism, 1976: 19.
49. Chinje, *The Media in Emerging African Democracies:...*, op. cit.: 52.
50. Wete: 177
51. Ibid: 177.
52. See special report in *Cameroon Life,* vol. iii, No 6, July 1992.
53. *Cameroon Life* 6, July 1992: 22-30.

54. *Cameroon Post*, Sept. 6-13 1991: 1.
55. *Cameroon Post*, Aug. 19-26 1991: 3.

CHAPTER 13

PROBLEMS OF PRESS FREEDOM IN COTE D'IVOIRE

Andre Jean Tudesq

POLITICAL HISTORY

Cote d'Ivoire has an area of 322.462 square kilometers, and an estimated 14.7 million people. The French made their appearance in the country as early as 1842, establishing military and trading posts. With the onset of colonialism, France governed Cote d'Ivoire as part of *Afrique Occidental Francaise* (French West Africa), a unit of its larger African empire.

In 1946, Cote d'Ivoire was granted the status of "overseas territory." It created an African farming union which after the 1945 election gave birth to Cote d'Ivoire Democratic Party (PDCI) initiated by Deputy Felix Houphouet-Boigny, a medical practitioner and planter who had been elected to the French Constitutional Assembly by the restricted African electoral college.

Cote d'Ivoire was proclaimed a republic on December 4 1958 and was granted independence on August 7 1960 with Houphouet-Boigny as president.

For more than three decades, Cote d'Ivoire had and knew only one president: Houphouet-Boigny. Opposition to one-man rule intensified in 1990 resulting in the government's acceptance of multi-partyism on April 30 1990. A presidential election in October 1990, allegedly rigged by the government, resulted in 81.7% of the vote for Houphouet-Boigny compared to a mere 18.3% for Laurent Gbagbo of the opposition Cote d'Ivoire Popular Front.

Since February 18 1992 when demonstrations for a more liberal and open society ended in the arrest and imprisonment of several opposition leaders, there has been a disillusioned mood prevailing within the divided and weakened opposition. The death of Houphouet Boigny in 1994 after more than 34 years in public office may well be the oxygen that the opposition needs to stay alive.

MEDIA DEVELOPMENT:
PRE- AND POST-COLONIAL ERA PRESS

The written press established in Cote d'Ivoire in 1893 was originally a monopoly of the French colonial administration. Publications by and for French settlers included *L'Independant Colonial* (1931) and *France-Afrique* (1933), later a daily in 1951 titled *Abidjan-Matin.*

The first newspaper published by an Ivorian was *L'Eclaireur de la Cote D'Ivoire* (1935) by Kouame Benzeme. From the early 1950s to independence in 1960, African-managed publications provided a forum for the discussion of the country's future, albeit along party lines. The Pan African Democratic Union's *La Voix de l'Afrique Noire* shifted from being critical of the colonial administration to being willing to dialogue. *L'Afrique Noire,* run by Houphouet Boigny of Cote d'Ivoire Democratic Party, advocated an evolution within the French Union (PDCI).

When the PDCI came to power after the attainment of national independence, it began replacing the multi-party press with a state information system. The establishment of Cote d'Ivoire Press Agency (1962) and *Fraternite Matin,* the first government-owned daily (December 1964), were the first steps toward government monopoly over information.

Radio

Radio broadcasting began in 1949 with a studio in Abidjan and another station in Bingerville from 1951. On October 31 1962 Radio Cote d'Ivoire was established as a public commercial company free from French control. Although the French were still responsible for the technical management of radio, Cote d'Ivoire has been training its own technicians at the Ecole Nationale Superieure des PTT.

In 1991 there were over two dozen radio stations in Cote d'Ivoire, including four medium wave stations, four short wave stations, thirteen HF stations and a few relay stations. With a 753 KW power, radio reaches virtually all of Cote d'Ivoire. There are eight regional production centers providing broadcasting in thirteen African languages. Although it is closely linked to the government, radio is truly a mass medium in Cote d'Ivoire, providing local entertainment programs and news, albeit good news.

Television

The birth and development of television in Cote d'Ivoire in 1963 was faster than in most African countries. Beginning with an hour and a half daily broadcasting time, television soon began penetrating the country's hinterland, a feat generally reserved for radio. Between 1964 and 1972, new stations were set up in Dotenzia to cover central Cote d'Ivoire, Mont Tonkoui to cover the west and several other stations to cover the east and north. Almost 70 percent of the villages could receive television broadcasts with state-owned sets under an educational television scheme.

In 1983, television reached over 60 percent of the country through twelve stations and five relays stations. In 1990, television coverage reached 90 percent of the country which now had sixteen stations and eight relay stations. In addition, a ground station in Akrako near Abidjan has made it possible to receive and broadcast satellite images from around the world.

Television is generally used for health education, entertainment, and news programs. The Community Television Experiment in Bonoua in 1977 was short-lived. Since 1987, however, "La Voix du Paysan," a program aimed at the rural audience, has been broadcast once a month.

MULTIPARTY POLITICS AND PRESS FREEDOM

Since independence, Cote d'Ivoire government, like its counterparts in other African countries, brought the media under its control. Such control is exerted by the Ministry of Information which holds a grip on *Fraternite Matin* — a government daily, the radio and television networks, Cote d'Ivoire Press Agency and Documentation Service, along with a photography service.

This take-over of public information by the state and the single party lasted almost three decades and was challenged in 1989 when the winds of multiparty politics began making their way to Africa from Eastern Europe.

Since 1990, multiparty politics has resulted in greater freedom of information, including the birth of many private newspapers, mostly partisan. New titles close to the opposition include *Nouvel Horizon* (1990), *Jeune Democrate* (1990), *Le Soleil d'Or, Cote d'Ivoire Nouvelle* (1990), *La Voie* (1991), *Changement (1992), L'Espoir* (1993).

The satirical press includes *L'Araignee and L'Agoutipenseur,* along with a radio and TV magazine, *Micro-Public,* and several sports newspapers, notably *Afrique-Sports.*

While the winds of freedom have roused the country's journalists and prompted them to begin publishing newspapers representing all sectors, the realities of publishing in Africa have set upon them. Many editors lack the working capital to sustain a publication for long. By the end of 1991, for example, about 25 newspapers still came out regularly whereas 37 had disappeared or were published irregularly.

Whatever freedom the Ivoirian journalists have enjoyed can perhaps be evaluated by examining the changes within the print and broadcast media.

The coming of the "new papers," often staffed by journalists with a commitment for political change, has changed the once government-owned and controlled media, particularly *Fraternite Matin,* the influential government daily, forever. In the early

1990s, the paper's circulation fell from 80,000 to 50,000. Advertising revenue also dropped, resulting in a ten-hour strike on January 7 1993.

Fraternite Matin, formerly a mouthpiece of the PDCI-led government, has undergone some significant changes. Not only does the paper now report on stories involving controversy, but it also dialogues with, rather than confront the opposition press. In fact, it even covers the activities of the opposition parties. On December 3 1991 it reported on a debate on 'Media and Democracy" in Yopongou.

On January 13 1993 the newspaper *Notre Temps* wrote: "We are forced to acknowledge that most of the colleagues and friends of the *Fraternite Matin* group have recovered their professionalism."

The broadcast media, on the other hand, have not been so free to experiment with the new liberalism simply because the government has attempted to maintain the usual controls, albeit loosely. In general, one can say the state monopoly over the airwaves has come to an end. Radio and television have made a tentative and somewhat difficult opening to representatives of the opposition, although in principle the state is still in control. A censorship committee set up on the eve of the October 1990 election, however, limited the opposition's TV campaign, banning an FPI program which mentioned a BBC poll favorable to the opposition. When FPI leaders staged a sit-in at the TV station on October 14 1990, police and the army forcibly removed them in a confrontation that was broadcast on television.

A comment by *La Tribune du Banco* that the TV broadcast had denounced the FPI activists "without reporting on the circumstances of the event" showed just how much government control remains over the media. Print, radio and TV journalists may have contributed to a wider opening of the state media but it will take time for the state's grip on the media to be completely untied.

Laws governing media development and performance still place much power in the hands of the government. In December 1991, a new law modeled after France and Senegal introduced a new framework for the creation of newspapers, which include a simple notification to be sent to the Public Prosecutor's Office. The same law also calls for the creation of a National Committee for the Freedom of the Press whose members are to be appointed by the head of state.

Despite protests from the opposition, the bill — popularly known as the December 21 Act — passed the National Assembly and became law. Provisions of the law require that the chairman of the National Committee for the Press be designated by the President of the Republic; that one member of the committee be designated by the President of the National Assembly; one representative from the Ministry of Home Affairs, one from the Ministry of Communication, one judge from the Audit Office, and two journalists.

In addition, the publication of a newspaper or periodical is only subjected to notification to the Public Prosecutor's office. The manager must be a Cote d'Ivoire citizen and can neither be a member of parliament nor a minister. The right of private persons and legal entities to reply or correct is to be provided free of charge. Provision is made for fines and prison sentences from two months to one year if a newspaper company breaks the law.

A newspaper can be suspended for three months or seized for libel against the head of state, the head of government or the presidents of institutional bodies, as well as in many cases such as "conspiracy against the internal and external security of the state." The act also provides for state aid to the press without specifying its form, except for preferential rates or tax relief.

With regards to broadcasting, the act officially put an end to state monopoly over radio and television, but retained, in principle, a shadow role over broadcasting. Infrastructures and wave bands remained "state property" (Clauses 3 and 4), but Clause 5 states in part that "the national state service for radio and television can be conceded to one or several private persons or legal entities."

Provision is made for preserving a share of the broadcasting time for national productions. Advertising and program sponsorship are acceptable.

On August 7 1992 the Minister for Communication issued an invitation to tender for the concession of one TV frequency and five radio frequencies. On December 23 1992 the five new radio frequencies were alloted to three foreign companies, Radio France Internationale, BBC, and Africa No. 1. The two Cote d'Ivoire channels are Jeune Afrique Musique (JAM), and Radio-Nostalgie.

In addition to the available frequencies, Radio Espoir FM (a Catholic radio broadcasting station close to Abidjan), has been broadcasting since 1990. Radio Paix Sanwi, another Catholic radio station, has been broadcasting from Aboisso since April 1992.

Television is still a government monopoly. Television Ivorienne, which has two channels, has been dominant since its inception in 1963. A private TV channel operated by Canal Horizon, a subsidy of Canal Plus (France), was expected to commence broadcasts from Abidjan during the early 1990s.

Direct access to TV satellites with dish aerials and wider use of video recorders have already counterbalanced the state monopoly over TV. But the state has no intention of conceding that monopoly easily. It plans to launch four rural radio stations, beginning with one in Tingrela.

Radio and television also plan to liberate themselves from their dependency on France. On October 29 1992 an agreement was reached with Comsat, an American company, to set up twelve satellite reception sites within the country, including the towns of Bouna, Diawala, and Kong, while thirteen other sites were to be renovated.

ASSESSING MEDIA PERFORMANCE IN A MULTIPARTY ENVIRONMENT

In general, the media and the government have been undergoing a transition of their own since the first signs of liberalizing the country appeared in 1989. On one hand, many journalists who once worked for the state, either became independent newspaper publishers or produced radio and television programs often critical of the government. On the other hand, the government has been trying to promote democracy without giving up control of what it considers state media facilities. For example, permission to operate private radio stations was granted to companies the government considered less threatening.

Newspapers, which are perhaps the only free media in the country, face many obstacles. First, they have a short life span. The winds of freedom rekindled the entrepreneural spirit within journalists, resulting in close to eighty newspapers. By August 1992, however, there were only 38 regularly published newspapers while the remaining 42 had either disappeared or came out irregularly.

By 1995, there were five daily newspapers. They include two government papers, *Fraternite Matin* and *Ivoir 'Soir*. The former does carry the most comprehensive information, including local columns, although not often the most desired information. The arrival of competing dailies providing coverage of subjects often neglected has caused a fall in the paper's readership. The remaining three dailies include *Bonsoir la Cote d'Ivoir, La Chronique du Soir and La Voie,* an opposition daily. The opposition, however, remains divided, resulting in numerous weeklies.

Cote d'Ivoire citizens have a keen interest in sports, hence several publications provide mainly sports news. Given the economic realities of newspaper publishing, however, the country may have to make do with a few dailies for now. The present newspaper glut, for example, is dangerous for two reasons: first, it breeds corruption among those who may look for secret funds when sales or advertising revenues are not enough; second, it leads to an escalation in sensationalism or coverage of controversial issues, sometimes resulting in heightened antagonism and a loss of credibility if information reported as being based on facts cannot be verified.

Lawsuits can also be initiated if newspapers denounce people without any evidence supporting alleged wrongdoing as was the case with journalists from *La Patriote* who were sentenced on May 15 1992 for libel in a January 16 article which accused a lawyer, without evidence, of embezzling five million francs CFA. The government also uses the legal route to crack down on the press. In 1991, *Notre Temps, La Nouvel Horizon, La Voie, and L'Independent* were either fined or given a two-month suspended sentence for articles which accused people close to the Prime Minister of buying up state companies about to be privatised.

In February 1992, journalists from *La Jeune Democratique*

and L'Oeil du Peuple were sentenced to eighteen months in jail for articles about the President considered unfavorable. The two newspapers were suspended for three months.

Journalists from *La Voie* were taken to court for accusing the ruling government of paying muggers to break up the February 18 1992 demonstrations which led to vandalism. One hundred and sixteen persons, including several journalists, were arrested after that demonstration. Seventy-seven were imprisoned and eventually released under the July Amnesty Act.

Many newspapers with tight budgets cannot bear the burden of lawsuits and heavy fines. The government does not only possess the political weapon to use against the press but it can also muzzle economic forces to work against independent newspapers. In 1990, for example, Cote d'Ivoire printing company SII canceled the printing contract of the opposition weekly, *Le Nouvel Horizon.* By the end of 1991, however, the company decided to accept printing orders from all newspapers regardless of political orientation.

Government and opposition newspapers do not enjoy the same operational advantages. *Fraternite Matin* is printed on tax-free paper imported by the government's publishing company. Independent papers pay more for their paper, including customs duties and VAT, because they buy it from an importer.

Access to information sources is also unequal. On June 22 1992 Paul Bouabre, formerly at *Fraternite Matin,* remarked in *L'Independent* that since multipartyism, departmental heads have been reluctant to disclose information, especially to opposition papers. Hence, government officials are able to control information reaching the public.

In short, newspapers not only face economic problems but they also have to wrestle the freedom to operate from the government. The enthusiasm that followed the newly discovered freedom of speech has subsided and journalists now face the reality of operating within the arena of a government in transition, one not willing to give up too much control of the media.

Journalists, particularly newspaper editors, have to win or keep their readers. They need to meet their readers' expectations which are often economic, social or political. In short, they need to be professional.

When the winds of change were blowing through Africa in late 1989, many activists or businessmen without any journalism experience launched new papers which eventually folded. It is now widely accepted that journalism training is necessary for any newspaper publisher.

A two-week training seminar was organized in April and May of 1993 by the Communication Science and Technology Institute of Abidjan and the Journalist Training Centre in Paris for some thirty young journalists.

The August 2 1983 Act, which introduced the Journalist's Professional Card, provided the first legal definition of a professional journalist in Cote d'Ivoire. In May 1993, a Cote d'Ivoire Press Association (ANEPEC) was formed. It includes 19 newspaper editors, among them Justin Vieyra from *La Nouvelle Presse*.

Journalists from the government-owned media, often used to self-censorship, are now experimenting with the freedom to speak as well as write. Cote d'Ivoire journalists in general also have to compete with foreign based media messages being beamed into the country.

Le Nouvel Horizon noted on November 29 1990 that Cote d'Ivoire citizens are increasingly attracted by foreign radios: the BBC, Radio France Internationale, Africa No. 1, La Voix de l'Amerique, and others. Even government officials still get their information from transistor radios.

The foreign media, mainly French newspapers, were introduced into the country long ago. There are also newspapers and magazines devoted to Africa which are published in France and often written by Africans. *Jeune Afrique* is one such publication. French publications easily available in Cote d'Ivoire include *Le Monde, Le Figaro, France-Football, Paris-Match, and L'Express.*

Radio, the most popular medium, reaches both rural and urban audiences. Radio broadcasts in local languages from neighboring countries such as Mali, Burkina Faso, Guinea, and Ghana are listened to and understood by some Cote d'Ivoire citizens.

The impact of Western media can be seen not only within

the population as a whole but also within Cote d'Ivoire media as well as the the ruling class. Western media influence is readily visible through the electronic media. Imported TV programs generally make up a significant portion of scheduled broadcasts. The availability of VCRs also makes it easier for citizens to watch imported programs. There were an estimated 31,800 in the country in 1982; 150,000 at the end of 1989. In 1992, at least 11.6 per cent of city households owned one VCR.

The ruling class often takes international opinion, particularly that of France, into consideration. The French press and most likely the French government's mild influence is believed to have contributed to the release in July 1992 of the opposition leaders arrested in February 1992.

CONCLUSION

Cote d'Ivoire's record of media development and press freedom has neither been revolutionary nor dictatorial compared to some of its neighbors and even other African countries. Despite decades of personal power wielded by the late President Felix Houphouet-Boigny, Cote d'Ivoire citizens seem to be aware that they can remain adversaries without being enemies.

The ruling class has come to the realization that any monopoly on the dissemination of information is futile and has been supportive of any dialogue which promotes media pluralism. When *La Nouvelle Presse* organized a conference on the press on August 24 1992, it extended a hand to journalists working for the government-owned media who accepted. The Ministry for Communication and the Journalists National Union also held a two-day seminar (August 28-29) in 1992 on "Cote d'Ivoire Press and the Challenge of a New Era" at Yamoussoukro. *Notre Temps* commented later that the goal of the seminar which brought together journalists from "all political creeds," was to reconcile the political class and the people of Cote d'Ivoire as well as to ban tribalism, intolerance and xenophobia.

The holding of this seminar was proof that the "official" media, including politicians, can cooperate with the independent press to establish a pluralistic media environment. The lack of unity among opposition parties more concerned with short term benefits such as winning elections, however, can generally lead to a government crackdown and more unrest as was the case in the early 1990s.

Like their counterparts elsewhere in Africa, Cote d'Ivoire journalists will just have to keep pushing for media pluralism and press freedom. While they strive to become professional so as to maintain the confidence of their readers, listeners, and viewers, they can only hope that the political climate will remain conducive for them to practice their craft.

REFERENCES

Akoun Serge, *Le Nouveau Paysage de la Presse en Cote d'Ivoire.* Memoire de l'Institut Francais de presse, Universite de Paris 11, 1992.

Cote d'Ivoire, Country Profile and Country Reports, 1992 - 1995. London: The Economist Intelligence Unit.

Europa World Yearbook, Vol. 1, London: Europa Publishers Ltd., 1995.

Faure Y.A. et Medard J.F., *Etat et bourgeoisie en Cote d'Ivoire,* 1980.

Gbagbo Laurent, *Agir pour les libertes.* Paris: L'Harmattan, 1991.

Handloff, Robert E., Cote d'Ivoire, a Country Study. Washington, D.C.: Library of Congress, 1991.

Marches Tropicaux, Special Cote d'Ivoire, 21 juin 1991: 1527-1561.

*Presse et Information en Cote d'Ivoire.*Abidjan: UIJPLF, 1983.

La Republique de Cote d'Ivoire, Notes et Etudes Documentaires #2588. Paris, 7 novembre 1959.

Tudesq A.J., *L'Afrique Noire et ses Televisions,* Economica, 1992.

Tudesq A.J., *La Radio en Afrique Noire,* Pedone editeur, 1984.

Yede N'Guessan, *Les Medias en Cote d'Ivoire.* Netcom IV2 juin 1990.

CHAPTER 14

CONGO (ZAIRE): COLONIAL LEGACY, AUTOCRACY AND THE PRESS

Minabere Ibelema

Ebere Onwudiwe

Eleanor Bedford, the Program Coordinator for Africa for the U.S.-based Committee to Protect Journalists, described the condition of the press in Zaire (now Democratic Republic of Congo) as "among the most repressive in sub-Saharan Africa" (Bedford, 1994). And the Freedom House's 1994 comparative rating of press systems places the Zairian press among the least free in the world. Indeed, the press in Zaire has been an instrument of power and impact from colonial times in the 1800s through the quest for independence in the 1950s; from the civil war of the early

1960s to the struggle for democracy in the 1990s. The goal of this chapter is to examine the impact of these historical and contemporary realities in the development of the Zairian press and to show how the press, in turn, has influenced the course of these events. The authors argue that the development and control of the news media in Zaire are inherent in the country's colonial experience and its post-colonial politics of fission and autocracy.

In a general sense, Zaire's experience is very much like that of most sub-Saharan African countries (Hachten, 1971; Wilcox, 1975), but a closer examination shows significant differences. To begin with, Zairian colonial experience under Belgium differs markedly from those of most other African countries, as will be elaborated on later. Also, its post-colonial civil war, the internationalization of the crisis, and the subsequent sustenance of President Mobutu Sese Seko by Western powers are also unique. So also is Mobutu's well-intended but heavy-handed attempt at cultural engineering. These experiences have uniquely defined the Zairian political landscape and the press in particular. Before the change of the country's name from Zaire to the Democratic Republic of Congo in May 1997.

HISTORICAL BACKGROUND

Following the Berlin Conference of 1885, during which European colonial powers formally shared Africa, the area that now constitutes Congo (Zaire) was "ceded" to Belgium, which was late in entering the colonization foray. The Belgians, under the personal directive of King Leopold II, immediately began a systematic exploration of the area's resources, ostensibly for scientific and humanitarian reasons (Leslie, 1993, p. 8). The "scientific" exploration was followed soon enough with military campaigns to control trade and mineral exploration and, ultimately, to bring the diverse ethno-political entities in the region under one administrative umbrella. In the process, existing political structures were overtaken, native and Arab explorers and merchants were displaced, and a new but uncertain order was imposed.

The direct involvement of King Leopold, whose power at home had been whittled by an increasingly powerful Belgian

Parliament, may have resulted in the especially repressive and brutal nature of Belgian colonialism. Natives were slaves of sorts. They were forced to work for the state under the command of "headmen" whose remuneration was pegged on the natives' productivity. "Accordingly, brutal methods—floggings, torture, and execution—were employed when villagers could not meet their assigned quotas" (Leslie, 1993, p. 9). By the end of the century, cultivation of crops needed in Belgium had become compulsory (Coquery-Vidrovitch, 1985). Following internal protests and international criticism, Belgium, in 1908, passed the Colonial Charter under which what was then called the Congo Free State was formally made a Belgian colony and brought under greater Parliamentary oversight. The ensuing mild reform notwithstanding, the Belgian colonial government remained one of the most repressive in Africa.

Following World War II and the resulting worldwide pressure for decolonization, nationalist sentiments began to grow stronger in Congo (Zaire), culminating in serious riots by the late 1950s. Unable to contain the pressures and responding to anti-colonial restiveness at home, the Belgian government hastily arranged for the independence of what had become Congo Leopoldville (as distinct from neighboring Congo Brazzaville). So sudden was the planned transition that there was hardly time to establish viable political parties and other necessities of democratic governance. Myriad ethnic-based parties hastily sprung up and, just before independence, several merged into three uneasy coalitions, with the National Congolese Movement of Patrice Lumumba and the BaKongo Alliance or ABAKO (led by Joseph Kasavubu) as the main contenders. When the elections of May 1960 failed to produce a Parliamentary majority or even a strong plurality for any party, a coalition government of the coalition parties became inevitable. The National party, which won the highest percent of the seats in Parliament (24 percent) reached an agreement with ABAKO that would have Lumumba become the prime minister and Kasavubu the president.

There hardly could have been a more untenable political marriage. Lumumba was a populist nationalist who wanted to steer an independent policy; Kasavubu was a conservative whose party was made up essentially of the BaKongos and who was inclined to maintain a strong alignment with Belgium and other colonial powers. The political gulf between them became evident enough during independence day ceremonies, when Kasavubu thanked the Belgians and Lumumba lambasted them. The gulf would soon become a major element in Congo's political convulsion.

The post-colonial government faced its first crisis in a matter of months, when the armed forces mutinied against their Belgian commanders. In the ensuing disorder, the region of Katanga declared secession under Moise Tshombe with the tacit support of Belgium, which had substantial investments in the mineral-rich area. With the military in disarray, the central government found itself incapable of putting down the rebellion. Lumumba and Kasavubu jointly appealed to the United Nations for help, unwittingly unleashing the forces of the Cold War in their country's affairs. With divided loyalties among the constituent powers of the United Nations, UN forces in Congo became entangled in the politics of the Cold War and failed to act to end the secession. Western powers viewed Lumumba's nationalist politics as inimical to their interests, and the Soviet block supported him for the opposite reason.

When Lumumba sensed a UN inclination to manipulate the crisis against him, he turned to the Soviets for help, thus giving the Western powers the pretext to turn decidedly against him (Onwudiwe, 1992). This development emboldened Kasavubu to dismiss Lumumba, who, in turn, announced Kasavubu's dismissal. Lumumba was formally reinstated soon after by the Parliament. A bitter power struggle thus ensued in the central government at a time when it was coping with secessions, not just of Katanga, but of at least two other regions which had followed suit. Thus, Congo became "one of the first countries to experience the bitter realities of the unresolved conflict between the demands of national liberation . . . and the strategic interests of the major powers in post-colonial Africa" (Nzongola-Ntalaja, 1994). The crisis culminated in Lumumba's arrest in January 1961—at the orders of Kasavubu—and his subsequent torture and assassination.

Access to radio broadcasting is said to have played a decisive role in the struggle for power between Lumumba and Kasavubu.

Each announced the other's dismissal in succession on Radio Leopoldville, the national network. Subsequently, UN forces barred both from access to the station. However, while Lumumba was thus denied access to a broadcast outlet, Kasavubu was granted access to radio broadcasting in neighboring Congo Brazzaville by premier Abbé Youlou, Kasavubu's friend and kinsman. The resulting imbalance in information-dissemination power is believed to have tilted the balance of political power in favor of Kasavubu (Ngefa, 1994, May; Hachten, 1971, p. 23).

In any case, with the Lumumba factor eliminated, the Western powers—working through the United Nations—proceeded to exert military and diplomatic pressure on Moise Tshombe, the leader of Katanga, to end the secession in 1963. But violence and political tension continued. In 1965, General Joseph Mobutu, the army chief who took orders from Kasavubu to arrest Lumumba, overthrew his erstwhile masters and began what to date has been about three decades of dictatorship. However, fueled by the repression and corruption of the Mobutu regime, several attempts at secession or overthrow of the government continued and were often thwarted by American, French and/or Belgian intervention.

As part of his consolidation of power and partly to build national cohesion, Mobutu immediately began to institute a three-pronged policy of "authentic" nationalism and cultural revolution. Politically, the policy aimed to concentrate power in one national party, the Revolutionary Popular Movement, created and headed by Mobutu. Economically, it meant the nationalization of key industries, especially mining, and the resulting transfer of greater economic power to the state—or more specifically to Mobutu. And socially, "Zairians decided to go back consciously to the cultural values of their ancestors and achieve a synthesis with what has been received from foreign cultures" (Bokonga, 1980, p. 10). In keeping with the cultural thrust of the policy, Congo Kinshasa (as the country was then known) was renamed Zaire, Joseph Mobutu renamed himself Mobutu Sese Seko, and all cities, streets newspapers and institutions formerly bearing European names were similarly renamed— by fiat. Katanga was renamed Shaba to erase a name that had come to memorialize the country's period of anarchy. And the Ministry of Information, which was charged with propagating the new policy, was renamed the Department of National Guidance. Thus, for more than three decades, Mobutu presided over the affairs of Zaire more as a monarch than as the head of a republic.

But early in 1990, Zaire joined other African, Asian, East European and Latin American countries in the quest for democratization, when Mobutu called on all sectors of the Zairian nation to submit recommendations for reform. The exact reason for the sudden spirit of democracy is not clear. Nzongola-Ntalaja (1994) traces the change to a 52-page letter to Mobutu in 1980 in which 13 members of Parliament, including Etienne Tshisekedi advocated major political reforms. Mobutu had responded then with repressive measures, but the spirit of the demand could not be quelled. Rather than bow to the pressures, the group went further in 1982 to establish the Union for Democracy and Social Progress in defiance of Mobutu's long-standing ban of opposition parties. Thus, Tshisekedi's personal courage, the tenacity of the movement itself, and the favorable global climate of democratization all coalesced to force Mobutu's hands. Some analysts believe, however, that Mobutu's pro-democracy gestures were merely a cynical attempt to find popular legitimization (see Turner, 1990). Whatever were Mobutu's motives, the response to his call for public input was overwhelming. By May 12 1990 he had received more than 6,000 memoranda (Turner, 1990).

In a speech on April 24 1990 Mobutu proposed a five-point political reform program which essentially reversed the consolidation policy he had begun in 1965. The two critical components were plans for multi-party elections and the establishment of a transitional government headed by a prime minister (with Mobutu remaining as president). When Tshisekedi handily won the election for prime minister in August 1992, however, Mobutu refused to surrender executive powers. Instead, he further polarized the Zairian polity by subsequently appointing another prime minister. The resulting power struggle left the country in political stalemate and chaos that approximates the Tshombe-Lumumba power tussle of the early 1960s. With the Cold War largely over, most of Mobutu's western supporters have now distanced themselves from him, but he managed to cling to power, albeit precariously until he was driven out of Kinshasa, the capital, by the forces of his long time nemesis, Laurent Kabila in May 1997.

The Colonial Legacy and the Press

The development of the press in Congo has followed the course of its political history and development. The country's colonial era, which lasted for about 80 years, set a pattern for press development which the country is yet to transcend. The repressive and brutal nature of Belgian colonialism set the overall pattern, but of particular significance are educational policies and use of the press as an instrument of control.

Belgian colonial rule deliberately kept the majority of their African subjects from attaining any form of higher education, even at the secondary school level. As one of the two poorest Europeans to operate colonies in Africa, the Belgians were paranoid about the possibility of losing power to Africans, and a policy of minimal education for Africans was intended to keep down nationalist agitation. Accordingly, at independence, less than one percent of the children of secondary school age were in school whereas about 65 percent of children of elementary school age were attending (McDonald et al., 1971, p. 157). And in a population of roughly 14 million people only 15,000 constituted the elites—tradesmen, lower-level civil servants, and other wage earners living in urban areas (Lierde, 1972, p. 6).

French, English, American and Swedish Christian missionaries played important roles in the early formal education for the Africans. As a result, education for the Africans emphasized Christian morality and religion, supplemented with instructions in agriculture, crafts, brick-making, housing construction and trades. The Belgian administration insisted that all educational programs conform with the overall policy of training Africans only for low administrative positions. For the most part, this policy continued from 1878 to 1922, when, after World War I, public opinion in Belgium forced colonial administrators to relax the policy of exclusion of Africans from higher education and skilled training. However, the reform notwithstanding, only 30

Congolese had a university level education by independence in 1960. Inevitably, the news media (especially publications) were of use only to a small proportion of Congolese. Accordingly, the press served primarily as a means of political communication among colonialists and the native elites who would soon replace them. It was ill-suited to serve as a watchdog of the government or as a unifying force, irrespective of the form of ownership and control, which were themselves far from libertarian.

Indeed, the other major colonial bequest to the Congolese press was government ownership and control—both direct and indirect. Until 1960, when Congo (then Belgian Congo) won political independence from Belgium, the press was an instrument of colonial rule. Its content was geared toward the needs of Belgians in the Congo as well as to propagate colonialism. Specially managed information was directed to the natives. A colonial agency, Service d'Information pour Africains, operated government radio stations, and prepared newsreels and news releases. This agency was directly responsible to the governor general. The post-colonial press continued its propaganda role, serving a different elite under the direction of a different master.

PRINT MEDIA

Newspapers were introduced in Congo at the turn of the century by Belgian publishers as colonial extensions of their home operations (Bokonga, 1980). Among the early papers were *Le Journal du Katanga* (founded in 1911), Essorial (1927)—which a year later became *L'Essor du Congo,* and *L'Echo de Stan* (1939). The largest daily, *Courrier d'Afrique,* was founded by the Catholic Church in 1930 while *Pres'ence Africaines,* a supplement to *Courrier d'Afrique* was founded in 1956. For the most part, the early papers were founded to support King Leopold. Though privately sponsored, these papers "catered for colonial society and defended their interests" (Bokonga, 1980, p. 13).

Until 1959, Congolese could not form political parties, join trade unions or own newspapers. However, among the newspapers published by the colonial government was *La Voix* du Congolais, which was set up in 1945 ostensibly to give colonial inhabitants an outlet for their views. When the nationals eventually established their own newspapers and began to call for self-determination, however, their papers were muzzled. For instance, *Horizons,* a paper founded by missionaries in 1936 as *La Croix du Congo,* and later turned over to Congolese, was shut down in 1959 for its nationalist agitation (Bokonga, 1980). Nonetheless, the growth of indigenous publications, especially after World War II, stimulated early interest in journalism, which was one of the limited number of professions open to Africans. This interest and the career opportunity facilitated the agitation for independence. Despite the political strife, the number of newspapers continued to grow after the attainment of independence. By 1965, there were about 90 newspapers and magazines. However, most were very short lived.

Communication Profile

Adult literacy rate: 72%

Daily newspapers
Number: 5
Total Circulation: 70,000
Circulation: 0.2 per 1,00 people
News Agencies: Agence Zaire-Presse (AZAP)
Documentation et Informations
Africaines (DIA)

Television
Networks: 1 government network,
TeleZaire
Sets: 62,000

Radio
Networks: 1 government network,
1 Catholic broadcasting service
clandestine broadcasting
Sets: 4 million

Sources: *Europa World Year Book* 1996: 3621-3623.
  World Media Handbook (1990); UNDP (1993)

As in all other African countries, communication between citizens living in different parts of the country was very difficult in the 1960s. It ordinarily took several days to deliver newspapers to remote areas of the country. With most colonial newspapers based in the major urban centers and given the low literacy rate in rural areas, newspapers had little direct impact in much of the country.

Reliable statistics on the circulation of colonial newspapers and periodicals are hard to come by. By 1969 circulation estimates varied from 120,000 to 170,000. However, the total audience including first- and second-hand access (sharing copies and reading for illiterates) was placed at about 2.5 million (McDonald et al., 1971, p. 274).

RADIO AND TELEVISION

From colonial times through the present, broadcasting has been strictly controlled—directly or indirectly—by the government. The first radio broadcasting service was established by the Jesuit College in Kinshasa (then Leopoldville) in the late 1930s. Though its mission was not directly political, like most colonial institutions, it was an instrument of the colonial order. In fact, the station was taken over by the colonial government in 1940 and made a voice of Allied support in World War II. Under the new name of La Voix de la Concorde, it was run by Radio-diffusion Nationale Belge. Following a few more name changes, it became Radiodiffusion Nationale Congolaise after independence was attained. At independence, the Ministry of Information also "inherited" other radio stations established during colonialism, operating a total of eight radio stations located in provincial capitals as well as Kinshasa.

By 1960, after over 70 years of colonial rule, the total number of radio receivers in the country was estimated at 35,000. Although most of the receivers were owned by Europeans, the number of African listeners, according to USAID estimates, was over 1.2 million at independence (McDonald et al., 1971, p. 275). By 1969, after just nine years of self-rule, the number of receivers in the country had increased to 800,000, and the audience had grown to an estimated 4 to 5 million.

Television service was relatively late in coming to Congo. The first station was established by the Ministry of Information in 1966. And about three years later, TELE-STAR, the first privately-sponsored television station was established by Catholic missionaries. Like its radio forerunner, it was taken over by the government in 1973 as part of Mobutu's cultural reform and political consolidation. Renamed Renapec and Ratelesco in succession, it has since become part of the national network run by Office Zairois de Radio et Television (OZRT).

THE MOBUTU LEGACY

While the colonial order and the subsequent political crisis in Congo set the stage for a restrictive press environment, Mobutu's autocratic leadership ensured pervasive control. Given that press freedom can only exist in the context of broader human rights and political freedom, Mobutu's blanket control of Zairian life precluded any meaningful form of press freedom. There has hardly been any separation of power in Zaire, although the veneer of democratic institutions have existed.

There has been a parliament, but its role has been more consultative than legislative, and its legislations have been subordinated to Mobutu's wishes—especially on sensitive and consequential issues. And although regional governments are supposed to have considerable authority over local matters, Mobutu ensures they follow his dictates, sometimes by fermenting uprisings and violence in areas that strayed (Africa Watch, 1993). In general, Mobutu has sought to equate his leadership to law and order, often playing on fears of the anarchy of the 1960s. Fermenting disorder in areas that deviate from his policy is thus a Machiavellian method of impressing this point on Zairians. So too are his brutal methods of quelling opposition, including the banishment of dissidents to remote areas (US Department of State, 1991).

The judiciary has been independent on paper, but in practice the courts have operated under Mobutu's spell. "Judges are free of direct political interference in most cases, but in sensitive or highly politicized cases they work under implicit or explicit constraints imposed by executive or security forces" (U.S. Department of State, 1991, p. 451). Salaries of judicial officers are so low that many augment their income by accepting bribes from defendants. Moreover, while Zairian laws specify due process, including requirement of formal charges within 48 hours of an arrest, in reality security forces operate by their own rules, often jailing suspects and dissidents in extra-judicial locations for indefinite periods.

Possibly, Mobutu's most far-reaching attempt at control came under his cultural authentication program. While the goal was ostensibly to shed Zairians of colonial mentality and to advance appreciation of indigenous culture, the policy also meant further incursion into individual rights and liberties. Zairians were required to change their names and the names of their institutions and communities. Even fashion was prescribed.

While other African countries have pursued cultural authentication policies, none has been as coercive or intrusive on personal choices. In Nigeria, for instance, traditional institutions, customs, and fashion have been elevated in part because of government reaffirmation of their inherent worth through promotions, funding, and other value-enhancement measures. But there has been little tampering with individual rights and choices, except for matters of corporate policy, as in the requirement that television newscasters wear traditional attire while on the air. Thus, the increasing popularity of traditional fashion, music and other cultural forms in Nigeria may be said to reflect genuine popular pride. While Zairians are just as proud of their culture and traditional forms and, indeed, embraced much of the cultural thrust of Mobutu's ideology, the political and dictatorial nature of the policy tarnished it. Zairians recognized cultural authentication as more than a nationalist ideology. It was also another dimension of Mobutu's political grip.

Not surprisingly, in the last years of Mobutu, many Zairians were reverting to their previous names, at least informally, and several newspapers and other institutions were once again bearing the once forbidden European names. Indeed, the transitional charter that emerged from Zaire's national conference of 1992 recommended that the country revert to its previous name,

Congo (Nzongola-Ntalaja, 1994). Such a rebellious retreat to the past can only be understood as a rebuff of Mobutu's dictatorial order, rather than a rejection of cultural authentication.

One area of Zairian life that witnessed remarkable progress under the cultural authentication program is education. Indigenization of the educational curriculum meant more instruction on Zairian life, history and culture. While the implicit ideological seeds of the educational reforms may have worked to Mobutu's favor, the overall advancement in literacy has been a phenomenal national triumph. In spite of Zaire's large rural population, the adult literacy rate had grown to 72 percent by 1990, an impressive figure by sub-Saharan African standards (UNDP, 1993).

The post-colonial advancement in education predated the Mobutu administration, however. Throughout the 1960s, Zaire substantially increased its education budget. In 1962 and 1963, for example, over 30 percent of the general operating budgets went to educational expenditures (McDonald et al., 1971, p. 160). Mobutu continued this policy by building educational institutions in rural areas and increasing post-secondary educational opportunities. The result was an expanded enrollment at all levels of education and subsequently an expanded market for the print media. The progress in education has been substantially halted since the late 1980s when the corruption of the Mobutu administration and other economic factors ravaged the Zairian economy. Today many schools are said to be in shambles, with teachers going for months without pay.

Mobutu's control of Zairian life naturally extended to the news media. His grip on the broadcast media is such that "the distinction between information and propaganda is more fictional than real" (Leslie, 1993, p. 91). By the early 1970s his government had taken a predominant position in information dissemination for other print media through its official news service, the Agence Congolaise de Presse (ACP), and his nationalization policy left little room for an independent press. Privately owned news media were required to become part of the mobilized press, which crusaded for Mobutu's policies and sang his praises. In return, the government subsidized them. *Afrique Chretienne*, a Catholic paper which resisted the policy, was closed down

(Ngefa, 1994, May). Meanwhile, the ACP, which later became Agence Zaire-Presse or AZAP, became the "official spokesman" for Mobutu until 1978, when a constitutional change gave that function to the Official Gazette (Bokonga, 1980).

Although Article 11 of Zaire's 1967 Constitution provided for the freedom of individual expression, it also subjected this right to strict regulation and prescriptive laws. In 1970, for instance, Mobutu promulgated Decree No. 70, 057 (reprinted in Bokonga, 1980, pp. 43-46) which set down the framework for press control. Article 10, perhaps the most significant of the clauses, states that:

> Quite apart from legal action, the Minister of Information may suspend for a maximum of six months the publication of any newspaper or periodical liable to endanger public order or the peace. In urgent cases the provincial governor may do the same, provided he informs the Minister of Information immediately . . . .

With no criteria for determining propensity "to endanger public order," the Minister of Information and provincial governors thus had unmitigated powers to shut down publications—for good, in the case of publications that could not recover from the inevitable financial hardship. And the decision was beyond judicial review.

Other significant requirements of the decree were that all newspapers must be registered; that a substantial amount of money (25,000 zaires at the time) must be deposited with the Exchequer; that members of the editorial board must submit their photos with the registration forms; and that, at the time of publication, specified copies of each edition must be deposited with a newspaper tribunal (or alternative judicial agency) and with the Ministry of Information. That these requirements were intended to facilitate the harassment of journalists is self-evident.

The ability of journalists to resist the blanket control of the press was hampered by the absence of an independent, professional union. Although several journalism organizations existed, they were closely tied to the government. This is evident in the manifesto of Union Nationale de la Presse Zairoise, the umbrella organization of all Zairian press associations (reprinted in

Bokonga, 1980, pp. 47-49). The introductory paragraph states:

> The constitution of the Union Nationale de la Presse Zairoise is a new landmark in the task of nation-building undertaken by Citizen-President J. D. Mobutu; it is one of the achievements of the new regime.

The first substantive clause of the manifesto was even more worshipful of Mobutu:

> Without the energetic and salutary intervention of Citizen-President J. D. Mobutu, the vicissitudes of the past would have brought about the disintegration of Zaire's national unity. The steps taken by the Mouvement Populaire de la Revolution (MPR) have since largely succeeded in rectifying this situation. The Zairian press rejoices at the results already achieved, and regards itself as mobilized to reinforce and support the campaign . . . .

Such declaration of commitment to an individual rather than a principle obviously does not point in the direction of an independent press. In the political climate of the time, the journalists had little choice. The Ministry of National Guidance had blanket control over all agents of information in much the same way that departments of agitation and propaganda functioned in Marxist states. Activities and declarations that were not explicitly supportive of Mobutu would probably have incurred government ire. In fact, the establishment of the union and the drafting of its manifesto were at the behest and under the oversight of the Ministry.

The resulting totalitarian press environment of the Mobutu regime may have resulted in the relatively stunted development of the Zairian press. For all its size (46.4 million people in 1996), natural resources, Western support, and high literacy rate, Zaire has had a small press relative to comparable African countries such as Nigeria and Kenya. With a 1988 daily newspaper circulation of about 0.1 copies per 100 people and television set ownership of 0.1 per 100 people, media reach in Zaire has remained far below the UNESCO-recommended standards of 10 daily copies and 2 television sets per 100 people. With 10.3

radio sets per hundred people, however, Zaire has surpassed the UNESCO standard of 5 per 100. Nigeria surpasses Zaire on all three counts (1.6 daily copies, 17.2 radio sets, and 3.2 television sets per 100 people). Kenya surpasses Zaire on daily copies (1.5) and radio sets (12.5). They are about equal on television sets (UNDP, 1993).[1]

THE ZAIRIAN PRESS AND THE DEMOCRACY MOVEMENT

The political turbulence that has engulfed Zaire since 1991 has left the news media in a state of flux. There is still no independent press in Zaire at this time, but a viable opposition press has emerged. Indeed, newspapers appear and disappear routinely as political alignments change and as the economic burden takes its toll. Others are forced to close by the heavy hands of state security or by politically inspired terrorism. Ngefa Atondoko, the president of the Zaire Association for the Defense of Human Rights, estimates that only about 17 newspapers and magazines were publishing in Zaire by mid 1994, down from about 150 at the height of the political activism of 1990-92, when several papers sprung up all over Zaire (Ngefa, 1994, April). Newspapers have been suspended or had copies confiscated, newspaper offices have been bombed or burned, and journalists have been murdered or forced underground (CPJ, 1994; Africa Watch, 1993). Yet the opposition press remained steadfast in its campaign for democracy.

According to Ngefa, the major opposition papers in the last years of Mobutu's tyranny include: *La Reference Plus,* a daily; Le Phare (light that can see) which is published twice weekly; *Le Forum,* also published twice weekly; and *Le Potential,* which is published twice or three times weekly (Ngefa, 1994, April). Also contributing to the opposition voice is *Periodique des Droits de L'Homme,* which is published six times a year by the Association for the Defense of Human Rights. This publication reports on abuses and educates Zairians about their rights.

The effort of the Zaire-based press was aided by Belgian papers and publications by Zairians abroad, which were often smuggled into Zaire. Their advocacy is exemplified by a front page editorial in the Belgium-based monthly *Zaire Info Plus* of Nov. 29, 1993. The editorial entitled "No to the Death of the State of Zaire" bemoans the flight of Zairians from "the country which they love dearly":

> Their state can no longer administer itself and uses the gun as law and the soldier in the place of the magistrate. The authorities in charge of the country: one refers to himself as the head of state, the other as the chief of government, but of what state? The Zairois government thinks it is in an age of gathering and in the Stone Age. They gather the diamonds and other minerals and run a printing press to produce money which never arrives at the Central Bank but goes directly to the military barracks.[2]

The editorial goes on to admonish Zairians and well-wishers alike to contribute whatever they can to forestall the imminent death of Zaire. "If not the future generation will spit on our tombs." Even with all the hazards of critical journalism in Zaire, such pointed commentary is not uncommon in the opposition press in the country. Such criticism is officially tolerated, especially if, as in this case, Mobutu is not attacked by name.

Broadcasting, however, is another matter. It remained under the tight control of OZRT, which ensured that the opposition voice was kept out. Journalists at the stations who wanted to assert even a modicum of professional independence were fired or jailed. Even the loyal ones did not escape danger, as marauding soldiers sometimes fired on broadcast stations. The regional broadcast stations continued to receive much of their programming from the national service and were, in any case, controlled by Mobutu appointees. Over a period of several months between 1991 and 1992, many local radio stations were turned off, apparently to keep locals oblivious of the political upheaval in Kinshasa (*U.S. News & World Report,* Aug. 10, 1992).

Some non-governmental broadcasting was offered by the Catholic church, which was not allowed to broadcast political news or commentary. However, there was clandestine political radio broadcasting by the opposition. Ironically, because they operated underground without concerns for professional ethics, the clandestine broadcasters were often more incendiary than they might have been if allowed to operate openly. On occasion they have precipitated major violence and bloodshed and have therefore been criticized even by pro-democracy advocates (Ngefa, 1994, April).

The near collapse of the Zairian economy has left the communication infrastructure battered even by the standards of sub-Saharan Africa. Few telephone lines are functional, postal services collapsed at some point, and even the national news agency, Agence Zaire-Presse, ran out of telex papers (*U.S. News & World Report,* Aug. 10, 1992). These and related transportation problems have kept the Kinshasa-based opposition newspapers from effectively reaching beyond the capital city to spread the message of democracy and the struggle to depose Mobutu.

CONCLUSION

The press in Congo is likely to remain in crisis and flux for quite some time despite the overthrow of Mobutu. With the political opposition highly divided and unable to develop a common agenda and strategy, Congo's political impasse seems destined to drag on even under Kabila. However, although the divided opposition could have lost a free election to Mobutu in 1996, it is unlikely that the country will ever again acquiesce to Mobutu's imperial presidency. No leader is likely to gain an unquestioned power again. Thus, it is a matter of time before democracy and relative press freedom arrive in The Democratic Republic of Congo.

REFERENCES

Africa Watch. Zaire: Inciting Hatred: Violence against Kasaiens in Shaba. *Africa Watch* 5. 10, 1993.

Bedford, E. Interview with one of the authors, Apr. 1994.

Bokonga, B. E. *Communication policies in Zaire.* Paris: UNESCO, 1980.

Coquery-Vidrovitch, C. The Colonial Economy of the Former French,

Belgian and Portuguese Zones, 1914-1935. In A. A. Boahen, ed., *General History of Africa VII: Africa Under Colonial Domination 1880-1935*. Paris: UNESCO, 1985: 351-381

CPJ *Attacks on the Press in 1993: A Worldwide Survey*. New York: Committee to Protect Journalists, 1994.

Europa World Year Book, 1996: 3261-3623.

Hachten, W. A. *Muffled Drums: The news media in Africa*. Ames, Iowa: The Iowa State University Press, 1971.

In Zaire, a Big Man Still Rules the Roost. *U.S. News & World Report* Aug. 10 1992: 31-34.

Leslie, W. J. *Zaire: Continuity and Political Change in an Oppressive State*. Boulder, Colorado: Westview Press, 1993.

Lierde, J. V. *Lumumba Speaks: The Speeches and Writings of Patrice Lumumba, 1958-1961*. Boston: Little, Brown and Co., 1972.

McDonald, G. C. et al. *Area Handbook for the Democratic Republic of the Congo; (Congo Kinshasa)*. Washington, D.C.: U.S. Government Printing Office, 1971.

Ngefa, Atondoko. Interview with one of the authors, Apr. 1994.

Ngefa, Atondoko. Interview with one of the authors, May 1994.

No to the death of the state of Zaire. *Zaire Info Plus,* Nov. 29 1993: (front page).

Nzongola-Ntalaja, G. Zaire I: Moving Beyond Mobutu. *Current History,* 93. 583, (May 1994): 219-222.

Onwudiwe, E. The United Nations Intervenes in the Congolese Civil War. In F. N. Magil, ed. *Great Events in History II: Human Rights*. Pasadena, Cal.: Salem Press, 1992: 1074-1072 (sic).

Turner, J. On the Threshold of Zaire's Third Republic. *International Freedom Review* 4. 1 (1990): 45-70.

UNDP. Human Development Report 1993. New York: Oxford University Press, 1993.

U.S. Department of State. *Country reports on human rights practices for 1990*. Washington, D. C.: Government Printing Office, 1991.

Wilcox, D. L. *Mass Media in Africa: Philosophy and Control*. New York: Praeger, 1975.

World Media Handbook 1990 Edition. New York: United Nations, 1990.

NOTES

1. All the figures are from the UNDP (United Nations Development Program) Human Development Report 1993, except the figure on Zairian daily newspaper circulation, which is from the World Almanac and Book of Facts 1996 and *Europa World Year Book*, 1996: 3261-3623.
2. Unofficial translation from French by Koryoe Anim-Wright.

PART 4

LUSOPHONE

Chapter 15

The Elusive Press Freedom
In Angola

Festus Eribo

Introduction

Angola, a former Portuguese colony with a long history of bloody struggle for independence, has found press freedom very elusive, a phenomenon also associated with other former Portuguese colonies, including Mozambique. The protracted colonial and post-colonial crises in Angola have for decades created a permanent martial condition for the fragile and underfunded press system in the country. The effects of colonialism on press freedom and the conflicts before and after attaining independence will be examined in this chapter.

Before colonialism, the traditional communication system was oral and may have been free by the standards of the communal life of the time. The African traditional communication system demanded social responsibility and utilitarianism. There were no censorship laws beyond the requirement to conform to social values or ethical standards and traditional rites (Birmingham,

1966, pp. 1-30). However, any claim to freedom of oral communication under the various Bantu administrations, including the Luba dynasty that ruled in ancient Angola, is arguable and inconclusive. But with the advent of the Portuguese and the introduction of the slave trade, new and alien values gradually crept into social interactions and communication.

The Portuguese started the slave trade in the fifteenth century and by the nineteenth century about 90 percent of Angola's economy depended on slave trade and sales of ivory. Under the catastrophic circumstances caused by frequent raids for slaves, the freedom of expression and indeed the freedom of the individual ceased to exist for the indigenous population (Henderson, 1979, pp. 99-103). The lucrative trade in slaves was stopped four centuries later by a British naval squadron which crushed the Portuguese-sponsored transatlantic slave trade between Angola and Brazil, and the shipment of Angolans for slave labor in European and Portuguese owned sugar plantations. Before this cessation of the slave trade, fear, insecurity, and destruction were the most common commodities for those who escaped slavery. Although there was trade in rubber, beeswax, ivory, diamonds, and cotton, the climate of terror engineered by the Portuguese slave and economic pursuits in Angola was incompatible with freedom of communication.

The colonial legacy and its impact on press freedom in Angola have received very little attention from communication scholars, partly because of the language barrier and Portuguese tight control of information about its colonies and activities in Africa. For a country such as Angola—the size of California and Texas combined with 10 million people—the dearth of scholarship on press freedom, partly because of its colonial past, is virtually inexplicable (U.S. Census Bureau 1994 and The World Almanac 1989, p. 650).

COLONIAL REPRESSION AND THE PRESS

The press in Angola under Portuguese colonialism was established for the colonial administrative machinery and domination. The majority of the indigenous population, which was largely illiterate, was left out in matters affecting the press. There were no newspapers in the local languages aimed at satisfying the interests of the local people. Existing papers had low circulation and were published in order to fulfill the information needs of the Europeans in Angola. As late as the 1960s, for example, all four major newspapers in Angola—*A Provincia de Angola, Diario de Luanda, Jornal de Congo, and Jornal de Benguela* - had a circulation of 39,000 copies a day.

All mainstream publications were published in Portuguese. In the 1960s, when the population of the country was about five million people, only 500,000 people lived in urban areas where the papers were circulated while more than four million people lived in rural areas where they were cut off from modern print media. Although Herrick et al. pointed out in 1967 that over 75 percent of the indigenous population relied on "direct and informal oral communication" for news and information, over 90 percent of the rural population did not understand Portuguese in spite of five hundred years of contacts with the invaders. The population lived in isolated settlements which were difficult to reach from the port cities of Luanda and Lobito. Accessibility to the people was a major problem. Even if there was the wish to circulate the newspapers to the hinterland, transportation was a major impediment (Gonzaga, 1967, pp. 54, 118-119). Describing the state of Angolan roads, Herrick et al. (1967, p. 23) noted that they were "poorly developed" and "concentrated in the coastal plain and central highlands between Luanda and Sa de Bandeira." The roads were single-lane dirt paths interrupted every few miles by rivers and streams without bridges. Despite the three unconnected Railroads linking the hinterland to the coast, the most reliable means of transportation is by air which is a costly means of transportation of newspapers.

The most influential daily newspaper in Angola before independence was *A provincia de Angola.* Another paper, *Diario de Luanda,* owned by Agencia de Noticias de Informacoes had the largest circulation. *Jornal de Congo,* published in Carmona outside Luanda, was the most outspoken while *Jornal de Benguela* was a sensational piece which relied on Portuguese and Angolan news agencies for its stories. Also published in the country were the following dailies and periodicals: *Boletim*

Oficial de Angola, Angola Desportiva, Angola Norte, Jornal de Huila, O Comercio, O Planalto, O Intransigente, Noticias, O Sul, O Lobito, O Namibe, O Estandarte, and *O Apostolado.* The circulation of these publications ranged from 1,000 to 9,000 copies. The papers mainly served the interests of the colonialists who were the major patrons of the media.

Interestingly, the ownership of newspapers in colonial Angola was private. The owners of the press were often close to the government and constantly practiced self-censorship in order to remain close to government officials. The colonial government did not tolerate any form of criticism of the Portuguese administration in Angola by the local or foreign press. In fact, the movement of foreign correspondents in Angola was restricted for a long time. Local newspapers were permitted to publish official police records, government job openings, items for sale, sport news, military operations and movement, religious news, entertainment, editorials, and news about events in Portugal. News of legislative, administrative, and personnel decisions in Angola was restricted to the weekly *Boletim Oficial de Angola.* Violations of government censorship were punished by the removal of government patronage and subsidies. Subsequently, the publishers would take neither the legal nor financial risk on behalf of the Africans. Thus, press freedom was virtually never conceived in colonial Angola.

The newspapers were usually full of praises for the government and its organizations. The papers relied on two Portuguese news agencies, Agencia Lusitania and Agencia de Noticias de Informacoes. These agencies were private but controlled by the Portuguese government. Thus the press in Angola was merely an extension of the press in Portugal. Portuguese newspapers, such as *Diario Popular* and *Jornal das Noticias,* were sold in Luanda and other large cities in Angola to bring home news to the Portuguese colonialists.

A major characteristic of the colonial press in Angola is that it did not represent the indigenous people. It represented foreign interests and was largely aimed at European audiences living in Angola as colonial representatives. Although the repressive colonial government expected total subservience from the press and the people, white or black, it did not receive the full co-operation of the neglected and exploited indigenous people. The Portuguese language newspapers were unpopular among indigenous Angolans since they could neither understand nor afford to buy the papers. Thus the papers were devoid of local participation and representation.

Another major characteristic of the colonial press period was the absence of resistance to censorship by the mainstream press owned by the Portuguese. The press was a natural partner to the government which did not welcome media criticisms. The acquiescence of the press was almost conspiratorial since the media owners were close to the government. The climate of voluntary press censorship may have been motivated by the need to support colonial domination in the interest of the Portuguese government and the owners of the newspapers in Angola. However, the result was that there was no press freedom for the Europeans, the Blacks, the mesticos and the assimilados in Angola.

Indigenous newspapers, representing the hopes, aspiration, and interests of the Angolan people were not tolerated in the country. It was common knowledge that the Portuguese used forced labor and paid miserable wages for work in cotton and coffee plantations and in the diamond mines in Angola. Not only were Portuguese oppression and over-taxation of the people never reported, the people's resentment of colonial rule could not be published within Angola. This attitude drove the opposition press underground. The oppression of the people led to passive resistance and later active resistance culminating in the 1961 Maria's war, the attacks on Sao Paulo and Luanda prisons, the sacking of several police posts including the killing of police officers, the rebellion of the Kongo people, and the subsequent guerrilla attacks on the colonial establishment (Kaplan, 1979).

Kaplan points out that heavy censorship of the Angolan media prevented the outside world from knowing the full extent of Portuguese vengeance and the indiscriminate massacre of Blacks by white groups roaming the slums of Luanda in a futile attempt to stop the rebellion. Gagging the press did not, however, prevent the news of the ferocious killing of Blacks from being discussed at the United Nations Security Council. The media blackout had encouraged the spread of rumors of Portuguese brutality among ethnic Angolans, precipitating further attacks by the Union of Angolan Peoples (UPA) on government institutions, farms and trading posts and the killing of Portuguese and mestico men, women, and children. More than 20,000 Blacks were reported killed by Portuguese forces within six months of the UPA rebellion (Jackson, 1982, pp. 53-91).

Clandestine publications challenging the colonialists were established outside Angola, in the neighboring countries of Congo and Zaire (now Democratic Republic of Congo). These publications were illegal in Angola where anyone found with copies of revolutionary newspapers was arrested. The tight control of the print media was extended to radio which has the largest audience in Angola. The Angolan freedom fighters also established their radio stations abroad. These stations provided the fillip and information needed by the urban and rural guerrillas. The final struggle for Angola's independence had begun and was spreading like a bush-fire across the country. Lisbon recruited and in many cases conscripted more than 50,000 troops to stop the guerrillas at a time when Portugal could least afford a foreign war.

The difficult terrain and vast plateau in Angola is traversed by multiplicity of radio transmissions from the numerous *radio clubes* or radio clubs owned by private cooperatives and individuals in Angola. The radio clubes were located in the cities of Benguela, Bie, Cabinda, Cuanza Sul, Huambo, Huila, Luanda, Lunda, Malange, Mocamedes, Moxico, and Carmona formerly Uige. There were 18 radio stations broadcasting on 19 mediumwave, 41 shortwave, and 5 FM transmitters in Angola in 1965. The stations were heavily censored, subjective, and, therefore, impotent in communicating effectively with the people of Angola. Furthermore, the majority of the stations were limited in their broadcast range. The radio stations had transmitters of about one kilowatt and served the immediate community. Some stations owned by Emissora Oficial and Radio Comercial de Angola had 10 kilowatt transmitters. However, no single radio station was powerful enough to broadcast throughout the country (Herrick et al., 1967, pp. 242-250). The stations and the broadcasters were guerrilla targets since Angolans were not satisfied with the role of this censored medium.

Although radio clubes transmissions crisscrossed the country, many indigenous Angolans were excluded from the audiences because of the scarcity and cost of radio receivers. The rural and urban poor could not afford to buy the receivers just as they could not buy the newspapers. In 1964, there were about 73,000 registered radio receivers in the country. The registered radio receivers were owned mainly by the Portuguese and other Europeans in Angola (Herrick et al., 1967).

Direct radio broadcasts from Portugal were often relayed to the limited elite audiences by the local stations. Other foreign radio stations such as the Voice of America, the BBC, Radio France International, and Radio Moscow can be received in Angola. The major barrier stopping the people from benefiting from the uninhibited and uncensored transmissions from Western radio was the paucity of receivers.

Like the print media, the majority of the radio stations were privately owned, with the exception of the stations operated by Emissora Oficial and Radio Eclesia, a religious station operated by the Catholic Church. The privately owned stations also depended on advertising and government subsidies and patronage. They were, therefore, obliged to practice self-censorship while avoiding criticism of the colonial administration (Herrick, 1967, pp. 241-255). Radio Angola—a government station operated by Emissora Oficial —broadcasts in Portuguese, French, and English. It has had the largest audience in the country in spite of the propagandistic nature of its broadcasts. Radio Clube de Angola based in Luanda was the leading private station while Radio Clube de Huambo had the strongest signals. Radio programming in colonial Angola included news, public announcements, interviews, and music—mainly European music.

Voices of dissent were not allowed on radio in Angola. And— like the print media—dissenting radio broadcasts had to be transmitted from abroad. The clandestine radio stations operated by revolutionary groups and freedom fighters demanding for independence for Angola were broadcasting from the neighboring countries of Congo and Zaire. Two major underground radio programs were established abroad—the MPLA (Movimento Popular de Libertacao de Angola) radio program operating from the government-owned station in Congo and the FNLA (Frente Nacional de Libertacao de Angola) radio broadcasting from the government station in Zaire. On the eve of independence, the Portuguese destroyed whatever they could sabotage and left Angola in bitterness and darkness. After independence day in 1975, surviving radio stations in the new Marxist Angola were nationalized and became the propaganda tool of the socialist government in Luanda (Hunter, 1993, p. 91).

POST-COLONIAL MEDIA AND PRESS FREEDOM

Angola became independent on November 11, 1975. The new MPLA-led government headed by President Agostinho Neto, a poet and medical doctor, abolished the colonial Ministry of Information and unleashed a new form of censorship, Marxist style (Jackson, 1982, pp. 53-91). The pro-Soviet government permitted the publication of two major dailies and eight journals. *Jornal de Angola* with a daily circulation of 42,000 copies was designated the government newspaper while *Diario da Republica* with a circulation of 8,500 copies was the official government news sheet, both published in Portuguese in a country with a 42 percent literacy rate (Banks, 1993, p. 28).

Other pro-government publications after the attainment of independence included *Angola Norte,* a periodical published in Malanje; *A Celula,* a monthly political journal of the MPLA; Lavra and Oficina, representing the Union of Angolan Writers; and *A Voz do Trabalhador,* a monthly journal of the National Union of Angolan Workers (Uniao Nacional de Trabalhadores Angolanos). Other post-colonial journals are *Jornal de Benguela, Correio da Semana, Noticia, Novembro, and O Planalto.*

All newspapers under the MPLA government were required to comply with the official government and party policies based on the Marxist-Leninist definition of the press as an agitator, propagandist, and organizer. The absence of private media resulted in the absence of alternative voices and the dissemination of managed news and information. Kaplan (p. 226) pointed out in 1979 that the news of the nationalization of ANGOL, a subsidiary of Companhiade Petroleos de Angola (PETRANGOL) owned by Belgian and Portuguese governments and private investors on February 25, 1977 lacked details. Such censorship was the result of directives from the ruling Angolan Political Bureau.

The definition of news events under the Marxist government in Angola was different from the Western concept of news. For example, a strike by workers leaving their jobs was reported by *Jornal de Angola* in 1978 as sabotage against the government. A law published on April 3, 1978, authorized the "death penalty for crimes against the state or against the revolution." The death penalty law included such offenses as "spreading false information that would endanger the good name of the state" (Kaplan, 1979, p. 195). The law was deadly and everyone including editors walked the tightrope of the censorship and repressive law. Editors and journalists depended on the official government news sources to avoid the death penalty. A presidential decree of April 1978, designated the Angolan Press Agency as the disseminator of official Marxist ideology. This centralization of news sources and media ownership in Angola is a major censorship instrument which has reduced the media to mere official megaphones.

The post-colonial press in Angola is different from the colonial press under Lisbon because it serves the interests of an indigenous Angolan government rather than Portuguese interests. But the government interests under the Marxist MPLA were influenced by Moscow and Havana before the collapse of communism and the disintegration of the Soviet Union. The ideological colonialism was indeed a form of Russian imperialistic and neocolonialist adventure with a fanciful sales pitch and name tag. Angola was a Soviet satellite with all the implications of national subordination and Soviet style press control and censorship. Thus, under both the colonial and indigenous administrations, press freedom eluded the Angolan people. It should be pointed out that although the post-colonial press was not free, it was managed by Angolans for the Angolan government in pursuit of a committed but futile communist paradigm to development in a country condemned to centuries of foreign exploitation.

Radio and television in post-colonial Angola are government owned. Radio Nacional de Angola, a government-controlled station, broadcasts three programmes and an international service. The station broadcasts in Portuguese, English, French, Spanish, and local languages, including Chokwe, Kikongo, Kimbundu, Kwanyama, Fiote, Ngangela, Luvale, Songu, and Umbundu. The indigenous languages on radio have brought the people closer to the controlled media. More Angolans can now listen to the barrage of merengue and lambada music on radio. The number of radio receivers had increased from 73,000 in 1964 to more than two million in 1990 (Bank, 1993). The flow of news and information to the rural areas has improved since the establishment of regional radio stations by the government. It should be pointed out that more access to government-censored media is not necessarily synonymous with press freedom. Television was established by the government in 1976, one year after the attainment of independence. Televisao Popular de Angola (TPA) transmits color programming from seven stations. The television stations depend on the Angolan News Agency (ANGOP) for local and foreign news while serving the propaganda goal of the MPLA. The television programming includes indigenous content and revolutionary messages for the mobilization of the people of this former guerrilla-infested country. There are now 290,000 television receivers in Angola (Europa World Year Book 1996).

Alternative news sources, via electronic media, are available to Angolans. The main indigenous news source not controlled by the MPLA government in Luanda is the Voice of the Black Cockerel, a radio station controlled by Jonas Savimbi's UNITA movement which waged a protracted guerrilla war against the MPLA. International media and news agencies are also serving as alternative sources of news in post-colonial Angola.

ETHNIC GUERRILLA POLITICS, IDEOLOGY, AND PRESS FREEDOM

Since the Maria's war of 1961 and the subsequent rebellions and guerrilla wars, Angola has been engulfed in one of Africa's most protracted armed struggles in the second half of the twentieth century. The post-colonial civil war in Angola may be characterized as an ideological war between forces loyal to Marxism-Leninism and forces sponsored by Western governments to overthrow the socialists. Another characterization of the civil war focuses on ethnicity. It is an ethnically motivated war between the MPLA led by the Mbundus or the Kimbundu-speaking people and the UNITA, the National Union for the Total Independence of Angola (Uniao Nacional para a independencia total de Angola) led by Ovimbundu people. The UNITA leader, Jonas Savimbi, holds a doctorate in political and juridical sciences from the University of Lausanne in Switzerland. He broke away from Holden Roberto whom he accused of racism, tribalism and pro-American philosophy. As a member of the Ovimbundu people, Savimbi is from a large ethnic group. He was originally supported by the Portuguese in order to use him against the Marxist MPLA. The Frente Nacional de Libertacao de Angola (FNLA), founded in 1962, was led by Holden Roberto, brother-in-law to President Mobutu Sese Seko of Zaire and a Bakongo nationalist. The FNLA troops were trained by the Chinese. However, the FNLA reconciled its differences with the MPLA and gave up guerrilla attacks on the MPLA targets at the intervention of President Mobutu Sese Seko (Jackson, 1982, p. 83).

The MPLA—founded in 1956 by young Marxists and former members of the Angolan Communist Party—is led by Jose Eduardo dos Santos, a Soviet trained engineer and successor of the late President Agostinho Neto who died in Moscow in September 1979. Since December 1977, after the first Party Congress, the MPLA was organized as a Soviet style socialist and workers party complete with a Political Bureau and a Central Committee (Martin, 1980, p. xx).

Although it is public knowledge that press freedom cannot flourish in a Marxist state, the censorship of the press in Angola was exacerbated by the internecine war between MPLA government forces and UNITA guerrillas led by Jonas Savimbi. The major victims of the continuous guerrilla warfare have been the freedom of the press, freedom of expression, and the pursuit of happiness which require a normal and peaceful climate, among other things, to flourish. Both parties in the civil war have their own media as allies in the war of words and guerrillas, and these media are tightly controlled. Since the 1980s, UNITA has received American support and the accolade of the Western press for opposing MPLA (Windrich, 1992). Savimbi's major media outlet is the ubiquitous radio station, the Voice of the Black Cockerel, which has built a personality cult for Savimbi.

The MPLA-led government in Luanda uses the Angolan Press Agency as the official mouthpiece and propagandist. Before the democratization process of the 1990s began, the directorate of the Angolan Press Agency was appointed by the Political Bureau from among the members of the Central Committee" (Kaplan, 1979, p. 142). According to Kaplan, the Angolan Press Agency was under the jurisdiction of the Revolutionary Guidance Department of the Central Committee which would enforce the "correct and effective participation" of the agency in raising the educational, cultural, and political standards of Angolans. The centralization and ideological control of the press deprived the media of any form of the democratic freedom which operates in Western libertarian and social responsibility press systems. The lack of press freedom engendered by the Marxist practices of the MPLA government was further compounded by the ideologically and ethically motivated guerrilla wars which forced the media on all sides to become more partisan and censored.

The Angolan civil war has had all sorts of foreign participation and intervention, including operation Carlota (the airlift of Cuban troops to Angola), the invasion at different times by South African troops and Zairean troops, and the presence of Soviet, Cuban and Western military advisers (Marcum, 1978). Moscow alone is believed to have spent more than $4 billion in military support for MPLA. The country is saturated with weapons and warring rebels, making any form of press freedom impossible.

In October 1992, the MPLA government conducted a democratic election under the watchful eyes of foreign observers and the world press. MPLA won the majority of the votes but UNITA claimed that the election was not free and fair. On May 19 1993 the U.S. government recognized the government in Angola after it had demonstrated that it would pursue democracy and press freedom. In the spring of 1994, a total of 14 political parties, four of which were represented in Parliament, formed a Democratic Civilian Opposition group against the MPLA government, its armed forces and police and demanded peace and national reconciliation (West Africa, 18-24 April, 1994, p. 697).

Angolan media are yet to experience press freedom despite the movement toward liberalization unleashed by the fall of communism in Eastern Europe. Savimbi continues to fight for his dream of Angola. The media in Angola have been caught in the crossfire. In the siege of the central city of Cuito, Abel Abriao, an Angola Radio reporter, received death threats from UNITA guerrillas for broadcasting four times a day the news of the casualties of the attacks by UNITA forces. His wife and child were also threatened and they had to go into hiding. Faria Horacio, another Angolan journalist, received death threats for broadcasting from Cuito while Abriao was in hiding (Sayagues, 1994). In June 1994, a BBC correspondent in Luanda was arrested for trying to interview South African prisoners in Angola.

Not only are journalists endangered by the war, the Angolan people are paying the supreme price with their lives. Starvation and destruction are the order of the day in this country where foreign guns and landmines are more available than food. International relief workers were unable to cope with the magnitude of assistance needed everyday by the victims of the war between MPLA and UNITA before 1997.

As Windrich pointed out in 1994, although "the MPLA had abandoned Marxism and a one-party system for pluralism and a market economy," UNITA is still a personality cult built around Jonas Savimbi by his guerrillas and the black cockerel. Savimbi's guerrillas control the Benguela, port city of Lobito and much of the country. Under the prevailing circumstances of invisible belligerence, press freedom continues to elude the people of Angola. Until the echoes of war are silent and major political and economic obstacles are removed, the press in Angola may never be free. At the request of the United Nations in June 1994, President Nelson Mandela of South Africa agreed to intervene and help negotiate a solution to the Angolan imbroglio. There has been some truce since the South African intervention. A long lasting peace and press freedom may be in the horizon if President Mandela continues to clean the Augean stable.

CONCLUSIONS

The media in Angola have never truly belonged to the people or served the interests of the people. The Angolan media experience has been dominated by foreign ideologies, culture, and values. The Portuguese colonialists were largely interested in what Angola had to offer them economically and not what they had to offer to Angola and Angolans. The goal of the colonial media was to perpetuate colonial rule and exploitation. Neither the colonial administration nor the expatriate press was interested in press freedom.

After the attainment of independence in 1975, the nationalization of the press was carried out under a different European maxim represented by Marxism-Leninism. The Angolan people and their media had exchanged the old Portuguese masters and their cruelty for a new ideological servitude and patrimony disguised in the name of Soviet style socialism. The post-colonial press in Angola was caught in a bloody civil war between MPLA and UNITA. This has perpetuated the climate of fear, destruction, and insecurity left behind by the Portuguese. The casualties of the protracted conflicts have been the people, the press, and the freedom to pursue a normal life.

REFERENCES

Banks, Arthur S. *Political Handbook of the World, 1993*. New York: State University of New York, 1993: 23-28.

Birmingham, David. *Trade and Conflict in Angola*. Oxford: Clarendon Press, 1966: 1-30.

Gonzaga, Norberto. *Angola: A Brief Survey*. Luanda: Agencia-Genal Do Ultramar, Centro De Informacao E Turismo de Angola, 1967: 54, 118-119.

Henderson, Lawrence W. *Angola: Five Centuries of Conflict*. Ithaca: Cornell University Press, 1979: 99-103.

Herrick, Allison Butler et al. *Area Handbook for Angola*. Washington,

D. C.: U.S. Government Printing Office, 1967: 241-265.

Hunter, Brian. *The Statesman Yearbook.* New York: St. Martin's Press, 1993: 91.

Jackson, Henry F. *From Congo To Soweto: U.S. Foreign Policy Toward Africa Since 1960.* New York: Quill, 1982: 53-91.

Kaplan, Irving. *Angola: A Country Study.* Washington, D. C.: The American University Press, 1979: 93-99; 175-240.

Marcum, John A. *The Angola Revolution, Volume II: Exile Politics and Guerrilla Warfare, 1962-1976.* Cambridge, MA: The MIT Press, 1978: 206-281.

Martin, Phyllis, M. *Historical Dictionary of Angola.* London: The Scarecrow Press, Inc., 1980: 5-9.

Sayagues, Mercedes. "The Siege of Cuito" *Africa Report* January/February 1994: 18-20.

The Europa World Year Book, 1996. Vol. 1. London: Europa Publications Ltd: 366.

The World Almanac 1989. New York: Pharos Book: 650-651.

U. S. Census Bureau, 1994. *World Population Estimate.West Africa,* 18-24 April, 1994: 697.

Windrich, Elaine. "Savimbi's Image in the U.S. Media: A Case Study in Propaganda." In Beverly Hawk, ed. *Africa's Media Image,* Westport, CT: Praeger, 1992: 194-205.

Windrich, Elaine. "Media Coverage of the Angolan Elections," *Issue,* Vol. XXII/1 (Winter/ Spring) 1994: 19-23.

APPENDIX

Festus Eribo

Africa: Socio-economic and Media Database

	Pop. 1997 (Millions)	Literacy Rate (%)	GDP ($Billions)	Life Expectancy (years)	TV sets (Millions)	Radio (Millions)	Dailies	Freedom*
Algeria	29.1	57	45	67	1.7	5.6	9	PF
Angola	10.3	42	8.3	45	0. 2	2.0	2	PF
Benin	5.7	23	2	51	0.02	0.4	1	F
Botswana	1.4	80	3.6	63	0.01	0.1	1	PF
Burkina Faso	10.6	18	2.9	52	0. 04	0.2	1	NF
Burundi	5.9	50	1.1	53	0.003	0.3	1	NF
Cameroon	14.2	56	11.5	58	0.2	1.5	1	NF
Cape Verde	0.4	66	0.3	62	0.005	0.05	n.a.	F
C.A.R.	3.2	33	1.3	48	0.001	0.1	1	PF
Chad	6.9	17	1.1	40	0.006	1.3	1	NF

	Pop. 1997 (Millions)	Literacy Rate (%)	GDP ($Billions)	Life Expectancy (years)	TV sets (Millions)	Radio (Millions)	Dailies	Freedom*
Comoros	0.5	48	0.2	57	0.0002	0.01	0	n.a.
Congo	2.5	57	2.4	54	0.001	0.2	4	PF
Cote d'Ivoire	14.7	54	10	55	0.6	1.6	4	PF
Djibouti	0.4	48	0.3	49	0.04	0.06	1	NF
Egypt	63.5	50	39.2	60	5.0	16.5	17	PF
Equatorial Guinea	0.4	50	0.1	51	0.003	0.1	0	NF
Eritrea	3.9	20	n.a.	n.a.	n.a.	n.a.	1	NF
Ethiopia	57.0	33	6.6	52	0.1	9.0	3	PF
Gabon	1.1	95	3.3	54	0.04	0.1	3	PF
Gambia	1.0	25	0.2	49	0	0.1	1	F
Ghana	17.6	50	6.2	55	0.2	4.3	3	NF
Guinea	7.4	24	3.0	43	0.03	0.2	n.a.	NF
Guinea Bissau	1.1	19	0.1	47	0	37	1	PF
Kenya	28.1	69	9.7	62	0.3	4.2	5	NF
Lesotho	1.9	59	0.4	62	0.005	0.1	4	PF
Liberia	2.1	50	0.9	57	0.04	0.5	4	NF
Libya	5.4	64	n.a.	69	0.4	1.0	1	NF
Madagascar	13.6	80	2.4	53	0.2	2.4	5	PF
Malawi	9.4	41	1.9	50	0	2.0	1	NF
Mali	9.8	32	2.2	45	0.004	0.3	2	PF
Mauritania	2.3	34	1.1	47	0.04	0.2	1	NF
Mauritius	1.1	83	2.5	70	0.1	0.003	7	F
Morocco	28.7	50	27	65	1.9	5.3	13	PF
Mozambique	17.8	33	1.7	48	0.04	0.6	2	PF
Namibia	1.5	58	2.0	61	0.03	0.2	6	F
Niger	9.1	28	2.4	44	0.03	0.4	1	PF
Nigeria	103.0	51	30	49	3.5	18.7	31	PF
Rwanda	6.8	5	2.1	53	0	0.4	0	NF

	Pop. 1997 (Millions)	Literacy Rate (%)	GDP ($Billions)	Life Expectancy (years)	TV sets (Millions)	Radio (Millions)	Dailies	Freedom*
Sao Tome-Principe	0.1	57	0.04	n.a.	0	0.03	0	F
Senegal	9.0	38	5.0	56	0.4	0.9	3	PF
Seychelles	0.07	58	0.3	70	0.008	0.03	1	n.a.
Sierra Leone	4.7	21	1.4	46	0.04	0.9	1	PF
Somalia	9.5	24	1.7	56	0.1	0.3	1	NF
South Africa	41.7	78	104	65	3.7	11.5	17	PF
Sudan	31.0	27	12.1	54	1.8	6.9	2	NF
Swaziland	0.9	55	n.a.	56	0.01	0.1	3	PF
Tanzania	29.0	46	6.9	53	0.04	0.6	3	NF
Togo	4.5	43	1.5	56	0.02	0.7	1	NF
Tunisia	9.0	65	13.5	72	0.6	1.6	6	PF
Uganda	20	48	5.6	51	0.18	1.9	5	NF
Western Sahara	0.2	-	-	-	-	-	-	-
Zaire	46.4	72	6.6	54	0.04	3.6	5	NF
Zambia	9.1	76	4.7	57	0.2	0.6	2	F
Zimbabwe	11.2	74	7.1	62	0.3	0.8	2	PF

Sources: *World Almanac*, 1997, Stevenson, R. L. (1994) Global Communication in the Twenty-first Century, New York: Longman, & Merrill, J. C. (1994) Global Journalism, New York: Longman, in press.

* 1992 data indicating freedom rating - free (F), partly free (PF), and not free (NF). Source: Stevenson, R. L. (1994) Global Communication in the Twenty-first Century, New York: Longman, pp. 127-132. Cited from Freedom House by Stevenson. Copyright (c) 1993, Freedom House.

The 1997 Information Please Almanac, New York: Houghton Mifflin Company.

SELECTED BIBLIOGRAPHY

Aboaba, Doyin. "The Nigerian Press Under Military Rule." Unpublished doctoral dissertation. Buffalo: State University of New York, 1979.

Adissoda, M.A. *La Presse au Dahomey (1890-1939)*. Mémoire de maîtrise d'Histoire. Université de Dakar, 1973.

Agbaje, Adigun A. B. *The Nigerian Press, Hegemony, And The Social Construction of Legitimacy, 1960-1983*. New York: The Edwin Mellen Press, 1992.

Ainslie, Rosalynde. *The Press in Africa: Communications Past and Present*. London: Gollancz, 1966.

Akhahenda, Elijah. *A Content Analysis of Zambian and Tanzanian Newspapers During the Period of Nationalization*. Ph.D. Dissertation. Southern Illinois University, 1984.

Allen, Chris, Michael Radu, Keith Somerville, Joan Baxter & Keith Somerville Eds. *Benin, The Congo, Burkina Faso: Economics, Politics and Society*. London: Pinter Publishers, 1989.

Almaney, A. Government Control of the Press in the United Arab Republic. In Alan Wells, ed. *Mass Communications, a World View*. Palo Alto: Mayfield Publishing Co., 1974.

Alot, Magaga. *People and Communication in Kenya*. Nairobi: Kenya Literature Bureau, 1982.

Altschull, J. Herbert. *Agents of Power: The Role of the News Media in Human Affairs*. New York: Longman, 1984.

Amin, H., "An Egypt-Based Model for the Use of Television in National Development." Unpublished doctoral dissertation. Columbus: The Ohio State University, 1986.

Ammar, S., *Censorship of English-language Books in Egypt*. Unpublished master's thesis. Cairo: The American University in Cairo, 1990.

Anderson, Benedict. *Imagined Communities*. London: Verso, 1991.

Argyle, W.J. *The Fon of Dahomey*. Oxford, Clarendon Press, 1966.

Article 19. *World Report*. London: Longman, 1992.

Atkinson, Norman. *Teaching Rhodesian*, London: Longman, 1972.

Austin, Reginald. *Racism and Apartheid in Southern Africa: Rhodesia*, Paris: The UNESCO Press, 1975

Babiker, M. *Press and Politics in the Sudan*. Khartoum: Khartoum University Press, 1985.

Banks, Arthur S. *Political Handbook of the World, 1993*. New York: State University of New York, 1993.

Barton, Frank. *The Press in Africa: Persecution and Perseverance*. New York: Africana, 1979.

Bechthold, P. *Politics in Sudan: Parliamentary and Military Rule in an Emerging African Nation.* New York: Praeger, 1976.

Bennett, W. Lance. *News: The Politics of Illusion.* White Plains, NY: Longman, 1988.

Betts, R.F. *Assimilation and Association in French Colonial Theory* New York: Columbia University Press, 1961.

Birmingham, David. *Trade and Conflict in Angola.* Oxford: Clarendon Press, 1966.

Biya, Paul. *The New Deal Message.* Yaounde: Sopecam Publications, 1984.

Boahen , A. A., ed. *General History of Africa VII: Africa Under Colonial Domination 1880-1935.* Paris: UNESCO, 1985.

Bokonga, B. E. *Communication Policies in Zaire.* Paris: UNESCO, 1980.

Boyd, D. *Broadcasting in the Arab World: A Survey of the Electronic Media in the Middle East.* Ames: Iowa State University Press, 1993.

Bourges, Herve. *Reflexion sur la Role de la Presse en Afrique.* Paris: Institut Francais de Presse, 1973.

Bradbury, R.E. *Benin Studies.* London: Oxford University Press, 1973.

Burns, Y. *Media Law.* Durban: Butterworths, 1990.

Codo, Bellarmin "La Presse dahoménne face aux aspirations des Evolués; La Voix du Dahomey (1927-1957)." Thése de doctorat. Université de Paris VII, Département d'Histoire, 1978.

Cookson, J.A., John, H.J., MacArthur, A.G., McEwen, J., MacGaffet, W. & Vreeland, M.C. *US Area Handbook for the Republic of Sudan.* Washington, DC: US Government Printing Office, 1960.

Cornevin, Robert. *Histoire du Dahomey.* Paris: Éditions Berger-LeVrault, 1962.

Coulson, Andrew, ed. *African Socialism in Practice: The Tanzanian Experience.* Russell Press Ltd.: Nottingham, 1979.

CPJ . *Attacks on the Press in 1993: A Worldwide Survey.* New York: Committee to Protect Journalists, 1994.

Curran, James and Jean Seaton. *Power Without Responsibility: The Press and Broadcasting in Britain.* London: Routledge, 1988.

Curry, J.L. and Joan Dassin. *Press Control Around the World.* New York: Praeger Publishers, 1982.

Davidson, Basil. *The Black Man's Burden: Africa and the Curse of the Nation-State.* New York: Times Books, 1992.

De Beer, A.S., ed. *Mass Media for the 90s. The South African Handbook of Mass Communication.* Pretoria: Van Schaik, 1993.

Decalo, Samuel. *Historical Dictionary of Benin.* London: Scarecrow Press, Inc., 1987.

Drost, H. ed. *World's News Media.* Essex: Longman. 1991.

Eribo, Festus, Oyeleye Oyediran, Mulatu Wubneh, and Leo Zonn, eds. *Window On Africa: Democratization and Media Exposure*. Greenville, NC: Center for International Programs, East Carolina University, 1993.

El Halwani, M.*El Izaat El Arabiah (Arab Broadcasting)*. Cairo: Dar El Fiker El Arabi, 1982.

El Halwani, M. and Atef El Abed. *Anzemat El Izaat El Arabiah (Arab World Broadcasting Systems)*. Cairo: The Arab Publication House, 1987.

Ellul, Jacques. *Propaganda: the Formation of Men's Attitudes*. New York: Vintage, 1965.

El Sayed, S.M. *Policy-Making in the Egyptian Broadcasting System: A Case Study Analysis*. Unpublished doctoral dissertation. Madison: University of Wisconsin Press, 1981.

Faringer, Gunilla L., *Press Freedom in Africa*, New York: Praeger, 1991.

Freedom House. *Freedom in the World: The Annual Survey of Political Rights and Civil Liberties*. New York, 1993.

Gellner, Ernest. *Nations and Nationalism*. Ithaca: Cornell University Press, 1983.

Ghai, Y.P. and J.P.W.B. MacAuslan. *Public Law and Political Change in Kenya: a Study of the Legal Framework of Government from Colonial Times to the Present*. Nairobi: Oxford University Press, 1970.

Gnonlonfoun, J. "Rapports Presse/Pouvoir Politique au Benin," *La Presse Beninoise Face aux Exigences d'Ethique et de Déontologie*. Cotonou: La Nation/Fondation Friedrich Naumann, 1993.

Good, Robert C., *U.D.I. The International Politics of the Rhodesian Rebellion*, Princeton: Princeton University Press, 1973.

Gouili, S.A. "Agenda Setting and Local Issues on Egyptian Regional Television Broadcasting." Unpublished master's thesis. Cairo: The American University in Cairo, 1993.

Hachten, William. *Muffled Drums: The News Media In Africa*. Ames: Iowa State University Press, 1971.

Hachten, William. *The Growth of Media in the Third World: African Failures, Asian Successes*. Iowa State University Press, 1993.

Hachten, W. & Giffard, C.A. *Total Onslaught. The South African Press Under Attack*. Johannesburg: MacMillan, 1984.

Hafez, S. *Ahzan Horriet El Sahafa (Anguish of Press Freedom)*. Cairo: Al-Ahram Center for Translation and Publishing, 1993.

Hamelink, Cees. *Cultural Autonomy in Global Communication*. New York: Longman, 1983.

Hansen, H, and Twaddle, M., eds. *Changing Uganda*. Athens, Ohio:

Ohio University Press, 1991.

Hansen, H, and Twaddle, M. eds. *Uganda Now: Between Decay and Development*. Athens, Ohio: Ohio University Press. 1988.

Haule, John. "Press Controls in Colonial Tanganyika and Post-Colonial Tanzania: 1930-1967." Ph.D. Dissertation. Southern Illinois University, 1984.

Hawk, Beverly G. ed. *Africa's Media Image*. West Port: Praeger, 1992.

Head, S.W. *Broadcasting in Africa — a Continental Survey of Radio and Television*. Philadelphia: Temple University Press, 1974.

Heath, Carla W. "Broadcasting in Kenya: Policy and Politics 1928-1984." Unpublished Ph.D. dissertation, University of Illinois, Urbana, 1986.

Henderson, K. *Sudan Republic*. New York: Praeger, 1965.

Henderson, Lawrence W. *Angola: Five Centuries of Conflict*. Ithaca: Cornell University Press, 1979.

Herbst, Jeffrey, *State Politics in Zimbabwe,* Berkeley: University of California Press, 1990.

Herman, Edward S. and Noam Chomsky. *Manufacturing Consent: the Political Economy of the Mass Media*. New York: Pantheon Books, 1988.

Herrick, Allison Butler et al. *Area Handbook for Angola*. Washington, D. C.: U.S. Government Printing Office, 1967.

Hobsbawm, E.J. *Nations and Nationalism Since 1780*. New York: Cambridge University Press, 1990.

Huannou, Adrien., *La Littérature Béninoise de Langue Française* Paris: Éditions Karthala, 1984.

Hughes, John. *The New Face of Africa South of the Sahara*. New York: Longman, Green and Co., 1961.

Hunter, Brian. *The Statesman Yearbook*. New York: St. Martin's Press, 1993.

Jackson, Henry F. *From Congo To Soweto: U.S. Foreign Policy Toward Africa Since 1960*. New York: Quill, 1982.

Kale, MacDonald N. "The Role of Public Address in the Search for National Integration in Africa: A Rhetorical Investigation of the Cameroon Nationalist Movement."Unpublished doctoral dissertation. Bloomington: Indiana University, Bloomington, 1985.

Kaplan, Irving. *Angola: A Country Study*. Washington, D. C.: The American University Press, 1979.

Kasoma, Francis P. *The Press in Zambia*. Lusaka: Multimedia Publications, 1986.

Keane, J. *The Media and Democracy*. Cambridge: Policy Press, 1991.

Khamis, S. "A Comparative Study on the News Credibility of Egyptian Television and Newspapers." Unpublished master's thesis. Cairo:

The American University in Cairo, 1989.

Kurian, G., ed. *World Press Encyclopedia.* New York: Facts on File, 1982.

Lahav, P. *Press Law in Modern Democracies.* New York: Longman Inc., 1985.

Lederbogen, Utz. *The African Journalist.* Bonn and Dar es Salaam: Friedrich, Ebert-Stiftung, 1991.

Lee, Chin-Chuan., ed. *Voices of China: The Interplay of Politics and Journalism.* New York: Guilford Press, 1990

Lenin, V.I. "Where to Begin." *In Lenin: About the Press.* Prague: International Organization of Journalists, [1901], 1972.

Lerner, Daniel *The Passing of Traditional Society: Modernizing the Middle East.* Glencoe, IL: The Free Press, 1958.

Lerner, D. and Wilbur Schramm, eds. *Communication and Change in Developing Countries.* Honolulu: East-West Center, 1967.

Leslie, W. J. *Zaire: Continuity and Political Change in an Oppressive State.* Boulder, Colorado: Westview Press, 1993.

Liebenow, J. Gus, *African Politics: Crises and Challenges, Bloomington and Indianapolis: Indiana University Press, 1986.*

Lierde, J. V. Lumumba Speaks: The Speeches and Writings of Patrice Lumumba, 1958-1961. *Boston: Little, Brown and Co., 1972.*

Lokossou, C.K. *"La Presse au Dahomey: 1894-1960. Évolution et Réaction Face a l'Administration Coloniale." Thése pour le doctorat. École des Hautes Études en Science Sociales. Paris, 1976.*

Louw, P.E. South African Media Policy, Debates of the 1990s. *Bellville: Anthropos, 1993.*

Man Chan, Joseph and Chin-Chuan Lee. Mass Media and Political Transition: The Hong Kong Press in China's Orbit. *New York: The Guildford Press, 1991.*

Manning, Patrick. Slavery, Colonialism and Economic Growth in Dahomey, 1640-1960 *London: Cambridge University Press, 1982.*

Marcum, John A. The Angola Revolution, Volume II: Exile Politics and Guerrilla Warfare, 1962-1976. *Cambridge, MA: The MIT Press, 1978.*

Martin, Phyllis, M. Historical Dictionary of Angola. London: The Scarecrow Press, Inc., 1980.

Martin, Phyllis M., and Patrick O'Meara, eds. *Africa,* Bloomington: Indiana University Press, 1986.

Matovu, Jacob. "In Search of Mass Communication Strategies to Facilitate National Unity in Uganda." Dissertation. University of Michigan, Ann Arbor, 1984.

Merrill, J. C., ed. *Global Journalism, A Survey of the World's News*

Media, New York: Longman, in press, 1994.

Muller, P. *Sonop in die Suide.* Cape Town: Nasionale Boekhandel, 1991.

Mwaura, Peter. *Communication Policies in Kenya.* Paris: UNESCO, 1980.

Mytton, Graham. *Mass Communication in Africa.* London: Edward Arnold Publishers, 1983.

McDonald, G. C. et al. *Area Handbook for the Democratic Republic of the Congo;* (Congo Kinshasa). Washington, D.C.: U.S. Government Printing Office, 1971.

McFadden, T.J. *Daily Journalism in the Arab States.*Columbus: Ohio State University Press, 1953.

Nasser, M.K. Egyptian Mass Media Under Nasser and Sadat. *Journalism Monographs* (No. 124). Columbia, S.C.: Association for Education in Journalism and Mass Communication, December, 1990.

Nordenstreng, Kaarle, and Lauri Hannikainen, *The Mass Media Declaration of UNESCO,* Norwood, New Jersey: Ablex Publishing Corp., 1984.

Nyerere, Julius K. *Freedom and Development.* Oxford University Press. Dar es Salaam, Tanzania, 1973.

Nyerere, Julius K. *Ujamaa: Essays on Socialism.* Oxford University Press. Dar es Salaam, 1968.

Ochieng', Philip. *I Accuse the Press: An Insider's View of the Media and Politics in Africa.* Nairobi: Initiatives Publishers, 1992.

Ochs, Martin. *The African Press.* Cairo: The American University in Cairo Press, 1986.

Ogbondah, Chris W. *Military Regimes and the Press in Nigeria, 1966-1993.* New York: University Press of America, 1994.

Ogbondah, Chris W. *The Press In Nigeria: An Annotated Bibliography.* New York: Greenwood Press, 1990.

Omu, F. I. A. *Press and Politics In Nigeria, 1880-1937.* New Jersey: Humanities Press Inc., 1978.

Oyediran, Oyeleye. *Nigerian Government and Politics Under Military Rule, 1966-79.* New York: St. Martin's Press, 1979.

Page, D.C. "A Comparative Analysis of Television and Broadcast Systems." Unpublished doctoral dissertation. Ann Arbor: The University of Michigan, 1977.

Parenti, Michael. *Inventing Reality: The Politics of the Mass Media.* New York: St. Martin's, 1986.

Prinsloo, J. & Criticos, C. *Media matters in South Africa.* Durban: Media Resource Centre, 1991.

Pye, Lucian., ed. *Communication and Political Development* Princeton: Princeton University Press, 1963.

Rodney, Walter *How Europe Underdeveloped Africa*. Washington D.C.: Howard University Press, 1981.

Rugh, W.A. *The Arab Press*. Syracuse: Syracuse University Press, 1979.

Saad, A.M. *Tarekh El Cinema El Mesriah (The History of the Egyptian Cinema)*. Cairo: Al-Ahram Publishing House, 1970.

Salih. M.A. "The Press in Sudan During Three Periods." Unpublished master's thesis. Indiana University, 1975.

Salih, M.M. *Al-sahafa al-Sudanya fi nisf quarn* [Half a century of the Sudanese press]. Khartoum: Khartoum University Press, 1971.

Schramm, Wilbur. *Mass Media and National Development*. Stanford: Stanford University Press, 1964.

Sid Ahmed, A. "Mass media and development in Sudan." Unpublished doctoral dissertation. Pennsylvania State University, 1984.

Siebert, Peterson and Schramm. *Four Theories of the Press*, Urbana: University of Illinois Press, 1956

Smith, Anthony. *The Shadow in the Cave: The Broadcaster, his Audience, and the State*. Urbana: University of Illinois Press, 1973.

Springborg, R. *Mubarak's Egypt, Fragmentation of the Political Order*. Boulder & London: Westview Press, 1989.

Sterling, C. *International Propaganda and Communications*. New York: Arno Press, 1972.

Stevenson, Robert L., *Communication, Development and the Third World*, New York: Longman, 1988.

Stevenson, Robert L. *Global Communication in the Twenty-First Century*. New York: Longman, 1994.

Stokke, Olav., ed. *Reporting Africa*. New York: Africana Publishing Corporation, 1971.

Sussman, L. *Power, the Press and the Technology of Freedom*. New York: Freedom House, 1989.

Swainson, Nicola. *The Development of Corporate Capitalism in Kenya 1918-1977*. London: Heinemann, 1980.

Tomaselli, K.G. & Louw, P.E. *Studies on the South African Media. The Alternative Press in South Africa*. Bellville: Anthropos, 1991.

Tripp, Charles., ed. *Contemporary Egypt: Through Egyptian Eyes*. London: Routledge, 1993.

Uche, Luke Uka. *Mass Media, People and Politics in Nigeria*. New Delhi: Concept, 1989.

Ugboajah, Frank O. ed. *Mass Communication, Culture and society in West Africa*. New York: Hans Zolt Publishers, 1985.

Unesco. *Broadcasting for Development in Zambia*, Volume 2, 1989.

Ungar, Sanford J.,*Africa*, New York: Simon and Schuster, 1985.

Vatikiotis, P.J. *The History of Modern Egypt*. London: Weidenfeld and Nicolson, 1991.

Walker, M. *Powers of the Press*. New York: Adama Books, 1983.

Wallbank, T. Walter. *Documents on Modern Africa*. New York: D. Van Nostrand Co., Inc., 1964.

Wete, Francis. "Development Journalism: Philosophy and Practice in Cameroon." Unpublished doctoral dissertation. Columbia: University of Missouri, Columbia, 1986.

Wilcox, D. L. *Mass Media in Africa: Philosophy and Control*. New York: Praeger, 1975.

Wiseman, John A., *Democracy in Black Africa*, New York: Paragon House Publishers, 1990.

Ziegler, Dhyana and Molefi K. Asante. *Thunder and Silence: Mass Media in Africa*. Trenton, NJ: Africa World Press, Inc., 1992.

Compiled by Festus Eribo.

CONTRIBUTORS

Hussein Y. Amin is visiting associate professor of journalism and mass communication at American University in Cairo. He is on leave from Helwan University in Cairo. Amin received his B.A. and M.A. at Helwan University and his Ph.D. at the Ohio State University. He has published extensively on mass media issues in Arabic and English. Among his areas of special interest are international and domestic television broadcasting.

Kwadwo Anokwa is associate professor of journalism and chair of the Department of journalism at Butler University, Indianapolis. He received his Ph.D. in mass media from Michigan State University and M.A. in journalism from the University of Wisconsin-Madison. Anokwa served as media practitioner and journalism educator in Ghana from 1965 to 1982 and has published several articles on the media in Africa.

Arnold S. de Beer, Ph.D. is director of the Institute for Communication Research and head of the Department of Communication, Potchefstroom University, South Africa. Professor de Beer has authored, edited or contributed to numerous scholarly journals and books, including *The South African Handbook of Mass Communication*. He is a member of the South African Press Council and the South African Broadcasting Board.

Festus Eribo is associate professor of international communication and coordinator of African Studies at East Carolina University, Greenville, North Carolina. He received his M.A. in Journalism from St. Petersburg University, Russia, and Ph.D. mass communications from the University of Wisconsin-Madison. He is co-author of *Window on Africa: Democratization and Media Exposure* and several scholarly articles on mass communication in Africa and Russia. He worked as a reporter, feature writer, public relations officer, communication consultant, and educator in Nigeria, Russia, and the United States.

Mohammed Galander (Ph.D., Howard University, 1993) formerly served as Editor of the only functioning (military) newspaper in the Sudan. He intends to teach mass communications in the Sudan.

Charles Anthony Giffard, Ph.D. formerly head of the Department of Communications at Rhodes University in South Africa, is now on the faculty of the School of Communications at the University of Washington, Seattle. He is the author (with William Hachten) of *The Press and Apartheid*, and of *Unesco and the Media*, as well as many articles on international communications. Giffard has worked as a journalist and academic in Britain, Germany, South Africa and the United States.

Paul Grosswiler is associate professor of journalism and mass communication at the University of Maine. He earned his Ph.D. in journalism at the University of Missouri in 1990. His research interest is communication in Third World socialist countries.

Carla W. Heath is associate professor at the Department of Communication, Randolph-Macon Woman's College, Lynchburg VA. She received her A.M. History and Ph.D. Communication from University of Illinois, Urbana-Champaign. Her Research interests are African broadcasting history and policy, specializing in Kenya; communication/media history; problems in international communication; modern media and the construction of national ideologies. In connection with the last topic, she is working on the production of children's radio and television programs in Ghana.

Minabere Ibelema is assistant professor of communication studies at the University of Alabama-Birmingham. He received his Ph.D. from Ohio State University. His research interests are in communication policies and media coverage of Africa.

William Jong-Ebot is currently a director at Alpha Communication and Consultants International in St. Petersburg, Florida. He was assistant professor of journalism and mass communication at the University of South Carolina at Spartanburg for five years. He received his Ph.D. in mass communications from the University of Wisconsin-Madison and M.A. from the University of Minnesota. His recent research interests include media law and ethics, communication policies in developing countries, and international flow of media products and programs.

MacDonald Ndombo Kale is associate professor and a member of the graduate faculty in the Department of Communication Studies at California University of Pennsylvania. Kale's undergraduate studies was done in Cameroon; graduate work was done at Governors State University in Illinois, University of Illinois, Chicago, Indiana University, Bloomington, and West Virginia University College of Law, Morgantown. Research interests are in the areas of political communication and law and communication in the Third World. Kale was a recipient of an NDEA Fellowship and a fellowship from the Annenberg Foundation and has participated in international and domestic summer workshop on communications law and policy in Washington D.C. Kale teaches courses in public relations, film, small group communication and media law.

Francis Kasoma is professor and Chair at the Department of Mass Communication at the University of Zambia. He was president of the African Council for Communication Education and a former news and feature editor at the *Times of Zambia*. He received his undergraduate education from Zambia and his graduate degrees from USA and Finland. He is author of several books and scholarly articles on communication in Africa.

Tendayi S. Kumbula, Ph.D., is assistant professor of Journalism in the Journalism Department at Ball State University, Muncie, IN. where he was coordinator of the News-Editorial Sequence.

James J. Napoli is lecturer and chair at the Department of Journalism and Mass Communication at the American University in Cairo. He received his B.A. and M.A. in English from Boston College and did further graduate study in mass communication at the University of Wisconsin-Madison. He has worked extensively in the United States as a newspaper journalist, including as chief editorial writer at the Hartford Courant in Connecticut. He has written extensively on issues of press freedom.

Ebere Onwudiwe is associate professor of political science and director of the Center for African Studies at Central State University, Wilberforce, Ohio. He received his Ph.D. from Florida State University. His research interests are in political issues in African development.

Allen W. Palmer is faculty member in the Department of Communications at Brigham Young University in Provo, Utah. Professor Palmer was co-director of a USIA-USAID sponsored seminar on economic reporting in Cotonou, Benin, in September 1993. He was visiting professor at the University of Mauritius in 1988. He is graduate of the University of Utah and the Annenberg School of Communication at the University of Southern California.

Melinda B. Robins is an assistant professor of mass communication at Emerson College, Boston, Massachusetts. She was Fulbright Scholar at Makerere University in Kampala where she helped in the organization of a new department of mass communications in Uganda in 1989. She returned to Africa in 1993 as a director of a workshop for junior reporters in Harare,

Zimbabwe, which was co-sponsored by the U.S. Information Service and the Cox International Center for Mass Communication Training and Research at the University of Georgia. She also conducted a pilot study in Tanzania for her doctoral program at the University of Georgia in Athens. Ms. Robins has 18 years experience as a professional journalist and educator in the United States and Africa.

William J. Starosta (Ph.D., Indiana University, 1973) is Graduate Professor of Communication at Howard University. He is founding editor of *The Howard Journal of Communications*. He received grant support to conduct field research in India, Canada, and Sri Lanka. He is Chair of the Speech Communication Association Intercultural and International Communication division. His work appears in the journals of six disciplines.

Elanie F. Steyn is a Researcher at the Institute for Communication Research at Potchefstroom University. She is currently working on her Masters degree on the 'South African media coverage of the 1992 Olympic Games'. She is Assistant Editor of Ecquid Novi, the South African journal for journalism and mass communication.

Andre-Jean Tudesq is professor of Contemporary History and Information Sciences and Director of the Center for Media Studies at the University of Bordeaux. He is a member of the National Council of Universities. He received his Ph.D. in Contemporary History. Tudesq has published extensively on Africa and the media and has conducted research in many French African countries.

INDEX